# Savage Constructions

## *The Myth of African Savagery*

WENDY C. HAMBLET

LEXINGTON BOOKS

A division of
ROWMAN & LITTLEFIELD PUBLISHERS, INC.
*Lanham • Boulder • New York • Toronto • Plymouth, UK*

LEXINGTON BOOKS

A division of Rowman & Littlefield Publishers, Inc.
A wholly owned subsidiary of The Rowman & Littlefield Publishing Group, Inc.
4501 Forbes Boulevard, Suite 200
Lanham, MD 20706

Estover Road
Plymouth PL6 7PY
United Kingdom

British Library Cataloguing in Publication Information Available

**Library of Congress Cataloging-in-Publication Data**

Hamblet, Wendy C., 1949– Savage constructions : the myth of African savagery /
Wendy C. Hamblet.
    p. cm.
Includes bibliographical references (p.   ) and index.
ISBN-13: 978-0-7391-2280-8 (cloth : alk. paper)
ISBN-10: 0-7391-2280-0 (cloth : alk. paper)
ISBN-13: 978-0-7391-2281-5 (pbk. : alk. paper)
ISBN-10: 0-7391-2281-9 (pbk. : alk. paper)
1. Africa—Colonial influence. 2. Violence—Philosophy. 3. Violence—Social aspects.
4. Civilization, Western. 5. Africa—Civilization. 6. Africans—Race identity. 7.
Blacks—Race identity. 8. Racism. 9. Philosophy, African. 10. Culture conflict. I. Title.
DT21.H25 2008
    303.6096—dc22

                                                                    2007049801
Printed in the United States of America

♾™ The paper used in this publication meets the minimum requirements of American
National Standard for Information Sciences—Permanence of Paper for Printed Library
Materials, ANSI/NISO Z39.48–1992.

This book is dedicated to Gladys and my other African "sisters" and "brothers" who, over the decades and across the miles in the West and in their own exotic world, welcomed this stranger into their midst, accepting me on my own terms despite the color of my skin and the brutal ignorance of my forebears. Regardless of all they have endured, these wise and long-suffering people continue to raise my hopes for a better human future, even against the realization, made stark at every new turn of my work as a scholar of violence, that the night of human darkness still drapes most of the human world. The kindness, the warmth, and the untiring graciousness of my African "family" have taught me lessons not easily learned in the brave new world of the West. They have shown me the unfaltering durability of friendship, the selfless generosity that makes for genuinely interwoven—if perilously unguarded—community, and the deep empathy and compassion that remain the sole hope for the flourishing of the family of humankind.

# Contents

# Preface

Four years ago, I shared a conversation with a very learned man, the Dean of Humanities at one of the most prestigious universities in the United States. That conversation disturbed me to such an extent that it clarified for me the focus of a philosophical mission that would carry me through the next four and a half years of my research life; it clarified for me in the starkest terms the need for the current book, a meditation that would tackle explicitly the prejudices still deeply embedded in the minds of some powerful and highly educated persons holding positions of authority in the West.

It was a spring afternoon. As I entered the Dean's office, I recall being struck by its sumptuousness. The bright sun flowed in the windows and danced across the softly tinted walls and plush furnishings of the spacious suite. I could hear the birds trill from the trees outside, despite the windows being boxed up tight as is the way in large institutions, in security-obsessive nations. This was the first time that we had met, he the distinguished man with thoughtful eyes and a timely frost at the temples, and I a simple philosopher not long tossed from the ivory tower of my graduate studies in philosophy into the cold realities of the academic marketplace.

We sat across from each other on matching lavender loveseats. The gentleman smiled amiably at me, and the conversation flitted breezily from topic to topic until it eventually settled on the subject of my research. At this point, I imagined the room to darken slightly, as it always seems to do when I attempt to explain my dark work to anyone outside my field. I shared with the man the burning question that had colonized my every thought and driven my thirst for study long before my doctoral studies forced the question into philosophical articulation for me.

My all-consuming research question is the perennial philosophical mystery: how do human beings, in seeming good conscience, come to do the dreadful things that they do to each other? How are we to explain the immense abyss that divides the lofty ideals that are purported to guide human societies from the stark fact of the bloody history of our species? Why, after these long millennia of "civilizing processes," does the madness of genocide and other crimes against humanity stalk innocents everywhere? I lamented to my host: "Violence floods the globe; bloodletting drowns the dreams of newly developing nations across the third world; misery and carnage undermine hopes for peace and progress in the poorest and weakest countries."

The gentleman in the plush office shifted in his seat; his eyes darted from left to right. He leaned forward, dropping his voice to a judicious whisper, clearly eager to share his wisdom with this naïve and artless philosopher. "Wendy," he said solicitously, "*These people* have always been killing each other. There is nothing you or I can do about it. It's just the way *these people* are."

*    *    *

This work composes a critical examination of the facile myth whispered to me in the plush office suite that sunny spring day by my sophisticated interlocutor, the myth that global violence can be explained entirely by reference to "the way these people are." I mean to challenge the popular assumption that violence is an essential quality of certain populations; it challenges the supposition, all too common in the West, that black- and brown-skinned bodies have always been killing each other. In place of this myth, I am offering an alternative, more sympathetic account of some of the world's current violences. My interpretation will be shocking to Westerners, confirmed as we generally are in the dual-ideology that asserts history as progress and social, intellectual, and moral evolution as culminating in white Western culture.

So I too have some "truths" to tell, though, as any philosopher trained within the humble Socratic tradition, I am loathe to make claims to truth. I doubt that any mere human being can know for certain the truth about something as cryptic and convoluted as the source and nature of the many evils that plague the world. I trust with the ancient philosophers that, about crucial matters, the best we can do is a likely story. Plato has Socrates state: "Enough if we adduce probabilities as likely as any others . . . for we must remember that we are only mortal . . . and we ought to accept the tale which is probable."[1]

Thus I offer here a "likely story" to explain postcolonial violence in Africa. I speculate upon the mystery of human subjectivity and its tendency to become transformed and disfigured by enduring long periods of oppression and suffering. This work represents an effort to explain, more sympathetically than previous accounts have done, how African peoples, the bulk of whom, it is now known, once gathered in simple kinship communities generally more democratic and egalitarian than modern states, came to the condition of abjection, misery, and fierce aggression in which we find them today.

I consider this to be a work of phenomenological ethics. It is phenomenological in the sense that the work seeks to trace from a most naïve attitude the experience of violence as it is lived in the human life and to appreciate the nature of that experience from the perspective of those who have suffered it and continue to suffer it. This method, I believe, will help me to arrive at a more sympathetic understanding of the war-torn peoples of Africa, because this method sets aside accepted accounts of African history recorded in history books by the victors of history's battles, and hearkens instead naïvely and uncritically to the people's own account of their experiences and histories.

I am naming this work a project of phenomenological ethics because this rethinking of violence is guided by an explicit moral objective. My purpose is to force the Western reader to recognize the debt that prosperous nations owe to Africa and other third world countries, whose cultural, political, and economic backs were broken on the altar of Western prosperity. My purpose is to expose the bankruptcy of the political and intellectual leaders of those countries, sitting smugly in their plush office suites and spouting self-congratulatory myths of historical progress and the "development" of lesser nations. I wish to expose that even the new enlightened discourses promoting peace and prosperity across the globe rest on a latent racism and ethnocentrism, lingering from the colonial period.

This work seeks to remind Westerners, whether indifferent to the tens of thousands of third world children dying daily from hunger's broad effects or conscientiously dedicated to third world charity and "development" projects, that the umbilical cord connecting first world privilege to third world abjection remains sturdy and intact. Western nations, fat with the ill-gotten gains of imperial triumphs, not only start all economic and political races ahead of the game; their hegemony in the global marketplace guarantees the continuance of the status quo of global inequity. The current global political and economic systems have been built upon slaughter, slavery, colonial oppression, and imperial triumphism, yet today the systems stride proudly toward the future without apology or reparation to history's victims. Attempts to relieve the suffering and poverty that still plague the vast majority of postcolonial peoples across that globe are deemed evidence of the generosity and moral worth of the West.

The violences we witness in third world countries in the modern era, I contend, are best understood in their historical context, as "reboundings" of earlier violences. I speak of reboundings of violence after the tradition of anthropologist Maurice Bloch in his *Prey into Hunter*, a fascinating study of ritualized violence and its capacity to sustain power relationships over vast periods across enormous historical changes. Bloch employs the term "rebounding" to describe the tendency of violence to repeat itself over generations and to configure population behavior patterns in victims as well as perpetrators, reconstructing the subjectivities of previously peaceful people so that, over time, victims come to mirror the brutality of the perpetrators under whom they previously suffered. [2]

Rebounding violence shows itself in the agonizing throes of "identity work" through which suffering populations express their abjection and dysfunction and struggle to reclaim their sense of self-worth in the wake of denigrating histories. Long oppressed people tend to emerge from those experiences divided from their neighbors, resentful and suspicious of their neighbor's successes, and unsure of their own self-worth. Victim populations have generally been submitted to long periods of denigration that cast them as morally wanting and deserving of the abuse they suffered. Denigrating myths are typically constructed by the oppressors to justify their privilege and domination over subgroups within the society. Therefore, the survivors of repressive and violent historical situations tend to suffer fundamental changes to their worldviews. Having witnessed the efficacy of violence in granting order and stability within the repressive society, victims as much as perpetrators tend to share the conviction that violence is a valuable, legitimate, and necessary political tool.

This shared worldview explains why, when colonial rule ends, indigenous leaders taking over the regimes of power tend to mirror the behaviors of the earlier repressors. Add to this problem the fact that the regimes they assume after independence have been historically designed expressly for rigid social control, and the harsh governing practices of the new leaders, as well as the ruthless practices of the minions of social order (armed forces and police), are often miserably consistent with the methods employed by the colonial predecessors.

In this work, I am focusing upon the violence in newly independent African nations and interpreting that violence as examples of pathological "identity work" of victim peoples working through their past violation and healing their present abjection. Just as early feminists donned masculine haircuts and men's clothing and aggressively spouted slogans such as "I am woman; hear me roar!" before they could reclaim their sense of power in more feminine forms, I understand postcolonial violence in the new nations as a power stage in the recovery of lost self-esteem. Victim populations feel the desperate need to re-empower themselves against a world they have discovered to be unforgiving to the disempowered. The violent upheavals of previously peaceful societies, I contend, are largely consequent of the existential damage wrought upon a victim population's worldview by suffering, disempowerment, and inferiorizing myths spun by powerful foreign invaders to justify their oppression and exploitation of indigenous peoples.

This work employs, as its primary example of the phenomenon of the rebounding of historical violences, the bloody conflicts we witness in newly independent nations of Africa, which continue to be interpreted by some Westerners as indicative of the essential inferiority of dark-skinned peoples, as "just the way these people are." By obliging a rethinking of the violences of modern Africa as pathologized responses to and re-enactments of the sufferings visited upon them during the colonial era, I seek to disclose Western implication in that violence and to argue for the reparations and ongoing support that victim peoples are due.

This work focuses upon Africa, but I mean this treatment of African rebounding violence as an instance of a much vaster phenomenon. Rich Western nations continue to sack poorer, weaker countries through covert intrigue, outright war, crippling debts, and unfair global labor and trade policies. The violences continue because many people still harbor, at least implicitly, metaphysical assumptions about the progress of history and the supremacy of white Christians on a natural scale of human worth. These assumptions depress the possibilities of minorities within the rich West; they continue to subtly influence Western foreign policy and frustrate global relations; they continue to ensure that the overwhelming collateral damage of modern wars is color conscious. I seek, through these pages, a rethinking of Western complicity in the miseries and violences tearing apart the worlds of foreign others.

I am indebted, in all my scholarly work, to my mentor David Goicoechea, for his invaluable coaching, support, and gentle but hearty critique over the years of my formation as a philosopher. I also owe an enormous debt to my children, Adam and Sarah, not simply for the personal sacrifices they have made in the interest of my work, but because their youthful but heartfelt compassion for the underprivileged children of the world has been crucial in fixing the trajectory of my research. This project has been immeasurably served by the tireless editing efforts of my friend and fellow Concerned Philosopher for Peace, Joseph Kunkel, whose patience, persistence, and stubborn doggedness saw me through four long years of revisions of this text.

# Notes

1. Plato, *Timaeus*, Benjamin Jowett, trans., 29cd.
2. Maurice Bloch, *Prey into Hunter: The Politics of Religious Experience* (Cambridge, U.K.: Cambridge University Press, 1992).

# Chapter 1
# The Savagery of "Civilizing" Forces

Philosophers are generally reluctant to step out from the sheltering canopy of Socratic ignorance and into the stark light of soul-endangering truth claims. The philosopher worries with good cause what grand and sinister edifices may arise on the most humble of grounding soils. However perilous, an argument must begin from some foundation. The fundamental assumption that grounds and guides the current project is what I am naming the "rebounding" nature of violence, after the expression coined by anthropologist Maurice Bloch in his fascinating study of the Orokaiva people of Papua, New Guinea, recorded in *Prey into Hunter*.[1] I am building my case for a more sympathetic re-reading of the violence witnessed in newly independent African nations on the assumption of the tendency for extreme experiences of violence to find repetition in victim populations.

My contention is that radical violence against innocent people is not merely a symptom of the modern devaluation of human life by those in positions of power across the globe; undeserved suffering of extreme violence, I am claiming, is also the recurrent cause of violence against new victims. When people are degraded, dehumanized, exploited, and demoralized for long periods of time, their wretchedness takes seat in their individual characters and invades their cultural and political forms. Simone Weil, a great defender of the oppressed, tells that when people are treated as if they were subhuman, they cease to think or behave as human beings. They cease to react to their abuse as though they have a right to more respect or better conditions. They behave, in Weil's terms, "as lifeless things" without value or right to dignity; "pushed, they remain fallen," she explains.[2]

This work seeks to highlight and to bring to public awareness the lengthy and manifold effects of historical violence that follow in the wake of one of the most extreme, longest-lived, and vilest episodes in human history—the imperialist era during which Europeans slaughtered, enslaved, and colonized the indigenous peoples of the African and American continents. My focus is the long-term effects of these "civilizing processes" on the indigenous peoples of the African continent. But it is important to note that their pain does not pale but highlights that of the Africans thrown into diaspora by the slave trade, who continue to suffer their own unique spectrum of destructive effects of the imperialist era. Subtle or overt, bodily, existential, political or social, violence transforms its victims, reshaping their subjectivity over time and across political eras. As sure as nighttime follows day, violence follows the sufferers long into their political and social liberation and drives them in the direction of a future that is deeply burdened by the past. Victims emerge from their histories of suffering scarred, wounded, and abject; their future behaviors often entail desperate efforts to bring closure to their suffering by projecting their miseries, their resentments, and their anger upon innocent others in their immediate vicinity.

In the glory centuries of the various European empires, modern "civilized" nations launched a vast assault upon small kinship groups of generally self-sufficient peaceful peoples around the globe. In the cause of moral and scientific progress and in the various names of king and god, about fifty million tribal peoples were forced to surrender half the globe to white Europeans bent on "civilizing" missions.[3] Though the invaders spoke of spreading the word of god and delivering the benefits of civilization to the far reaches of the globe, in fact much of this assault composed deliberate extinction—murder undertaken on a mass scale as a blatant act of political and economic purpose.

National and papal policy endorsed this global slaughter. The killing missions required then, and have to this day been given, no justification or apology. The remaining fraction of the indigenous peoples of the invaded lands that survived the bloody onslaught of "civilization" were then conscripted into murderous militaries to prey upon their former neighbors, enslaved for cost-free labor, or were "hired" to work themselves to exhaustion or death as ambiguously "free" people, toiling under the most miserable of conditions for ridiculously deficient wages and all the humiliation they could stomach. Long after the mass graves had been transformed into cotton and sugar farms, long after the good Christians had rediscovered their consciences and abandoned their colonial holdings, and long after capitalist merchants had found new, more profitable ways to organize the armies of laborers for the strip-mining of their vast homeland territories, the conquests and slaughters of the imperialist era continue to be rejoiced in songs, films, and history books as grand episodes in the history of Western pioneering heroism.

The indigenous victims had no recourse; they were effectively politically invisible: sovereign nations, they were permitted no sovereignty; landed peoples, they were left no lands. Cultures were shorn of their cultural value; ancient artistic, organizational, and medicinal wisdoms, deemed barbaric superstition, were left to wither and die. Without histories, the populations were "primitives"; without culture, they were "savages." No voice was raised in defense of these peoples, no humanitarian appeal was sounded, as "civilization" swept through their ancestral lands and massacred their populations, usurping their bodies, their territories, their histories, and their pride. This global bloodletting composed more than mass murder, more than multiple genocides. It composed an assault upon humanity, a vast raid on the human world. Inimitable artifacts vanished forever; traditions of peaceful trade and non-hierarchical governance were crushed. Lost forever were endowments of knowledge and expertise—natural medicines, fine arts, music, and dance. Vanished were the farsighted resource-utilization practices that guarantee low consumption and sustainability, the social traditions that render longevity and stability of cultural forms, the naturally egalitarian democratic institutional forms, and the complex self-sustaining networks of social and economic exchange that promise self-reliance and political autonomy alongside sound neighborliness.[4] A wealth of human life, social tradition, political skill, and artistic talent was crushed by ethnocentrism, cultural ignorance, and capitalist greed.

## 1. An Extreme Example of a Common Plight

In this work, I concentrate my attention upon the continent of Africa, one of the areas of the world worst hit by, and still suffering from, the multifold effects of imperialist violence, masked behind a rhetoric of "civilization" of the world's "savages." The taming of the "dark continent" was deemed a work of *karitas* by the Christian invaders, just as the Muslim invaders of earlier centuries had seen themselves in the service of their god as they slaughtered and enslaved their path across northern Africa. When it came to the exploitation and butchery of god's *other* children, the conscience of at least two lines of Abraham's seed awakened only very late. In many lands, it still sleeps soundly.

As late as the 1980s, Africans were still seeking liberation from their European invaders. Some parts of Africa continue yet the struggle. The colonial powers only slowly and reluctantly withdrew from their colonies, leaving behind a continent carved like a great bleeding carcass into political territories whose borders have no significance for the people trapped within them. The institutions of oppression they left in their wake sat ready to be taken over by some new tyrant. The communities of white settlers, who in many independent nations still own the vast majority of the most arable land, carry on neocolonial master-slave relationships with the still impoverished local indigenous.

The colonials left behind poverty, abjection, and resentment in the indigenous populations. Child had been turned against parent, sibling against sibling, and tribe against neighboring tribe, in the fierce wars for slaves, in the contention for privilege under the oppressive colonial regime, and in the bloody struggles for independence. Culturally raped, habituated to war, existentially exhausted, economically depleted, and psychically disfigured by generations of insecurity, abuse, and denigration, the people of the newly independent nations set out to reconstruct their lives and salvage their sense of self-worth. The colonials promised financial aid to facilitate in this reconstruction, but those promises, more often than not, turned out to be hollow or simply connected to some further neocolonial scheme to enrich the colonial mother-country. In most cases, previous colonial masters simply became more insidious neocolonial tyrants, levying power from a safer distance through the more sanitized, institutional coercion of the World Trade Organization, the International Monetary Fund, and the World Bank.[5]

In the mid- and late-twentieth century, many African peoples found themselves achieving their independence from oppressive foreign rule. But Africans had long been excluded from participation in economic or political activity in their countries, so they are discovering that they are ill prepared for the rigorous tasks facing them as newly independent nations in a fast-paced global market system. Political and economic struggles and collapses are completely foreseeable results of the failure of colonial regimes to share their technical skill and economic expertise with the indigenous subgroups. Collapse is also entirely predictable given the current international system of trade, which is rigged to serve the interests of super-profitable multinational corporations rather than the nations that must prostitute their laborers or their environment simply to get into the game. When new Africans nations falter politically, Westerners have a ready explanation for the failure: political ineptitude is further proof of the essential inferiority of African peoples, their unfitness for self-rule. When the new nations founder economically, their neocolonial masters quickly exploit their failures as new opportunities for profit.

New masters move in where old masters move out. New "investment" schemes are hatched to "develop" the "underdeveloped world," and new "military aid" programs, sponsored in the name of "freedom and democracy," keep the impoverished populations in check or embattled, while the new masters execute new projects to plunder the human and natural wealth of the third world. New, more subtle violences take the place of the former, more overt ones, demonstrating for those who will see that the sun is only ostensibly setting on the colonial glory days of Western imperialism.

For the colonial rape of the third world, no apologies are issued, no reparations offered, and no aid extended to the victims that does not intend the further benefit of the imperialist home countries and their corporate neo-extensions. According to the foreign invader, a great favor had been done these simple peoples by the colonial era: underdeveloped peoples have been ushered into the modern era from a Neolithic existence. By European reasoning, indigenous peoples, before the time of colonial rule, had accomplished nothing of any value or worth preserving—no culture, no traditions, no artifacts, nor innovations. Their lands, rich in resources, were wasted in small-scale holdings, where "outdated" traditions of painstaking hand-tilling, biodiversity pest-control methods, and rotating field cultivation were still practiced, or in the passing use by nomadic hunters and traders. Genocide, enslavement, exploitation, and oppression were, for the colonists, the unfortunate by-products of a noble enterprise—the taming of "savages" through the expansion of powerful "civilizing" forces, the modernization of outdated systems, and the development of a backward world.

## 2. Diverse Agents of Colonial Violence

The colonial project could not have succeeded without the combined agency of a full cast of diverse players. The soldier, the governor, the clerk, the scientist, the merchant, the full retinue of settlers, and their various attendants all played their diverse roles in tearing the continent from its deep cultural rootedness and reconstructing it into a little Europe complete with its servile class.

Anthropologists played an early and integral role in the success of the colonial project. Curious observers of the human world, the earliest scholars of the budding science of anthropology were often guided by the prevailing pseudo-scientific evolutionary theories, which posited a hierarchical ordering of the various human cultures of the world. Anthropological projects served to conceal the purely exploitative nature of the new political and economic arrangements of colonial rule. Their studied observations of African groups suggested discreet and distinct cultural traits that easily hardened in ethnocentric minds into morally and culturally "inferior others" beside whom the mediocre colonial clerks could feel superior. Anthropological reports of the colonial period were snapshots of oppressed sub-peoples and tended to reinforce the colonialists' claims that "primitives" had no histories or cultural traditions worth preserving. Measured against distinctly European standards of appropriate social intercourse, anthropological reports tended to bolster colonialist arguments that European "civilizing" influences were desperately needed.

Western medical and religious discourses, too, aided the colonial project by providing dark metaphors of sin. The Christian theory of history promoted the further oppression of the African populations since the "fallen" sinner could only be saved for ultimate redemption and reunion with the god by prior purification through earthly sufferings. Christian teachings were degrading, biased, and alienating to the African "sinners" but since religious practitioners were often the sole source of medical help provided for the Africans, who were constantly struggling against the panorama of new diseases imported from Europe, their Christian moralizations often colored their medical diagnoses. Medical hypotheses often cited sinful tribal customs and decadent familial practices as the reason for the high incidence of disease among the Africans.

Another disturbing discourse of denigration that promoted the vast abuse of the people of Africa comes to us from Western philosophers of the era who provided the conceptual tools and logical paradigms for analyzing—and morally condemning or justifying—colonial and imperialist projects. There exists, since René Descartes, a modern prejudice in favor of reason, a distinctly white male European brand of rationality that allowed all other forms of reason to be judged as lacking in rigor, intelligence, and moral value. Since Western rationalist philosophers elevate reason and devalue the bodily as a faulty source of knowledge, they deemed people who live close to the soil as devoid of the reason that would separate them from animals.

The modern prejudice elevating mind over matter, rational beings over less rational, scientific method over ancient lore culminated in the Enlightenment. It impelled a philosophical tradition that paralleled the social Darwinist tradition in anthropology, a tradition that posited as self-evident a "natural hierarchy" of human cultures. Since reason is the distinguishing mark of the human being and reason unfolds in the world *as human history*, then surely those humans *with histories*—the Europeans—were rationally superior to those without histories— the subhuman "primitives."

Modern philosophy did not recognize its implicatedness in the violences of imperialism and colonialism. It did not see that its grand metaphysical constructions and its epistemological projects provided powerful paradigms structurally analogous with the European projects of "civilization." It was not until Adolph Hitler's racist ideology compelled a rethinking of what Europe meant by "culture" and "civilization" that philosophy's ancient metaphysical traditions and modernist rationalisms came under scrutiny by postmodern philosophers. Could Plato's "blueprint of the ideal city," Saint Augustine's *City of God*, and Georg Wilhelm Friedrich Hegel's "divine Reason" unfolding from savage primitivism into Western logical purity have contributed to the justifications for global slaughter and exploitation of simple indigenous communities? Could the grand philosophical edifices of Beauty and Truth be driven by a will to power, which come to be modeled by the Fuehrer?

European anthropology, medicine, religion, and philosophy, esteemed institutions of the Western world, are, each in its own unique way, implicated in the histories of exploitation, enslavement, and slaughter that ravaged the African continent and crushed its proud peoples. Each had its integral role to play in the seemingly senseless attacks upon the value, the integrity, the psyches, and the bodies of peoples whose only failing was to be culturally and racially different. Our European ancestors did perform these crimes against humanity and they did so in good conscience. Ethically blind they were, and ethically blind many of their descendants remain, inheritors of their ethnocentric worldview today.


## 3. Rebounding Colonialist Violence

People who have suffered deeply need time and understanding, and material and physical security to come to terms with, and to conquer, the manifold and persistent effects of their violent histories. They require liberation from oppressive regimes. They need safe and secure conditions of life. They need the trust, protection, and compassion of bystanders to overcome the ill effects of generations of oppression. They require these varied supports in proportion to the length and depth of the oppression they have suffered. Many Westerners are ready in theory to accept as just the concept of reparation for criminal abuses—in domestic abuse cases, in neighborhood gang violences, in business rackets, and in political fraud. We rally behind our criminal system because it promises retributive justice to victimized citizens. Frightfully rare, however, are lobbies demanding just repayment for life, land, and labor stolen from native peoples. Though Western nations were built upon the sweat of slaves, the blood of the indigenous, and the rape of their territories, the descendants of victim peoples still compose the have-nots of the world. They look on at the ongoing prosperity of the conquering nations and await their crumbs of charity.

Material reparations are unlikely to be forthcoming. My concern in this project, however, is with an equally crucial reparation. Generally victims who have been long subjected to abuse by foreign powers have absorbed the worldview of their oppressors and adopted the myths of their inferior status. They have long been under the thrall of powerful narratives that projected responsibility for the abuse upon the victims themselves. This means that victims must wrestle with erased identities and disfigured images of themselves, with degraded visions of their ancestors and heroes, and with alienation from their neighbors and their kinship groups.

All too often victims work themselves free of their sense of vulnerability and powerlessness, and break from their entrancement by their oppressors' denigrating myths only through exaggerated counter-mythologies of their own. They often mirror the practices of their abusers by positing their victimizers as "demonic" and by essentializing hyper-elevated moral images of themselves as innocent victims "purified by their suffering."[6] This mechanism is a common response to violent pasts because it proves effective in re-empowering the victim group. Victims often resort to starkly polar opposition to their historical abusers in their redemptive "identity work." In defining themselves as "us innocent victims" over against "them monstrous perpetrators," victims often exaggerate their moral purity, and assume superiority over others. Victim groups may be left with a sense of entitlement to practice the violence they once suffered. The newly independent are often prone to violent acts of self-empowerment because re-enacting their abjection upon less powerful others gives release to their pent-up frustrations and satisfies the need for overt and powerful demonstrations of their newly acquired strength.

Suffering teaches its victims that brutality is the only effective defense against a threatening world. It further teaches that violence is legitimate in the hands of "rightful" powers. The victimized therefore often continue forth from their cruel histories locked psychically within a dialectical identity, trapped within the violence-legitimating myths of domination, and enamored of the methodologies of cruelty bequeathed to them by their oppressors. Especially during the early phases of their independence and sometimes long after they are freed from their repression, victims can turn to the pitiless practices of their oppressors to seek re-empowerment. They reconstruct their identities and establish a secure place in their worlds by aggressively expressing their strength against proximate others. In the worst cases of historical abuse, violence rebounds in frightening force from oppressor to victim populations.

Because of the tendency for violence to rebound, victim populations run a considerable risk in the wake of their suffering. They risk their moral character in transforming from victim to victimizer. The rebounding nature of violence is the lens through which I am here reinterpreting the abusive histories of Africa and Africans. Tracking signs of this rebounding, I hunt through Western and African conceptual histories, pore over the works of philosophers both African and Western, colonial and African religionists, as well as social scientists, political leaders, and other authority figures. My objective is to discover what features of recent upheavals on the continent of Africa remain consistent with earlier imperialistic brutalities that characterized the colonial era. I analyze instances of radical postcolonial violence in localized African contexts, such as Rwanda and Zimbabwe, to demonstrate the degree to which the new violences remain logically and symbolically consistent with past abuses against those populations. I conclude with an interpretive tour of African philosophy of the post-independence era, decoding its difficult and struggling course as the battleground of identity work, where African thinkers seek to overcome the multiple disfiguring effects of denigration and abuse upon African subjectivity and self-identity.

Anthropologists of violence like Jeffrey Sluka have demonstrated that violence is not merely an externally administered socio-cultural phenomenon that remains outside the arena of everyday existence.[7] Violence is an integral productive component of life and a reconstructive phenomenon within those lives. For the millions upon millions of people who have suffered, and continue to suffer under repressive and exploitative regimes the world over, violence continues to function as a powerful force that undermines their future possibilities for peaceful coexistence. Violence takes place within societies, and therefore its disfiguring effects are deeply embedded in social realities—in bodies and psyches of individuals, in patterns of interaction and exchange, in methodologies of control within the group, in the shared worldview of the victimized and abusers, and in the mental attitudes and dispositions for action that are lodged in the progeny of all societal subgroups for generations to come.

Individuals and collective identities come into being within concurrent, overlapping, and conflicting arenas of power. Idealized identities struggle to unfold in the daily lives of individuals, families, cultural communities, and nations. These multiple and often contradictory fields of engagement compose conflicting arenas of power. Identity is negotiated and ever renegotiated in an existential terrain somewhere among the competing authorial forces of popular knowledge, cultural tradition, and formalized institutional doctrine and dogma. These forces are themselves continually evolving and restructuring themselves, each seeking unique yet overlapping politico-economic and social goals, each served by self-justifying mythologies.

People are (quite literally) "definitively" marked by the effects of these struggles at each of these identifying centers. Individual and collective identities are shaped and reshaped according to the mythologizing forces at work within them. Myths, as narratives of origination and legitimation, make ideological claims upon subjects, reconstructing them on their own terms, reshaping them in the image of their own logic, and embracing or marginalizing them accordingly as they name them "belonging" or "deviant" from the reigning norms.

Violence to bodies is only one of the many ways these powerful fields of engagement theatricalize their ideological assumptions and manifest their mythologies. Tortures are only the most obvious of aggressions upon victims. The effects of physical tortures are easy to see. Whips and chains leave visible scars. However, ideological violences can cut much deeper, last much longer, and are harder to root out. The degree to which powerful mythologies invade the conceptual and existential terrain of victims and alter the lifeworlds of oppressed subcultures is exceedingly difficult to gauge with any degree of accuracy. Myths of moral and substantial inferiority are expressly designed to invade the victim subgroups and corral them into beliefs and behaviors that make almost inevitable their psychic, cultural, and moral collapse.

We can hardly imagine how radical violence is lived by people caught in its throes, how deeply and unpredictably they are molded within its disfiguring clutch, and in what ways they are marked beyond the visible scars of the tortures and the span of the diaspora they suffer as families and cultural groups. How do the victims act out their pain and their abjection in the aftermath of their sufferings? How long after their release from oppression does their cruel past continue to torment and distort their sense of self-worth, to frustrate their sense of security, to configure their patterns of behavior, and to predispose them toward pathological responses to threatening situations? How do the wounded throw themselves into the task of reconstructing their damaged worlds? How do they go about rebuilding their families and recreating their destabilized communities, resurrecting their traditions, and recapturing their lost pasts?

Once victims have been indoctrinated into dark logic that underlies the law of "civilization," they have a tendency to learn all too well the lessons of their subjection. They tend to absorb, over their long suffering lives and across the generations of lives of their people's collective victimization, the ideology upon which that law rests, the ideology that "might is right" in the world of political realities. How do victim peoples overcome that logic when they come to rebuild their future worlds? How long will they mirror the repressive methods of their conquerors in the management of their families, their clans, and their newly independent nations? How will the victims of repressive regimes find their way "home" to their traditional, highly democratic ways, and resurrect the long-dead alliances with kin and neighbor that were not configured by the twisted ideals of capitalism nor grounded upon divisions of wealth? How long after they escape the raids upon their bodies until the victims find release from the raids upon their consciousness?

Long-term violence rears different kinds of subjects. Repressive regimes nurture different kinds of citizens. Suffering shapes different kinds of people, hardens and desensitizes them. Where violence has been a powerful component of life by an allegedly *morally* superior elite, violence becomes a socio-cultural reality that configures everyday thought and action across the cultural reach.

## 4. Difficulties in Charting Rebounding Violence

In charting the flow of violence and the effects of that flow upon victims, the scholar encounters an elemental problem. The very attempt to plot the effects of politically and culturally functional mythologies implies an original purity from systematic violences across the collective cultural terrain of victim populations. The project necessarily therefore risks preserving a further myth—the notion of an uncorrupted innocence, a sanitized *arche*, in the victim people's traditional ways of being-in-the-world. It assumes a prior discrete and static identity in the original peoples which is later corrupted. The claim of identity damage inexorably denies the dynamism of identity-constructing forces. Ironically, the scholar cannot avoid a critical logical error that repeats the anthropological blunder that prepared the groundwork for the colonial violences that the scholar seeks to comprehend and help heal.

No matter how the scholar takes care, all descriptions of identity are constructed through the use of language, a medium of communication that freezes dynamic realities into solid, static forms. Furthermore, though the scholar attempts to resist the tendency toward oversimplified polar characterizations of the very sort employed to denigrate subpopulations, the inclination to radical polarity is embedded in language, in logic, and in the will to comprehend that drives every scholarly project. The parsing and probing of complex human phenomena necessarily impel the scholar in the direction of oversimplification and conceptual polarization.

The Aristotelian-Cartesian method of clear and distinct definitions grounded in a logic of identity and non-contradiction that provides the framework for scholarly investigations in the Western world frames and limits the scholar's every attempt to make sense of the conflicting forces that propel the human world. It stalks all scholarly investigation and, at least to some degree, falsifies all findings. Scholarly descriptions are compromised because the language and logical categories of the investigator are limited to systems of value-ridden binaries. In short, scholarly investigation is inevitably played out upon a pre-established field of falsifying assumptions. The violence scholar is dogged at every turn by a performative contradiction embedded in investigative work *as such*: the impossibility of condemning violence without enacting the mechanism of "demonization" that is the essence of the problem being addressed.

Another problem, a problem of moral myopia, stalks the success of the project of understanding the suffering of abused populations. Because the institutional violences from which Western populations suffer are not readily visible to the observer, we in the West, finding ourselves at a safe spatial distance of oceans and a safe temporal distance of decades from the concrete manifestations of the more obvious violences of war, starvation, and disease, are condemned to be *voyeurs* peeking and listening in on the distant spectacles of violences of foreign others. That safe distancing permits and even impels a strong tendency t blame the victims for the violences they suffer. The strong predisposition exists for observers in distant peaceful lands to wonder whether the violence we are observing in distant populations is a function of some failure in those populations to behave in a neighborly fashion. It is easy to leap from this speculation to the "evolutionary" prejudice that a general barbarity infects foreign cultures who have not yet learned, as we have, to get along with each other. Perhaps, as our ancestors claimed, foreign others are not fully "civilized" after all.

Carefully protected within the moralistic sheath of our elite, well-fed, (somewhat) crime-free "first world" identity, violence comprises, for us, a perpetually elusive and always abstract phenomenon, alien to our everyday experience of Western being-in-the-world. As a consequence, tales of the violences of foreign lands can easily collapse into oversimplifications and facile moralizations. Either all contenders can come to be seen as "savages" incapable of "civilized" behavior, or we may begin to make sense of distant conflicts by casting the opponents into the stark binaries of "good guys" against "bad guys," savages and civilized, or the god's chosen against the demonic infidel. Either way, the news of the miseries of distant others tends to trivialize into tired morality plays, themselves mythological constructions, from which our flourishing Western lifeworld can hardly avoid emerging the moral victor.

This prejudice is constantly confirmed and promoted by the print and visual media that tend to reflect the interests and prejudices of their readers and those of the ruling global elites. There exists little good journalism these days that escapes servitude to the agendas of powerful governments and big business.[8] Even the best journalism may present to its audience a picture of foreign battles that feature clear ideological truths motivating starkly obvious opponents, visibly delineated and distinct politically, socially, and morally. Though conflicts, wherever they occur, tend in reality to be highly complex and ambiguous, the press strives to describe and interpret foreign conflicts in clear and distinct terms to suit the intellectual capacities of their most average readers. This permits the outsider the illusion of a clear understanding of the influences, forces, and devices at work in conflicts oceans away. It permits a vision of the here and now that all but blocks out the rebounding forces of the past and that occludes the more subtle influences of less obvious agencies and exigencies.

What is crucial is that the media be fair in its reporting. If people are to heal from their histories of violence, they need their pain to be heard. Yet how is this fair hearing to be accomplished? Fields of meanings are socially constructed, and all claims of fixed and stable identities, good or bad, compose cultural myth. Mythical discourses, local prejudicial reality postulates, cut deep, persist long, and are exceedingly difficult to heal. Social prejudice and stereotyping linger and fester long precisely because they cannot be effectively rooted out by the most sensible and rational counter-arguments. Once accepted within a community, social myths become embedded in concept and language, and ritually conveyed across the full extent of the system. Even the most radical suffering of a society's subgroups can seem to make perfect sense to non-sufferers, and indeed often to the sufferers themselves, because that suffering fits within the dominant worldview that grants meaning to all that occurs.

Ironically and sadly, suffering all too often makes sense for people within their meaning systems. Furthermore, systems of meaning are ultra-conservative and resistant to updating to suit new empirical realities. It is an exceedingly slow and difficult process to change the direction of the mythical tide of a society—to teach old dogs new tricks. However, violence teaches sufferers quickly and deeply that violence is an effective tool for gaining power over others and freedom from suffering.

Violence is also a useful means for expressing one's abjection. Healing requires the outward expression of one's misery but suffering is often difficult to communicate directly. Language fails, words falter, syntax deserts the speaker, in her attempts to articulate the worst of events. Violence provides a most effective means whereby abjection and despair can be expressed. Lashing out at others is a well-practiced way of acting out terror and pain, displacing one's suffering onto another's body, and projecting one's wretchedness upon other psyches. Those who have suffered through violent histories are prone to maintain the traditions of demonizing discourses and scapegoating mechanisms, because demonizations of their adversaries make facile "identity work" in persons whose self-images have been corroded, and because demonized images of an opponent provide readily visible enemies to blame for their feelings of inadequacy and vulnerability. In dysfunctional human communities, developing a strong sense of belonging is a process well served by scapegoat mechanisms. Locating and isolating those who do not belong gives robust meaning to one's home group. Thus is the chain of violence maintained over time, rebounding over shifting national consciousnesses, over evolving historical circumstances, and across the transformation of individuals and cultures. Violence rebounds by re-enactments of the mechanisms of demonization and countercultural rejection.

The violences witnessed in newly freed but long and violently oppressed peoples often compose the agonizing labors of the creative reconstruction of their lifeworlds, the more or less pathological "identity work" through which people heal from their histories of abuse. Reconstructions always imply destructions. In the newly independent nations of Africa, much therapeutic "identity work" has been accomplished to deconstruct the residue of colonial violence. Much remains to be accomplished. In taking up their places within the systems of their oppressors, the new rulers all too often take up too the cruel methods and the repressive traditions of their predecessors. They take up the illusions that structured the colonist's reality, and adopt the myths that undergirded imperialism—the myth that violence is legitimate in the hands of legitimate authorities; the myth that some human beings are "naturally" destined to lead while others must follow; and the myth that some are more deserving of the privileges denied to their neighbors. The new leaders assume the elitisms and the ideological fantasies—the social "myths"—that drove the colonialist invaders in their violences.

Colonial systems in Africa are founded upon social myths that hierarchize populations into worthy and less worthy. Those myths are held in place by radically uncompromising mechanisms of control. Mechanisms of control tend to proliferate and to replicate themselves with ferocity. The purpose of regulatory mechanisms is to channel public rage—always lingering just beneath the surface of the most "civilized" of peoples—and to expel it onto the marginal and most vulnerable within the society. Mediocre clerks and other unremarkable colonials assumed pretensions of superiority that helped relieve their petty frustrations and sense of inadequacy. The baseness and brutality they projected upon the Africans in rituals of social and physical cruelty. Now those cruelties are being re-enacted by the African leaders of newly independent nations upon scapegoats within their new nations or on foreign groups beyond their borders.

Violence is a dynamic and complex socio-political phenomenon, experienced and re-enacted by human subjects in fluctuating interplays of power, expressed and deflected across time and history in multiple arenas of public and private discourses. Political, social, and economic anxieties are articulated in cultural performances in a wide variety of ways. Each person, family, clan, *ethnos*, and nation must work out its pain, reconstruct its unique self-identity, salvage morally and ascetically its public image, and reconstruct its traditions, through sometimes lengthy, but always agonizing "identity work." Sometimes this work will get messy, sometimes bloody and, yes, sometimes "savage." Seen in the context of the savagery of their histories and measured against the defeating neocolonial forces that continue to suppress their possibilities for independence, security, and peace, African nations must be credited with the courage, integrity, and spirit that now carry them through these difficult tasks.

## 5. Collapsing the Myths That Justify Violence

The project of this work is to offer a counter-theory to modern ethnocentric myths that continue to flourish in great popularity in the Western world. Those myths permit the Western observer to interpret conflicts in the third world, and in particular in modern Africa, as yet one more proof of the savagery of "those underdeveloped people." Myths abound that posit the economic and cultural underdevelopment and general inferiority of third world nations; they enjoy a robust following in discourses of charity as much as in propaganda supporting the current "free trade" system. This is because those myths serve important functions in the West. Westerners are persuaded that third world countries are underdeveloped and culturally inferior, so they do not tend to question foreign investors' claims that their investments in poor foreign nations are purely altruistic.

As long as Westerners can buy the myths that third world nations are underdeveloped, our consciences can be satisfied that there exists a reason, apart from the grossly swollen ecological footprint of Western nations, for the poverty and wretchedness of the vast mass of the world's peoples. The world's 36,000 daily deaths of children from hunger and hunger-related diseases ceases to become a problem of Western greed or a function of the maldistribution of the world's "common wealth." The deaths can be conveniently attributed to the snail-paced development of the world's "inferior" peoples and the "cultural backwardness" that drives them to overpopulate their infertile lands. Under the thrall of these myths, Western bellies can be stuffed and Western heads put to comfortable rest each night in the self-assurance that we are doing what we can to rush "civilization" across the oceans of despair to aid these sorry peoples.

The economic realities of globalization have proven bleak for third world peoples. Communication and transportation technologies leap forth in new directions every day. Many people across the globe for the first time in human history are appreciating a sense of global connectedness. Their engaged cosmopolitanism is witnessed in the concerted outcries of the millions of people who took to the streets around the world in the months leading up to the United States' invasion of Iraq in 2003. The strengths of global identity are seen as well in the myriad non-governmental organizations (NGOs) that have cropped up in the past decade and dedicate themselves to improving health, education, peace, and justice on a global scale. Some of these groups, such as the San Francisco-based Global Exchange, provide critical information to educate Western citizens about the cruel realities of global economic tyranny. Many provide informative books, CDs, and videos for use in classrooms; some arrange guided tours of troubled areas of the world to help connect peoples face to face with their global neighbors. Other NGOs work as alternative middleparties to provide Westerners with access to third world products at fair trade prices. Yet others raise funds to supply small loans to farmers, craftspeople, and traders in poorer countries so that third world peoples will have alternatives to neo-enslavement in Nike sports gear factories and other sweatshop industries.

These developments are hopeful signs that change in the direction of a more just and peaceful world can be effected. Justice begins with reparation for past injustices. Justice begins when global relations are taken up on a truly fair and level playing field. History's victors owe that reparative justice to the poor peoples of the third world who helped them to build their prosperous empires. They do not need charity handouts of rice; nor do they need to be taught to fish. They need to nationalize their country's rich resources and feed their own people before they prepare the desserts and exotic coffees for our Western tables.

A Ugandan friend once related to me a tale, popular in his country, that tale expresses succinctly African wisdom regarding modern "development" schemes on their continent. The tale describes a monkey dancing down to the river's edge and looking about. Spying a fish thrashing about in the water, the monkey cries, "I will help you!" He wades into the river, catches the fish, and brings it to the sandy riverbank, where he lays it on the burning sands, saying, "There, now you'll be alright!" When he returns the next day, the monkey finds the fish has died. Scratching his head, he spies yet another fish flopping about in the river. Wading in, he proceeds to "save" another and another. The moral of the story is contained in the closing question the Ugandans pose: "How long will it take the monkey to figure it out?" Their charitable interpretation of the global community's (imaged as the monkey's) intentions as an innocent misunderstanding of reality is yet another witness to the time-honored generosity of Africans.

# Notes

1. Maurice Bloch, *Prey into Hunter: The Politics of Religious Experience* (Cambridge, U.K.: Cambridge University Press, 1992), 3.

2. Simone Weil, *Intimations of Christianity Among the Ancient Greeks*, Elizabeth Chase Geissbuhler, ed. and trans. (London, U.K.: Routledge and Kegan Paul, 1957), 28.

3. John H. Bodley, *Victims of Progress* (Mountain View, Calif.: Mayfield Publishing, 1990).

4. See Chancellor Williams, *The Destruction of Black Civilization: Great Issues of a Race From 4500 B.C. to 2000 A.D.* (Chicago: Third World Press, 1987), 21, 26.

5. See John Madeley, *Big Business, Poor Peoples: The Impact of Transnational Corporations on the World's Poor* (London, U.K.: Zed Books, 1999); c.f. Oswaldo De Rivero, *The Myth of Development* (London, U.K.: Zed Books, 2003); and Justin Rosenberg, *The Follies of Globalization Theory* (London, U.K.: Verso, 2000).

6. Wendy C. Hamblet, *The Sacred Monstrous: A Reflection on Violence in Human Communities* (Lanham, Md.: Lexington Books, 2004).

7. Jeffrey Sluka, ed., *Death Squad: The Anthropology of State Terror* (Philadelphia: University of Pennsylvania Press, 2000); see also Carolyn Nordstrom, Jo Ann Martin, eds., *The Paths to Domination, Resistance and Terror* (Berkeley, Calif.: University of California Press, 1992).

8. Noam Chomsky, *Media Control: The Spectacular Achievements of Propaganda* (New York: Seven Stories Press, 2002); and Noam Chomsky, Edward S. Herman, *Manufacturing Consent: The Political Economy of Mass Media* (New York: Pantheon Books, 2002).

# Chapter 2
# Orienting Notions

My research as a violence scholar convinces me that the violence, which we witness repeated again and again in the world throughout the history of human-kind, testifies to the recurrent, regenerative nature of violence itself. In making this claim, I am not proposing that violence is substantive or metaphysical. I am not subscribing to the recently repopularized notion of evil that sees brutality as something larger than human action that acts through, but somehow does not originate with, a human agent. A substantive view of violence emanates from the religious notion of "evil." Many religious theories continue to explain evil as a dark force more powerful than human action that looms on the cusp of the world of decency and civilization, waiting for an opportunity to creep inside and contaminate the pure.

On the contrary, I am certain that *people* harm people, often cruelly, in many cases knowingly, and very frequently in good conscience. In *The Sacred Monstrous*, I rally a spectrum of social scientific theories alongside philosophical treatments of ideas about self and world, in order to demonstrate that the archaic view of evil is not only unhelpful in explaining violence; the concept of evil is often itself a cause of much of the violence that occurs in the world.[1] I suggest in that work that one important method for minimizing the violence that we commit lies in conscious acts of questioning those things that we hold most sacred in our traditions, institutions, values, virtues, and ideals. Sacrosanct notions must be robbed of their aura of infallibility because they serve as powerful forces that orient thought and guide behaviors in all our most sacred "home-spaces" of family, religious group, culture, and homeland. Where elements of the lifeworld are considered infallible, and where ideas about identity are rendered clear and distinct, all too often calls for purity rally exclusionary missions to cast out those who do not fit well within the group's norms. Purification rituals often entail expulsion and murder of alienated components who are seen as outsiders to the group—the profane "nonbelonging." The false dichotomy of sacred and profane needs to be dispelled. People need to recognize that what we hold most sacred can propel us to perform the most monstrous deeds—hence the "sacred monstrous."

Western anthropologists insist that *human* communities originated in bloody sacrifice rituals. Brutal murder rituals were practiced with the intention of purifying the in-group of external contaminants seen to corrupt the purity of the group. Sacrifice rituals also served to secure a firm definition of the group's identity—as *this* because *not that*. When Western anthropologists posit examples of the "primitive" mentality, they turn for their illustrations to simple tribal communities of the third world, peoples they label "primitives." Ironically, these scholars practice the very sorting ritual they are describing, when they cast primitivism as something exotic, something "over there" to be overcome by (white Western) rationality. They do not consider the possibility that murder sacrifice rituals may be peculiar to the Western tradition. There exists much evidence to militate against the notion that native peoples of Africa followed the archaic and bloody path of identity formation which included human sacrifice. Africans may well not share this violent history for several reasons. First, Africans gathered in kinship groups that remained, for the most part, relatively small, and their primary struggles were crop failure and child mortality. Therefore, their traditional communal rites tended to focus upon weather, fertility (of soil and mothers), initiation of newborns into the group, and rites of passage (that prepared responsible parents and caretakers for the weak of the society). Chapter 5 takes up more fully the question of the lifeworld and practices of precolonial Africa and provides alternative discourses about African history.

Eli Sagan helps us to understand how small African kinship communities differed from larger militaristic communities. In his influential book, *At the Dawn of Tyranny*, Sagan explains that, as long as communities remained relatively stable in population, tied to the land, and focused upon feeding themselves, they stayed small enough for each member to know intimately the others of their group. As long as the communities recognized the benefits of trade and intermarriage with their neighboring communities, they continued to live in relative peace and harmony with their neighbors.[2] Simple native cultures tended to stress the values of stability, community, and fertility. The virtues they practiced and esteemed reflected their communal ethos—sharing their meager goods and welcoming freely the journeying stranger.

Undoubtedly the peace was broken from time to time, within these early simple communities and among the various communities. At those historical moments, sacrifice rituals may indeed have been taken up, as such rituals are highly functional in channeling aggressions and restoring peace in and among the groups. After all, the purpose of ritualized violence is to defuse aggressive urges by submitting them to the rigid yoke of ritual regulation. Sporadic ritual practice may have helped to minimize the number and intensity of outbreaks of violence among small communities. Once the community feels safe and solidified again, it can go back to its more peaceful traditions.

In the case of the larger, more aggressive state, however, rituals of violence tend to grow in intensity and frequency in accord with the burgeoning size of the structure. Internal scapegoating practices in developed states are paralleled by external overflow of ritual violence upon neighboring states and peoples. Famed anthropologist Maurice Bloch argues for a direct relation between the state's self-perception of its power and the aggressions a state will levy upon its neighbors. The degree to which the state believes itself capable of getting away with aggressive violences, unavenged, for Bloch, parallels the degree of likelihood that the state will commit aggressions against its neighbors.[3]

Sagan's theory of the parallel evolution of state size and state aggression is convincing. Once innovative technologies of production and storage of foodstuffs propel the sudden explosions of population, their numbers necessitate the development of correspondingly huge armies. Then, with standing armies, there arises the possibility of year-round wars of aggression and raids that bring in booty in all seasons. With these developments, tells Sagan, the state proper comes into existence, with its rigidly hierarchical structure and the typical tripartite class divisions—the worker masses who perform the menial labors of the system; the priestly/kingly class which rules; and the permanent warrior class who manage internal dissent and bring in and share the booty of war.[4]

As the state becomes numerically distended, the ritual life that organizes, conveys, and affirms the power hierarchy becomes concomitantly distended, and the aggressions that enrich the whole from the coffers of the neighbors become institutionalized into seasonal practice. As the state flourishes, so burgeon forth the rituals of containment that serve crucial functions both within and without the state. Institutionalized aggressions and external wars aid in maintaining the status quo of power relations within the group, increasing the wealth and power of the elites, and expanding the territorial holdings of the state. Even the most oppressed members come to support the system that oppresses them, because they take great pride in being a small cog in a strong chain of power that instills fear and respect in its neighbors.

Sagan's theory of the link between size and aggressiveness of early states supports my theory that the violence Western anthropologists attribute as endemic to *human* community may actually be a feature peculiar to their tradition alone. My theory is supported as well by the Pulitzer Prize-winning scholar, Jared Diamond, who argues in his winning masterpiece *Guns, Germs and Steel* that European societies developed the guns, germs, and steel with which they slaughtered other indigenous peoples as a result of the geographical conditions which permitted them to share seeds, domesticated animals, and various other transferable ideas and technologies across the broad latitudinal stretches of Eurasia.[5] Diamond sets out in this book to discover the reason why some indigenous peoples of the earth lived in small peaceful communities and focused upon their crops and their animals, while others (Europeans) built ships, invented guns, and exported their germs and their violent "civilizing forces" to slaughter, enslave, and seize the territories of their generally more peaceful neighbors.

Sagan, Diamond, and African historians grant credence to the suggestion that Western "civilization" is configured for brutal slaughter by the long millennia of bloody pasts. Western anthropologists insist ritual violence is universal to *human* communities, rather than peculiarly Western. There is good reason to believe, however, that our present traditions and institutions, our noble ideals, and social and political practices may well be founded in violent murder-sacrifice rituals that demonize the different. Perhaps the discrete socio-political meanings to which we cling for our identifying markers today date back to murderous practices that marked out the familiar as sacred and the unfamiliar as demonic.

Anthropologists of the Western tradition tell that archaic communities practiced common and pervasive human sacrifice rituals for millennia before the arrival of our Greek ancestors, who were themselves male-skygod-worshipping, horseback-riding, heavy-armored, marauding invaders from the Russian steppes who pillaged, raped, and raided their way across the European continent before settling in Greece. Anthropologists are convinced that violence-legitimating practices are deeply embedded in the structures and forms of *human* cultural systems and institutions. However, if Sagan and Diamond are correct, war and pillaging are practices that began with overblown city-states whose male-dominated, rigidly hierarchical political orders venerated hypermasculine virtues. These societies saw rigid class structure, coercive leadership, war, and the raiding of neighbors as legitimate exercises of masculine courage and prowess.

Many of the anthropologists of violence explain that long millennia of human sacrifice rituals caused violence to become embedded in the genetic structure of *human* bodies, predisposing all people toward violent behaviors today. We may believe that acts of barbarity are the function of *human* frailty, which has long ago been overcome by our superior "civilizing processes" but perhaps the propensity for violence is a peculiarly Western phenomenon, hailing from our Indo-European (cum Greek) ancestors. Perhaps their war games and hyper-masculine military ideals of the nobility of battle are only sublimated into more subtle forms of countercultural violence that we continue to practice today. Mechanisms that legitimate murder of different others, dating back to the earliest progenitors of our Greek ancestors, may still linger on the cusp of the "civilized" lifeworld, waiting for an opportunity to leap forth and justify violence against people seen as differing from the glorified homegroup. Certainly much of the current propaganda about "axes of evil" and "corrupt foreign civilizations" suggests that primal dread of the "demonic other," seen as infecting from within or lurking on the borders of the sacred home-space, may still orient our political activities in the world.

The solution to the paradox of the violent forms that Western "civilizing processes" have assumed over the past several hundred years might be found in the proud elitisms that motivated their expansion. Western imperialists have been diligently identifying, enslaving, and sacrificing the wicked "uncivilized" peoples of this world from the time of their earliest empires. Locating evil in different others can be experienced as deeply "purifying" for the home group. However, locating evil in others tends to increase hysteria over pollution and propel violence more than it cures it. Locating and illuminating the moral failings of our human neighbors is a source of misplaced glory and is simply a poor way to cure violence. Rarely is escape from evil secured through murderous acts. Projecting evil onto a "demonic other" does not reduce the violence in the world; indeed, it merely serves to legitimate violence against those others. This fact recommends that, if the Western world were less certain of its status as a beacon of civilization, Western leaders might prove less ready to take up arms against other political and economic systems and other brands of civilization.

Much evidence exists to support the shocking claim that Western value systems, ideas of right and wrong, virtues extolled as exemplary, codes of prescriptions and prohibitions, and the lofty ideals guiding communities may themselves have been configured by, and remain consistent with, archaic murder rituals. Violence may well be the catalyst of Western civilization. The bloody onslaught of Western civilization across the globe throughout the era of imperialist slaughter may indeed be explained as proof of the self-legitimating and self-perpetuating violence ingrained in Western systems.

Human and animal sacrifices, excruciating mutilations, cruel expulsions, war games, war raids, pillaging one's neighbors—these are the traditions that connect the people of the Western tradition in a common violent history. That violent history may be, as the anthropologists suggest, common to all *human* communities, or perhaps that history is peculiar to the Indo-European tradition who compose the cultural ancestors of today's Western societies. The social-scientific jury remains out on this crucial question but one thing is agreed—violent ritual pasts continue to dictate overserious responses to the human condition. That overseriousness may still drive us to desperate and violent acts when our worlds become chaotic and threatening. Africans and other simple communities of tribal peoples may have avoided the violent ritual pasts of the Indo-European tradition, but the violences they have suffered at the hands of imperialist warriors may have destined them for a similar future.

An easy and convenient way that people make sense of their individual and collective lives during times of social chaos is to sort out clearly the elements of their world in categories that are simple, clear, and distinct. They will undertake to distinguish in starkly simplistic and polarized categories what is known from what is confusing, what is common from what is strange and foreign, and what is familiar from what troubles and bewilders them. Empirical data will be re-sorted into clear and distinct categories accordingly as they fit the communal sense of familiar or threatening: safe or perilous; good or evil; friend or foe; pure or impure; sacred or profane. When evil is located and isolated, set apart from the hallowed homespace, it can more easily be eliminated. Location of guilty others and conceptual isolation and articulation of their malevolent features allows people to make sense of their chaotic worlds. Clear and distinct identities point toward the remedy for social chaos.

The disposition to demonize difference lurks deep within the psyche of every human being. Studies in the phenomenon of "pseudokinship" suggest that the disposition is universal. However, raising that disposition into people's conscious self-awareness can do much to disarm its power. Far more insidious are the forces that serve in legitimating violence, forces that lie deeply embedded in the very processes, traditions, and institutions that we name as "civilizing."

# 1. Truth and Phenomenological Method

Coupling the evolutionary journeys charted by Jared Diamond in *Guns, Germs, and Steel* and Eric Sagan in *The Dawn of Civilization*, the most victorious civilizations of the human species have been those that have ridden upon waves of aggression into the Common Era.[6] Small, relatively peaceful agricultural communities developed along their own ritual paths—ceremonials focused upon fertility focused upon the successful proliferation of crops and human offspring. These locally focused, earthy, mother-goddess-worshipping peoples were gradually destroyed by, or assimilated into, larger states that eventually developed into, or were devoured by, massive empires. Where the geography permitted travel across extended latitudinal stretches, seeds, domesticated animals, and ideas were shared, new technologies of cultivation and storage developed, and population booms resulted. Where population burgeoned, germs too proliferated and waves of plagues controlled the population, until antibodies slowly developed and the plagues slowly disappeared.

Once germs were under control, population surges necessitated more territory, and also made standing armies both possible and necessary to citizenry and food-store security. At this point, the overblown city-states began to look longingly at their neighbors' lands, and their colonial aspirations wandered far across the seas. Just as the axes and hoes of soil-bound peoples of Europe had proved a hopeless match for the waves of barbarian Indo-European horseback-riding, heavy-armored, male-skygod-worshipping bands from the Russian steppes, indigenous peoples of Africa and the New World were unprepared for such wild aggressiveness as faced them during the colonial era. *Steel* (ships) brought the *guns* of overflowing nations to their distant unsuspecting shores. The *coup de grâce* was dealt when the imported *germs* from the distant lands infected unaccustomed, unprotected bodies and completed the cruel slaughter. Over fifty million tribal peoples were murdered, worked to death, or fell to disease. The victors seized their territories, totaling more than half the area of the globe.

Western histories of violence and the "civilizing forces" that propelled them have prepared people poorly for peaceful coexistence today. Ritual histories in the West being rites of war and pillage, rather than fertility and nurture, are deeply engrained in Western notions of right, progress, and justice. Their histories have taught Westerners to purify their actions and legitimate their violences by projecting the causes of social chaos—"evil"—onto those alien to the home group. The history of their brand of civilization teaches modern Western states the crucial lesson that those who are slow to swallow weaker states will themselves be swallowed without remorse by greater powers. The combined lessons of history have been learned well in the Western world, and the ethnocentric prejudices that ground the "success stories" of the era of imperialism continue to be called upon to justify new violences upon weaker populations. The violent histories of the West have fostered in modern Western nations the tendency to see one's own community as wholesome and benevolent, one's own practices and traditions as civilized and modern, and to see others different from one's own as underdeveloped, uncivilized, malevolent, and threatening to social order. This tendency comes into clear view when worldly truths are reconsidered from the "phenomenological position."

By the phrase phenomenological position, I am referring to the field of philosophy descending from two German philosophers, Georg Wilhelm Friedrich Hegel (1770-1831) and Edmund Husserl (1859-1938). Husserl's later arrival upon the scene of philosophy's transition to this new perspective on truth may seem to militate against his being considered the father of phenomenology. Husserl was not the first to coin the term "phenomenology" but scholars nevertheless consider uncontroversial the claim that he is the father of the philosophical movement known as phenomenology. Phenomenology can be generally described as the attempt to express reality through the lens of human experiences without resorting to metaphysical or theoretical assumptions about the truth of those experiences.

Hegel is the first to take up the new orientation and explore truth as a phenomenological occurrence, rather than as an absolute fact of empirical reality. In his *Phenomenology of Spirit*, Hegel traces the evolution of truth as the conflict across time of a *thesis* with its *antithesis*, until the struggle results in a higher revelation of truth, a *synthesis* of the two lesser, incomplete truths.[7] Hegel shows that truth arises always in the living moment of the subject's "now" and that notions of truth shift over time with the historical evolution of the subject's consciousness and with new information gleaned through intersubjective encounter.[8] Hegel demonstrates that all meanings and notions of truth, indeed all identities, change *essentially* over time. Truth is temporal and relational, an intersubjective and historical phenomenon, not a stable, eternal fact. Hegel illustrates that identities are not stable in either meaning or essence. Over time and in confrontation with other subjectivities "masters" shift subjective places with their "servants" in ever-contesting networks of social reality.

Hegel's phenomenology may be understood as a reformulation of the ancient notion of a Great Chain of Being that substitutes ideas for beings and sorts them along a valuational chain. But because Hegel sees his particular path of truth as universal and *human*, he does not appreciate that he elevates white European reason above other diverse ways of knowing the world and reasoning about what is true and good. But Hegel goes farther, dangerously farther. For Hegel reality does not simply *have* a logical structure; it *is* logical structure unfolding into the incontestable excellence of logic. Reason *is* history.

For Hegel, one need only note the cultural differences in the world to witness reason's stages, unfolding into differing historical moments. The world's various cultures mark the notches of reason's unfolding development and sophistication. Cultural distinctions, according to this evolutionary philosophy, separate the more reasonable peoples from the less or unreasonable, the advanced cultures from the underdeveloped. For Hegel, as for Immanuel Kant before him, simple tribal people suffer not only a diminished rational ability in comparison with the Europeans; they suffer *ontological* inferiority, an immutable deficit that is significant intellectually and, because Being is good, morally.

Hegel states of Africans:

> The characteristic feature of the negroes is that their consciousness has not yet reached an awareness of any substantial objectivity—for example, of God or the law—in which the will of man could participate and in which he could become aware of his own being. The African, in his undifferentiated and concentrated unity, has not yet succeeded in making this distinction between himself as an individual and his essential universality, so that he knows nothing of an absolute being which is other and higher than his own self. [9]

The father of modern philosophy, René Descartes had established in the sixteenth century that human beings are simply "thinking things." In Hegel, the Cartesian *cogito* becomes governor of the world, and since every governor needs its subordinates, simple tribal peoples serve nicely as the primal point of reason's unfolding. Hegel's grand ontological schema is the exemplary "metanarrative," a Great Chain of Being that captures the spirit of modern times, permitting white Europeans to name themselves winners in the ontological race, teetering on the brink of rational perfection. A very small and predictable step separates Hegel's unfolding Reason from Adolph Hitler's overblown nationalisms and Aryan fantasies.

Hegel's phenomenology is invaluable in carving out a new evolutionary notion of truth, thus overcoming Aristotle's long-reigning laws of identity and non-contradiction, which together did not allow truth to change with evolving historical circumstances—in short, did not allow theories of truth to explain the thinkers that created them. But this early phenomenology has serious ethical flaws in the universalist metanarrative structure that assumed European reason as the only form of rationality worthy of being designated *human*. Husserl takes up the phenomenological orientation toward truth, as a localized phenomenon of subjective experience, but insists on some grounding rules to guard against ethnocentric assumptions. All metaphysical and theological assumptions must be abandoned at phenomenology's door. It is for this standing rule of method that Husserl is considered the "father" of phenomenology.

Phenomenology offers a point of entry much humbler than other approaches to truth that largely rest upon claims of "objectivity." With Husserl, phenomenology sets aside questions of truth, whether absolute or relative, scientific or magical, rational or emotive, objective or subjective, and considers the question of the nature of a "phenomenon" as it comes to appearance in the lived experience of a subject—truth as it is encountered in the event of its *self*-disclosure before a witnessing person.

The phenomenological encounter is of such a nature that to speak in terms of truth or falsity becomes logically impossible and phenomenologically inappropriate. Phenomenology employs a naïve attitude and a careful, "stumbling" language that attempts to describe phenomena candidly and non-judgmentally. Phenomenology is interested in *how* an encounter is lived, how something comes to appearance for a subject as "this" and "not that." The phenomenologist therefore must set aside questions of truth or falsity, abandoning any will to absolute truth. In Husserl's terms, the phenomenologist must learn to "bracket" any assumptions and preconceptions she might have, because these are necessarily calibrated according to some implicit set of measures deemed "universal." The phenomenologist *listens* simply and ingenuously, and *records* candidly and honestly the features that come into view as characteristic of the subjective experience.[10]

No "objects" ever arise without "subjects" who observe their self-disclosure, even if those subjects are scientists by trade. The lived encounter is all we really have. The attempt to contrast the features of the lived experience of a phenomenon with some less "subjective," more "objective," or less relative, more reliable "scientific" truth rests on inappropriate distinctions. These distinctions compose altogether deceptive and existentially groundless divisions.

Husserl, in many respects the father of phenomenology, affirms the *a priori* nature of the phenomenological account. He explains, in his introduction to *Ideas Pertaining to a Pure Phenomenology and to a Phenomenological Philosophy*, how phenomenological investigation composes the underlying method of research in each of the allegedly "objective" sciences. Husserl shows that their very claims to "objective" truth are *a posteriori* to, and derivative from, the data collected in phenomenal experience. He states:

> Pure phenomenology . . . is an essentially new science which, in consequence of its most radical essential peculiarity, is remote from natural thinking. . . . It is called a science of "phenomena." Other sciences, long known, also concern phenomena . . . [as] psychology is designated as a science of psychical "appearances" or phenomena; likewise on occasion historical phenomena are spoken of in the science of history, cultural phenomena in the science of culture; and something similar is true of all other sciences of realities.[11]

Every investigation by every science within every diverse field in the edifice of knowledge assumes an objectivity cut off from, and purified of, subjective bias, and yet every instance of the supposedly objective data issues *a priori* from a consideration of phenomena. That is, all information is derived "originarily" (to use Husserl's terms) from a consideration of the experiential data supplied by experiencing subjects. There is no data that can sidestep the subjective stage of collection. In speaking of the supposed "primary data" that is the object-province of every scientist and gathered through the "natural" or "theoretical" attitude alleged to be objective, Husserl states:

> there correspond, as primal sources of the grounding which validates their legitimacy, certain intuitions in which objects belonging to the province become themselves given as existing, and at least some of them, *given originarily*. The *presentive* intuition belonging to the first, the "natural" sphere of cognition and to all sciences of that sphere, is natural experience; and the natural experience that is presentive of something *originarily* is *perception*, the word being understood in the ordinary sense.[12]

What this difficult passage affirms is that, before all scientific observers interpret their objects in this or that way, perception delivers up the world and its phenomenal contents to observing subjects. The phenomenal experience is fundamental to, and *a priori* of, the objective knowledge claims of the sciences.

Though a phenomenological treatment may appear as a shift in perspective from an objective truth, it is the very stuff from which objective truth-claims derive. Phenomenological treatment is more honest than scientific inquiry since the phenomenological method takes up the event or phenomenon under consideration in an "absolute poverty" of assumptions, "in an absolute lack of knowledge," and "aiming at the ultimate conceivable freedom from prejudice."[13] Phenomenology seeks to set aside those judgmentalisms that inhibit a nonprejudicial observation.

Regarding phenomena that are violent in nature as the events of colonial oppression under observation here, the claim that scientists have utterly missed the mark in their investigations would be a false and unjust charge. Much valuable analysis has been conducted by historians and political scientists to record the events and examine the effects of colonial expansion and rule. Here the difference between the phenomenological approach and the scientific comes into clear view. The allegedly objective records of battles and conquests recorded by the historian and the political scientist generally fail to reach the more subjective aspects of the violence—the effects of the oppression upon subjects, both perpetrators and victims, and upon the nature of their subjectivity—because those accounts aspire to the scientific and objective "distance" that grants them credibility in their various fields.

Research into histories of violence by sociologists has been invaluable in locating the victims and the perpetrators of violence, in helping them to overcome the devastating effects of those histories, and in identifying the signs by which we might detect in advance when future atrocities threaten. Sociological explanations of violent events, however, share with historical accounts a common weakness that removes them from the immediate and stark reality of those phenomena, profoundly limiting their philosophical and ethical usefulness. In the variety of formal scientific and historical studies of violence, a misleading uniformity exists: the clarity of these accounts. The ideologies driving violence are too often presented as crystalline; the opponents of the frays are obvious; the struggles are staged along clear battlelines between delineated factions that are essentially distinct and readily recognizable. Social and political conflicts *make sense* to sociologists where those events remain baffling, inchoate, and chaotic for subjects caught up within those conflicts.

The lived experience of violence is rarely neat and unambiguous. In some cases, the complexity of issues is such that no clear understanding of events is possible. Outbreaks of sporadic violence are experienced as meaningless, even to the most aware victim. In the worst cases where violence stretches into long years of oppression, intense abuse may utterly reconstruct the subjectivity of the victim and erode the possibility for any rational interpretation of the abuse.

Power twists the charcter of those who wield it. Suffering reconfigures the spirit, disposition, and moral make-up of victim populations. Violence changes those on both sides of its cruel event. Often those in control enjoy such a profound monopoly over the interpretation of local events that their victims are rarely able to maintain a healthy perspective on their situations, and often end up sharing the perpetrator worldview that justifies their abuse. Victims, whether oppressed subgroups, battered spouses, or mistreated children, generally come to adopt the viewpoint of their oppressors. Over time, the victims often find themselves guilty of deplorable behaviors or objectionable characteristics, and sometimes they accept the myth that their faults and imperfections are not occasional lapses in judgment or behavior but essential and immutable characteristics that prove their subhuman status. Victims come to agree with their oppressors that their imperfections are the cause of their troubles. In many cases, the victims come to find themselves blameworthy for the abuse that they are suffering.

This situation is exacerbated by the fact that those with obsessions of control often make use of the strategy of "divide and conquer" so that their victims are effectively cut off from any access to alternative worldviews. The likelihood that myths justifying abuse will be readily adopted as the victim's own reality increases in proportion as victims are separated from alternative interpretations of their situation, that is, in proportion as victims are separated from potential supporters—family, friends, and neighbors. In the separation, corroborations concerning traditionally established certainties about real or ideal selves disappear, and alternative orienting truths from outside supporters cease to become unavailable, at the precise moment when they are most needed. When traditional self-understandings and conventional behavior practices have lost their ring of certainty, denigrating myths imposed by the powerful can become overwhelmingly convincing. When these myths are repeated in isolation from more positive ideas and supportive input, they can over time become self-fulfilling prophecies.

Much has been written by social scientists to track, through the alleged objective data of empirical reports, the disfiguring effects of violence upon individuals. What is needed for a more genuine understanding of the effects of violent histories upon human beings and human lives is a more primordial perspective that seeks the lived experience of violence's event. Some may ask: what is to be gained through assuming the subjective position? Subjects may know firsthand the sting of victim abuse and the ironies of perpetration, but their experience is hardly unbiased. Subjects are nothing if not partial in their views. Their peculiar access does not issue in any universal truth that can be valuable to other members of their species. The phenomenologist would argue that a certain universality is at play in all subjective experiences. Events are experienced by individual subjects, and their individual experiences are in many ways unique. Indeed they are so unique that they often defy articulation to others. This explains why the most arresting events can effect such a rupture in individual lives. However, phenomenologists believe that at a certain level, subjective experience is universally shared. Human subjects experience similar events in typically human ways. An example will help to demonstrate.

Imagine an alien watching the earth from a distance and observing the human species in its natural habitat. The alien notices that the species forms groups grounded in birth identity within which mothers and fathers tend and feed the young offspring. The aliens note that parental care is given freely and generally with great enthusiasm. The favor is generally returned and, when the children grow, the children in turn care for the ageing parents. The cycle of mutual care makes perfect sense to the objective observer.

Now imagine that the alien observes one of these family cycles broken by the untimely death of a child. It witnesses the parents grieving inconsolably and wonders at this new development. The alien might explain the grieving by saying that the parents feel cheated, since the cycle of care is ruptured and the child has expired without fulfilling its duty, leaving the parents without caretakers for their old age. Only a human being would understand the hollowness of the alien's conclusion. Only a human being could appreciate the gross perversity that the untimely death of a child would represent. Only a human being would feel the scandalous injustice of parents outliving their young. It would take a human being to understand the anger and resentment that would arise against a god that could order a universe so perversely as to make possible such an outrage. Only a human being could appreciate the self-hatred with which the parent would cry out to the heavens: It ought to have been me!

However unique the circumstances of the death, whatever the quality of the parent-child relationship, however many the remaining children, whatever the unique characteristics of the child, the loss experience is likely to be deeply appreciated by most parents in the human world. The experience of the sorrow and the course of the mourning process may be played out uniquely with each set of parents and may defy communication with other human beings, but these uniquenesses do not militate against the existence of certain elements of the experience that are common across the species; there exists a shared and undeniably "human" response to the most wrenching tragedies of life.

Common sense seems to dictate that people acknowledge the existence of a generalizable *human* response to phenomena, but how would I know whether the truth I discover in *my* mind is *human* or simply a local or cultural phenomenon? There exists a fundamental epistemological flaw in a project of philosophy that seeks to map the logical layout of truth as it is experienced in *my* mind and to assign that truth to all human beings. The flaw is more than epistemological, however; it is an error of great ethical significance. Thus the universalizing claim is precisely what brings Husserl to criticism by other scholars.

Postmodern philosophers have simply connected the dots from European universalist metanarrative to Hitler's racist fascism. Now philosophy takes a dramatic and radical shift in its labors, in an effort to unseat the arrogance of Descartes' "thinking things" and Hegel's monumental edifice of Reason. They seek to return philosophy to the radical skepticism of its humble Socratic roots. Derrida's insistence that "all is text" reminds thinkers that their ideas are infinitely removed from "objective" knowledge; all knowledge must be seen as subjective "phenomenal" experience, interpretation, text, hermeneutic elaborations of a concrete immediacy that is never securely grasped and remains ever vulnerable to error. Lyotard shows that secure knowledges have a way of rising up into formidable edifices that weigh heavily upon individuals and freedom. Foucault demonstrates that the societies that most celebrate individualism and freedom may be the most "disciplinary" of all, because their oppressive structures of citizen control have grown subtle, cunning and seductive.

Martin Heidegger, Maurice Merleau-Ponty, and Hans Georg Gadamer take up the problematic of universalization through the metaphors of "language" and "text" in the context of phenomenological inquiry.[14] Michel Foucault broadens the focus of the critique, extending the analysis from the nature of language and discourse to an exploration of culture, historicality, and identity. Foucault demonstrates that the governing notions concerning appropriately "human" ways of being are always embedded in lived experience and reflective of the power relations that compose power-knowledge networks in socio-political lifeworlds.[15] In Jacques Derrida and his wealth of followers, we witness the linguistic metaphor taken to its most radical phenomenological form.[16] Derrida's work confronts and challenges the assumptions underlying and embedded in the works of Husserl and Heidegger, positing that "all is text" and, with Emmanuel Levinas and Paul Ricoeur, that "radical alterity" separates and alienates contending discourses of truth.[17]

Derrida challenges Husserl's claim that signification in language is primarily a function of consciousness and intentional experience. As Heidegger, Merleau-Ponty, and many other philosophers of the postmodern era, Derrida opposes the idea of the "transcendental ego," the locus of the "universalizing move" in Husserl. However, where Heidegger turns to the "question of Being" and Levinas to the paradoxes of subjective violence, the enigmas of the knowing within subjective lifeworlds, and the conflicting arenas of freedom and ethics, Derrida expresses ethical concern through the metaphor of text, insisting that meaning systems remain always primarily linguistic in nature. Meaning remains invested in language and thus is a feature of the text, rather than being within the conscious control of an autonomous subject, or embedded in life experience. This radical denial is established in his famous claim that there is "nothing outside of the text." Intersubjectivity remains, for Derrida, always intertextuality.[18]

Over against Husserl's indubitable grounding of human understanding in universalized human knowledge gleaned in the common lived experiences of the subjective *cogito*, then, Derrida posits the essentially unstable and inchoate character of human understanding as guaranteed by the trembling ground of knowledge—the evolving, deficient, capricious linguistic "signs" that compose our texts. Echoing and extending Socrates' meditation on verbal and written speeches in Plato's *Phaedrus*, Derrida insists that the meaning of any text, written or spoken, enjoys an autonomy of its own, independent of both subjective intention (in an author or a reader) and external reference contexts. The text, for Derrida, as for Plato, is truly a "bastard son."[19]

Through the method of deconstruction, Derrida shifts the terrain of critical discourse to establish, not simply the variance within the category of human phenomena, but the *essential* variance, self-contradictoriness, and fluctuating murkiness of language and therefore all meaning—what he names in his notion of "differance." [20] The replacement of the *e* in "difference" with an *a* renders a new word, "differance," whose meaning is different from "difference" but whose difference from that original meaning resides both in exaggerating and undermining the meaningfulness of the original term. The difference indicated in "differance" remains undetectable by the ear, undetectable in face to face communication, rendering communication itself impossible, without differentiation. Only a visual examination of the two words can locate the difference between "differance" and "difference." By illuminating the existence of a difference—"differance"—that is more different than "difference" itself, Derrida highlights the fragility of meanings in any supposedly meaning-controlled discourse. "Differance" is a sign, an indication of a difference that necessarily destabilizes all meaningfulness and upsets all certainties of definitive meaning that ground all identity systems.

French philosophers of the postmodern tradition, to the great chagrin of many philosophers of analytic training, replace clear philosophical analysis with difficult, highly poetic rambling that acts out and subtly gestures toward, rather than states, their intended meanings. The new philosophical style composes a wrestling with ideas that exposes less a definitive new philosophical position than a display of the linguistic problem—a spectacle that reveals the shiftiness of language, the inherent instability of identity, and the fragility of language's meaningfulness. Much postmodern philosophy is so opaque as to frustrate those of bravest heart who enter its murky waters. Levinas maintains a degree of intelligibility in his written style throughout much of his early work until Derrida eventually challenges his method in the famed article "Violence and Metaphysics." [21] This challenge resulted in Levinas' much more difficult, much less transparent style in his final work, *Otherwise Than Being*. [22]

Derrida leads a decisive charge against Husserl's over-certain transcendental ego on the argument of the essentially destabilizing nature of language that undermines stable meaning and makes fragile all identity claims. Other critics, such as Levinas, oppose Husserl's notion of the transcendental ego because of their weddedness to an ethic that posits the "radical alterity" of subjects. The universalizing move in Husserl, Levinas argues, betrays the sovereignty of individual subjects. [23] Once Husserl identifies the subjective experience as a universal *human* experience, that experience becomes existentially leveled, indistinguishable in structure and disclosive content from person to person and from culture to culture. The shared common human experience of Husserl's transcendental ego has the practical effect of leveling differences of identity. Levinas resurrects those differences and raises them to the highest degree in elevating the ego's uniqueness to a *transcendental* mystery, a divine spectacle, a miracle of difference. Levinas signals the divine aspect of the stranger (and the best known of our familiars remains ever a stranger, by his theory) by elevating the case of the other to a properly eminent "Other." When we respond to the widow, the orphan and the alien in appropriately ethical ways, God "passes by."

Husserl and Hegel are the twin fathers of phenomenology. Indisputable is the value of their contributions to the history of thought and to the philosophical understanding of how truth happens. But both thinkers make grave "modernist" errors, valuing universalism over uniqueness and sameness over difference. Hegel's errors reside in his affirmation of the hierarchical nature of truth, his notion of history *as truth* unfolding into its more and more perfect forms. Husserl's use of the notion of a transcendental ego also remains true to the modernist tradition that values universalism over uniqueness, and sameness over difference. The errors of Husserl and Hegel are not simply logical errors to be sorted out on the road to phenomenological truth; they are ethical errors that keep the faith with a logic of European reason as right and just. The failures of these two seminal thinkers raise a great many questions about whether phenomenology can overcome its founding flaws. Postmodern philosophers worry that a *careless* phenomenology might end up, as earlier Enlightenment philosophy had done, serving as a justification for violence against subjects who fit less well the universalist mold ascribed to a *human* subjectivity. Perhaps people who do not experience phenomena as Husserl says humans do, or who fail to progress up Hegel's ladder of history, will be deemed "less human" than others who better share the common lived experiences phenomenology describes. This concern opens the tradition of postmodern philosophy, signaling a radical shift in philosophical focus from metaphysical and epistemological questions to explicitly ethical ones.

Levinas has a finely tuned sensitivity to the ethical challenges that arise in speaking of collective human experiences. In asserting that infinitely radical differences separate all subjective experiences, Levinas is affirming difference, rather than sameness, as the grounding truth of subjectivity, rendering each ego utterly sovereign and unique in identity, each as in effable to other subjects as a god is unknowable to human beings. The notion of the "radical alterity" of the subject describes an ethical position for Levinas because, in affirming the infinite un-know-ability of each subject, the impenetrability of each to the grasp of the inquiring observer, Levinas elevates the uniqueness of the ordinary subject to a godlike singularity, a parallel that highlights the value of difference and calls forth from his readers the ultimate respect for others. The elevation of the different other offers a salutary and dramatic departure, not only from the troubling universalization found in Husserl's notion of the transcendental ego and Hegel's universal Reason, but from the entire modernist tradition of Western philosophy, which culminated in an elevation *as universal* of their peculiar European brands of scientific and philosophical investigation and culture, reformulating these as *human* rationality and *human* civilization.

The concern for the foundational errors of phenomenology drives me, in this work, toward a careful phenomenology in the tradition of Levinas, one that seeks to speak of human ways of experiencing phenomena without sacrificing the radical uniquenesses of either individual experiences of phenomena or shared cultural representations of truth. Postmodern phenomenologists of "radical alterity" and African philosophers of the last few decades demonstrate that careful and faithful descriptions of the shared lived experiences of subjects can indeed be achieved.

Bénézet Bujo, Congolese Roman Catholic priest and moral theologian, claims that a human way of experiencing phenomena is fundamental and universal in the ethical sphere, providing a consistency to ethical insights across cultural and linguistic barriers. His notion of a "minimum moral code" preserves individuality, even in maintaining the notion of "human" *ethoi*, when he states:

> African ethics recognizes a *minimum moral code* which, "formally" speaking, deserves recognition in every human group, even if [the code] is expressed variously in keeping with specific cultures and communities . . . there is no "moral Esperanto," but only a plurality of languages, inspired by the common experiences of different persons. This minimum must certainly be preserved in all cases. But the minimum moral code also includes the right of each particular community to translate its laws into practice in a substantially different manner, provided that this praxis does not "morally" injure the minimum itself.[24]

Assuming the phenomenological position to understand the violent experiences that have been endured by indigenous peoples offers a further advantage over the sheer fact of empirical data and the truth-claims rallied by the historical and social sciences. History records the rise and fall of military and political battles, and the shift of political boundaries. The victor's truth invariably becomes the truth for posterity. In abandoning the claim to an absolute truth and attending to a lived truth—as an experiential event arising between subjects— the phenomenological account permits the abandonment of notions of absolute truth and allows a new perspective on the events of history, a firsthand report of the successes and damages from the position of those who experience them. Phenomenology serves to give voice to the subjects of experiences that lie outside the dominant truth, voices that have long been suppressed or silenced.

What is needed to disclose the disfiguring effects of violence upon oppressed peoples is a phenomenological description of the lived experience of oppression from inside its event. This permits an understanding of violence not as a cold fact long dead in a history book, but as a dynamic socio-cultural event that shapes collective mental worlds and individual psyches within those worlds, mapping, determining, and limiting future responses to challenges that arise and paradoxes that characterize the human condition. This work rethinks the effects of violences upon individuals and upon cultural entities, attempting to explain, from the inside of the victim position, the psychic and cultural consequences that arise during, and follow in the wake of, events of radical violence.

Much valuable work has been accomplished by phenomenologists who have considered the ideas and the actions of subjects from the phenomenological position. Treatments of subjects carving out their identities in the world reveal some fascinating and telling features. What might be named a certain phenomenal blindness in subjects comes to light under the phenomenologist's gaze. One fact that comes to the fore when the phenomenologist naïvely considers willful subjective acts is that subjects rarely see their own actions, however violational of other subjects those acts may be, as unjustified or malicious. Phenomenological accounts expose that the world is experienced as immediately true and certain to a subject, however ill-conceived the subject's conception of reality may seem to others. A subject's acts are grounded in this self-certainty and so rarely come into question as dangerous or violent.

Inside the subject's strictly controlled lifeworld—what Levinas names the "domicile"—the subject is for the most part safe and secure in grounding truths that make action possible and reasonable. Levinas does acknowledge, however, that from time to time subjects encounter unknown phenomena that challenge its security and cause it to lose its grip upon its world. The world can become increasingly menacing beyond the borders of the "known" territory. Levinas employs the notion of the "elemental" to speak of the threatening aspect of the environing unknown, echoing archaic notions of pre-creation chaos before the advent of the god(s) who bring cosmic order and meaningful world.[25] The subject overcomes this occasional menacing by appropriating difference in knowledge and representation, so difference disappears and ceases to menace. The task of re-securing the domicile is one of "appropriating" the "sides" of environing others and objects. Levinas uses the term "sides" to highlight the un-knowability of the radical other, whose reality escapes the appropriative grasp of knowledge, and extends off into an infinity of incomprehensible difference. The subject's belief that it can fully know environing others allows it to once again feel safe and strong. Others assume places and functions that serve the subject's domicile; the "uses" others serve and the "pleasures" they bring become the standard modes of relation with others. Levinas states:

> Man has overcome the elements only by surmounting this interiority without issue by the domicile, which confers upon him an extra-territoriality. He gets a foothold in the elemental by a side already appropriated: a field cultivated by me, the sea in which I fish and moor my boats, the forest in which I cut wood; and all these acts, all this labor, refer to the domicile. Man plunges into the elemental from the domicile, the primary appropriation.[26]

The domicile, throughout this bold adventure of living, represents comfort, pleasure, and the happiness of separation and interiority; it remains ever a safe harbor and a pure site. What cannot be gathered into the meaningful domicile by acts of appropriation lies menacing beyond the doors and windows, but difference can be subordinated to sameness, infinite "depths" to manageable "sides," difference to "use" and "pleasure" objects. Openings to exteriority can become barred shut against the threatening world.

Levinas reinterprets Hegel's idea of the historical nature of truth when he describes the imagined stability of the subject's lifeworld as an incarceration in an endless "now." In place of Hegel's powerful edifice of knowledge, Levinas substitutes truth that looms and suffocates, truth that menaces as an endless burden, an incarceration. That imprisonment can only truly be broken by permitting ethics into the lifeworld, letting difference invade the safe domicile. The arrival of the radical other lets in the fresh air of difference, allows god to invade (bless?) the sovereign territory of sameness. Levinas names the stranger "Other" to indicate the extramundane status of a presence that has the power to rupture static lifeworlds and to demand sacrifice of sovereign right.[27] The sacrifice of the ethical encounter in Levinas is no useful or pleasurable encounter; it composes an obsession, a possession, and an incarceration to the limitless needs of the Other. But ethical response does have a payoff. It rescues the ego from a timeless and suffocating existence.

This account of the safe domicile of subjective life testifies to the self-possessed nature of subjectivity, and the difference-phobia that guides our representations in knowledge and truth. It testifies to the potentially violational nature of all relations with otherness, and it witnesses that subjects are blind to the harm that they do to others, as they go about their business securing their domiciles and carving out their identities in the world. Levinas insists the subject is always innocent in its appropriations: "innocently egoist and alone."[28] The domicile is the place where "the unreflected and naïve consciousness" enjoys absolute sovereignty in a voluptuous world.[29] A naïve blindness that does not reflect upon itself shields the agent from the dark reality of its cruel effects in the world of its use and enjoyment. The phenomenological position exposes that, when violence threatens from the environing world, we feel it acutely, but we lose sight of it *as violence* when it rebounds through us, and when we displace it onto others. That is to say, a huge phenomenal gap yawns between the victim's experience of abuse and the experience of the perpetrator.

Phenomenological accounts are most instructive in helping us to understand how violence happens, and such accounts illuminate very effectively how violence transpires without ill conscience on the part of the perpetrator. Little phenomenological work has been done to disclose the other side of violence's event—the experience of abuse and oppression from the perspective of the ones abused and oppressed. This book seeks to fill that void.

## 2. My Theory of Rebounding Violence

My plunge into the dark *arche* of human history has convinced me of the assumption that grounds the current investigation: violence begets violence. Violence "rebounds" because violence composes an altogether functional phenomenon, an event that works to alter human beings on *both* sides of its event—perpetrator and victim alike. Since the phenomenon of violence has as many global forms as individual modes, the current project is grounded in the further assumption that the "civilizing processes" that have, historically, formed the logical ground of Western claims to superiority are fundamentally militaristic, ethnocentric, and dangerous. Phenomenology shows perpetration to be myopic and self-justifying. Violence has the tendency to rebound across generations, turning victims into perpetrators. Once people have been disfigured by their experiences, their trust in their neighbors becomes distorted, and their self-images despoiled. Thus, across the historical trajectory of the bloody imperialist history of Western civilization, we may expect to find brutalized peoples securing their futures with pathological earnestness, obsessive about their security .

If we accept this premise, then we are bound to its necessary conclusion—that the only hope that exists for mending this wounded world lies in healing yesterday's victims before they turn to violence to heal themselves. Fyodor Dostoevsky has Ivan Karamazov laments that the earth is "soaked from its crust to its core in the tears of a suffering humanity." [30] The task before us is monumental in magnitude. We must seek to break the cycle whereby the violences people have suffered in the past are likely to rebound upon others who appear as threatening to their security. If we could guarantee to the victims of violence simple public acknowledgment of their historical injuries and attention to their continuing plight, a protected space for healing their wounds, and the concrete materials to rebuild their shattered lifeworlds, they would pose less of a threat to others in generations to come. Apology, security, and reparations are a simple but crucial remedy.

Many will respond to this plan for healing by asking: Why should *I* take on the monumental task of healing the wounded of the world? What moral debt do I *personally* owe to suffering others? In the West, where most people are well fed and well sheltered, safely tucked away in the secure domiciles of their capitalist heaven, people tend to be well convinced of the disconnectedness of first world abundance from the miseries of third world poverty and abjection. We feel assured that our material abundance is a function of our cultural and technological supremacy. This assurance permits us a comforting distance from the miseries of the world.

We reaffirm this moral distance and teach it to future generations in school history books that boast our illustrious pasts, extol the virtues of our heroic forefathers, and applaud their "taming" of the New World. If we could drop the veil of innocence a moment and attend to our histories, we would be forced to admit that first world wealth is a direct function of past violences against the indigenous and present and ongoing violences against the third world. Our European ancestors and their modern-day neocolonial counterparts are largely responsible for the impoverished lives of the majority of people around the globe. Centuries of colonial and imperial adventure established a political and economic connection between the first and third worlds that cannot be easily dismantled. When our ancestors finally discovered their Christian consciences and released their slaves and their colonies, the oppression did not suddenly cease; colonialism simply morphed into new more insidious forms that remain in full play today.

Global institutions that determine the rules of trade today continue to protect the right of rich Western corporations to exploit the natural and human wealth of the third world. The World Bank (WB) and the International Monetary Fund (IMF) have, ostensibly, been created to aid struggling third world countries into the allegedly level playing fields of global trade markets. In most instances, these institutions have served only to burden the needy countries with immense high-interest national debts. To repay those ever-growing debts, these poorest struggling nations are forced to shift from producing local foodstuffs that feeds their hungry people to producing desserts for export to the rich nations of the world, since export sales bring in the much needed hard currency that enables indebted countries to meet repayment requirements.

Global trade rules backed by the muscle of the World Trade Organization (WTO) and the structural adjustment policies of global loan institutions (IMF and WB) cripple the "developing" world. They require the opening of local markets to the flood of cheap, often subsidized products from rich countries with which local producers simply cannot compete. The SAPs then seal the fate of the third world by forcing them to devalue their currencies to attract foreign investors who buy up their national patrimony at bargain-basement prices. Separately, these policies might make some economic sense in stimulating investment and currency flow in struggling nations, but together they are a recipe for economic disaster. The forced program of devaluation of currency, coupled with the mandatory privatization of public goods and the abandonment of trade tariffs, reinstates, in more subtle but equally devastating ways, the colonial "extractive model" that crippled the third world in the first place. Wealth continues to drain from struggling third world nations in the direction of the rich first world. The allegedly level playing field promised by global trade regulations guarantees continuing hegemony to the strongest players on that field.

Current global trade policies serve to further enslave the poor of the world to their historical abusers. But economic winners leave a growing body of sore losers. When the poor recognize the futility of their plight under the burden of existing policies, they rise up and call for land reform, unionization of their labor forces, nationalization of their common wealth, and safeguards of their natural resources. Only then does the fist inside the ostensible glove of global policy show itself to the downtrodden peasants of the third world. Under the guise of the battle for "freedom and democracy," third world demands for national rights to ownership and self-determination of their national wealth, collective bargaining rights for their workers, and unfettered exercise of their democratic prerogative to elect their officials of choice are answered by military interventions, and replacement of their elected officials with bloody dictators more sympathetic to Western business interests. Ongoing "military aid" ensures the "insurgents" are kept in their places and business continues as usual.

There exists, even today, active training centers for assassins, dictators, and death squad fighters who are needed to control the growing armies of the poor and dispossessed of the third world. The euphemistically labeled "School of the Americas" of Fort Benning, Georgia, is one such state-funded training school that continues to produce assassins for distribution in Central and South Americas. Their graduates are trained in the latest methods of control, then they are released upon democratic leaders, peasants, human rights activists, and church workers who demand changes to the neocolonial system.[31]

Western nations are deeply indebted to the poor of the world whose misery and slaughter continues to support first world abundance. The inequities of global wealth are directly purchased through the violence that drenches the globe. Westerners continue to enjoy the ill-gotten gains of the violent histories upon which the current global order rests. The continued and collective failure of Western peoples to see cultural and racial others as fully human continues to legitimate violences against the third world. That failure nurtures hotbeds of religious fanaticism and ethnic hyper-pride which eventually rebound within broken societies and onto those societies' neighbors.

The violence has begun in the last decade to turn back upon the West. The historical and neocolonial violences are coming home to roost in the terrorisms that now explicitly target sites that symbolize Western trade and military might. Across the Middle East, across post-socialist Europe, across India and Pakistan, across Central and South Americas, across the continent of Africa, in New York City and London, in Afghanistan and Iraq, people are caught in the agonizing throes of rebounding violence. Where the violence will rebound in coming generations is unknown, as victims work free of their violent histories by throwing themselves into their futures with a zealous and ruthless vengeance.

Recognizing, from inside the self-purifying phenomenal space, the harm that we effect upon collateral others as we pursue our projects in the world can prove an undertaking extremely difficult to accomplish. To the subject, all acts are "innocent." Subjectivity is an amoral space. As Levinas states, the subject is "innocently egoist and alone. Not against the Others, not 'as for me'—but entirely deaf to the Other, outside of all communication and all refusal to communicate—without ears, like a hungry stomach."[32] Had we ears for the victims of atrocities, then perhaps the atrocities would not continue to be repeated—year after year, decade after decade, and century after century. If we could see beyond our myths of innocence, if we could recognize the vast web of abuses that links our smug abundance to the miseries of the world, if we could face the fact that, when our ancestors collectively ravaged the ancestors of others, they left their progeny to fester and grow bitter toward us, we might hope to begin the monumental task of mending a wounded world. Easier by far is the facile dismissal of these discomfiting facts by repeating the perennial mythical mantra: *These people have always been killing each other. It's just the way these people are.*[33]

Our ancestors' historical crimes set the moral course for the Western ship of state. In strong keeping with tradition, Western nations turned away when, in genocidal waves at the turn of the twentieth century, the Turks exterminated the Armenians. The West also looked blankly when Adolph Hitler was rounding up Jews and other minorities for slaughter. Under the auspices of the United Nations, we turned away again, quite recently, when Rwandans rose up to butcher their neighbors. We stood by and watched as the United Nations ordered Belgian peacekeeping forces to drive their tanks off into the sunset, leaving innocent families to the surest and cruelest fate under the blade and club of their tribal others.

More recently, Western nations remained comfortably disconnected from the famines across the African continent. For much of the 1970s and 1980s, parts of Africa experienced a crippling drought that resulted in death by starvation of over a million people. Now researchers know that sulfur dioxide from smokestacks in Western nations contribute to these tragedies. The compelling proof resides in the fact that the drought conditions in Africa improved in the 1990s, when Western nations started cracking down on industrial polluters.[34] Global analysts further report that recent famines in the "breadbasket" of Africa is a direct result of the debt obligations of those countries to the World Bank. In order to come up with the hard currency to fulfil their repayment commitments, these countries are forced to produce desserts for the rich of the world rather than staple foods for their own populations.

The United States and Great Britain set the (a)moral tone of world priorities. They plunge their monies into weapons of mass destruction and wars of economic aggression. Less powerful countries like India and Pakistan believe they must follow suit, if they are to protect themselves from these global giants. After all, the United States military and the CIA never attack those who can defend themselves.[35] The world races toward further disaster instead of addressing its historical crimes or the continuing woes of its historical victims. The only countries that are wealthy enough to make a difference in the sad realities of global affairs are busy scrambling to secure their continuing hegemony in the global marketplace. A chorus of global humanitarian agencies and non-governmental organizations plead for a change in global priorities and a redressing of the global inequities that fuel terrorism today. The Culture of Peace Program, under the auspices of UNESCO, promotes a decade of peace initiative that focuses public attention on the plight of the children of the world, their families and futures torn by wars of economic and political aggressions. The initiative is given lip service by the United Nations but is not awarded a penny of funding.

The new U.S. "War against Terrorism" is already being exploited, by much of the free world, as a convenient means of closing down borders to suppliants and of denying legitimate asylum claims from endangered individuals and groups. Terrorism has become the latest excuse for the burgeoning war arsenals of the United States. It has also provided a handy justification for the latter's increasing military presence around the globe. Today's fearsome discourses on terrorism eclipse the fact that terrorism is nothing new in the global arena. Terrorism remains the sole means of communication for the vast majority of depressed peoples of the world. Individuals and subgroups of oppressed societies express their refusal of oppressive global and national forces by high profile spectacles of pain projected onto innocent foreigners.

In most cases, terrorist groups arise in states where state-sponsored terror has long been the norm. Anthropologists of violence indicate that state terrorism has for decades been most prevalent in client states of the United States and Great Britain.[36] Often puppet elites enjoy "military aid" from the United States and Britain in exchange for keeping their populations in check so that business interests in the region continue untroubled by pesky local insurgents. The rhetoric of the "war against terrorism" replaces the "fight for freedom and democracy" (against communism) in justifying the violences that flood the globe in the third millennium of the Common Era. Both provide apt demonstrations of how demonization of the different promotes countercultural rejection and justifies murderous response. People in the Western nations accept the facile proposition that the moral failings of other countries' leaders, whether Idi Amin, Robert Mugabe, Yasir Arafat, Osama Bin Ladin, or Saddam Hussein, are responsible for the burgeoning levels of global violence. However, it was Britain and the United States who showed contempt of international law when they teamed up to invade Iraq in 2003.[37] The Geneva Convention continues to be willfully ignored and torture continues without apology at Guantanamo Bay and in U.S. prisons in Iraq.[38] The latest incident, the U.S. Invasion of Iraq, served so clear a case of the flouting of international law by serving leaders of Western countries that, throughout 2004, an International Criminal Tribunal on Iraq, a peoples' court, held public trials and hearings in a variety of locations throughout Japan. On 12 December, 2004, the tribunal delivered a preliminary damning judgment against U.S. President George W. Bush, Tony Blair, Prime Minister of Britain, Koizumi Jun-Ichiro, Prime Minister of Japan, and Gloria Arroyo, President of the Philippines.

The people's court is not to be confused with the International Criminal Court of Geneva, but the court retains, nevertheless, great moral import, following a tradition of peoples' tribunals dating back to the Vietnam War Crimes Tribunal of the late 1960s. The International War Crimes Tribunal on United States War Crimes against Iraq followed in 1992, then the Women's International War Crimes Tribunal of 2000, and finally the International War Crimes Tribunal on Afghanistan in 2003. Such tribunals represent the world's outcries of moral indignation at the excesses of major world powers, affirming the right of the earth's peoples to condemn criminal activity by heads of state, and to judge them in the discerning light of international justice and to sentence the culprits to ignominy in the annals of world opinion. The four nations condemned by the latest peoples' court in Japan are well aware of the world's general opposition to their roguish behavior.[39] This explains why none of these except Britain has to date ratified the existence of the International Criminal Court in Geneva.

The rich West is thoroughly implicated in the violence and the misery that floods the globe. Our lack of bad conscience over the inequities of the global system proves that we are no more "civilized" than our forefathers were, if by civilized we mean more humane. The histories that record the alleged progress of civilization continue to chart the triumphs of the winners and to ignore the sufferings and losses of the weak and powerless masses. Violence is not simply a term in a history book. It is a term that defies firm meaning, and escapes scientific analysis. Violence is assumed irrational and unreasonable; yet violence is driven inexorably by *someone's* reasons, and often follows a very rational, predictable, and resolute course. Violence, in its lived reality, is elemental and constitutive. It composes not simply a destructive burden under which subjects must bear up and endure, but it is a constructive phenomenon by virtue of which subjectivities are recreated. The composition of subjects is altered and the flow of their histories set on new paths by the life experiences that confront, confound, condition, and transform people. The recomposition is all the more profound the more those experiences are painful or terrifying. Violence begets violence. Cruel experiences often produce cruel people.

Experts in the psychological effects of disasters report that violence has a profound power over people's future behaviors and attitudes. Catastrophic events can rob the sufferer, the perpetrator, and even the witnessing bystander of the ability to "humanly" respond to others. Those who are close to disaster often cease to empathize with sufferers. Sympathetic responsiveness toward others in suffering is the very emblem of humaneness, but this responsiveness turns out to be very fragile. Caring about other people and responding to their needs becomes nearly impossible under prolonged exposure to cruelty or carnage. Sociologists of disaster tell us that sufferers, witnesses, and perpetrators of brutality grow hardened by the experience of suffering. This process sociologists name "dehumanization" because events of extreme cruelty or devastation reduce the humaneness of participants and onlookers by reducing the human connectedness of those on all sides of such occurrences.[40]

The process of dehumanization is actually an adaptive mechanism that prepares the nervous system for emotional survival, and for effective participation in difficult life circumstances. The process curtails full emotional responsiveness where that responsiveness would likely crush the participant and paralyze the ability to act. At least temporarily, the capacity for "normal" responsiveness, typical of healthy human beings, is interrupted in order to prepare the subject to survive the emotional task at hand. Witnesses of terrible affliction experience a sudden, often profound, and sometimes enduring desensitization. Crises trigger an emotional shut-down that can last for short periods or persist for a lifetime.

One of the most famed records of the dehumanizing effects of disasters comes from the work of research psychiatrist Robert J. Lifton.[41] Lifton has recorded the reactions of Hiroshima survivors to the mass death and devastation in the aftermath of the atomic bombings. At first, reports Lifton, witnesses were overcome by the utter horror of the carnage. The dreadful burns and disfigurements, the skin-stripped carcasses, the bodies torn limb from limb and strewn about—these horrors initially left witnesses stunned and speechless. No words could be found to articulate their horror. However, a remarkably short time later, reports Lifton, people overcame their initial paralyzing dread and began to feel quite comfortable in their surroundings. Lifton states of the witnesses: "Each described how, before long, the horror would almost disappear. One could see terrible signs of human beings in extreme agony and yet feel nothing."[42]

Lifton's is one of many such disturbing reports that demonstrate how emotion and compassion very quickly harden over into that numbed non-responsiveness that sociologists call "dehumanization." Where suffering has been long-lived and the brutality intense, adaptive mechanisms can turn maladaptive. Years or even a lifetime may be required to cast off the hardening effects that are triggered by the suffering or the witnessing of cruelty and horror.

I claim in this book that the civilizing processes whereby Westerners lay claim to cultural superiority are themselves fundamentally violent. This claim will no doubt be found discomfiting by modern readers. The nature of Western civilizing forces is crucial to my argument. It is critical to understand the differences that separate typically Western from African patterns of power relations and the histories of their development.

When I claim that Western civilizing processes are inherently violent, I do not mean to imply that everything that has been accomplished in the name of civilization is devoid of value or necessarily vicious. I do intend that the forces that people extend for the sake of ordering their worlds and the worlds of others are always potentially oppressive because they stem from a perspective of dominance that names itself fit to do the ordering. Ordering forces are always potentially violent. At times their oppressive nature may be deeply sublimated, at others controlled by careful mediation, but the will to order is a tyrannical drive and always stands ready to spill out in bloody and murderous manifestations. Tsenay Serequeberhan offers:

> Indeed, in Europe social contradictions are mediated. In the medieval age religion served this purpose, and in modern capitalist Europe the liberal abstract discourse of rights and the ideals of "liberty, equality and fraternity," which animated the French Revolution, still fulfill this task. In the colonies, on the other hand, the dialectic of social existence has no middle term, or, to be more precise, this dialectic is mediated by violence.[43]

The claim that ordering forces are potentially violent is offensive and scandalous because we have been schooled to believe that the normal state of human affairs is peaceful and cooperative, ordered and not chaotic. In a nutshell, this describes the structuralist or functionalist theoretical position in social science. Violence, according to this position, becomes seen as an episodic deviance from the normal course of events, a lapse in the otherwise healthy engagements that characterize human communities. Virtue resides in stability and integrity.

This assumption is deeply embedded in the Western philosophical tradition. In the fifth century B.C.E., one of the earliest Greek philosophers, Empedocles of Akragas describes the movement of cosmic history in terms of great cycles of divine hegemony.[44] The goddess Love comprises Empedocles' gathering force that draws the varying entities of the cosmos into peaceful—albeit ultimately lethal—harmony. The god Strife breaks apart that suffocating oneness and divides it again into the individual beings that make for the diversity of the current world. During this era of colorful difference, Strife remains in sway, interrupting the peaceful coexistence of those individuals and making them discordant, hateful, and ultimately murderous.

Socrates, according to Plato's account, continues in the conceptual tradition that identifies perfection in terms of order and stability. Justice, according to both the *Phaedrus* and the *Republic*, describes the fully human state of soul when reason, the soul's charioteer, imposes order upon the troublesome passions and the chaotic appetites.[45] The social contract theorists, such as Jeremy Bentham and Thomas Hobbes, who posit an essentially competitive and hostile character to human beings, propose the civilizing institutions of contracts for the sake of rendering the naturally brutish human world to a mutually beneficial order.[46] All of these thinkers believe violence to be a phenomenon eradicable by civilizational processes. None seems to consider that violence itself may compose the civilizing force called upon by those in power to impose a pocket of stable order where business may continue unfettered.

Few philosophers are ready to entertain the idea that the civilizing forces themselves may be fundamentally maladaptively aggressive and agonistic, though modern history seems to point toward this discomfiting conclusion. Violence may not merely be a destructive force that infects healthy communities from outside the social fabric, not simply an unfortunate side effect of happy ordered homespaces. Violence may compose the very force that holds the social fabric intact. To the degree that a society is well ordered, violence or the threat of violence may be the catalyst of the social order. Coercive interrogations by armed police, detainment in cold dank cell blocks, airport security forces with sub-machine gun power at their fingertips, midnight roadblocks, humiliating security checks, the shocking spectacles of death row—these savageries may compose the ordering forces that render modern societies civilized.

Granted, the forces holding intact the social fabric are more overtly violent in some societies than in others. The violence seems to escalate the more that the social order is a hierarchy grounded upon wealth, as in tyrannies, military dictatorships, and hyper-capitalist states. In any system, but especially in hierarchies of wealth, cruel inequalities compose the integral vitiating ground whereupon the micropolitics of power are played out. The violent forces that maintain the system intact proliferate and become more openly manifest, the more unequal the society.

This fact should concern us more than it does, since our societies fit the dangerous pattern: hierarchies based upon distinctions in wealth. Nowhere do those distinctions imply such radical inequities than in modern societies of the industrialized West. By comparison with the overt physical oppressions characteristic of tyrannical and militaristic societies, the more subtle but deeply vicious structural violences of modern Western systems may not be recognized *as such* from inside their own event. Through conflict and exploitation, citizens vie in continual competitions to hold their positions at the peak of the social and political ladder within their systems. Through conflict with, and exploitation of, foreign systems, capitalist democracies struggle with other merchant economies to maintain their hegemony in global markets. The survival of nations in the modern era depends on their economic survival in the global marketplace.

Hegel's master-slave dialectic, Karl Marx's theory of history, and Friedrich Nietzsche's genealogy of morals are philosophical theories which have brilliantly disclosed, in diverse yet resonant ways, that human communities, as they evolve, reveal themselves to be escalating episodes of socio-political conflict, shifting battles that mark out the contentious terrain that separates the haves from the have-nots.[47] Each of these genealogical theories also shows that the battles of history may be fought over material wealth and power, but the human *experience* of the battle involves an evolution of consciousness in which the victimized, as much as the dominant, engage in mythologies that first position the powerful as rightfully dominant and then, ultimately, depose them.

Hegel's master-slave dialectic provides the clearest example of this evolution. A loose paraphrase of his theory follows. The master wins the place of domination precisely because masters experience no fear of death when facing the enemy in battle. The enemy, in fear for survival, assumes the position of slave and cowers before the greater might and fearlessness of the master. Over time, the master grows dependent upon the slave; the master is unable to manage daily routines without the slave's constant aid. The master cannot eat; cannot dress; does not know where the bread is stored, never mind the weapons. The master grows soft, reliant, useless, and fearful of death.

The slave gradually realizes that the slave's life is barely worth the living; so his fear of death soon subsides. As a result, the slave grows cocky indeed, running the household as though it is slave property. The slave can steal all the eggs one could want and even borrows the master's boots on Sundays. Hence, time inverts the master-slave dialectic and the conflict relation is raised to a higher power: no longer clear are the responses to identity questions such as who is working whom, who is running the estate, and who is the beneficiary of its wealth.

The optimism in all three of these great genealogical thinkers (Hegel, Nietzsche, and Marx)—that the powerful will always meet with eventual deposition and the exploited receive their due recompense—while deeply satisfying to our sense of justice, remains historically unsubstantiated. Masters never seem to get so soft that they give up the farm, nor slaves so bold that they cannot be beaten into submission. Perhaps the failure of politico-economic structures to evolve into fairer and more just forms over time is to be explained by the functional utility and sheer relentlessness of violent forms upon human bodies and psyches, in the power struggles of the real world. Theories of history with happy endings seem to ignore the sorry fact that violence rules from the summit to the dregs to maintain the inequities of the system, and violent rituals re-form the thought processes of those at every level of the system.

One of the greatest ironies of oppressive systems is that the most avid supporters of the system are often those who are most oppressed by it! This is because no one needs the approval of the group more than those who have been shoved to its margins; they crave identification with the oppressive system in order to satisfy their yearning for belonging. If the oppressed do not realize that they are oppressed or if they have been persuaded that their oppression is well deserved, those systems may take far longer to evolve toward more benign social and political models than the genealogists calculate. Some systems may never evolve beyond simple tyrannies of power. Violence rules more subtly and insidiously in some systems, more brutally and overtly in others. Wherever inequities exist, violence lurks, maintaining the status quo of power relations.

Harmonious integrity is an illusion in all systems, especially those grounded primarily in distinctions of wealth. That is why Hannah Arendt states: "There is no document of civilization which is not at the same time a document of barbarism."[48] Precolonial Africans had no documents of civilization. They needed none to keep their societies intact. Africans could boast stable and relatively harmonious social forms from time immemorial. But their social structures had not developed by way of the violences that, in European systems, elevated some members and subordinated others. For this lack, they were thought crude and savage by the foreign invaders. Insofar as traditional African societies granted increasing benefits of the system in accord with increased age and responsibility toward the societies' weaker members (the young and the old), those societies remained naturally democratic and thereby avoided the gross inequities that demand the violent processes that come to be named "civilizing."

## 3. Terms of the Discussion

In this work I employ the word "tribe" and its derivatives freely. I recognize that this term is highly problematic because such references have historically been employed only pejoratively. The term "tribe" is generally applied to peoples of color, whereas the expression "ethnic group" is used to speak of white European cultures. The term tribe has historically been employed to signal a people's inferiority by reasserting a less evolved, less civilized form of social organization.

This negative connotation persists today in general parlance. When Westerners speak of conflicts, say, between Europeans (as in the Balkans), the term tribal is never used. "Ethnic" remains the preferred term for describing conflicts among Caucasians. Tribal has taken on genetic overtones and suggests immutable and inferior mental and moral characteristics across a human group. Tribal suggests distinctions of "race." However, race is itself nothing more than a social construction, having no biological or scientific meaning. An analyst cannot study the blood or brain cells or DNA of human beings and arrive at information that will grant racial identity.

Though there exists no difference between tribal and ethnic in meaning (each denoting no more than a social group that identifies itself as such), and since recent sociological theory has shown that none of these terms has any fixed meaning or signals any firm identity features, all social groups being dynamic, evolving structures that remain in constant flux, the distinction is without meaningful ground. Still, the tendency in the West persists for people to use "ethnic" when referring to those groups about whom the speaker is more culturally approving. This persistent prejudice causes some scholars to shy away from use of the term "tribe" and its derivatives altogether.

Since most people are fully cognizant of this linguistic history, the reader may be struck by my choice to employ a term so steeped in negative tradition. I employ the term not simply in consistency with the language of many of the Africanist scholars whose works I employ extensively, but because I note that African people themselves speak of their cultural identity and describe their social origins with reference to the term tribe. I am not convinced that we scholars have a right, even in the interest of political correctness, to impose an anachronization of the term by eliminating its usage from scholarly discourse.

So long as people continue to employ the term in their *self*-descriptions—to designate themselves as belonging to this tribe and not that, as having descended from this common tribal origin, or as having tribal connections with this or that other group—I hold social analysts and other researchers presumptuous to say their usage is inappropriate. I am intending that my conscious and positive use of the term pay tribute to the right of African peoples to determine their self-descriptions as they, and not we scholars, see fit. The positive employment of terms of abuse has been known to turn the terms against their own histories and cleanse the words of their negative overtones. "Black" and "native" are two examples of terms that have been reclaimed. "Nigger" is another, and far more problematic, term that is being reclaimed by the people it had formerly victimized.[49] Since this work itself seeks to force a rethinking of the terms of our social and historical discourses *per se*, my employment of the term tribe is meant to constitute a kind of affirmative action to disabuse the reader of any linguistic prejudice regarding these words.

A further problem with my terminology may arise for the reader with regard to what may appear to be a totalizing language. References to African peoples, African customs, and the indigenous African may seem to deny the radical uniqueness of differing individuals and differing social groups across the broad continent of Africa. My use of this totalizing language may seem to imply an under-appreciation for the vast differences that divide the peoples of the African continent. This language may seem to underplay the uniquenesses that distinguish each African nation from the others, not to mention each sub-national division, each clan, and each family on the African continent. Such linguistic references may also threaten, on a grander scale, to reassert, after the tradition of the early anthropologists, the mistake of naming human groups as pristine, detached entities. All namings imply stable, fixed units of identifiable features, detached from their histories and their environing pressures. They resonate with the essentialist claims that were historically employed to justify exploitation of these peoples.

For several reasons, I consider both fitting and appropriate to my project my practice of referring to Africa as a unity. First of all, my practice is grounded in an African practice. Africans themselves employ the motif of African concord, arguing that there are many binding features among African communities and many resonant worldview postulates binding tribe to tribe and nation to nation across the continent, if not across the global diaspora of African peoples. There exists a shared self-definitive unity to Africanism that causes people who name themselves African peoples to celebrate that unity at Kwanzaa.

Fabien Eboussi-Boulaga observes that Africa, as "an assembly of heterogeneous countries and realities," can hardly unproblematically claim "the integration of its components or of its contents" but, for philosophical research to begin, asserts Eboussi-Boulaga, the "wish of unity" must be postulated.[50] "Africa has a tendency to claim to be an autonomous assembly of internal dependencies in which we can observe the concentration of the global at the local level, the passage from an ordered state to a chaotic state, and the reverse of this passage."[51]

I claim legitimacy for speaking of Africa as a unity because unities exist in nature, despite the undeniable diversity that characterizes the individual parts of systems. Features of unification can be plotted and demonstrated in phenomena where diversity is nevertheless pervasive. To demonstrate how unities in diversity occur, I adapt for my own ends an analogy from the scientific theory of dynamic systems, employed by Eboussi-Boulaga to serve his different purposes.[52] Scientists map models to typifying dynamic systems. These mappings provide evolving blueprints of diversity in unity that help to chart how diversity and unity can coexist in the same geographical and multicultural space:

> In the beginning, there are various elementary modules. Among the many figures that their free association produces, many disappear. Left are only those which are stable, those which resist randomness of all sorts. The forms thereby spared and favored form complex structures through coupling. By connections and interrelations, these forms become integrated into a vast organism, which develops according to the criteria of immanent optimality, according to its own law—escaping individual mastery and intent.[53]

To apply from this general scientific model to African cultural particulars, Africa can be said to compose an "inside"—a "field of transformations" or a "framework"—in and from which take rise the varied and multifarious mechanisms promoting the birth of new forms.[54] We may safely assume that the transformations that occur, or the new forms that may arise within the field of transformations in no way negate but instead confirm the existence of the field or framework that hosts their arising. Africa and Africans can, therefore, be legitimately spoken of as a cohesive group, without denying the possibility for dynamic internal differentiations.

# Notes

1. Wendy C. Hamblet, *The Sacred Monstrous: A Reflection on Violence in Human Communities* (Lanham, Md.: Lexington, 2004).

2. Eli Sagan, *At the Dawn of Tyranny* (New York: Knopf, 1985); contra Keeley, *War Before Civilization* (Oxford, U.K.: Oxford University Press, 1996).

3. Maurice Bloch, *Prey into Hunter: The Politics of Religious Experience* (Cambridge, U.K.: Cambridge University Press, 1992).

4. Sagan, *At the Dawn of Tyranny*; see also Jared Diamond, *Guns, Germs and Steel: The Fates of Human Societies* (London, U.K.: W. W. Norton & Co., 1999) and Bruce Lincoln, *Death, War and Sacrifice: Studies in Ideology and Practice* (Chicago: University of Chicago Press, 1991).

5. Jared Diamond, *Guns, Germs, and Steel*.

6. Diamond, *Guns, Germs, and Steel*.

7. G. W. F. Hegel, *The Phenomenology of Spirit*, A. V. Miller, trans. (Oxford, U.K.: Oxford University Press, 1979).

8. Hegel, *Phenomenology*, B. IV. A, 111-119.

9. G. W. F. Hegel, *Lectures on the Philosophy of World History: Introduction*, Hugh Barr Nisbet, trans. (Cambridge, U.K.: Cambridge University Press, 1989), 177.

10. Edmund Husserl, *Ideas Pertaining to a Pure Phenomenology and to a Phenomenological Philosophy*, F. Kersten, trans. (Dordrecht: Kluwer Academic Publishers, 1998).

11. Husserl, *Ideas*, xvii.

12. Husserl, *Ideas*, 5.

13. Husserl, *Cartesian Meditations*, Dorian Cairns, trans. (Dordrecht: Kluwer, 1995), 1–6.

14. Martin Heidegger, *Poetry, Language, and Thought*, Albert Hofstadter, trans. (New York: Harper-Collins, 1975); Maurice Merleau-Ponty et al, *The Primacy of Perception*, Nancy Metzel and John Flodstrom, trans. (New York: Routledge, 2002); Hans-Georg Gadamer, *Truth and Method*, Joel Weinsheimer, trans. (New York: Continuum, 2005).

15. Michel Foucault, *The Order of Things* (New York: Vintage Books, 1994).

16. Jacques Derrida, *Writing and Difference*, Alan Bass, trans. (Chicago, Ill.: University of Chicago Press, 1978).

17. Paul Ricoeur, *The Symbolism of Evil*, Emerson Buchanan, trans. (Boston, Mass.: Beacon Press, 1967); Emmanuel Levinas, *Otherwise Than Being*, Alfonso Lingis, trans. (Dordrecht, Netherlands: Kluwer Academic Publishers, 1991).

18. J. Derrida, "Structure, Sign, and Play in the Discourse of the Human Sciences," *Writing and Difference*, 278–295; and H-G. Gadamer, *Philosophical Hermeneutics*, David E. Linge, trans. (Los Angeles: University of California Press, 1977), 59–68.

19. Plato, *Phaedrus*, 277e, R. Hackforth, trans.

20. Jacques Derrida, *Speech and Phenomena*, David B. Allison, trans. (Evanston, Ill.: Northwestern University Press, 1973), 88–104.

21. Derrida, *Writing and Difference*, 79–153.

22. Levinas, *Otherwise Than Being*.

23. E. Levinas, *Discovering Existence with Husserl*, Richard Cohen, Michael Smith, trans. (Evanston, Ill.: Northwestern University Press, 1998), 47–89.

24. Bénézet Bujo, *Foundations of an African Ethic* (New York: Crossroads Publishing, 2001), 9–10.

25. Levinas, *Totality and Infinity*, Alfonso Lingis, trans. (Pittsburgh: Duquesne University Press, 1969), 130–132.

26. Levinas, *Totality*, 131.

27. E. Levinas, *Otherwise Than Being*, 93, 94, 148.

28. Levinas, *Totality*, 134.

29. Levinas, *Totality*, 139.

30. Fyodor Dostoevsky, *The Brothers Karamazov*, Constance Garnet, trans. (New York: Barnes & Noble, 1995), Book V, Chapter 4.

31. Leslie Gill, *The School of the Americas: Military Training and Political Violence in the Americas* (Durham, N.C.: Duke University Press, 2004); and Jack Nelson Pallmeyer, *School of Assassins: Guns, Greed, and Globalization* (Edinborough, U.K.: Orbis Books, 2001).

32. Levinas, *Totality*, 134.

33. See preface of this book, x.

34. "Study: Pollution is a possible cause of African Famine," *USA Today*, Weather, 7/22/02.

35. John Stockwell, *In Search of Enemies* (New York: Replica Books, 1997).

36. Jeffrey A. Sluka, *Death Squad: The Anthropology of State Terror* (Philadelphia: University of Pennsylvania Press, 2000), 8.

37. See "The New Rules of War," *World Press Review* (December, 2002), 7–9.

38. Michael Ratner and Ellen Ray, *Guantanamo: What the World Should Know* (White River Jct., Vt: Chelsea Green Publishing, 2004).

39. Richard Falk, "The World Speaks on Iraq," *The Nation*, 281: 4 (1–8 August, 2005), 8–10.

40. Viola W. Bernard, Perry Ottenberg, Fritz Redl, "Dehumanization," *Sanctions for Evil*, William E. Henry, Nevitt Sanford, eds. (San Francisco: Jossey-Bass, 1971), 102–124.

41. Robert J. Lifton, *The Nazi Doctors: Medical Killing and the Psychology of Genocide* (New York: Basic Books, 1986).

42. Robert J. Lifton, "Failures of Identification and Sociopathic Behavior," in *Sanctions for Evil*, 125–135.

43. Tsenay Serequeberhan, *The Hermeneutics of African Philosophy: Horizon and Discourse* (New York and London: Routledge, 1994), 68.

44. Empedocles, *On the Nature of Things*, as *per* Diogenes Laertius VIII, 77, G. S. Kirk, J. E. Raven, and M. Schoefield, *The PreSocratic Philosophers* (Cambridge, U.K.: Cambridge University Press, 1957), 282.

45. Edith Hamilton and Huntington Cairns, *The Collected Dialogues of Plato*, (Princeton, New Jersey: Princeton University Press, 1961), *Republic*, 575–844, 253c–??; see also *Phaedrus*, 475–525, 246 & ff., 253c & ff.

46. *Jeremy Bentham, Collected Works*, J. H. Burns, ed. (London, U.K.: Athlone Press, 1968), 199; and Thomas Hobbes, *Leviathan* (New York: Penguin, 1982).

47. G. W. F. Hegel, *The Phenomenology of Spirit*, A. V. Miller, trans. (Oxford: Oxford University Press, 1979), B.IV.A, 111–119; Karl Marx, "Marx on the History of His Opinions," *The Marx-Engels Reader*, Robert C. Tucker, ed. (New York: Norton, 1978), 3–6; Friedrich Nietzsche, *Thus Spake Zarathustra*, Thomas Common, trans. (New York: Tudor Press, 1934), 21.

48. *Illuminations*, Hannah Arendt, ed., Harry Zohn, trans. (New York: Schocken Books, 1968), 256.

49. See Randall Kennedy, *Nigger: The Strange Career of a Troublesome Word* (New York: Pantheon, 2002).

50. F. Eboussi-Boulaga, "The Topic of Change," in *African Philosophy as Cultural Inquiry*, Ivan Karp and D. A. Masolo, eds. (Bloomington, Ind.: Indiana University Press, 2000), 187–214, 194–195.

51. Eboussi-Boulaga, "Change," 187–214.

52. Eboussi-Boulaga, "Change," 187–214.

53. Eboussi-Boulaga, "Change," 204–205.

54. Eboussi-Boulaga, "Change," 193.

# Chapter 3
# The Truth of Myth, the Myth of Truth

The power of myth has long been recognized by anthropologists, classicists, literary theorists, and philosophers. In this work I am employing the term "myth" in its broadest sense, as an instance in the body of a culture's understandings of self and world. Myths compose a people's truths; social truth denotes the accepted body of reality postulates adopted by a certain social group. A society's myth/truth grounds its identity, and configures its social behaviors. Myth/truth comes to be acted out in everyday social rituals and expressed in verbal and written narratives.

Social myths are locally accepted as truth, but they come to be accepted as universally and eternally true by becoming traditional, that is, by proving their timeworthiness through repetition and persistence over time. The content, symbols and images (mythologems), and governing logic of social myths gain greater factual status and become more powerful—more "true" for the group—the more the tale is reiterated across time and evolving historical circumstances. By repetition in public and private discourses across diverse and overlapping social arenas and over multiple generations, a myth is adopted within a culture's foundational assumptions. Over time and cultural space, a myth wends its way into the very being of its cultural audience.

Because myths/truths tend toward greater credibility for the society the more that they are repeated, they are highly functional within communities and their function is rigorously conservative. Whatever their temporal or spatial point of origin, they serve crucial purposes in the social group in which they take their rise. Because they are doggedly conservative and because their content links with cultural identity, a society's myths/truths reconfirm the legitimacy of the social structure with every fresh repetition. They confirm the rightness of the group's traditions, values, attitudes, and beliefs. They buttress the very foundations of the worldview shared by the group, the sense of belonging and non-belonging that defines legitimacy. Myths identify social actors, and define and justify their positions within the social arena. Therefore, the power of myth over a people's modes of being-in-the-world can hardly be overrated. Cultural myths both express and shape people's psyches, for better or for worse. They are the very fabric from which a people carve out their identities in the world—who they are, whence they have come, and what is their destiny. Myths reassert the governing logic and reaffirm the powerful symbolics that orient the power relations that hold within the group, granting metaphysical reasons for system inequalities. Myths affirm the rightness of the methods of social control, however brutal.

Over time, myths transform and evolve, but one of myth's greatest and most mysterious powers resides in the fact that, throughout the elaborations and distortions of the tales, their omissions and additions are generally incorporated into the legitimate body of "truth" with remarkable ease. This astonishing power to absorb transformations and accept omissions and even self-contradictions, while yet maintaining a reputation for eternal validity, is perhaps the greatest mystery of the truth-production process in human societies. The elemental messages, underlying cultural myths, exercise an uncanny longevity and a functional persistence throughout the discontinuities and transformations that occur over time. The mystery of myth's persistence is resolved not by reference to specific details of content that rest at the essential core of social belief, but by the persistence of powerful nuclear symbols and an organizing logic that undergirds and orders those symbols. There exists an ideological continuity in the symbols and structure of the tales despite the cosmetic mercuriality of their content.

Well-deserved attention has been afforded, in recent anthropology, sociology, and philosophy, to tracing the social myths/truths expressed in cultural narratives and their sociological effects in communities. Experts have long acknowledged the importance of understanding the mysterious powers that cultural myths exercise within populations, over vast expanses of time and across immense socio-historical and physical distances. Scholars have long been seeking the key to this power in order to determine how cultural narratives configure thinking and behavior—how, as Walter Burkert says, they structure a people's "common mental world."[1]

In most cases, a people's cultural myths/truths are entirely pervasive of their lifeworld, inscribed in their everyday language, encoded in the proverbs and their codes of behavior, embedded in the fairy tales and parables that morally educate new generations. Myths/truths undergird peoples' political forms and economic practices. To fully appreciate how human beings function and where that functioning goes right and wrong, we must comprehend how their cultural myths establish the horizons of possibility for moral decision-making.

## 1. Western Notions of Myth

I am deliberately interchanging the terms "myth" and "truth" in this work to undermine a distinction deeply embedded in the Western hyperrational, scientific worldview—the belief that myth and truth are two distinct and separate entities, one (myth) that represents consciously crafted stories, the other (truth) that maps perfectly onto empirical reality and comes to be recorded as "history." History, in the Western worldview, denotes a linear and progressive chronology of *true and actual* events. Myth signifies phantasmagorical inventions having no connection with reality and its messages are seen as inconsequential to the *real* world of human action and experience. This radical juxtapositioning of myth and historical reality itself represents a mythical dichotomy, a fiction born of Western rationalism. People in the West are convinced that their worldview, though simply one of many possible sets of reality postulates, one among many "common mental worlds," comprises the *normal*, scientifically *accurate*, properly rational worldview shared by all reasonable people of the earth.

The juxtaposition of myth and truth composes an utterly false dichotomy, as false as the "theoretical attitude" assumed by the "objective" scientist who believes that science overcomes the biased "subjective" position. People have no access to truth except as perceiving subjects and their most creative and radically novel ideas rarely extend outside their always culturally and historically configured perceptions of phenomena. The most rigorous scientist or the most objective historian is involved in a project of judicious construction, selecting from a wide spectrum of the variable data at hand, arbitrarily electing, on the basis of prior assumptions, the test results and the historical facts that will be deemed legitimate truths and jettisoning those that will become deemed misfired experiments and faulty interpretations. We are all involved, albeit unconsciously, in selecting our reality postulates from a much broader range of interpretive possibilities for understanding the phenomena of our lifeworlds.

Because of the Western conviction that but one "correct" schema of reality matches up exactly with empirical reality, we are bound to an ethnocentrism, and to an anthropological ignorance that necessarily limits our effectiveness in dealing with culturally different others. We must collapse the false "myth versus historico-scientific truth" dichotomy, and realize that the one world recognized by Western science is no *more* "objectively" and "absolutely" real and true— and also no *less* locally real and true —than any other culture's schemata of reality postulates. The Western worldview is no less partisan and no more myth-free than any other worldview. Richard Stivers convincingly argues this point in his *Evil in Modern Myth and Ritual*.[2] Every cultural group is essentially ethnocentric. Every group is trapped within its own lifeworld, and thinking and behavior patterns within the group are configured according to their culture's unique schemata of truths. For Westerners, too, their phenomenal experience of world, oriented by their local reality postulates and their historical horizons of truth, is the only one available to them. The subjective experience of world, with all its biases, prejudices, and blind spots, is, for every individual and for every human community, primordial and foundational. Even the Western scientific and rational view of the world composes a subjective experience of world. This is the fundamental and essential discovery celebrated most emphatically in the works of Edmund Husserl.[3]

All people live within unique, self-confirming, morally significant, and evaluative universes, a fact ever present to the phenomenologist whose task is begun in the "bracketing" of cultural preconceptions.[4] The fact that people's lifeworlds are preconstituted and morally expressive is occluded from view by Western science that posits facts as autonomous from value. Bracketing the truth/myth dichotomy prepares the way for a more promising approach to the discovery of cultural truth. This bracketing permits a sincere listening to the peoples of Africa, emphasizing the deconstructive (destructive and constructive) powers of cultural myths (their own and those of their colonial invaders).

The rationalizing tradition composes a persistent feature of Western philosophy from its early roots in the Greeks. The Greek philosophers, however, do not share in drawing the sharp distinction between myth and logos insisted upon in the modern era. The Greeks in fact often elevate the notion of myth as a source of higher, deeper truth. They acknowledge that myths reach far deeper into a people's being than rational arguments can. Plato, despite his love of dialectic and his appreciation of the power of rational argument to divide and define the elements of the world, defers to *mythos* once *logos* has taken its course and collapsed on the hard rocks of absurdity. The *Phaedrus*, the *Symposium*, and the *Republic* defer to myth once the rational argument has been exhausted. The fundamental Socratic dictum recognizes that nothing is certain for reasonable beings. The wise know only that they cannot know. The best one can do, Plato has Timaeus assert in the dialogue bearing his name, is a likely story—a myth. "Enough if we adduce probabilities as likely as any others. . . .We ought to accept the tale which is probable and inquire no further."[5]

Rational certainty is an arrogance—a *hybris*—that stands in the way of human wisdom. In the dialogue *Theaetetus*, Plato depicts Socrates explaining to the young Theaetetus why the *elenchus* (or "emptying out") of arrogant assumptions is so important to ethical development. After the repeated failure of the young mathematician's attempts to discover the definition of knowledge, Socrates asserts:

> Supposing you should ever henceforth try to conceive afresh, Theaetetus, if you succeed, your embryo thoughts will be the better as a consequence of today's [failure], and if you remain barren, you will be gentler and more agreeable to your companions, having the good sense not to fancy you know what you do not know.[6]

The failure of rational certainty brings with it the ethical success of humility. Traditional myths, by their very form, encourage humility and discourage hardened dogmatism. Platonic myths are directed toward the end of this humility, defeating through their elusiveness and ambiguousness the possibility of rational certainty about things most important. Plato's myths may not give clear and distinct understanding about their subjects, but they frequently dramatize the benefits of gentleness and agreeableness over arrogance and self-certainty, juxtaposing the profound unhappiness of tyrants over against the happiness of the humble philosophers.[7]

Despite his emphasis on Socratic irony, Plato nevertheless plays a significant role in the establishment of the notion of an absolute truth to be sought by rational inquiry. Though Plato agrees with Socrates that humility is best, it is the notion of the rational quest that sticks as a worthy—and perhaps as the supreme—philosophical task. Myth is forgotten and the quest for rational certainty becomes the model for philosophical investigation for the Western tradition, finding its most arrogant expression in Enlightenment certainties of the rational power of the human mind. For millennia since Plato, rational arguments are the very stuff of philosophical discourse. Despite Socrates' emphasis upon the wisdom of humility, philosophers remain dogged in their pursuit of absolute objective reality. Desperate to hold on to that comforting illusion that objective absolute knowledge can be had, thinkers posit, throughout the millennia of philosophical speculation, rigorous theoretical discourses to guide thinking toward certain and stable truth that will resolve human differences and overcome the discomfiting flux of opinion (*doxa*).

The trend to accept scientific method as revelatory of certain truth begins slowly to take hold after Plato. Aristotle begins to consign "substance" to worldly things, in an effort to bring truth down from the distant heavens (where Plato had posited truth). However, philosophers continue to be troubled by the fact that no amount of rational inquiry can reduce the troubling differences of perspective. No common *logos* unites the cosmos or brings all rational subjects together in universal agreement. There can be found no way to resolve the paradox of subjective differences in perceiving different things. Differences in reality postulates cannot rationally be overcome. That means that, ultimately, for human beings, no reliable means exists to distinguish between truth and opinion.

## 2. Phenomenological Truth

The epistemological quest for ultimate truth has been misguided—as a quest for truth certainly, but more importantly *as a moral quest*. Emmanuel Levinas suggests as much when he states: "A philosophy of power, ontology is, as first philosophy which does not call into question the same, a philosophy of injustice."[8] Levinas and many other postmodern philosophers abandon the modern Western dichotomy between *mythos* and *logos* when, post-Holocaust, they begin to recognize the structural analogousness of philosophy's metaphysical adventures and Nazism's metaphysical ethnocentrism.

The dangers inherent in metaphysical thinking drive Levinas and other postmodern philosophers to the radical move of abandoning the notion of a "common mental world" in favor of the notion of individual lifeworlds. Levinas names the world of each subject, caught up in unique projects and enterprises according to particular and morally significant visions of things, the "ontological adventure." Levinas is, by this stunning reformulation of subjectivity, attempting to open his reader to the fact of the radically individual nature of truth.

The subjective experience of world, Levinas demonstrates, is characterized by a sense of sadly limited epistemic power within a limitless cosmic space and time that Levinas names "the elemental." No one subject can fully know the phenomena of its own world, let alone peek into the truths of other subjects' worlds. Levinas is attempting to expose that there exist worlds as many as there are subjects, each utterly unique and irreplaceable, each equally valuable and worthy of merit.[9] Discussions of truth or falsity, or the drawing of distinctions between mythical fantasies and scientific truth make no sense from a phenomenological perspective that seeks only to disclose the defining assumptions of subjective realities. All that matters within this view is what the subject experiences as true. This experience of truth exposes a corollary fact—the incapacity of the subject to reach outside the singular ontological realm to gather true knowledge about other subjects.

Individual worlds are irredeemably closed, closed for exit to other worlds and closed to entrance from without. The subject's necessary epistemological failure simultaneously predetermines its *ethical* failure. The closed horizons of the lifeworld make extraterritorial knowledge impossible. There is no accurate cognition of the otherness outside one's monadic world. Fair and accurate judgment of others remains impossible, for Levinas. He states: "To measure a man by his works is to enter his interiority as though by burglary. . . .Works signify their author but indirectly, in the third person."[10]

For Levinas, re-presentations cannot do justice to the original and dynamic event of any presence. Judgments are always misguided, self-interested opinions formed on the basis of partial knowledge. The problematic question of a subject's epistemic and ethical limitations in the knowing of other subjects is highlighted by Levinas's description of subjective relations as an appropriation of the "sides" of whole others. Others are grasped only by superficial "sides" while their infinite reality beyond the subject's grasp stretches forth into an infinite unknown.[11]

Beings remain inestimable in their subjective "depth" beyond the superficial perceptions others have of them. Since reality is always the intuition of a subject about radically transcendent objects, my best actions toward others are always misplaced, always off the mark of good behavior. However well-intended, my kindest acts are ever doomed to epistemological and therefore ethical failure. Ontological myopia determines in advance the ethical myopia of subjects, and predetermines the ethical failure of all subjects in regard of all others. The situation remains ever, as Fyodor Dostoevsky's Ivan Karamazov describes: "We are all guilty of all, and for all men, and I more than all the others."[12]

This pessimistic claim about the predetermined ethical failure of all subjects may seem to sound the death toll for ethical projects *per se*. If one cannot know who the other truly is, if one cannot surmise what the other needs, what is best for the other, one can never determine accurately what the best course of action is. This seems to pose an epistemological roadblock that sabotages ethics as it sabotages absolute knowledge. The myopia of subjects also sounds the death toll for all claims of absolute knowledge. No certain truths exist for the phenomenologist, no matter with what certainty truth is lived by individual subjects. Truth has no capacity to reach beyond the lifeworld of the individual subject.

Levinas's intention is not to paralyze thought by naming all truth subjective, nor to paralyze action by naming good action impossible. Levinas' phenomenology is essentially marked by his violent history. Levinas was a Holocaust survivor who lost much of his family to Adolph Hitler's madness. He is driven by that history in the direction of a new philosophical project, a project that is nothing if not ethical. For Levinas, "ethics is first philosophy."[13] For Levinas, the fact of the Holocaust has rendered starkly urgent the task of a post-Holocaust philosophy: ethics must compose the primary and most important branch of philosophical inquiry and the place where all philosophers must begin.

Levinas' ethics is not an ethics in the popular or traditional sense of the term—as a study of the set of rules or standards that are (or ought to be) applied in human communities. For Levinas, ethics is closer in meaning to its ancient Greek root in the word *ethos*. The term *ethos* was taken literally to mean custom, usage, manners, or cultural habit, but this narrow definition fails to capture the ethical breadth of the word, though it does explain how the word came to be translated into the Latin *more* where it was employed to speak of ethnically defined behavior codes and local patterns of conduct, a meaning that comes down to us in our English words "mores" and "morals."

In the ancient world a distinction was drawn between local customs practiced in human communities—the term *nomos* was used—and *ethos*, that larger, all-embracing reality that expressed the more holistic "enworldedness" of all beings sharing earthly existence alongside each other. *Ethos* was deployed to speak of the way that beings (human and otherwise) dwell (or ought to dwell) together in the ordered harmonious wholeness of the cosmos. *Ethos* is a broader term, embracing the whole of being, and it addresses the question of how all beings, "the many," may successfully come together to make "one" world.

The problem of the "one and the many" is not simply an epistemological challenge and a metaphysical paradox; the problem represents an ethical dilemma. That dilemma is explored throughout ancient Greek philosophy from Heraclitus and Parmenides, to Plato and Aristotle. Since crafting a peaceful sublime changeless singularity from the chaotic and troubling many of worldly things is a monumental feat given the plethora of earthly beings, ethics implies the cultivation of a certain art of appropriate cosmic "co-dwelling-ness" whereby all creatures constrain themselves fittingly that all might co-dwell in harmony.

When Levinas insists that ethics is first philosophy, he is calling the reader to a new orientation; he is making an ethical demand upon us! He is lobbying for a human rethinking of the way that we share our earthly dwelling place. In particular, he is petitioning for the cultivation of a new art in the modern era, one that responds to an ethical call that hears the needs of all kinds of earthly dwellers. Furthermore, Levinas' ethics beseeches that we remember, within the closed security of our private worlds, that other beings have a right to earthly happiness as well. Because Levinas' call to ethics is about remembrance of the rights of forgotten others, and because that call is so relentless and demanding, it fits well within the project of this work.

## 3. African Philosophy and Living Truth

The Greeks elevate the notion of *hybris* to promote an ethic of humility in the human world. Post-Holocaust Jewish thinkers, like Levinas, suggest that guilt should promote a sense of responsibility for suffering others. The Greek masters and their postmodern counterparts have labored to promote philosophies of humility to undermine the arrogances of rational certainty. However, African thinkers have long recognized that responsibility is grounded in social truth. African philosophers show that traditional African wisdom is rooted in this insight. African modes of thought were denigrated as "pre-logical" by colonial era anthropologists like Lucien Lévy-Bruhl. However, African philosopher Bénézet Bujo disputes this characterization by challenging the metaphysically based idea that there exists only one correct and viable *human* logic that governs and directs all human thought. He challenges the notion that only the goal-oriented, formal-logical, future-oriented mode of thought peculiar to the West is truly logical.[14]

Teleological thought and thought that emphasizes the argumentative power of reason, contends Bujo, is too narrow a definition of rationality to be accurately applied to all forms of thought and communication across all human worlds. It is not even the healthiest form of thought. Bujo recommends, over Western hyper-rational modes of thought, an alternative African mode of thought because, far from pre-logical, it is more holistically logical, embracing in its *logos*, the whole of the human person.

> Black African rationality is much more inclusive. In the process of establishing norms for ethical-moral conduct, it admits the contribution of that which cannot be justified in terms of reason. This is because it wishes to consider the human being holistically—and the mystery that surrounds the human person cannot be grasped by reason alone.[15]

Thinkers of the African tradition, as the Greek philosophers of ancient times, do not draw firm boundaries of distinction between what is known by the body, the emotions, and the passions, the imagination, and intuitions, and what is known through rational inquiry. As the ancient Greeks, Africans too are skeptical of disembodied thought. The most certain facts of life are lived truths, lived differently by different humans in differing realities over time and space.

For the African as for the Western phenomenologist, a person's worldview evolves over time. So too do a person's orienting notions, a person's obligations and responsibilities to self and social world. Speaking of absolute truths ascertained by rational exercise alone is ethically fruitless. The timeless truths of social groups are dispensed in social realities. Social constructions of reality are not the false other to reason, but form the very core of the living truth of communities. Perhaps Africans value their mythical heritage of social truth so highly because of their unique conception of time. For the Westerner steeped in the myth *history as progress*, time flows forward into a future and leaves the past forever behind. For an African, time flows backward—from the young toward the adult and into the elderly (the *Sasa* dimension), and on into the living world of the ancestors who have passed from earthly existence and live in timeless company (the *Zamani* dimension) with the god. Human lives follow this backward flow, growing from weak and helpless members to more and more responsible adults, unfolding toward the wisdom of age and finally remaining, even after death, in the extended "living death" of an ancestral caretaker watching over the kinship fold.

As with the phenomenological view of truth, the African view of truth is not posited as a radical other to myth or social belief. Truth is recognized as created by human communities; truth is historical and intersubjective. Truth has to do with the passage of time, evolutions in subjective identity, and changes in the social world. Truth becomes myth and myth remains true, even as it passes into temporary remission with the evolution of the singular life into the past of ancestral eternity. The *Sasa* represents the present truth of the past of the *Zamani*, a past awaiting in every future.

All myths are persuasive, and some myths are ethically persuasive. They alter people's lifeworlds, their characters, and their social patterns. They change what people value, their notions of truth and falsity. Myths become truth and truth becomes myth. Both shape people for good or for ill. Both a people's myths and their truth-claims can reach beyond the merely rational, and thus dangerous mythologems cannot be extirpated by reasoned arguments or reckonings of truth or falsity. This explains why people are rarely seduced by rational arguments to do the "right thing"—to open their wallets to the needy or to leave the safe comfort of their homes to battle injustices in the world. A powerful story of heroic valor, the sad music of a hungry child's cry, or the pleading tears of a damsel in distress can reach into the soul and tug at the heartstrings and rouse people to ethical action far more effectively than reasonable arguments.

If a culture's myth/truth narratives help determine the ontological shape of their members' subjectivity, then it is crucial to ethics that those narratives open subjects to ethical life. A culture's narratives—its mythical truths—must be ethically oriented and, in Levinas' terms, they must work toward restructuring merely "living beings" (focused merely upon survival of the self) into morally awakened "thinking beings" (concerned about the survival of others).[16] To restate this urgency in Bujo's terms, human beings approach ethical/moral conduct and develop their cultural responsibilities holistically and in community with others, not as free autonomous individuals.[17] Our cultural myths have an ethical responsibility: to predispose subjects to an appreciation of diverse modes of being. Our cultural myths can prepare us so that the experience of difference can be joyfully anticipated or they can harden us to difference and ensure that the alien appears as an object of dread.[18]

Truth is historical and intersubjective. All people believe they have truth cornered, while others entertain their myths to the contrary. People always labor under the truth assumptions imposed within their lifeworlds by that world's histories and by their fellows. Their truths include the prejudices and bigotry, the myths that denigrate foreign lifeworlds and designate their own as worthy of their particular loyalty. All truths are myths constructed at the home site of identity to maintain order and harmony, and to guarantee the longevity of the home site. All truths entertained within that site are as morally significant as the lifeworld itself. The dominant behavioral and cognitive truths of a society can predispose its members toward peace. Others, often those of history's victimized peoples, may dispose them in favor of war. Whether a people adopt a worldview that welcomes difference or one that finds otherness threatening is fatefully important. Fear and distrust tend to lodge in people's social and political institutions, causing those people to reject differences as deviant and expel them to the margins of social worlds, or murder them out of existence.

## Notes

1. Walter Burkert, *Creation of the Sacred* (Cambridge, Mass.: Harvard University Press, 1996), 24ff., 32, 84, 151, 161, 171.
2. Richard Stivers, *Evil in Modern Myth and Ritual* (Athens, Ga: University of Georgia Press, 1991).
3. Edmund Husserl, *Ideas Pertaining to a Pure Phenomenology and to a Phenomenological Philosophy*, F. Kerston, trans. (Dordrecht: Kluwer Academic Publishers, 1983).
4. Husserl, *Ideas*, 57–59.
5. Plato, *Timaeus* 29cd, Benjamin Jowett, trans.
6. Plato, *Theaetetus* 210bc, Howard North Fowler, trans.
7. Plato, *Republic* 587c–e, c.f. 580bc. Paul Shorey, trans.
8. Levinas, *Totality and Infinity*, Alfonso Lingis, trans. (Pittsburgh, Penn.: Duquesne University Press, 1969), 46.
9. Levinas, *Totality*, 110–120.
10. Levinas, *Totality*, 66–67.
11. Levinas, *Totality*, 131.
12. Paraphrase from F. Dostoevsky, *The Brothers Karamazov* (New York: Barnes & Noble Inc., 1995), 275. Repeated in E. Levinas, *Ethics and Infinity*, R. Cohen, trans. (Pittsburgh: Duquesne University Press, 1985), 98, 101; *Otherwise Than Being*, A. Lingis, trans. (Dordrecht, Netherlands: Kluwer, 1991), 146.
13. Levinas, *Totality*, 42.
14. Lucien Lévy-Bruhl, *Primitive Mentality*, Lilian A. Claire, trans. (New York: MacMillan, 1923); see also the remarks of G. W. F. Hegel, *Vorlesungen über die Philosophie der Geschichte*, Theorie Werkausgabe 12 (Frankfort, 1970), 120 & ff.
15. Bénézet Bujo, *Foundations of an African Ethic* (New York: Crossroads Publishing, 2001), 10.

16. Levinas, "The Ego and the Totality" in *Collected Philosophical Papers*, A. Lingis, trans. (Dordrecht, Netherlands: Kluwer Academic Publishers, 1993), 25–46.

17. B. Bujo, *Foundations*, 8–13.

18. Plato, *Symposium* 206, Michael Joyce, trans.

# Chapter 4
# Rebounding Violence in Social Rituals

In the previous chapter I argued that the distinction between myth and truth is a false distinction. What people name "truth" is a collection of reality postulates that are *lived*—made "real" in the living. Truths are not something stable and eternal, set up in the stars for all people to share but always have a local texture, a meaning within the common mental world of a particular group. Myths may be empirically faulty at the moment they are first articulated, but over time they become cultural truth, social *facts*, for the people who share them, from the most powerful articulator to those most oppressed by the truth system.

The way that myths and other social truths come to expression in societies repeats the way they arise—through ritual. Historically, rituals precede myth. There exists evidence of a rich palette of ritual observances in early human communities, long before hominids developed the physiological equipment that make possible speech and story-telling. In order to fully comprehend the functions that myths perform in a social milieu, we must understand their ritual bases and their ritual expressions.

## 1. Rituals of Domination

Rituals are obsessively repeated sequences of behaviors. Early humans practiced elaborate rituals at grave sites, and on territorial borders, and in their villages. The rituals marked out the most important events of their lives. Rituals helped to prepare individuals for life's most anxiety-ridden events. Feeding and eating, sex, marriage, childbirth, passage into adulthood, war, death, the hunt and its consequent distribution of meats all involved highly complex sequences of ritual events. Rituals brought to the forefront of social life its most crucial realities. Rituals precede myth. They also arise after the fact of myth, cropping up to express performatively the ideological assumptions embedded in both. Social "truths" underlie the rituals, and mythical articulations put those truths to word and legend. Myths articulate the anxieties of life's crucial events, celebrate the crucial life transitions, welcome newcomers into the group, bid farewell to the deceased members, and in all these functions, myths reconfirm the value and the legitimacy of the group's most sacred beliefs and practices.

Social scientists agree that people learn best what is taught through terror and pain.[1] Truths that are etched through the body into the psyche by sequences of terrifying and painful experiences carve themselves deep into a person's being. The painful and terrifying lessons of life are the most difficult to dislodge. This is why many anthropologists, such as Walter Burkert, René Girard, and Maurice Bloch, believe that the ritual practices repeated for millennia in early human communities convey across the generations and into the present world ancient ancestral truths about the world. The persistence of myth and ritual, the dogged conservatism of social truth, suggests that our histories have far more moral weight than we are generally prepared to admit. Whether our ancestors practiced primarily human and animal sacrifice or fertility rites and rituals of passage seems crucial in determining the moral direction in which our societies would proceed.

Since terror and pain teach best, and since they teach domestic truths that come to be applied to the world at large, a society's truths, though always local, are for the most part understood as universal and self-evident to all human beings. Where pain and terror are the methods of inscribing cultural myth, where people are abused physically and denigrated by myths of inferiority, those people learn most deeply the fact of their powerlessness. They learn that the world is a terrifying and brutalizing place where only the powerful survive and prosper. Without access to alternative voices or counter-myths and without social or legal recourse to defend their dignity or their bodies, a people's self-esteem and sense of worth are slowly whittled away under the constant and daily repetitions of their essential inadequacy and moral/human failings. Victim sub-populations can become convinced of their inferiority on the scale of human substance. A generally accepted social scientific fact declares that victims, over time, absorb the myths of their oppressors.

This tendency of victims to adopt the worldview of their oppressors is evidenced most disturbingly in domestic violence cases. There exists the strong propensity in battered spouses and children to believe that they themselves are the cause of their own battering. This tendency also explains the shocking fact that children raised by violent methods, whether psychically, physically, or sexually abused, often have a predisposition to the same cruel methods when rearing children of their own. Violence begets violence because it teaches its victims that the world is a brutal and menacing place. It teaches that mirroring the methods of the powerful provides the greatest assurance that one will survive the rigors of the harsh environment. It teaches that those incapable of internalizing the violence aimed at them and turning that violence upon their oppressors soon fall by the cosmic wayside. Those who adopt the ways of the brutalizing world will be the ones to prevail.

The tendency to adopt rather than challenge environing truth assumptions is universal to the human world in all forms of communities. Primo Levi, Italian chemist-philosopher, survivor of Auschwitz, and Holocaust autobiographer, is convinced that all socio-political systems share a common ideological power to persuade and manipulate the behavior patterns of insiders. All systems, for Levi, are dehumanizing, to greater or lesser degrees. They bend their members and shape their modes of interaction toward its ruling logic. In *The Drowned and the Saved*, Levi contends that the more brutalizing the system, the more deeply etched and manifestly apparent are the disfiguring effects of the logic of the system upon the moral character of the inmates.[2]

Levi argues that, in the Nazi lagers, the good rarely survived long.[3] In fact, moral strength soon proved to be a burden that incapacitated the prisoner for survival in the brutalizing system. Scruples rendered the individual incapable of internalizing the ways of the system and adopting the only methods available for survival: stealing, cheating comrades, turning in others for favors, and offering oneself as local minion to execute Nazi power (*kapos*). In the rigors of the most decadent—though structurally typical—human community, self-preservation is the only order of the day, and most prisoners soon adopt the logic of the system as the only available means to eek out another hour, another day, in their hell.

As ever new abject modes of dwelling were invented in the Nazi camps, the human beings there—the definitively social animals—became ever more dehumanized by the system, till their sociality was corroded and their animality was all that remained. From the moment of their entry into the camp through every daily selection for death, the body of sufferers watched their numbers dwindle, and, simultaneously the possibility of "community feeling" among the surviving. There was no time, no breath, no spark of hope—between the meaningless labors and the freezing marches, the agonizing hunger and thirst, the soul-draining exhaustion—for a smile or a word of consolation, never mind for fraternity and compassion. There was no energy left for moral reflection or for empathy for the suffering others.

Levi finds this absence of community feeling not in the least surprising or censurable. He states: "It is naive, absurd, and historically false to believe that an infernal system such as National Socialism sanctifies its victims; on the contrary, it degrades them, it makes them resemble itself."[4] Victims in Nazi camps became living corpses, isolated skeletons. Human community was an impossibility for the most part. Only ruthless strangers could struggle over scraps of food or clothing. There existed few social valences within which human connections might be struck or maintained. There was only the nagging hunger, the endless labor, and the terror of the next selection.

## 2. The Violence of "Identity Work"

What is most disturbing about this vision of human community is Levi's claim, echoed by anthropologist Eric R. Wolfe, that the moral impoverishment witnessed in death camps is the identifying mark of human community *per se*.[5] For these thinkers, violence is not the sign of communal collapse; it is the very fabric of human systems. Extermination camps are, according to Levi, utterly typical, if extreme, examples of a common, very human, phenomenon. Cruelty in gaining power over others and securing one's place in a system are common features of all systems. That truth emerges readily and reveals itself clearly when the polite civil *push* of civilized human communities comes to bare survivalist *shove*. The Nazi death camps disclosed to Levi an alarming revelation: that an atrocity like the Nazi slaughter was possible everywhere because cruelty and inhumanity are "dreadfully exemplary" of all human communities.[6]

Adolph Hitler was only one man. Yet he was able to rouse an entire country and seduce to his mission of genocidal horror populations many nations removed from German soil. Across the stretch of Hitler's Europe, young men and women became caught up in his utopian promises of a "New World Order," homogeneous nationhood cleansed of its racial contaminants and fulfilling its bright and glorious destiny. In many places of execution across Hitler's Europe, mothers with babes in arms and old folks with picnic baskets emerged in festival masses, thronging to witness the executions of their neighbors—mothers, old folks, and babies named outsiders to the fêted race. Many scholars consider one of the greatest mysteries of the Nazi phenomenon to be the apparent ease with which Hitler enlisted into his reprehensible project the passionate support of so many otherwise decent people. However, this is less of a mystery than it may appear; the disposition to mirror the powerful, to align oneself with the dominant worldview, and to pattern one's behavior according to the logic of the prevailing system is a feature pervasive of the human world.

Everyone wants to be a winner. By attaching themselves to the powerful elites, people join the winning team; it is the most reasonable thing for people to do. Following the footsteps of those who head the social ladder offers the only way up the ladder, a very seductive option for the many resigned to the ladder's base. The conversion to open violence from social myths and political propaganda is for many people a small step, which takes place on an existential level far deeper than the merely rational. Songs and tales of glorious histories and brave, illustrious ancestors, pledges of allegiance, national anthems, flag waving, and cheers for the homeland ring deep and true in a people's hearts, exciting national pride and rousing morally blind virtues like loyalty, courage, and vengeance. To betray the homeland is unthinkable, whatever mischief the state may be doing. The possession of authority can authorize the most questionable actions, and afford a sense of righteousness to whatever the rightful powers deem politically necessary. The people's sense of the legitimacy of the status quo of power relations and their conviction of the rightful authority of the state authorities is difficult to unseat. Violence always has reasons.

Levi and a host of other thinkers are convinced that dehumanization of the lesser members is a sweeping effect in all social orders *per se*. The very politeness of our social worlds masks the violence upon which those systems are founded and indeed our polite social rituals are one powerful medium through which inequities are confirmed and communicated. Those polite niceties that are considered to be the signs of civilization—from infant circumcision to the polite

"Good afternoon!" and the "After you" at the doorway—may simply provide a human face that masks a general institutional cruelty born of the will to order and organize. Social rituals may provide a shroud that is fundamental to and amplificatory of the system's cruelty.

The polite mannerisms of the politico-economic elite, their codes of etiquette and protocols of behavior and dress, easily occluded the fact of the colonizers' mediocrity and moral poverty. Though the manners and dress of the powerful are often cited as proof of their essential superiority, cultural knowledge (language, social bearing, eccentricities of dress and manners) is often employed to justify wanton injustices, economic disparities, and cruel treatment of the system's weaker members. Polite manners form a conceptual veil fundamental to the cruelty. Cults of elitism arise around cultural mannerisms. Since possession of this unique cultural knowledge proved people to be more civilized, then everyone, even those most oppressed of the system, would scurry to take up the ridiculous pretensions and to mirror the habits of the mediocre few.

This tendency reveals one of the most ironic features surrounding cultural myths in oppressive communities: the harsher the system, the more pervasive among the oppressed is the readiness to accept the prevailing habits as morally acceptable, the prevailing social prejudices as fact, in order to find a place of belonging within the alienating system.[7] Persons confined to the bottom rungs of the social ladder often voluntarily collaborate with the system's terrorisms and readily place themselves in subordination, often without experiencing any overwhelming sense of coercion or self-betrayal. Human beings are hardwired for survival. People can unhesitatingly opt for, and even embrace, the alienating aspects of their lives, if it means securing the sense of belonging they so desperately crave. Those most alienated by the system crave most desperately this feeling of belonging, so they often submit themselves willingly to the system that oppresses them.

Mental health cannot be long maintained if one is constantly, deeply focused upon the miseries of life. In most stable societies, the myth that firmly prevails declares that the system and its divisions of power are the entities that take care of people, providing gratification of particular needs and fulfillment of group expectations, and regulating mutual obligations among the various strata of the society. A system tends to be rationally supported by all who live under its thrall, sharing its ideological assumptions in their common mental world, framed by the myths that legitimate the status quo of power relations.

This tendency in the oppressed to accept as right and good the eccentricities of the dominant is as strong as the tendency to accept as right and just the inequities of the system that oppresses them. These tendencies are cultivated in deeply insidious ways. They are the work of the ritual traditions spawned within the power structure. Anthropologist Maurice Bloch, a specialist in the ritual systems of early and modern cultural groups, describes, in *From Blessing to Violence* and *Prey into Hunter*, features of ritual systems that he claims so broadly practiced in human communities as to be "quasi-universal."[8] Bloch, like most anthropologists today, sees both mythical truths and cultural reality postulates originating in, and reconveyed through, the culture's ritual systems.

Rituals and their mythical elaborations comprise the means by which societies dramatize their patterns of domination and repression, and the way they reinforce and theatricalize the rightness of the status quo of power relations. Oppressed groups at large are included in the community's ritualized activities, whether those activities compose floggings or celebrations, public hangings or feasts, because the active participation of subgroups in the rituals of the system enlists the powerless in reaffirmation of the processes dictating their own degradation.

Bloch explains that patterns of domination and oppression are reinforced through a culture's rituals. This occurs because there exists a common patterning to ritual that Bloch believes to be quasi-universal to human communities. Bloch demonstrates this patterning through a detailed exposition of the circumcision ritual of the Merina tribe of Highland Madagascar. This ritual event begins with an incident of social disorder, always initiated by a subordinated subsection of the population, such as women or children. This group steals grain or fruit from their fellows or neighbors. They may even whip, beat, or torture other members of the tribe. Then, the initial victims turn upon the attackers, beating, humiliating, and torturing them.

The sequences of violence mount to a frenzy until some person or group is singled out and marked off as inassimilable. To be inassimilable is to prove unresponsive to the violence meant to order the rebellious. The ritual reaches its climax in the murder or metaphorical murder of the inassimilable ones. Metaphorical murder may take the form of some physical torture that causes unconsciousness, as in the Merina circumcision ritual.[9] It may mean a terrifying abduction of adolescents from their homes to dark huts in the forest where ancestor spirits teach the secrets of the tribe, as in the Orokaiva tribe of Papua, New Guinea.[10] It may even mean permanent expulsion from the community. But, Bloch is clear on this point: an occasional real murder is necessary to maintain the seriousness of the event.

Bloch believes the underlying message of such rituals communicates the claim that mischief-makers, inassimilable ones, are enacting a breakdown in the social codes. The rituals are meant to dramatize the chaos that can be relied upon to ensue when rightful social order is lost. This explains why the inassimilable ones marked out for ritual discipline are always subordinates of the society—women or children. The climax of the event returns the society to order and stability by returning the subordinates to the bottom of the social ladder. Then, beginning with the final "murder," a festival breaks out. All members share in the celebration of the return to status quo with song, dance, distribution of meats, and often drunken revelry. The group is rejuvenated, its social forms and patterns of power reconfirmed. The illusion is conveyed to the entire group that all members of the society have their turn at domination, but the ritual also communicates the fiction that the group is at its strongest and most stable when the rightful powers are in place.

# 3. Rebounding Violence

The oppressed members of the community believe that their willing submission to their assigned social roles is what makes the social order the powerful and stable unit that it is. This belief is embedded in the most archaic social rituals and remains a powerful constant in the ritual lives of many societies today. Maurice Bloch traces affirmations of social hierarchy and the latter's connection to system power into the "core messages" of many social rituals. His study of the Orokaiva "Pig People" of Papua, New Guinea, and other simple modern tribes reveals that many rites of passage and initiation rituals close with active demonstrations of the necessity of rigid social hierarchy. When social place has been confirmed, the aggressiveness of the tribe is exhibited to neighbors through provocative and hostile gestures. The boundary stones may be moved outward, and insults, war cries, and spears may be jettisoned toward the external world. This closure often leads to hostilities and provokes open warfare with neighbors. This tendency for internal violence to fulfill itself in external aggressions Bloch calls the "rebounding" of violence.[11]

Rituals that legitimate the status quo of power and reaffirm the traditional system may change their form and intensity over time, but they very rarely change their underlying meanings and structure. Bloch names the underlying logic re-legitimating the violences of the powerful and justifying the inequities of the system "a logic of domination."[12] The externally aggressive phase of the ritual, where internal violences are turned outward upon neighboring groups, demonstrates explicitly how violence rebounds. Victims are profoundly affected by the suffering they have experienced; their subjectivities come to be reconstructed by those experiences. Then their abjection is given reasons by being projected onto their neighbors. Surrounding persons become the new victims of old social rituals of violence.

The logic of domination, Bloch contends, confirms a shared mental world within which subordinates can wear their humiliation with pride because they have been convinced that the strength, longevity, and stability of their powerful social order is preserved by their willing submission to the system. The rituals mask the purely exploitative nature of the social arrangements. In the celebratory denouement to the rituals, the precursory violence is forgotten, eclipsed by the dance, music, and drunken revelry. The violence, however, endures long after the ritual closure. It endures within the social system in the internal violences against the subordinates, and outside the system's span in relations with neighboring peoples. Bloch concludes with a frightening claim: "Ritual does its ideological job and carries at its core a simple and general message which can be received and used to justify almost any type of domination."[13]

Ritual evolves in its outward forms and expressions but across these evolutions the logic of domination remains persistent and conveys a consistent message: violence is legitimate when conducted by legitimate authorities. This message endures through changing historical situations, unaltered across vast upheavals in politico-economic circumstances. Far from the evolving historical forms composing alterations in the logic of the system, they actually come to being as elaborations of that logic. However varied those elaborations, the underlying logic maintains throughout, in the form of what Bloch calls a minimal "structural core."[14]

Historical forms arise, evolve, and transform radically, as do ritual practices and their mythical expressions, but the evolving forms continue to express and elaborate the minimal core. Across the most varying socio-political landscapes, the rightful traditions and rightful authorities of the evolving systems are reasserted, and the truths that compose the horizons of the people's common mental world remain intact. Rituals, and their mythical expressions continue to function inclining people to accept, if not celebrate the internal injustices practiced by the current power nodes and their aggressions upon external others.

Since the truths that underpin the system (the logic of domination and its rebounding violence toward external peoples) orient the outlook of the entire system, the violent practices of the socially and politically dominant are emulated and mirrored in social attitudes and everyday practices. The system's ideological assumptions seep down deep within a people's being and disposes them to echo the violent behaviors of the current power nodes. Since pain and terror teach more deeply than other methods, we can reasonably conclude that the myths and rituals legitimating current power relations are carved most deeply into those most cruelly oppressed by the system, those who are persuaded into the system's truths by terrorizing and painful methods.

Bloch describes violence as rebounding to indicate his deep awareness that victims rarely suffer oppression, torture, and exploitation without that violence reconfiguring their worldview and causing them to carry the effects of their abuse into their understandings of self and world, and to manifest those worldview assumptions in their future behaviors. People who suffer deeply redefine the world as threatening; they see phenomena that arise to confront them as menacing, and measure neighboring forces as malevolent. These negative expectations become self-fulfilling prophecies. When neighbors find themselves viewed with suspicion, they often respond suspiciously.

The most innocent gestures can be mistaken as menacing if the observer is sufficiently paranoid. This often leads the observer to respond-in-advance to a perceived menace with acts that are understood as retaliatory but actually comprise instances of blatant unprovoked aggression. This is the meaning of pre-emptive attack that is employed to justify unprovoked attacks on national neighbors in the world. People who have suffered a history of violence, as individuals or as social groups, can go forth from their experiences with a great chip on their shoulders, daring all others who enter proximity to knock it from its precarious perch. Children who have been beaten often grow into adults who beat their children in turn. Wives who have been abused often turn to their children and repeat the abusive behaviors they have suffered.

Violence teaches people that the world is ruled by the powerful. It teaches that if one does not want to continue to be a victim, then one had better become a perpetrator. Those who have historically been abused come to understand power in very simplistic terms. They know it simply as top-down coercive power. They seek this form of power to protect themselves from future abuses. Taking up the forms of power they have witnessed in their own histories, they work out their abjection by recreating their own abuses upon the bodies of neighboring others. Violence comes to rebound from husband to wife to children, from generation to generation, from abused people to their new neighbors, from the ghettoized social misfit to society at large. Violence reconstructs subjectivities, turning victims into perpetrators, and innocents into victims.

Given the rebounding nature of violence, the observer of history may assume that violent histories will repeat themselves in ever-broadening circles of violence, as subjectivities of victim populations reconstruct themselves in more powerful images to withstand and combat the reigning order. The victims who achieve release from the tyranny of a dominant elite, as the victims of colonial power in Africa, will continue, at least for a time, to pay homage to the truths of the abusive system under which they have historically suffered. They continue to mirror the patterns of behavior they have witnessed in the powerful elites. They continue to accept the logic compressed and conveyed in the institutions and traditions of those repressive systems. The historical victims continue to adhere to the truth assumptions and behavior rituals of their previous masters.

Healing time is required before the myths of domination, thrashed into the bodies and etched in the psyches of the degraded and downtrodden, can be expelled to make way for healthier self-perceptions, social practices, and codes of behavior. Free and independent Africans may put their national houses in order, but those new houses will likely continue to mirror the colonial systems until the thrall of the reigning worldview, the logic of domination, is broken. And the methods adopted by the rulers within the newly independent states will tend to mirror the ruling methods of the colonial oppressors, at least for a time after independence. The logic of domination continues to rule the new system and its citizens remain predisposed to rebound the violences they have suffered in their colonial past upon their national and external neighbors.

## Notes

1. Walter Burkert, *Creation of the Sacred* (Cambridge, Mass.: Harvard University Press, 1992), 29.

2. Primo Levi, *The Drowned and the Saved*, Raymond Rosenthal, trans. (New York: Vintage, 1989); cf. Michel Foucault, *Discipline and Punish, The Birth of the Prison*, Alan Sheridan, trans. (New York: Random House, 1995).

3. Levi, *Drowned Saved*, 9.

4. Levi, *Drowned Saved*, 40.

5. Eric R. Wolfe, *Envisioning Power: Ideologies of Dominance and Crisis* (Berkeley, Calif.: University of California Press, 1999).

6. Levi, *Drowned Saved*, 19.

7. Viola Bernard, Perry Ottenberg, and Fritz Redl, "Dehumanization" in N. Sanford and Craig Comstock, eds., *Sanctions for Evil* (San Francisco: Jossey-Bass, 1971), 102–124.

8. Maurice Bloch, *From Blessing to Violence* (Cambridge: Cambridge University Press, 1986); *Prey into Hunter* (Cambridge: Cambridge University Press, 1992).

9. Bloch, *Blessing*, 195

10. Bloch, *Hunter*, 37.

11. Bloch, *Hunter*, 37–43.

12. Bloch, *Hunter*, 37–43.

13. Bloch, *Hunter*, 195.

14. Bloch, *Hunter*, 13–15.

# Chapter 5
# Precolonial Africa

To place in historical context the colonial exploitation of the continent of Africa requires a brief overview of the history and peoples of Africa before the colonial era. Much fine work has been accomplished in this regard in the last two decades, challenging previous Eurocentric interpretations of the history of the continent. To provide a historical framework for my inquiry into the existential effects of colonial violence in Africa, I draw on both traditional and recent studies of the continent and its peoples.

## 1. A Common Human World

I shall begin where human life began, in the Paleolithic era, when we find Africa assuming central stage in the ancient record of humanity. "Archaeologists, paleontologists, and molecular biologists have amassed overwhelming fossil and genetic evidence that Africa is indeed the sole birthplace of humankind . . . the womb of humanity."[1] The continent of Africa is the cradle of civilization. It provided the stage whereupon the first of our species would emerge from the primeval forest, stand upright, and walk across the savannah.

A common theme in African folktales is the primordial break between gods and humankind. Many tales picture the beginning of the human world in terms of a fateful break with the gods. Often the notion of a heavenly fire comes into the tales, sometimes as a divine gift to humans, sometimes as a symbol of raw power or eternality. The Chaga, a Bantu people occupying the slopes of Mt. Kilimanjaro in Tanzania, tell the tale of Murile, who brought fire to the Moon God and was blessed many times for his gift.[2] The story begins when Murile, a mere child himself, sang a magic song and turned a particularly beautiful taro root tuber into a baby. He hid the infant in a hollow tree, telling no one of his creation, and growing thinner and thinner each day from secretly feeding the babe his own dinner.

One day, Murile's mother followed him, hoping to discover why her son was growing so thin. When she learned the truth, she strangled the little child. Thereafter, Murile grew terribly melancholy and raised himself up into the heavens where he worked his way to the Moon God's village by helping wood gatherers, grass cutters, herders, harvesters, and water carriers. Murile finally reached his destination and there won the favor of the Moon God by teaching him how to make fire by twirling a pointed stick atop a second flat one. Murile then cooked the Moon God a fine meal of roasted plantains and meat. The Moon God was so pleased with the "wonderful doctor" that he had the moon people give Murile gifts of cows and goats and whatever else they had in their storehouses. Murile became a very rich man, and in time had many wives and many children.

In the Western tradition, the old Greek stories tell a similar tale. The gift of fire set the human world apart from that of the beasts, but that gift was stolen and so simultaneously alienated humans from the gods. According to Hesiod, fire was the ambiguous gift of Prometheus the Trickster. Prometheus stole this precious commodity, symbol of the eternal energy and immortality of the gods, hid it in a hollow fennel stalk, and gave it to humankind.[3] The gift made possible warmth and cooked food and protection from the savage beast, but humans would not have needed these things had Prometheus' trickery not caused them to be cast from the heavens to wander the harsh earth and scratch out a meager living from its unwelcoming crust.

Clearly the African tale has advantages over the Greek version. The divine theft that alienated humans from the gods is replaced by a human fire-gift to the god that seals a bond between human and divine. In the Greek tale, humans are innocent of any wrongdoing, making this alienation ambiguous and the human world ambivalent toward its gods; sometimes the gods are jealous and angry, sometimes fatherly and just. In the Chaga tale, humans are starkly presented in the chiaroscuro of the mortal struggle for existence, where babies appear virtually out of a song, and are quickly eliminated when the food grows short. Murile is a hero precisely because he sets himself apart from the harsh realities of everyday existence. He sings life into whatever he finds beautiful, he starves himself to feed hungry children. He is a giver and not an undeserving recipient of stolen gifts.[4]

Whatever the source of the earliest flames that sparked human *technos*, the propensity for the crafting stone and metal tools defines the distinction between human and beast, and separates modern man from other hominids. No doubt even at the dawn of human time each family and clan varied immeasurably from the next. Nonetheless, from the time (four to five million years ago) that the first of our ancestors stood upright and walked out onto the savannah of east and south Africa until the end of the Middle Paleolithic period (about thirty thousand years ago), humans were relatively singular in kind. This is considered anthropological fact.

## 2. Peaceful Beginnings

That the earliest human groups composed relatively peaceful communities is fairly certain. Their peaceful orientation composes a compelling mystery given the hardships and terrors facing them in the environing world. Anthropologists agree that, as long as communities remained small and their needs for land did not overflow their traditional borders, social groups tended to live alongside each other in peaceful communities, trading and intermarrying. This seems to be the general scholarly consensus regarding people occupying the African continent.[5]

Anthropologists agree that Africa composes the "cradle of all civilization" and they commonly assert that civilizations remained almost pervasively peaceful and naturally democratic across the African continent. However, when we consider the theories of anthropologists of the Western civilizational tradition, a paradox emerges. Anthropological tracings of Western communal beginnings deem the earliest "human" clans fundamentally intraspecifically aggressive. Walter Burkert, anthropologist of culture and violence, posits the Paleolithic hunt for large carnivores as the "civilizing" moment for the species. He claims that, from pre-hunt rituals that were developed to ease the anxieties associated with this highly emotional event, arose all manner of political configuration and all patterns of exchange, along with the full range of prohibition and prescription, grounded in the appropriate religious justifications, that formed the social codes of these early communities.[6]

René Girard, as well, makes universalist claims about violence as the catalyst of human communities. Girard believes that certain anxieties that motivate human rivalry are ever present in human communities. Girard's notion of "mimetic rivalry" explains, in decidedly Freudian terms, that individuals form desires by mimicking those they model, and in seeking to possess the objects of their desire run into conflict with their heroes. The model becomes an ambiguous hero, and their relationship an ambivalent contest. Rivalries inevitably escalate until there is no way to distinguish between good models and evil rivals. The community is forced to develop elaborate rituals to re-establish identities that make sense of the communal identities again, distinguishing each from another. Ritual expulsions achieve this end.

Deviants, for Girard, are purified from the communities by scapegoating rituals that funnel the members' natural aggressions upon those marginal within the group.[7] The *pharmakon* of the ancient world, the cripple or village idiot of the dark ages, the witch or warlock of the medieval world, the jungle savage of the imperialist era, the dark-skinned, black-eyed Muslim of the neo-imperialist world—all these figures of non-belonging serve the purpose of the communities that demonize them, binding those communities together in a firm identity and unshakable solidarity that is purchased through self-distinction from an alien outcast.

Many would say that religion soothes the savage beast. In most religions, in fact, the god is understood to name all people brothers and sisters and to require them to live in peace. Many anthropologists argue convincingly that religion arises to mask the fact of universal human aggressiveness, and to suppress and channel those aggressions upon unsuspecting victims, providing the conceptual machinery to figure the deviant as demonic in order that the god's vengeance can be guiltlessly dished out upon those who fail to assimilate.[8]

Western anthropologists are faced with a paradox: they must explain how Western communities came to a general state of intraspecific violence that require elaborate ritual systems to channel and civilize the aggressive urges, while African peoples—and other indigenous communities—remained peacefully co-existent with their neighbors. Applying the conclusions of Eli Sagan's compelling work, *At the Dawn of Tyranny*, we may assume that African and other simple tribal societies resist the urge to tyranny because they are small and intimately connected. In these smaller communities, people maintain the face-to-face connections with each other and with their neighbors that compel them to their best ethical behavior.

Anthropologists find it difficult to explain how humans form peaceful communities because those experts accept the assumption that aggressive urges are encoded in human genes and acted out in violent rituals throughout the archaic histories of their communities. The problem suddenly disappears if we consider the early communities of the West as a special historical case—if we consider that people of the Western tradition developed along particularly violence-prone trajectories.

One fact that may explain why overwhelming communal violence is a uniquely Western phenomenon is that, beginning many millennia before the Common Era and lasting well into the Middle Ages, wave after wave of Indo-European barbarians descended from the Russian steppe lands into Europe. These peoples were a new breed, very different from the indigenous populations that they slaughtered or assimilated. The barbarians were worshippers of a male sky-god; the political structure of their communities was rigidly hierarchical; their lifestyle, as mounted warrior castes, suggests ritual lives that were highly militaristic and violent. The indigenous Europeans were relatively peaceful agrarian folk who worshipped the mother goddess and built their communal life around human and agrarian fertility rites, some of which were undeniably sacrificial but rarely aggressive toward neighbors.

The original tribal peoples of Europe may have shared in many features of the peaceful lifestyle of their ancestors and contemporaries on the African continent, but centuries and millennia of imposed subjugation to the brutal warrior tribes from the northeast of their continent probably reconstructed their identities and gave rise to a general culture of violence. This explanation would also elucidate why the people of Europe, exemplified in the Hellenists, though in many respects ethically and socially regressed, deem themselves more civilized than other peoples. Civilization implies hierarchical rankings and rigid orderings; it implies the creation of a military class and the seasonal practice of war. These characteristics were common features of European communities from the classical era onward.

People in Africa maintained over long stretches of time benevolent connections with neighbors that made the creation of armies and the waging of war unnecessary. I contend that the Africans and other simple indigenous communities retained their peaceful ways in direct relation as they managed to retain their sacred connections with the earth, practicing fertility rites instead of violent rituals.

Chancellor Williams is an African American historian who revolutionized public perceptions about African history, shifting the focus from Arab and European adventures in Africa to the history of black Africans themselves. Williams attempts a scholarly reinterpretation of traditional Eurocentric accounts of African history, seeking to read between the ethnocentric lines and produce a more authentic understanding of the patterns of life and interethnic relations in early African societies.[9] Williams believes the achievements of early Africans to be prodigious. He is clear: Africans lived in relative peace and stability, a crucial factor in the development of their stable and democratic societies. Africans were among the first to invent writing, tells Williams. They also evolved uniquely African systems of philosophical thought, ethically superior life-principles, and highly evolved value systems. Africans developed economic traditions that were exceedingly egalitarian and political institutions that were decidedly liberal and independent. Williams tells:

> A continent wide study of the traditional customary laws of the Blacks . . . enabled us to learn, for the first time, that a single constitutional system prevailed throughout all Black Africa, just as though the whole race, regardless of the countless patterns, lived under a single government. A similar continent wide study of African social and economic systems through the millenniums reveals the same overall patterns of unity and sameness of all fundamental institutions. . . . there [exists] a historical and fundamental basis for real brotherhood and unity of the black race [that] could not have escaped the notice of those Europeans who have been investigating and writing about Africa over the years.[10]

Cheikh Anta Diop reports a similar bias in African historiography, stating, in his *Precolonial Black Africa*:

> Until now the history of Black Africa has always been written with dates as dry as laundry lists, and no one has almost ever tried to find the key that unlocks the door to the intelligence, the understanding of African society. Failing which, no researcher has ever succeeded in revivifying the African past.[11]

Diop also confirms that the historical documents at the disposal of the researcher demonstrate indisputably that the greater number of African societies, from early human time until the colonial era, prospered in relative peace and stability, without a break in their stable continuity, for most of those thousands of years. Diop corroborates that African political regimes, despite their mostly monarchial form, were exceedingly democratic in both structure and practical functioning.[12] That is to say, early African peoples tended to be gathered into kingdoms, but the kings were not chosen according to family pedigree, but according to their merit and record as wise and beneficent leaders. The monarchies could not become tyrannous because of deeply engrained practices of shared leadership: most of the important decisions the king faced required the agreement of a council of elders, which drew from and represented all the various villages of the territory and the many households of the kinship group.

Diop's project is to highlight the integral role played by Africans in the genesis of human civilization. To the purpose of demarginalizing Africa and relocating it at the center of the universe of human evolution, Diop rediscovers ancient Africa, positing new truths that for some dogged historians are found scandalous: for example, Diop insists that the pharaohs of Egypt were black Africans.[13] Proof that Diop's work is revolutionary comes in the virulent critique he endures from more traditional scholars; he is challenged on the basis of his "sweeping generalizations" and "the weakness of his arguments."[14] However, a full appreciation of Diop's work requires that one recognize the political and ethical intent of Diop's work. Diop is not writing *only* to address a scholarly audience and to challenge as Eurocentric previous scholarly readings of African history (though this too is undoubtedly an important aspect of his scholarly mission).

Diop is also directing his scandalous truths toward a general Eurocentric audience, to disabuse them of their ongoing prejudices about the civilizational backwardness of African peoples, when measured against white Western notions of *human* progress. Diop is addressing as well Africans in turmoil on the continent today and Africans in diaspora, to awaken them to alternative understandings of their traditions and their pasts, to afford them a clearer appreciation of the deep cultural and political losses exacted by slavery and colonialism. Though his scholarly critics may object to his theories as inadequately rigorous and scholarly—as overgenerous and impassioned speculation, founded on weak evidence and questionable sources—Diop's theories have been met with much applause by his Africanist audiences and by those scholars who trust that a little generosity is due in historical reinterpretations of African history. Diop's work represents a commendable contribution to the new literature on Africa.

Henry Olela expands Diop's claim of the significant African contribution to human evolution with his assertion that the birthplace of philosophy is older than the Greeks, to whom the Western tradition pays homage. "The ancient Greeks themselves often credited Africa with being the source of foundations of philosophical knowledge."[15] Olela asserts that regions of northern Africa and the island of Crete were inhabited by Africans who migrated north during the expansion of the Sahara Desert around 2,500 years B.C.E. The awesome magnificence of ancient Egyptian kingdoms Olela claims for the descendants of the Gallas, the Somalians, and the Maasai. According to Olela, civilization began in the interior of Africa and shifted northward, through descent and diffusion, to engulf the north of the continent and regions around the Mediterranean Sea. Ancient Egypt in all its magnificence is, for Olela, ancient Africa—the kingdom of Sais in Olela's terms—and that places "Black Africa" at "the intellectual center of the world," inventing the mathematics, philosophy, astronomy, science, and medicine that would be passed, through the Pre-Socratic philosopher Thales of Miletus (around 640 to 546 B.C.E.), to the secondary "cradle" of civilization and philosophy, ancient Greece.[16]

Many Africanist scholars demonstrate that there were striking consistencies in the way African peoples organized their societies and lived their lives, across the continent. Diop and Williams note broad consistencies of social and political forms across the diverse African cultural landscape. In his thorough study, *African Religions and Philosophy*, John S. Mbiti, too, traces thought patterns, social understandings, and worldview features that he holds pervasive of African cultures and consistent across the diversity of African peoples.[17] If Africans did not share a thoroughgoing "common mental world," at least they demonstrated abundant symbolic resonances with each other, according to Mbiti's account. I consider these features in order to provide a backdrop against which colonial effects might be measured and the rebounding nature of colonial violences might be conjectured.

There exist as many as twelve hundred tribes in Africa today. Across this vast human landscape, with all its profound differences, religion permeates and guides all aspects of tribal life. Africans make no formal distinctions between the sacred and the profane, the spiritual and the material. Religion is an integral feature of community. A full understanding of African cultural ways recognizes that the goal of African religion is the good of the whole social group, in radical opposition to secular Western liberal capitalist ideals of autonomy and individualism.

For the African, the individual person takes shape and comes to human fruition only within the social context. Since ancient times, the African has been deeply aware that an individual is socially constructed, a fact that has only begun to occur to Westerners with postmodern reformulations of theories of self.[18] Only in the context of family, surrounded by the ancestors and the god, connected with the past and the future, does the present and distinctly individual person emerge most fully. The common Swahili proverb *Mtu ni watu* (A person is people) affirms the contextual nature of individual life for the African.

Social life, on its many levels and across its diverse dimensions of time, is what issues in the full human life that embraces, creates, and gives issue to the whole of a person's possibilities. In traditional African societies, these other dimensions of life include the past generations of ancestors and the beings yet to be born to the community. The spirits that have passed and those that await future birth are believed to dwell in the present, albeit invisibly, alongside the present social actors. African ethics is deeply intertwined with the present, because the present enjoys broad temporal and existential reach; the immediate family extends back into the past and forward into the future. Mbiti can thus say that, for African peoples, religion permeates existence. Religion occupies the whole person, affects the whole of social life, and extends across the multidimensionality of time and existence. Religious conviction configures everyday life patterns, shapes language, informs thought patterns and social relationships, and dictates fears, attitudes, and social dispositions. "Everybody is a religious carrier," states Mbiti.[19]

One might wonder how religious ideas come to resonate across such a wide diversity of peoples and across such a massive expanse of territory, given the fact that the African religious universe is not universal, national, or tribal. The religious universe is bound entirely by, and limited to, the people among whom it has evolved. There exist in precolonial Africa no missionaries, no preaching, and no evangelism since no benefit derives from imposing local beliefs upon outsiders to the group. Religious notions spread spontaneously, as social groups migrate, intermarry, and trade with other groups, or as one group conquers, or is conquered by, another.

One of the common notions shared across tribal boundaries is the conviction in life after death. This is understood far differently from the utopian or millenary obsessions of Judaism, Christianity, and Islam. Westerners tend to shift the import from the here and now of human existence to some future and glorious time when the god will raise up the righteous and cast the wicked into eternal torment. For the African, there exists no messianic hope, no apocalyptic vision. Since there is no distinction between the spiritual and the material, the soul has lost no primeval home. It is not lost, wandering, or alienated from its earthly dwelling place. It does not long for reunion with the god nor for redemption from earthly degradation. The African notion of an afterlife boasts the highly positive effect of configuring the here and now of human existence as the most important of human times. Earthly matters are crucial, not for their redemptive value in a glorious hereafter, but because the earthly life is the richest and fullest dimension of human existence.

Many Westerners believe that Africans worshipped a myriad of gods and ancestors before the white man brought to the continent the more advanced notion of a single god. This claim is altogether false. All Africans have long accepted the notion of a single deity—omniscient, omnipresent, omnipotent, just, and good.[20] Ancestors have never been worshipped in any common sense of that term. Even worship of the god is entirely pragmatic and utilitarian, since the god is not understood to stand in an ethical or spiritual relationship with human beings. The god does not "love" humans, nor do the Africans speak of love for their god.

The African holds the god to be simply the creative force of the world, responsible for the laws and customs and for human creation. The cosmic drama is the god's drama. Like most peoples, Africans speak of the god as male. Like the Hebrew god, the African deity has various conflicting aspects: the god can be persuaded through prayer to heal and to soothe human ills, or can punish with epidemics and widespread misfortunes. In other words, like lightning or fire, the god can punish or purify.

Worship for African communities is no adulation or prostration before an almighty, but takes the form of utilitarian acts to draw the god's favor. These are practiced mainly in times of shortage. When African communities enjoy ample amounts of the necessities of life—food, rain, children, wealth—they have reached the "promised land." The god confronts the African as mysterious and unknowable, so there are no images or physical representations of the god. Westerners would be hard pressed to understand the African placement of the god; though in theory the African god is transcendental, in practice the god is entirely immanent, often metaphorized as the wind or the air or other natural phenomena.

To understand the African perception of the relationship between humans and the god, one must consider the African ontological vision. In the African worldview, the god composes the ultimate explanation of all things, genesis and sustainer of all beings. Beneath the god, on the ontological scale, resides the spirit world—composed of superhuman beings who, with the god, dwell in the shadowy realm of the past (the *Zamani*). These superhuman spirits were once ancestors of the tribe, but they are now forgotten. When their personal names are no longer mentioned by the living members of the tribe, the ancestors are understood to lose their individual identity—their *personal* being. Forgotten ancestors, lodged in the impersonal realm of the *Zamani*, are thought to become resentful and malevolent toward their living relatives.[21]

More recent ancestors, the ones not long dead and still remembered by name, compose the "living dead" of the tribe. These are the newly departed of several recent generations. For up to five generations, an ancestor is thought to dwell among their living families in the now of human existence (the *Sasa*). They are kept alive through rituals of respect in the food offerings and libations of the living, and especially through the repetition of their names in the genealogies and stories recounted in the present. As long as they continue to be named by the living, they are maintained in a living and personalized state, inhabiting the forests and mountains surrounding the family homes, acting as mediums between the spirit world and the human—hence, the import of rituals of respect, burial rites, tales, and genealogies. Africans have a delicate sense of the necessity of appropriate ritual since improper burial and neglected rituals of respect toward the spirit-dead are understood to risk their resentment and revenge, understood to arrive in the form of illness, misfortune, or death.[22]

Human beings inhabit the realm of the living, ontologically positioned above animals and plants. At the bottom of the scale rests phenomena and objects without biological life. Human beings are understood to live the richest of lives among all beings, as they exist in the *Sasa* where life is concrete and tangible. The living-dead share somewhat in their lively existence, though once-removed from its fleshy palpability. Both dimensions of time (the *Sasa* and the *Zamani*) have quantity and quality, but the *Sasa*, which includes the immediate past of the recently dead, the present, and the very near future of the not-yet-born, is the focus of all dimensions of being. Eternity resides in the *Zamani*, a hazy mythical realm, but the *Zamani* exists neither as a future nor as a goal at the end of history. The *Sasa* feeds upon, and then disappears into, the *Zamani*. The *Zamani* serves as a foundation for the present, giving meaning, security, and depth to those currently enjoying life. The *Zamani* is the dimension of existence thought to bind all living creatures in the *now*, even while drawing them backward into its eternal embrace.[23]

This peculiar understanding of time is a feature of African religious belief that tends to be common across the diverse tribal landscape. The same can be said of the mysterious African notion of material space. Westerners, with their notion of property as economic asset to be bought and sold for profit, find the African understanding of land as the sacred domain housing the roots of social existence difficult to comprehend. In direct contradistinction to Western understandings, in Africa, the land is understood to belong to no one, but people belong to the land. If a people lose their land, it can mean existential disaster for family and communal life. Abandonment of the burial grounds and lurking spots of the living-dead ancestors and other sacred spaces can mean not only territorial loss but existential and moral catastrophe for the tribe—a loss of cultural identity, a loss of the connection with the forefathers, a moral loss in abandoning their duties to the dead, and a loss of meaningful existence in time. The African has always maintained a mystical relationship with the land of the ancestors. The land, for these ancient peoples, represents the most concrete manifestation of life, the meeting ground of the *Sasa* and the *Zamani*.

The uniquely African way of conceptualizing time and space explains another important and widespread aspect of African cultural identity that prevailed in the precolonial world and still maintains in many African social groups today. Despite the great number of tribes, each with its own language, territory, and socio-political organization, there are extensive commonalities in cultural traditions that revolve about the common importance placed upon the ancestors and the land. These commonalities include tightly bound kinship relations, the social emphasis placed upon the institution of marriage, the meaningfulness and elaborate nature of ritual practices, and the custom of raising large families to ensure the fulfillment of the strict requirements of communal responsibility.

The communal responsibilities served by the above social practices include the various aspects of tribal education administered to subsequent generations. Often misunderstood by Westerners, initiation rituals and rites of passage initiate young tribal members into the multiple functions and duties of adulthood. These rituals teach the budding adults to care for the more helpless of the community, the young and elderly. They learn to uphold tribal custom and recite and transmit tribal lore. One important function learned in initiation rites is the traditional recitation of names of the recently departed. This tradition holds great weight since it is the guarantee that community elders will themselves be rightfully remembered in death.

For the African, kinship extends not only horizontally across families and clans in the present, but vertically up and down the ontological scale including the newly departed and the yet-to-be-born. For this reason, many tribes practice the recitation of long genealogies to keep the people focused upon and oriented toward the *Zamani*. Kinship obligations impose a sacred responsibility to extend the genealogical line through the cultivation of rich family ties, and the human resources of the family and clan through raising large families. Family to an African means all the members caught up in this genealogical line. It can denote between ten and a hundred members. There may be several wives per husband. If a husband dies, the wives and children are taken by a brother of the deceased and accepted as his own.[24]

One household or joint households gather to form a village which includes houses, gardens, fields, cattlesheds, and granaries. African huts, themselves circular and made of the most natural of substances—sun-dried bricks formed of the dung from the precious family cow—are placed in a circular or semi-circular formation in the compound, facing its entrance. The arrangement is curious and provocative to the observer: a symbol of the endless rhythms of cosmic order? A micro-model of the god's universe? Whatever may be the architectural or existential meaning, the arrangement of the village exhibits the corporate nature of life in Africa. Each individual being finds a place and owes survival to other beings—from the plants, the animals, other humans dwelling round about, to the living-dead who wander the vicinity.

In the West, we understand kinship as blood relationship and biological connection. For the African, kinship extends beyond the usual blood lineages, and ties of family loyalty reach outward from the local family group to neighboring tribes and ultimately the whole human world. Kinship, for the African, ultimately finds its orienting parameters in the outer and final circle of life that includes all beings.[25] Alexis Kagame too confirms this beyond-the-blood understanding of kinship, adding that, even in modern African states, a conscious attempt is made to cultivate notions of kinship relation, addressing strangers as "sister" and "brother," or "mother" and "father."[26]

Ritual customs incorporate the individual into full communal being and create the person each is to be, defining the existential possibilities for each and delineating the horizons of the lifeworld. Rites of birth, naming, nursing, initiation, marriage, death, and corpse disposal define the community, and define the individual within the community. Only in terms of social others can the African realize true individuality, by accepting individual privileges and rights within the community, and individual responsibilities to it. Only within the group can one's truest destiny unfold.

African life is deeply religious in its most trivial and mundane everyday practices, because mere life is always a supermundane calling to enter the moral life. Under the witnessing eyes of the god and the proud sentinel of the revered ancestors, individual lives are taken up and dedicated to posterity. Africans hold no separation between profane life and sacred life; all life is fundamentally sacred, and all life's activities moral significant.

Mbiti, a deeply Christian thinker, is ultimately critical of African belief systems, and forces a comparison of African with Western religious systems in which the African systems come up wanting. He complains: "African religions and philosophy must admit a defeat: [the fact that] they have supplied no solution [to the problem of death composes] the greatest weakness and poverty of our traditional religions compared to world religions."[27] Mbiti sees the universal appeal of Judaism, Christianity, and Islam as proof of their superior ability to deal with the human dilemma of mortality. Without a means of escape, a redemptive getaway, Mbiti feels that traditional tribal belief systems are doomed to tribalistic, or at best nationalistic, appeal.

Mbiti's criticism is, I believe, misconceived. Traditional Africans enjoy a sense of deep-rootedness and historical belongingness that the relatively culturally superficial Westerner can never fully appreciate. The fact that broad, even continental, continuities of ritual and belief form the markers by which Africans locally define themselves demonstrates that their belief system has more than tribal appeal. The shared conviction that the individual is an organic member and product of the wider social world that is ultimately cosmos-embracing, including non-human beings, renders a worldview in which the world's humans and other creatures are deeply connected and interdependent.

Such a worldview issues in self-definitions that tie individuals to their families and bind people across extended families, bonding the groups to the land and the land to their histories. The eternal rhythms of life are rendered stable and familiar over against the violent vicissitudes of human history. African belief systems deliver a deep sense of rootedness in the earth and an intense belongingness within the family of humankind, features sadly and conspicuously absent from the mindset of the European colonist, and from modern Judeo-Christian notions of self impoverished by capitalist competitivism and isolationism.

## 3. Violence Enters Africa

Traditional scholarship places a synchronous human world on African soil until movement across and eventually out of the African continent caused that original syncretism to diversify into the various races we now know.[28] Particularized environments had genetic consequences and different racial or physical types emerged, though at first in only the broadest categories. According to traditional theory, north of the Sahara and east of the Nile, the medium-height, brown-skinned Afroasian appeared, forefather to the Caucasian. In the sub-Saharan savannah and forest fringes, tall, fine-featured, dark-skinned people with wooly hair emerged, forerunner of the African black. The true forest people, short and pale, evolved into the Pygmy. In the east and south savannah, medium-height, yellow-skinned Bushmen with tuft-like hair turned up. Thus an original human syncretism mushroomed into racial types.[29]

Having admitted the emergence of racial difference into this discourse, the impossibility of speaking in terms of distinct racial types needs to be stated unequivocally. Albert Memmi explains succinctly in *Racism*: "In truth, with the exception of chemistry, the very idea of purity is either a metaphor, a prayer, or a fantasy . . . pure races do not exist, but humans differ."[30] That human beings differ qualitatively is empirically verifiable. Nevertheless the most astute scientist with the finest tools and the most exact categorical system could not in any comprehensible way divide and define the human race into discrete entities that we might call races.

By the close of the Upper Paleolithic era, there occurred an economic revolution. Hunting and gathering practices in human communities gave way to the cultivation of food, and agricultural and stock-raising villages arose. These villages are similar in construction to the simple cities that Plato has Socrates assert as his preference over the city "fevered" and "swollen" with luxury goods and thus, significantly, prone to greed and war and requiring an army.[31] As surely as the youths of the *Republic* insist that a town without couches and exotic foods composes a "city of pigs," the simple mud-brick towns of craftsmen, potters and artists gave way to the cities swollen with nobles, priests, and divine kings—and then came slavery. Those still living in simple towns, bartering and tending their crops, soon fell prey to the marauding bands from the fevered and swollen cities.

Between the seventh and the thirteenth centuries of the Common Era, Muslim Arabs overran all of Africa north of the Sahara, raiding and plundering in the name of Allah, to the *jihad* war cry: *Écrasez l'infidel*! In the writings of the ninth century, we find the first Arabic reference to trans-Saharan trade in black slaves; by the twelfth century, such references are commonplace. This verifies that trade in slaves began very early and continued in waves for over a millennium.[32] The earliest waves of oppression and slavery are evidenced in Swahili and other languages now used on the continent. Many of the local words are adapted from Arab terms, and many black Africans and Africans in diaspora today maintain the Muslim religion as a result of their people's conversion during that early oppression. Thus it is important to understand that, as Oliver and Fage state, almost apologetically: "There had been slavery in the Kongo, as in every other part of Africa, long before Europeans began to export slaves overseas."[33]

By the sixteenth century, the burgeoning European demand for slave labor established the trade in African slaves as a massive global enterprise. English and French became the principal competitors in the slave trade, furnishing young, strong, black bodies to serve the home demand and that of their colonies in the Americas. Britain, boasting naval hegemony, carried nearly half of the slaves taken to the Americas.[34] Perhaps in part to escape this fate, the Bantu from West Tanzania pressed, by the eighteenth century, into the southern part of east Africa. With this movement was opened the first long-distance trade routes across the continent. Methods of weights and measures and West African money systems soon developed to serve the demands of the cyclical markets along these trade routes that offered many of the luxuries to which Plato refers in his account of the "fevered" and "swollen" city of the *Republic*: salt, cattle and horses, gold, nuts and ivory.[35]

It is important to note that, invariably, during this period, African slaves were purchased from African kings or merchants who delivered them to the Gold Coast. It was not until the nineteenth century that Europeans evolved from mere peripheral exploiters of the budding continent, slave-trading and operating plantations in coastal areas only, to invasive intruders prepared to penetrate Africa's "dark" depths to secure a greater share of the spoil. The forging of trade routes meant that eventually the "dark" continent would be opened to the "light" of full exploitation by the European capitalists. Africa could be penetrated and this meant that African peoples, targeted for the enslavement, had nowhere to retreat.

The moral ironies of the enslavement of the god's other children did not trouble "civilized" Europeans all through these early centuries. Oliver and Fage state: "the absolute wickedness of slavery was a late discovery of the Christian conscience."[36] The trade in slaves remained in full force for as long as there were markets for them in the Americas or until capitalist producers decided it was more practical to hire hourly wage-workers than to buy slaves, and keep their families in sickness and in health, through troubled youth and old age. The analogy between hiring a prostitute for occasional use and keeping a wife and children for a lifetime was one capitalist argument that could be rallied against slavery. Not until the victory of the North over the South during the American Civil War in 1865 and the abolition of slavery in Cuba and Brazil in the 1880s did the demand for slave labor wane and the slave trade finally die out.

The close of the slave trade did not mean the end of exploitation of the Africans. European colonial powers remained in control of most of the African continent into the twentieth century, periodically battling each other for hegemony over the most bountiful territories. Not until the middle of the twentieth century did movements toward independence begin in full force. By the 1980s, most of the continent had secured freedom from colonial oppression. They were freed to face the sad consequences of colonial invasion. Long excluded from participation in government and economic ventures, the African talents at these arts had grown fallow. Africans lacked the technological expertise to face the demands of their suddenly postcolonial world. These demands were many: ongoing internal problems of poverty and disease, over-rapid population growth, civil disorder, archaic and repressive systems, and famine and refugee crises, to name but the largest.

A full appreciation for the ill effects that these decades of continental rape produced in African communities requires some basic understanding of the traditions prevalent in African communities before the Arab and the European onslaught. The fundamental existential and cultural differences that separate African societies from the Western capitalist world must be appreciated before the African losses can be successfully recognized. I have stated in chapter two of this work that nowhere is the moral aspect of social reality more profoundly recognized and practiced in everyday life than in traditional African communities. I qualified this sweeping generalization with the disclaimer that I do not mean to deny the radical differences that divide the reality postulates of each and every tribe, not to mention each clan, each family, and each individual on the African continent.[37]

The blood and tears of colonial oppression have undoubtedly done serious damage to this worldview. The long-term abuse and denigration has weighed heavily upon the once contented, stable, democratic, highly social African peoples, and the divisions and humiliations that the people suffered have robbed them of much of their connectedness.

Their resistance fighters have been slaughtered or their heroic energies corroded in long incarceration in prisons. Their villages have been burned out, entire families laid to waste, their lands appropriated, and their sacred spaces despoiled. Without apology, African labors have, over centuries and across the globe, been extracted and exploited. The long-term suppression and the intense humiliation of widespread mythical denigrations of their peoples cannot but have cut the individual African loose from the social anchors, undermined the proud sense of history, kinship and self, and bankrupted the secure constancy afforded by traditional beliefs and ritual life. In the simple displacement from the land of the ancestors, Africans lost much in terms of their identifying bases and markers—the foundation of eternal time, the contact point with the god, the communal dwelling place, and the focal spot of identity. Lifeworlds became corroded and lives lost their ancient meanings.

Whether the stable order so prized by societies could be expected to occur under any political form without social inequalities, without the oppressions and exploitation of subgroups and the concomitant injustices that undermine the structure's commitment to justice is certainly highly questionable under the best of historical circumstances. But, in systems whose stratifications and power strangleholds are widespread and intense and whose patterns of privilege are harshly enforced, there will be corresponding incremental increase in the intensity and the scope of the conflict required to overthrow the system. There will be corresponding increase in the mechanisms of oppression that remain in the ruptured post-revolutionary systems, as well as corresponding increase in the psychic damage done to those who have suffered the violences of the colonial system, as well as those who had taken part in the bloody wars of independence. Simone Weil explains the tendency of violence to dehumanize all those whom it touches:

> Such is the nature of [violence]. Its power to transform man into a thing is double and it cuts both ways; it petrifies differently but equally the souls of those who suffer it, and of course those who wield it . . . this double ability of turning men to stone is essential to [violence] and a soul placed in contact with it only escapes by a sort of miracle. Miracles of this sort are rare and brief.[38]

The violences that the African peoples suffered at the hands of colonial oppressors is beyond all calculations. The physical violences that the African colonized endured, because directly and overtly degrading, were possibly less damaging than the more subtle violences that reached into the very psyches of the people: the mythical legitimations that justified the oppressions on the basis of essentialist assertions of inferior and immutable characteristics. The denigrating myths assigned by strangers who knew nothing of African histories, the richness of African cultures, and the complexity of African traditions undoubtedly did immeasurable damage to the self-image of these proud and ancient peoples. The capacity of the dominant group to prevail in the general constitution of truth, and in the defining of subgroups, can hardly be overrated. No myth has endless conceptual power. Every truth has a limited life span in the evolving common mental world of a social group. No configuration of reality postulates remains stable and unaltered beyond a given period of duration.

# Notes

1. Clyde W. Ford, *The Hero with an African Face: Mythic Wisdom of Traditional Africa* (New York: Bantam Books, 1999), 12.

2. Ford, *Hero*, 45–51.

3. Hesiod, *Theogony* IX, lines 507–616; *Works and Days*, lines 50–105.

4. Story told in full in Ford, *Hero*, 45–51.

5. Cheikh Anta Diop, *Precolonial Black Africa*, Harold J. Salemson, trans. (Brooklyn, N.Y.: Lawrence Hill Books, 1987); See also Harold J. Salemson, Marjolin de Jager, *Civilization and Barbarism*, Yaa-Lengi Meema Ngemi, trans. (Brooklyn, N.Y.: Lawrence Hill Books, 1987).

6. Walter Burkert, *Homo Necans: An Anthropology of Ancient Greek Sacrificial Ritual and Myth*, Peter Bing, trans. (Berkeley: University of California Press, 1983), 1–17.

7. René Girard, *Violence and the Sacred*, Patrick Gregory, trans. (Baltimore: Johns Hopkins University Press, 1979).

8. Girard, *Violence*; see also Paul Radin, *Primitive Religion, Its Nature and Origin*, (New York: Dover, 1957); and Walter Burkert, *Homo Necans*, trans. Peter Bing (Berkeley, Calif.: University of California Press, 1979).

9. Chancellor Williams, *The Destruction of Black Civilization: Great Issues of a Race From 4500 B.C. to 2000 A.D.* (Chicago: Third World Press, 1987).

10. C. Williams, *Black Civilization*, 21.

11. Diop, *Black Africa*, xi.

12. C. Diop, *Black Africa*, xi, 72 & ff.

13. C. Diop, *Black Africa*; See also C. Diop, *Civilization and Barbarism*, Harold J. Salemson, Marjolin de Jager, eds. Yaa-Lengi Meema Ngemi, trans. (Brooklyn, N.Y.: Lawrence Hill Books, 1987).

14. D. A. Masolo, *African Philosophy in Search of Identity* (Bloomington: Indiana University Press, 1994), 18–19.

15. Henry Olela, "The African Foundations of Greek Philosophy" in *African Philosophy: An Introduction*, R. A. Wright, ed. (Lanham, Md.: University Press of America, 1984), 80.

16. H. Olela, "Foundations."

17. John S. Mbiti, *African Religions and Philosophy* (New York: Frederick A. Praeger, 1969).

18. See for example Emmanuel Levinas, "The Ego and the Totality" in *Collected Philosophical Papers*, A. Lingis, trans. (Dordrecht, Netherlands: Kluwer Academic Publishers, 1993), 25–46.

19. Mbiti, *African Religions*, 4.

20. Mbiti, *African Religions*, 29-38.

21. Mbiti, *African Religions*, 29-38.

22. Mbiti, *African Religions*, 29–38.

23. Mbiti, *African Religions*, 27–29.

24. Mbiti, *African Religions*, 83–91.

25. Mbiti, *African Religions*, 104–5.

26. Alex Kagame, *Comparative Bantu Philosophy* (Paris, 1976), 289, as cited in Bujo, *Foundations of an African Ethic*, 86.

27. Mbiti, *African Religions*, 99.

28. Oliver and Fage, *A Short History of Africa* (New York: Penguin, 1962), 105-107.

29. Oliver, Fage, *History*, 107.

30. Albert Memmi, *Racism*, Steve Martinot, trans. (Minneapolis: University of Minnesota Press, 2000), 7. Emphasis Memmi's.

31. Plato, *Republic* 372ab; 374a.

32. Oliver, Fage, *History*, 107.

33. Oliver, Fage, *History*, 107.

34. Ieuan L. L. Griffiths, *The Atlas of African Affairs* (London, U.K.: Witwatersrand University Press, 1994), 48–51.

35. Plato, *Republic* 374a.

36. Oliver, Fage, *History*, 115.

37. Oliver, Fage, *History*, 24–26.

38. Simone Weil, *Intimations of Christianity Among the Ancient Greeks*, Elizabeth Chase Geissbuhler, trans. & ed. (London and Henley: Routledge and Kegan Paul, 1957), 44–46.

# Chapter 6
# Colonialist Constructions of Africans

When a stranger, completely disabled, weak and disarmed, appeals to a warrior, he is not by this act condemned to death; but only an instant of impatience on the part of the warrior suffices to deprive him of life. This is enough to make his flesh lose that principal property of all living tissue. . . . Alone, the hopeless suppliant does not shudder, does not cringe; He no longer has such license.

Simone Weil[1]

In the previous chapter, I broadly sketched a precolonial portrait of African communities. That portrait is meant to serve as a backdrop against which colonial reconstructions of Africa may be reckoned. The portrait also suggests certain features of simple tribal community that rendered those communities vulnerable to attack and subordination by invading Europeans. Traditional Africans looked upon members of the environing territory as extended family, with mutually designated responsibilities of social engagement, dictated and enforced by powerful ancestral overseers. Europeans suffered under the illusion of no such moral forces. Certain of their technological superiority, they felt confident of their moral superiority over native populations. This chapter offers an anthropological account of how people develop a sense of superiority, how they weave their cultural myths around their sense of superior worth, and how they use those myths to maintain dominance over sub-populations.

This chapter traces the unique ways that European invaders explain to themselves and the world their treatment of those peoples they slaughter, exploit, and abuse. This chapter unfolds the dominant myths, the reality postulates that held sway in the worldview of colonialist rulers, under which these simple peoples labored to maintain their dignity, their self-esteem, and their ancient tribal pride. Since the governing powers have control over the dominant discourse, the power of their myths is formidable. Their reports of the indigenous people they rule greatly influence popular beliefs about Africa and Africans, back in the European home countries and among incoming colonial settlers.

## 1. Anthropology of Western Naming Rituals

I have stated that human beings are, by nature, namers. Ever since we developed the physiological equipment to articulate our thoughts, we have been making sense of our world, carving cosmos out of chaos, through a process of identification, and sharing those identifications with our fellows through linguistic and artistic representations. Identifying a thing as a discrete entity and labeling the entity with a name permits the sorting and ordering that renders categorizations that give meaning to the absurdity of experience. Konrad Lorenz claims that the success of this sorting and ordering process is the key to advanced social life in higher vertebrates.[2] Walter Burkert unfolds Lorenz's claims by demonstrating that this skill was first developed in Paleolithic hunting communities. The processes that we today name "civilization" compose the ripened fruit of rituals of meaning sortings by which earliest hominoids made sense of a confusing and threatening world.[3]

We enter into life already fully immersed in meaningful and coherent worlds. Our social codes, prescriptions and prohibitions, rules of etiquette, and political and economic patterns of exchange are in place long before our arrival on the scene. This is not to deny that these traditions are themselves always under construction, constantly being renegotiated in the light of changing historical conditions and politico-economic exigencies. Burkert, René Girard, Maurice Bloch, and other prominent anthropologists have shown that throughout the evolving forms of our ethical codes and our institutions, there persists an underlying, unrelenting logic that orients thought and predisposes people toward certain kinds of behaviors.[4] For Burkert this logic is founded in the rituals practiced by the first hunting communities.[5]

According to Burkert, the hunt for large and dangerous carnivores by men armed only with fire-hardened weapons is so anxiety-producing that pre-hunt rituals develop to ease the tensions evoked by the prospect of the upcoming kill.[6] Pre-hunt rituals are intended to charm the beast into the territory and to solicit the favor of the ancestors and the gods so that the prey, and not the hunters, will meet with the desired end. Pre-hunt rituals are also intended to draw the community into a solidified unit, focused upon the success of the hunt. They help each individual find his rightful place in terms of a singular function within the community.

Pre-hunt ceremonies multiply in form and ideological content, extending into post-hunt festivities, so that eventually the event evokes in the participants a full range of emotional and psychic responses. The hunt ceremonies become the most important gathering of the community, so entirely unifying and homogenizing that they come to be practiced outside the hunt, whenever the community is seen in need of rejuvenation or reunification. According to Burkert's theory, the hunt rituals eventually lead to the development of every form of social code and institution—prescriptions delineating proper mating custom, feeding habits, political arrangements, patterns of social subordination and domination, and prohibitions outlawing inappropriate behaviors.

Burkert's speculations culminate in the claim that the Paleolithic hunt, evoking in the community such fiercely emotional and highly symbolic ritual activity, induces in the group a kind of creative confusion. The image of the prey becomes exaggerated in character and potency and conceptually confused as simultaneously victim, animal, and enemy. The animal becomes humanized and finally deified. The creative confusion of contrasting images then begins to defeat clear and stable identity in the population. The animal-prey comes to be seen as simultaneously friend and enemy, god and demon, male and female, benefactor of the community and grim reaper of its hunters.

The hunt ritual, with its evolving and expanding forms, ultimately brings sense out of the confusions. Though the kill of the animal is clearly the desired end of the hunt, a happy ending, there is also emotional and psychic contradictoriness in the slaying of such a symbolically potent being. Therefore post-hunt rituals come to express apologies and denials after the fact of the kill. The culminating festivities, with their feasting and drinking, music and dance, celebrate the self-sacrifice of the god. The distribution of meats following the kill establishes patterns of exchange and socio-political pecking orders that are believed to be ordained by the animal-god for the good of the community.

In the earliest hunting communities, the pivotal figure around which the community builds its identity is highly ambiguous and self-contradictory. But the world cannot be reasonable; it cannot be conceptualized, spoken about, or made sense of, where identities collapse into paradox. Contradictory imagery defeats all reasonable identifications. The necessity of community meaningfulness dictates that the incompatible features of existence be sorted. The chaotic, dialectically intertwined, polar oppositions that become attached to the demon/god expose the problem of unsorted experiential data, but they point the way toward the solution of the problem as well. Burkert tells us that the solution to conceptual chaos was accomplished in early communities by the positing of dual containers, and the orienting logic of the sorting system was clearly provided by the polar aspects of the demon/god. Things could be named good or bad, right or wrong, friend or enemy, victim or perpetrator, ruler or subordinate, but one entity could never be both opposites at the same time.

This sorting and ordering process issues in a common mental world shared by the whole community.[7] Names break through the chaos of meaninglessness and render comforting coherence of world. Top this neat worldview with a god or other transcendental signifier, and sense can be made of the most contradictory facts of life—economic and political inequalities, unstable and unequal distributions of goods, wars, plagues, and other communal tragedies. With a divine overseer to dish out punishments and rewards in a transcendental gift system, even the cruelest dominations and the most offensive injustices can be made reasonable and easier to bear.

The polarizing, simplifying, sorting logic in place, hierarchies can be constructed, causal connections forged, and meaningful identities carved from the chaos of existence. Communities can establish a firm self-sameness that holds steady against the flow of time, connecting them with the changeless, eternal realm of the ancestors and the gods. Identities are able to ossify, harden into concrete self-images that deny the deathly character of life.

This enormously creative process, identified by Burkert as spawned by murderous rituals, accomplishes two ideological tasks. It communicates to people a logic of domination. The polar logic confirms to the community that ordered, unified community life becomes possible only when rightful patterns of domination and suppression, established in natural hierarchies ordained and maintained by the gods. The polar logic also supplies what Bloch names an "idiom of conquest" that communicates to the community that the powerful have a natural right to rule over weaker populations; powerful identity rightfully fulfills itself in aggressive overflow onto neighbors and surrounding peoples.[8]

According to prominent anthropologists, modern social, economic, and political systems, our ideas of good and evil, our codes of etiquette, and our prescriptions and prohibitions remain poised toward clear and distinct valuations on the basis of starkly polarized, oversimplified understandings of the world. According to the experts on humankind, we achieve conceptual clarity, find our unique places in the world, distinguish our friends from our enemies, and chart out our existential possibilities and political necessities by affixing clear and distinct definitions to the chaotic forces of life.

Disturbingly obvious to the critical eye is the fact that the dangerously simplistic worldview of ritual creation which polarizes worldly entities into starkly clear and distinct definitions still lurks behind claims of legitimacy in the modern era. We still sort the known in contradistinction to the unknown, and represent this polarity in terms that betray the persistence of the archaic ordering mechanism—good/evil, freedom-fighter/terrorist, beacon of freedom and democracy/axis of evil. In the modern era, clear signs indicate that a ritualistic worldview continues to orient thought and dispose people toward overly simplistic and radically polarized understandings of self and world.

We continue to hold order to be morally superior to chaos, and one to be better than many. We make sense of things and events by extracting them from their chaotic context, freezing them into readily identifiable entities, and naming them self-identical across the flux of time. If their identity features do not conform to our own, we label them threatening and dangerous. We seem driven to make sense of the confusing data of experience—people and events we do not understand—by applying the sorting and murdering practices bequeathed by ancient rituals.

A feature that remains disturbingly common to human beings is our love of rigid order and our contempt for disorder and multiplicity. But we are not simply content to have order instead of chaos. We crave a world in which our voices are dominant, our interests most strongly represented, our loyalties the only legitimate ones. We want not simply the camaraderie of the ghetto, not the commonality of the alley. We desire, in the words of Pascal, to build a tour which reaches to infinity (*edifier une tour qui s'élève à l'infini*).[9] People desire the solidarity of the citadel and the legitimacy assigned by the gods. They do not simply engage in a logic that separates good from evil. They name the good as definitive of the home site of identity and name the alien evil. They engage in a logic of inclusion and exclusion that is always hierarchical and morally significant. Because definition can only happen through opposition and dialectic, dominance is purchased dialogically, through demonization of the non-belonging.

The myths invented and shared by colonial rulers are especially important to our understanding of the harms done to Africans because myths supply foundational truths that serve multiple important functions within the colonial world. First, the myths provide a justification for the crimes that the rulers commit against native peoples. Colonialist myths work within the dominant group to justify the oppression of African bodies, the exploitation of African labor, the displacement of families and clans, and the seizure of sacred lands.

The power of dominant colonial myths is not confined to the immediate colonial lifeworld. The colonialist myths had command that extended well beyond. The myths spun by powerful foreign invaders positing the moral and cultural inferiority of the Africans extended across the entire colonial world. They provide a foundational truth world, a common mental world, for each new wave of incoming colonials, upon which each could construct unique interpretations to justify their exploitations of the native folk. Ultimately, the myths take root in the worldview of the victim people. The peoples of Africa, alleged uncultured, ahistorical, and primitive, eventually adopt the dominant myths. They forget their histories, lose their love of the ancestral lands, abandon their traditions, and depart from the deeply moral social rituals that once welded their communities in peaceful harmony. The colonial myths ultimately become self-fulfilling prophecies that reconstruct the identities of their victims.

Long centuries of victimization and long submission to the dominant myths ultimately convince the Africans that they are unworthy peoples; they have no moral fiber, no dignity, and no decency to lose. These ancient and gracious peoples, with their deep sense of generosity, their ethos of humility and welcome, their intense respect for life in all its myriad forms, and their ancient conviction of the connectedness of life, are subjected to centuries of abuse. They steep their abjection in centuries of resentment and ultimately become what they are named; they are reconstructed into savage and bloodthirsty warriors, ready to attack any passerby that appears on the horizon of the lifeworld to further threaten them with abuse.

## 2. The Slave Trade and African Identity

From the end of the fifteenth century into the early twentieth century, only Portugal, of all the Europeans caught up in the slave trade frenzy, ventured from the relatively safe coastal holdings into the interior of the African continent. The small Portuguese holdings of the 1490s marked the first European presence in Africa at which time evangelical missionaries, skilled artisans, masons, and carpenters composed a small army of Christian settlers in Africa. The missionary efforts paid off with few dividends in souls until the great Congo sovereign Nzinga Mbemba, baptized "Afonso" in 1491, succeeded to the throne in 1507 and made substantial efforts to remodel his kingdom after Western European systems.

Early into this period of European entry into the interior of Africa, capitalist greed eclipsed any more altruistic Christian motivations. The slave trade composes the primary interest of the foreigners, until profits in ivory and later gold caught their avaricious attentions. Even Mbemba, opposed to slavery on Christian principle, had lucrative connections with the slave market, paying for European goods and services with slaves. The huge Portuguese appetite for slave labor to feed their Brazilian colonies soon overrode any more Christian motivations as Portugal spread its influence across the extensive Congo kingdom. With the colonial drive inland, there occurred a significant shift in policy; traditional slave-gathering practices were systematically replaced by more violent and more effective means.

For more than four hundred years, Sierra Leone and the Upper Guinea coast remained a major slave center and thus a site of continual bloodshed. This long-standing bloodbath had profound effects upon the societies caught up in those regions. What Rosalind Shaw names "a habitus of war" reconstructed the social practices of the local people, causing them to aggressively cultivate warlike qualities in their members and to practice guerilla tactics, along with techniques of concealment to preserve their lives and their freedom.[10] For example, some native peoples began to build underground places in their villages, fully equipped with all the necessities, in case a siege required them to disappear for extended periods. They also developed cunning deceptive strategies, such as walking backward in order to conceal the paths into their secret villages. Africans across this wide region begin to practice a general and purposeful deceptiveness as many of their everyday rituals were redesigned in an effort to secure their safety from marauding slave-hunting parties.[11]

The voracious demand for slaves resulted by 1575 in mandates to *conquistadors* like Paolo Diaz to open up the interior of the continent. These early colonies were designed for one express purpose: to supply the need for slaves. To this end new, more diabolical methods of slave collection were adopted. Roland Oliver and John Fage report: "the new Portuguese method of colonization, aimed principally at supplying the slave trade, was to train and arm bands of African 'allies' to make war on the peoples all around the slowly expanding frontier of the colony."[12]

Over centuries, the lives of vast masses of indigenous peoples in the slave collection areas of Africa grew increasingly chaotic. Beyond all other deleterious consequences effected during the colonial/imperial period, the method of securing slaves left the greatest and most enduring scars on the African people. Hiring African mercenaries to hunt slaves meant the introduction of firearms and gunpowder into the African interior. This new development proved lethal to intertribal connections. It broke with ancient African taboos condemning violence against one's neighbors.

Christian Africans eventually addressed impassioned appeals to the Holy See about the new slave-gathering practices, and a few popes seem to have communicated the appropriate disapproval to the Portuguese government.[13] That government's response was to declare that the government was hardly to be held accountable for the overzealousness of enterprising nationals overseas. This impunity emboldened other European entrepreneurs to follow the aggressive slave-gathering policies initiated by the Portuguese.

The first European colonies were aimed almost exclusively at gathering slaves. Christian values stepped aside and sheer economic profit provided the stimulus behind the opening of the Atlantic coast and then the penetration into the territories beyond. The Portuguese held control of the vast Luba-Lunda lands (which composed southern Zaire, western Angola, and northern Zambia). By the beginning of the sixteenth century, they were making their way up the lower Zambezi. The lust for gold and ivory took them into the hinterlands of Sofala and across the gold-laden plateaus of Zimbabwe, and eventually they founded the Sena and Tete river ports or expropriated existing ones from Arab and Swahili traders.

Portuguese activities in Africa, from the fifteenth through the eighteenth centuries, brought no constructive material or humanitarian advancements to the indigenous peoples of the continent. Not even Portuguese missionary work was of any great benefit to the African locals. The Portuguese clergy fit the generally mediocre mold typical of the European colonial presences in Africa. Africa seems to have supplied a conveniently distant and broad mat under which to sweep its undesirable and undistinguished.

Angola, in particular, was left in shambles, not only because the slave trade and early introduction of firepower into the area turned the people against one another, tribe against tribe and family against family. The area was especially ravaged because early settlements in the Angola region were begun with a criminal class of settlers placed in the region for the explicit purpose of inciting local natives to war on their neighbors for Portuguese profit. The situation in Mozambique was only "a shade less bloody" but equally vicious.[14] Oliver and Fage conclude, "The effect of the two [Portuguese] penetrations into the African mainland was almost wholly injurious to the African societies with which they came into direct contact."[15]

The Portuguese territories remained the only European colonial holdings until the middle of the seventeenth century, when the Dutch learned how to sail east on the trade winds, and the Cape of Africa acquired importance as a halfway stopping house en route to the Indies. Though colonial myths generally marketed the notion that the European presence in Africa was a benefit to the "underdeveloped" peoples of Africa, that myth masked a horrific reality. In most places, their presence caused nothing but bloodshed. Still today many white South Africans hold tenaciously to their dominant cultural myth—that they are the first inhabitants of the Cape area. However, this myth too is not in the least true. Cape Province west of the Kei was inhabited by Khoisan hunter-gatherers and, east of the Kei, Xhosa, Tembu, Pondo, and the Anguni ancestors of the Zulu made their homes.[16]

The seventeenth century saw other Western European nations race for their cut of the profits of the lucrative slave trade. English traders, during the eighteenth century, took the lead in this commerce, which reached its peak in mid-century. By this time, between four and six thousand sturdy young black bodies were being dispatched annually from the Sierra Leone area. The broad slave raids led to a state of insecurity in the indigenous that, according to Walter Rodney, "bordered on anarchy."[17] Personal safety for Africans was precarious at the best of times, and alliances among them unreliable because in constant flux. The overwhelming degree of daily risk meant that no one could be trusted. Friendships could at best be fluid and shifting; family ties necessarily grew strained, as family members turn in others for ransom or sacrifice others' security to save their own lives.

Under the new conditions of secrecy and insecurity, raiding, and outright war, new social actors and political subjects were constructed. From out of this horror, families, friends, and neighbors began living new existences, their new social rituals grounded in feelings of fear, suspicion, doubt, and deceit. Neighborly relations of trade and intermarriage were replaced by a general socio-pathology of suspicion under the reigning habitus of war. Lives were reconstructed to fit the new atmosphere of mistrust. Old cultures were transformed, and old social hierarchies undermined and restructured. New styles of leadership were developed, more appropriate to the new environment of generalized war. Modes of habitation, strategies of defense and attack, and methods of social production underwent radical revolution. Soon the simple people who had once lived peaceful existences alongside one another were hardly recognizable as neighbors.

The British finally outlawed the Atlantic slave trade for all British subjects in 1807 and then turned their attention to developing what they term "legitimate trade" with the African continent. Groundnuts, timber, and palm products become the coveted harvest. The illegalization of slavery, however, did not mark the awakening of the European conscience in regard of the Africans. In reality the shift from trade in bodies to trade in other resources was not primarily motivated by a change of heart about the treatment of the god's darker-skinned children, or by the desire to silence the loud criticisms being raised by slavery's critics, largely working-class Englanders.

The abolition was simply a pragmatic capitalist strategy. Why bring home slaves to house, feed, attend medically, discipline in their rebellious youth, and nurse in their old age, when you can leave them in the squalid conditions of their own shattered lands out of sight of critical eyes, and import at greater profit the finished product of their labor? Products produced in local areas by the labor of slaves collected nearby found ready and profitable markets in home countries. Slave-purchasing countries recognized that renting good workers by the hour is simply more profitable business practice than keeping slaves and their families twenty-four hours a day for their entire lifetimes. It is eventually accepted that the problems and expenses of keeping slave families was eating into the profits of business ventures.

Further proof that awakening European conscience was not the motivation for the abolition of slavery comes eighty years after the abolition, when European capitalists, conscience-free, gathered in Berlin. At this famed meeting, the imperialist giants of Europe mapped out their interlocking business interests, and aligned their various penetrating strategies. Among them they carved up Africa, like a vast continental cake, dividing up the massive mineral resources, the rich territories, and the abundant labor capital of the continent. From the lands and the lives of defenseless foreign others, they set out to build empires.

The shift from slave trade to legitimate trade may suggest an improvement in the lives of African villagers. In reality, the shift from slave trade practices outside the African continent served only to foster the growth of the slave industry in the interior of the continent. The new trade in goods brought new local conflicts in the form of trade wars fought for the control over river depots and access points that brought resources and products to the foreign buyers. The lived effect of the abolition of slavery proved to be anything but a relief and a benefit for the Africans.

Europeans explained the new conflicts as tribal wars. This interpretation was readily accepted both in the home countries and in the colonies. This myth purified the new industries of any implication in the ongoing bloodshed. Trade wars increased the socio-pathology of suspicion that set family members against one another, and neighbor against neighbor. There reigned throughout Africa a general atmosphere of suspicion, resentment, and fear.

Colonial Africa was built exclusively upon the desire for slaves. The slave trade in fact discouraged other sorts of contact and commerce, since trade in human bodies is both easier and immensely more lucrative than any other venture. Only after the close of the slave trade were other kinds of connections explored. Since slaves could be had without the perils of entry into the "dark" interior of the African continent, Africa remained an impenetrable, mysterious unknown for most Europeans into the late eighteenth century.

The northern part of the continent was absorbed into a Muslim world and was effectively closed to European interests for centuries, despite the general stagnation of the Arab world after the fifteenth century. The first European penetrations into northern Africa were from the north and west in movements generally motivated by humanitarian motives, if ethnocentric. Christian evangelists sought to wipe out the remnants of the slave trade and to evangelize the African native populations. And thus it was that Christian missions came to replace slave collection posts, and commerce in souls came to replace the previous commerce in bodies. Which of the two forms of slavery—physical or religious— enjoyed the longest duration of power over the Africans is a compelling subject of debate.

## 3. Colonial Rule and African Identity

By the nineteenth century, European powers had established informal and over-lapping interests across much African territory, but these did not become formal empires until the last quarter of the century. In the closing decades of that century, there was still little actual colonial penetration beyond the coasts, except in Afrikaner communities stretching into the interior from the Cape. However, by the beginning of the twentieth century, European governments were clamoring for a slice of the African pie, claiming sovereignty over all but six of the forty political units into which they had carved the continent.

The European colonists tended to find the dark continent and its strange people unworthy of that scientific curiosity that had driven the early explorers. African languages and traditions, their vision of reality, and their mysterious understanding of the backward flow of time and of the profound significance of sacred spaces were taken by the colonials as simply the weird practices of underdeveloped minds. Europeans did not find the Africans worth inquiry. The African's mystifying ways fell outside the European's notion of human existence.

The biggest mystery for the European was why Africans were not more easily persuaded into abandoning their "primitive" customs and adopting the European's more "civilized" ways. The cultural impenetrability of the African, likely the mark of deep cultural heritage and richness and profundity of tradition and institution, was taken by the invader as proof of their cultural poverty. Instead of approaching these ancient peoples with a sense of anthropological wonder, Europeans, bankrupt of the existential funds that grant a good-natured cultural curiosity, were incapable of broadening their narrow perceptions to include alternative kinds of human beings, or alternative ways of living human lives. To abandon the quest for real cultural knowledge and to dismiss the African native as unworthy of interest or concern—as "savage" and "primitive"—proved much easier.

Europeans did not try to understand the African people because they believed they already knew all there was to know about them and indeed all simple natives. They considered Africans primeval forerunners of the European civilized and cultured person. The African was seen as what the Europeans would have been if evolution had left them behind, if history had never happened to give the European a boost up the evolutionary ladder. Africans were a radically ahistorical people, according to the European. Steeped in the tradition of the popular social evolutionist theories prevalent at that time, Europeans declared Africans simple, primal, brutish, and uncultured. In the earliest colonialist myths, the Africans were named lazy, slow-witted, good-natured primitives, childlike and simple—dull-witted but irresponsibly happy. Perhaps they might be urged up the ladder of human evolution in the exemplary company of the more civilized. Regarding their pathetic and dangerous inferiority, they needed, for their own sake and for the safety of proximate others, to be guided, controlled, and educated into more suitable, more civilized habits.

The Europeans had plenty of argumentative ammunition to "prove" the Africans' inferiority. *Are these people not too simple for their own good, failing to exploit the full value of their rich lands, living in humble huts like animal dens? Are they not like beasts awaiting domestication through the civilizing effects of rigorous modern trainers?* After all, the tale went, *the Africans virtually allowed themselves be colonized. They welcomed armed invaders into their midst. They had not the sense to fight for their freedom. They have neither the capacity nor the inclination to defend their lands and their families. Militarily and technologically, they are pathetically inferior to us. Have you noted the beastliness in their very smell, the savage look in their eyes? They are comfortable lying and even sleeping in the dirt, among their domesticated beasts.*

*Are we cruel to keep the Africans in their poverty and ignorance?* the Europeans asked themselves. *Animals do not know poverty,* they reasoned. *They do not know of better lifestyles and higher ideals. Africans laugh at the slightest provocation, no matter how miserable their circumstances. They have not the awareness to know their wretchedness, never mind the motivation to rebel against it.* These self-serving arguments formed the core of the colonial case for their presence in foreign lands. The persuasive force of these self-justifying arguments was so great that they persist yet today among many colonialist defenders across the world.

How do such obviously flawed arguments come to hold such weight in people's lifeworlds? According to Albert Memmi, denigrating myths take hold at a deep level in dominating regimes because they are of crucial necessity to the continuance of those regimes. They serve not merely to justify the invasion and oppression of subject peoples, but they effect the necessary psychological changes in perpetrators to permit them to carry out vicious cruelties that would otherwise be impossible. By constructing the Africans as animals, the colonials could overcome the inhibitions against violence against one's own kind that nature instills in every creature. Denigrating myths helped the colonials make sense of the moral ambiguities of their situation, reconstructing the cruel colonial "civilizing methods" as unfortunate but necessary duties. Memmi states:

> Accepting the reality of being a colonizer means agreeing to be a nonlegitimate privileged person, that is, a usurper. To be sure, a usurper claims his place and, if need be, will defend it by every means at his disposal. This amounts to saying that, at the very moment of his triumph, he admits that what triumphs in him is an image that he condemns. His true victory will therefore never be upon him: now he need only record it in the laws and morals. . . . [The colonial] endeavors to falsify history, he rewrites laws, he would extinguish memories—anything to transform his usurpation into legitimacy.[18]

Denigrating myths serve a multitude of purposes in the often struggling, isolated colonies. They permit a solidarity among the colonizers that eases their collective consciences and holds them unified against a native population of vastly greater numbers and incomprehensible strangeness. Denigrating myths are highly functional because they permit the creation of a thought world in which the privileged elite come to be understood as indispensable to law and order, to the continuity of civilized communal order, and to stable functional operation. Of course, order and stability are only ever illusions, mere abstractions from the dynamic reality of people's social and political lives. The ruling elite need desperately to maintain these illusions to bear the paradoxes of their positions.

# 4. Reconstructions of African Identity

Cultural myths are mostly the work of the dominant elite who hold monopoly over the ear of the society. They rarely fail to elicit a response, of one kind or another, from those they inferiorize and demonize. Memmi writes: "It is not easy to escape mentally from a concrete situation, to refuse its ideology while continuing to live with its actual relationships."[19] Myths constructed by the dominant provide a meaningful collective existence, a common mental world for colonizer and colonized. They make a certain narrow sense of the absurdities and ambiguities of the colonial situation.

Colonialist myths help to provide the Africans with resolutions to the immensely contradictory social realities that they witness in their immediate lifeworlds. Myths confirm the rightness of social realities as social realities confirmed the myths. The grand lifestyle of the foreigner stood as proof of the superiority of the white European, while the inferiority of the Africans was substantively manifest in the contrary social facts; the masses of beggars, the children ragged and half-naked, the hunger and disease, and the muddy huts gave justification to the colonists' open contempt, the wanton beatings, the rapes, and myriad other humiliations.

Where broad and dramatic differences radically divide the sectors of the society, often the ostentatious ways of the cruelest tyrants become the focus of emulation for the downtrodden. The strange skin color and often flamboyant dress, the pretentious mannerisms and eccentric codes of etiquette made the European cultural superiority visibly evident. The lavish lifestyle of the foreign invader contrasted painfully with the wretchedness of the indigenous and divided the colony's populace into distinct, mutually exclusive elements. Myths of domination provided the means of transcending that cultural gap and establishing a strange sense of community between the belonging and the non-belonging. Since myths map out a cognitive field that makes sense out of the injustices and inequalities that define the system, even the oppressed find cultural myths cognitively functional for ordering their violated worlds. Once the natives accept the argument of their substantive inferiority, their worlds gain a meaningfulness and a coherence that make comprehensible the stratifications of the society and the injustices that configure the relations between the strata.

The loss of meaning and coherence in the lifeworld is an existential crisis that is profoundly damaging to a people's functional viability and to their sense of self and world. The African was predisposed, like many oppressed peoples of the world, to accept the denigrating myths propagated by their colonial oppressors. Acceptance gained them entry into the truth world of the colonials and made them privy to the community's system of meanings. To the disenfranchised and wretched of the world, inferiorization and marginalization can be accepted and indeed willingly embraced as preferable to outright social expulsion.

The colonized, as readily as the colonizer, in the earliest stages of the colonial invasion, are wont to accept the new standards of meaning compressed in the denigrating myths, in order to cope with the crisis of reality-incongruent data that arise in the radical clash of traditional African understandings and the imported enlightened European truths. The traditional African narratives—illustrious histories, tales of glorious ancestors, heroes and kings, sacred customs, practices, and homelands—out of which tribal identity had historically been carved eventually gave way to the new myths, new understandings of self and world more in tune with current politico-economic realities.

The most denigrating cultural myths can serve to bind radically diverse people into a cognitive coherence, by supplying reality-congruent truths that are functional for the whole society. Such myths do not necessitate or favor a social binding. Instead, myths that elevate one segment of the society at the expense of others almost invariably enhance the divisions among the social strata. Through cultural myths, identities become ever more radically polarized and subgroups become more and more demonized, and this growing division of subgroups cannot facilitate tolerant relations, nor foster dialogical exchange among the social strata.

Cultural myths offer explanation for the fate of the oppressed, making sense of their disordered and wretched worlds, and providing them a social place to fit—if only at the base of the social ladder. This is no small factor in their acceptance by the marginalized. A culture is a system of radical singularities bound in union by collectively held beliefs, understandings, ideas, and dispositions. Differences are rendered a structural unity by its myths and their consequent rituals. Whether the myths have any degree of accuracy does not matter in the least. What matters is that they provide a common mental world in which all can share, and that they serve efficiently the purpose of deflecting attention from the abuses of the dominant elite and the injustices of the system. Cultural myths are conservative in this sense.

Myths are dynamic, evolving, and unstable. Myths, as most cultural entities, are perpetually recreated in response to evolving circumstances in the historical world. A people's worldview and self-understandings evolve as the cultural myths that express these realities evolve, creating and recreating a social field within which social actors, their attitudes, behaviors, and self-conceptualizations constantly evolve. As the culture self-generates, absorbing and exhibiting new meanings and new values and recalling the forgotten or refashioning the historical, cultures *in toto* develop, change, diminish, and enhance their being over time.

Because of the dynamism characterizing all social systems and all individuals within the systems, and because of the simultaneous evolution of cultural myths and the rituals that arise to confirm them, the most oppressed and denigrated in a society have the hope that they can reconstruct their identities. They can rediscover their uniqueness and value by becoming witnesses to past and present injustices and bearers of social and moral worth. They can regain a sense of cultural self as members of an eminent group with a history and traditions worth preserving.

The stark irony surrounding cultural myths is that, because myths are constantly evolving, they come to contradict themselves over time. They often evolve to reconstruct those they originally inferiorized in more and more exaggerated scale. Generally, the potency and malevolence of the unknowable becomes inflated and embellished. In the case of the African, the denigrating myths that described the indigenous as the lazy and foolish primitive evolved into more intimidating descriptions of the loathsome irresponsible savage. Over time, simple savages became seen as evil and cannibalizing demons whose wickedness and malice demanded their suppression by morally superior forces.

The mechanism of demonization over time triggers a revolutionary response in the stigmatized subgroups. The oppressed do not simply tire of the insults and rebel against the imposed identifications. On the contrary, the abused are likely to accept the demonic role assigned to them. The tendency in victims to adopt the myths of the powerful reaps ironic consequences. The Africans, eventually convinced of their malevolence and potency, overcome the paralysis generally typical of the hopeless, and regain their sense of empowerment.

Cultural myths are intuitively constitutive of a people's vision of self and world. Myths absorbed are intimately bound to a people's behavior patterns and attitudes. The anthropologists insist that attitudes and behaviors are shaped by symbolic and emotive persuasions of rituals and myths than by rational arguments and utilitarian calculations.[20] The memories of grander times and illustrious histories had, for a time, been chased from the African mind, but the new myths of hidden potency and malevolence triggered in the native once again intimations of powers dormant, but functional and nascent within. John S. Mbiti is convinced that the Africans, for all the abuse they have suffered, remain fundamentally connected with the greatness of their past and wait to rediscover that greatness. He states: "On the surface, tribal [identity] is disrupted but beneath lies the subconscious mind of the traditional *Zamani*. . . [T]he subconscious of tribal life is only dormant, not dead."[21]

Demons and savages are mythically created, that is, people emotively persuaded to behave in malevolent and hostile ways. They can become potent, threatening, and capable of heroic or heinous deeds; they can reconnect to powerful ancestors and gods who enhance their powers and favor their projects over invasive aliens in their world. A new identity of malevolent potency arises and recalls from the distant past of cultural memory indigenous myths—myths of consecrated territory, sacred soil upon which kings and heroes made history, and hallowed spaces where the bones of ancestors are secretly stowed and where purificatory ceremonies cleanse the community from alien invaders. They recall ancient rituals that demonize the external infection that has entered the home site from without and contaminated its original purity.

African people for the most part welcomed European strangers into their midst. They soon witnessed the horrors of colonial rule and then, out of existential necessity, adopted the myths that justified those horrors in order to make sense of their worlds. But in time the myths evolved into a source of strength for the downtrodden native, revealing the deep fearfulness and ignorance of the invaders and the inexhaustible power of the African people.

# Notes

1. Simone Weil, "The 'Iliad', Poem of Might" in *Intimations of Christianity Among the Ancient Greeks*, Elizabeth Chase Geissbuhler, ed. & trans. (London and Henley: Routledge and Kegan Paul, 1957), 24–55.

2. Konrad Lorenz, *On Aggression*, Marjorie Kerr Wilson, trans. (New York: Harcourt, Brace, and World, 1966), 40–42.

3. Walter Burkert, *Savage Energies: Lessons of Myth and Ritual in Ancient Greece*, Peter Ling, trans. (Chicago, Ill.: University of Chicago Press, 2001); *Creation of the Sacred*, Peter Bing, trans. (Cambridge, Mass.: Harvard University Press, 1996); *Homo Necans: An Anthropology of Ancient Greek Sacrificial Ritual and Myth*, Peter Bing, trans. (Berkeley, California: University of California Press, 1983).

4. Maurice Bloch, *From Blessing to Violence* (Cambridge: Cambridge University Press, 1986) and *Prey into Hunter* (Cambridge: Cambridge University Press, 1992); Walter Burkert, *Savage Energies: Lessons of Myth and Ritual in Ancient Greece* (Chicago, Ill.: University of Chicago Press, 2001); *Creation of the Sacred* (Cambridge, Mass.: Harvard University Press, 1996); *Homo Necans: An Anthropology of Ancient Greek Sacrificial Ritual and Myth* (Berkeley, Calif.: University of California Press, 1983); René Girard, *Violence and the Sacred*, Patrick Gregory, trans. (Baltimore: Johns Hopkins University Press, 1979).

5. Burkert, *Creation*, 24–27.

6. Burkert, *Creation*, 24–27.

7. Burkert, *Creation*, 24–27.

8. Bloch, *From Blessing to Violence*, 27.

9. from Blaise Pascal, "*Misere de l'Homme sans Dieu*," *Pensées Les Provinciales* (Paris, France: Bookking International, 1995), Article II, 31–71 (translation mine).

10. Rosalind Shaw, "'Tok Af, Lef Af': A Political Economy of Temne Techniques of Secrecy and Self" in *African Philosophy as Cultural Inquiry*, Ivan Karp, D. A. Masolo, eds. (Bloomington and Indianapolis: Indiana University Press, 2000), 25–49, 33.

11. Shaw, "Tok Af."

12. Oliver and Fage, *A Short History of Africa* (New York: Penguin, 1962), 107.

13. Oliver, Fage, *History*, 108–109.

14. Oliver, Fage, *History*, 114.

15. Oliver, Fage, *History*, 114.

16. Oliver, Fage, *History*, 115–6.

17. Walter Rodney, *A History of the Upper Guinea Coast 1545-1800* (Oxford: Clarendon Press, 1970), 259, cited in Shaw, "Tok Af," 33–34.

18. Albert Memmi, *The Colonizer and the Colonized* (Boston: Beacon Press, 1991), 52.

19. Memmi, *Colonizer*, 20.

20. Burkert, *Creation*, 30-31.

21. John S. Mbiti, *African Religion and Philosophy* (New York: Frederick A. Praeger, 1969), 22.

# Chapter 7
# Anthropological Constructions
# of Africans

Virtues, values, ideals of behavior, mechanisms of identity, and processes of tradition have enormous significance for the ways in which human beings live their lives. None of these features of the lifeworld are encompassed by rationality. They remain largely hidden from the conscious life, concealed from rational scrutiny. However irrational these aspects of the lifeworld may be, however inconsonant with empirical realities, these covert mechanisms and processes compose the very fabric of people's social worlds, manifesting reality and determining the biases, prejudices, and absurdities that are constitutive of, and fundamental to, a people's worldview. These hidden symbols and their underlying logic are encoded in cultural narratives that are passed across the group and conveyed across continuing generations. Cultural myths compose one of the crucial methods by which human groups convey their governing truths.

Myths compose a crucial instrument in a people's lifeworld construction, establishing and maintaining the foundations of their being, and carving out and expressing their identities. They compose a functional tool that creates a universe of shared meanings within the social group, their "common mental world." Myths arise to express and ground a people's systems of meanings and values, to delineate their social codes, to justify the reigning prescriptions and prohibitions, and to express and validate the underlying assumptions upon which their lifeworld is configured. Distinctions between good and evil, normal and strange, rightful and wrongful are communicated across the group in evolving myths. In this fashion, communities come to formation out of the mass of radically diverse individuals who share the same geographical space.

# 1. Identity Crisis in the Colonies

Strangers in a strange new land finding themselves suddenly immersed in a vast ocean of radical otherness, the white Europeans who first entered Africa felt understandably threatened by their new situation. The Europeans' own identity, heretofore taken for granted, suddenly came into relief *as different* and into question as *normal*. Far from the shores of the homeland, far from the site of belonging, the relatively miniscule band of European newcomers, wildly outnumbered by radically different peoples, experienced an "identity crisis."

Every group, at times of identity crisis, has its radical others. The non-belonging come to the existential foreground when identity comes into question because the non-belonging serve the home group in very practical ways: helping the group to find itself, re-establish its self-meanings, and distinguish its borders of legitimacy by distinction from those who do not fit. The identity crisis faced by the European colonials was exacerbated by the moral paradox of their minority but elite status in foreigners' land. They understood their mission in Africa in starkly moral terms—as a "civilizing mission" to underdeveloped peoples. However, the manner of their presence in the colony, the fact of their privilege, stood as undeniable proof and continual reminder of their neglect of the express moral duty to the indigenous that, by their own political rhetoric, granted their presence in Africa.

By what right, according to what lopsided moral code could the striking paradoxes of their situation be resolved? Their self-conflict could be resolved and their self-definitions salvaged only by gathering the sea of terrifying unknown "otherness" into a meaningful representation radically polarized in both moral and existential terms from their own self-identity. Africans offered themselves as stark "radical others" because of their readily distinguishable characteristics—black skin, curly hair, strange languages, ragged clothes, humble living conditions, easy-going nature—over against which features the Europeans with their white skin, straight hair, "civilized" languages, fancy dress, and polished European manners could reconstruct their identity and justify the privileges they enjoyed.

Gathering the unknown into a meaningful cognitive representation with a readily identifiable character allows one's self-image to stabilize, permitting one's distinctive characteristics to emerge into relief. When the other can be definitively known, categorized, and analyzed according to cultural and moral criteria, the identity crisis of the struggling knower can be resolved. The work of self-identity and the resolution of moral paradoxes about one's situation are crucial to psychological well-being of persons under the healthiest of historical situations. New social truths—"myths of domination"—arise to make sense of the players within the social field of engagement, and the rules of their engagement. Social myths resolve even the most drastic inequities of the social field by assigning to each player a crucial role in the successful functioning of the whole. Myths make sense of the existing political and social forms, provide a foundation for the rankings and orderings within the population, and assign the logic that assigns the duties and the responsibilities that link social actors in functional networks. Myths come to be accepted by powerful and powerless alike because they make sense of the social hierarchy.

Myths of identity permit the social order to coalesce and stabilize; thus, in any system, order tends to be acknowledged as a value *in itself* needing no further justification. Order is understood as beneficial to all players within the system. Because distinctions are crucial to order, and order crucial to the stability and security of the system, all players at every level of the social hierarchy tend to understand as valuable the reigning order of power relations, just as they tend to understand themselves, whatever position they occupy in the society, as essential links in a powerful social chain of which they may all be collectively proud. The question of *whether* a social order is desirable, whether it ought to be considered worthy of continuance, is a question seldom raised in any system.

Various processes manipulate the cultural imagination of a group and give rise to the dominant myths. One only need inquire who enjoys dominance within the group to determine whose myths will dominate. The power nodes of the society have the ear of the lesser interest groups and, through the manipulation of economic and political forces, they control the general perceptions shared within the group. Myth creates a field, a hazy discursive field. Precisely because this field is "hazy," its truth parameters and content claims do not require rational justification or compelling empirical evidence. Mythical discourses dominate the cultural imagination because they do not aspire to prove objective truth. The function of cultural myths is to articulate the moral superiority of the powerful, and thus the rightness of the configurations of power that exist within the system. They are seductive from the pinnacle to the dregs of the social ladder because the least members of the society most need to feel they form a crucial part, however minor, in the smooth operation of their powerful system.

## 2. Anthropology and "Truth"

Anthropologists are scientists. Fundamental to the scientific orientation is the insistence on the distinction between truth and myth, a distinction I am not honoring in this work. Anthropologists claim to deal in truth, not in myth. They see their noble task as the investigation and articulation of social truths by identifying and reporting the identity markers of social groups. In this quest for social truth, anthropologists enjoy a reputation for, and indeed aspire toward, a high ideal of descriptive purity in their articulations of social identity. Their express goal, not unlike that of the phenomenologist, is to leave behind, to the greatest extent possible, their ethnocentric prejudices and inherent preconceptions about how human lives ought to be lived. They set aside their own social myths that dictate the legitimacy and non-legitimacy of social parameters, in order to discover naïvely and without bias the parameters of other people's lifeworlds.

The anthropologist attempts above all else to describe honestly and frankly the practices of their studied group from within their living worldview, offering description without prescription. The task of the anthropologist is fittingly described by George Marcus and Michael Fischer thus: "to enlighten us about other human possibilities, engendering an awareness that we are merely one pattern among many, to make accessible the normally unexamined assumptions by which we operate and through which we encounter members of other cultures." This goal renders a strict anthropological ideal. Marcus and Fischer continue: "Anthropology is not the mindless collection of the exotic, but the use of cultural richness for self-reflection and self-growth."[1]

Despite the ostensibly noble nature of the anthropological calling and the purely descriptive intentions of the anthropological quest, Western anthropology played a crucial role in the violence levied against indigenous populations, since the ethnocentric descriptions of native otherness proved highly serviceable in justifying European colonial rule over Africans and other indigenous peoples during the imperialistic era. Anthropological work in fact composed a necessary step in constructing and legitimating the hierarchies of power that would hold sway in the colonies. Their descriptions would prove crucial to the assertion of European identity as morally superior and to the denigration of indigenous identity as morally flawed.

The anthropologist's descriptions of strange and exotic societies would provide scientific and ontological substance to back the theories of natural hierarchy that would eventually be employed to justify the slaughter, the enslavement and the subjugation of indigenous peoples, the destruction of their ancient cultural assets, and the confiscation of their lands. Anthropology in Africa aided in a most practical way in the cultural denigration and the moral alienation of the indigenous peoples of the continent, despite the noble intentions of their discipline.

The task taken up by the anthropologist in Africa is to observe, record, and articulate the location, social habits, and essential distinctiveness of the diverse tribal groups on the continent. The anthropologist would note distinctive qualities, common features, and general social traditions practiced within each group, drawing the connections that determine identity within the community and establishing disconnections from other neighboring groups. By identifying peculiar traditions and practices, anthropologists could analyze demographics, categorize continuities and discontinuities, assign reasoned explanations for the links and disconnections among the groups, and speculate about the histories that give rise to the cultural peculiarities.

In the doggedly causalistic mode of Western scientific inquiry since its roots in Aristotle, anthropologists explain what a thing is by reference to its historical causes. They posit historical origins and trace historical tracks in an effort to explain the peculiarities of physical and social traits in various groups, and the ethical and political traditions that distinguish these groups. This genealogical approach enables links of causality to be mapped backward into time to account for the advent of the distinguishing features.

Finally, connections and disconnections among the differing tribes come to be explained by reference to genetic causality. This group is different from that group because their more or less evolved genetic codes dictate those peculiarities. Broken and unbroken lines of heredity are accepted across the anthropological community as primary in accountability for the distinctive cultural features separating one cultural group from the next.

These genetic differences are then plotted onto historical charts that map the progress of the human species from extremely primitive to more evolved modern groups. A lack of evolutionary progress could be cited not only to account for the general differences between people: the technologically advanced, industrialized, urbanized European seen as far advanced beyond the people of Africa, living in their simple huts in the sun and scratching out an existence from the land. Evolutionary distinctions are also cited to explain the differing features of appearance and cultural traditions among various African tribes.

Entities become less troubling for the observer when they can be made meaningful, when they can be analyzed and categorized, and when clear and distinct definitions can be articulated. Vast masses of different others can appear threatening by the simple fact of their elusiveness, but the threat disappears once the groups can be defined, when certain features can be identified as coextensive within the group, and as discontinuous with other groups. Where ethnic distinctions would suffice to explain the differences in customs and traditions among European social groups, genetic explanations would be posited to explain the distinctions separating African groups. Thus could individual tribes be located, distinguished, analyzed *as distinctive*, articulated clearly and explicitly, and, most significantly, given reasonable cause.

When solid identity—cultural meanings—are affixed to peoples, it is almost always the dominant powers who determine what meanings are affixed, and the less powerful, more vulnerable, that become victims of the affixing. The power of naming is, in the reality of political worlds, the instrument of the oppressor. The powerful name; the powerless are named. Because the anthropologists' identity myths are given historical causes in the form of imagined lines of descent—genetic reasons for the differences—those myths equipped the powerful European invaders with the full range of explanatory tools necessary to racism and all its accompanying horrors. The anthropologist's genetic explanations provided the convenient conceptual foundations that supported the notion of a natural hierarchy within the human world. In turn, the claims of a natural hierarchy could be rallied to validate the natural rightness of social processes of control and the moral necessity of the more civilized to rule over their human inferiors.

Anthropologists may have understood their work to respond to a humanitarian calling—to discover and articulate eccentricities distinguishing human groups. They may have understood themselves to be attending to that task without importing external valuations or imposing prescriptive recommendations. They may have been seeking to promote understanding and mutual appreciation among human groups and to be fostering cross-cultural tolerance and thus global human compassion. However, in the long run of human history, the science of anthropology has proven itself to serve the purposes of oppression as much as those of toleration. This dark secret is visible in the origins of the discipline. The anthropologist's discipline blossomed alongside, and was an integral feature of, European imperialism.[2]

This identity-substantiating naming act, this mythologizing of the identity of the other, composes the first movement of oppression—the location and identification of the alien. Thus was cognitive order imposed upon the fluctuating, constantly evolving, dynamic reality of African cultural life and identity. Internal differences were suppressed or confined to the margins of the group's identity, the parts were melded into a comprehensible whole that could be identified, labeled, and analyzed. Rigid classifications of fluid realities resulted. Complete the myth with its causal dimension: the group had formed as a "descent group."

Thanks to the anthropologist's careful work, the distinctive features of African peoples became differences in breeding—differences in "breed." Like cattle, their heads could be measured and charted; their limbs, their strong backs, and even their genitals could be put on "scientific" display. In the notebooks of early anthropologists, as in the circuses of the homeland, the African could be cited as a genetic freak, a people left behind by evolution, lost ancestors who had escaped evolution, a Neanderthal forerunner of the infinitely more advanced European specimen of humanity.

No matter how benign differentiating characterizations may appear, they are always valuational, always morally significant. This is why Salman Rushdie claims in *Imaginary Homelands*: "description itself is a political act."[3] Descriptive distinctions explained as genetic allow the positing of a natural order to the human world. Natural differences are rallied to explain differences among the alien cultures observed, and are also employed to distinguish between belonging and non-belonging, and between those deemed savage and those deemed civilized, providing not merely cultural or ethnic distinctions but value-laden ontological distinctions attributed to varying qualities of human substance.

Identifying processes comprise, in their first and fundamental movement, a kind of self-othering, a countercultural rejection that is always morally significant. Self-identity and self-legitimation is accomplished in a single cognitive movement: by juxtaposing what is mine over against what is not. The ritual of identity logic embedded in our psyches and issuing as the "common mental world" of our shared cultural vision dictates that what is mine is experienced as good and safe and true; what is not mine is experienced as alien and dangerous.

The first Europeans, in a tiny minority, looked out upon a vast sea of dark human otherness and experienced the natives' differences as ambiguous. The land was beautiful, seductive, exotic, thrilling but, like its inhabitants, the continent was also threatening, disease-ridden, and lethal to the unwary traveler. The ocean of dark bodies surrounding the early European colonists, the diffident looks in their eyes, the inexplicable fits of laughter, dance, and music, and the strange superstitions and secretive rituals carried on in their villages at nights led the Europeans to interpret the native peoples as exaggerated in potency and malevolence, chaotic and demonic. Despite their unchallenged technological and political prowess, the Europeans felt vulnerable and continually menaced by the radical differences confronting them. For the threat of radical differences to be diffused, they need to be understood, embraced by knowledge, and captured by the mind. Otherwise, the threatening will be confronted with force, engaged in war, suppressed, and perhaps even murdered.

## 3. Early Anthropological Myth

The negative descriptions of the African continent and its peoples had begun early. Before Europeans even entered Africa, the first naming had been accomplished: Africa was the "dark" continent. Europeans were not simply noting the color of the indigenous peoples in contrast to themselves. Nor were they expressing what more generous observers have noted: the impenetrability of African cultures by European ideas and traditions. John S. Mbiti, for example, tells that African cultures were already so richly developed, so deeply rooted and interwoven with their neighbors and the land, that European values had little hope of upsetting the rich tapestry of African life, of *culturally* colonizing the African.

One might argue that the success of the European conqueror was largely attributable to the African himself and the strong indigenous values that connected across tribal realities and indeed across the spectrum of the human world, values that ordained unthinkable the possibility that newcomers would not be welcomed as friends. Still today, after all the historical abuse at the hands of "strangers," Africans generally consider it only proper that strangers be taken in, fed, bedded, and treated with respect.[4]

When Europeans named the continent "dark" they were naming the territory impenetrable, the life-forms disease-ridden, and the travel treacherous. Naming the continent "dark" also had the further effect of implying European superiority in relation to African inferiority. The use of the metaphor constantly reminded Europeans of long journeys through sunless but steamy, vine-slung jungles, long nights with only campfires to penetrate the gloom and ward off the terrors of the black night. It reminded them of their own safe and happy worlds, "civilized" by technological advances that did not exist for the African. The darkness metaphor was meant to recall the enlightening knowledge of modern industrial society and its edifying customs. Europeans were celebrating their own cultural habitat and traditions by highlighting the African lack of such features as industrialization, urbanization, and technological dependence. This celebration is ironic in view of the ambivalence with which those same features have since come to be viewed—as both the boon and the disaster of the modern world.

When the Europeans finally entered the dark continent as settlers and conquerors, they still only knew the African native through a very narrow mode of representation, a myopia typical of invading powers. Measuring the worth of the indigenous peoples by the scale of their European industrialized and urbanized values, it did not occur to the colonists that the invasion itself had disrupted the indigenous spatial and cultural terrain. Having no prior acquaintance with the local populations, no knowledge of the interwovenness of peoples before their arrival, and not the slightest understanding of the importance of the land in the African self-understanding, the Europeans had no idea how their very arrival fragmented and isolated—divided and conquered—the local people. Anthropologists set about observing the local folk, mapping out their cultural features, distinguishing this group from that one, and assigning to each a cultural definition—an "ethnicity." Substantialist thought always finds what it seeks, and so anthropologists found, in the fragmented and disparate peoples, discrete groups that were easily identifiable by traits deemed quasi-universal across the ethnic group.

The anthropologist's task is, in theory, to observe and describe the cultural object without resorting valuational judgments. In the case of African cultural groups, anthropological descriptions were especially deceptive. Their discrete namings not only solved the identity crisis of the displaced European invader and established the ontological superiority of the observer, but their explanations concealed the fact that the invading process itself was responsible for much of the anthropological evidence rallied to support the claims of native inferiority. The influx of European settlers, the carving up of the continent from a distance of millions of miles, and the furious collection of slaves from the continent had utterly disrupted African populations, traditions, alliances, and lives.

Previously contiguous and interactive groups had, over time, been displaced and disconnected as a result of the very processes of invasion and colonization. Neighbors had been lost, allies alienated, families thrown into disarray, and tribal cousins thrown into suspicion. What the anthropologists observed in their careful records—peoples unable to cooperate with their neighbors, alienated from their families and their clans, practicing peculiar and sometimes antisocial rituals (deceptions, lying, and hiding)—had been forcibly created by their history's cruelties. The anthropological descriptions completed the alienation of tribal groups. Over time, evolving, dynamic groups of peoples who had traded and intermarried with their neighbors for centuries would take on the distinct and discrete characteristics imposed by the powerful authorities. Descriptions of alienated neighbors, displaced and suspicious of the others, can reify over time and the fictions become cultural fact. Definitions can become self-fulfilling prophecies. When the definitions are morally and ontologically negative, the effect can be culturally disastrous.

The identity-substantiating act that was performed by the anthropological myths about African identities composed the first movement of oppression. The alien was located and specifically identified. In naming common features across distinctive groups, cognitive order could be won for the European invader. Meaningfulness could be imposed upon the fluctuating, constantly evolving, dynamic reality of African cultural life. Its unique parts and internal differences could be suppressed or confined to the margins of the group's identity, and the parts could be fused into a comprehensible whole that could be identified, understood, and labeled. Rigid classifications of fluid realities result. Then the myth can be advanced that the group observed has formed as a "descent group," their distinctive features explained as differences in breeding—differences in "breed." Rigid definitions with historical and genetic underpinnings serve an indispensable function to the invading powers; they support myths of cultural progress that found their claims of rightful hegemony over primitive others.

Already by high Victorian times, European anthropologists had written extensively of the savage African natives. Europeans back in the homeland devoured the exotic tales. At first, Europeans generally understood Africans in the patronizing terms of mental retardation, as children who would never grow up. Later descriptions, like Samuel Baker's diary of 1863, would give the African reputation a more objectionable and moralizing spin by affirming that the African was morally inferior to the European, not simply innocent and naïvely free of higher cultural norms. The exotic African would come to be seen by European readers as capable of "neither gratitude, pity, love, nor self-denial" and as having "no idea of duty; no religion" but only characterized by "covetousness, ingratitude, selfishness, and cruelty."[5]

## 4. Late Anthropological Myth

Africans would be further inferiorized in the European imagination when sociologists and philosophers on the European continent, never having entered Africa, would analyze from afar anthropological descriptions of African "thought systems" in the light of the social Darwinist hypotheses popular during the Enlightenment. For example, French philosopher and sociologist Lucien Lévy-Bruhl sets forth his theory of the "prelogical" African mind in his famed works *The Mental Functions in Inferior Societies* (1910) and *The Primitive Mentality* (1922).[6] Lévy-Bruhl's account had great weight for European readers because he had devoted the last thirty-nine years of his life to the study of African thought systems, mapping out the "primitive mentality" of the Africans by examining the structure and order of their reasoning procedures. His theory claims that an individual's thinking patterns are predetermined by the collective representations shared within the society. Social traditions are credited as the formulative power behind the representations.

According to Lévy-Bruhl's theory, human societies are classified into two broad categories—the primitive and the civilized—with distinctive patterns and methodologies of thinking characterizing each. Africans, Lévy-Bruhl holds, compose the primitive. Primitives are marked by their tendency to attribute explanations for events to supernatural and occult powers. Only long acquaintance with scientific modes of thinking, reckons Lévy-Bruhl, can transform people's thinking into a form that is logical, procedural, and truly rational. Lévy-Bruhl's distinctions leave African peoples millennia behind the scientific European in the evolutionary race for rational thought. The African is "prelogical," his religion is "prereligion," and his thinking is prerational—mystical, not logical and reasoned. Lévy-Bruhl states:

the superabundance of . . . mystic data, and the existence of dominating preconceptions between the data afforded by the senses and the invisible influences. . . prevent the primitive mind from adding to its mental stores by means
of its experiences . . . Moreover, the primitive mind is not like our own, oriented to cognition, properly so called. It knows nothing of the joys and advantages of knowledge. Its collective representations are always largely emotional.
The primitive's thought and his language are but slightly conceptual, and it is in
this respect that the distance which separates his mind from ours may perhaps
be most easily estimated.[7]

Since these demeaning accounts of non-Europeans elevate and self-
congratulate the European mentality, reports like this one by Lévy-Bruhl found
enthusiastic welcome in the home communities. The anthropologists' descriptions compose the first movement, the unilateral first wallop, in the substantialist
attack. As long as the definitions and their ontological explanations remained in
place, Europeans could justify their forced control of others' lands, resources,
and bodies, no matter how brutal their methods or how unjust their appropriations.

The first blow is never the whole battle. The *coup de grâce* of European
"identity work" is accomplished once the indigenous too are persuaded by the
dominant prejudices, and adopt the myths of their oppressors. The knock-down
occurs when the myths of inferiority take hold in the self-understanding of the
oppressed group. With this adoption, the raid on the victim is complete. The
victim populations, described as retarded, fragmented, and isolated from their
neighbors, now assume the reality that has been assigned them by their social
superiors. A tribe, a discrete ethnic entity disconnected from its neighbors, alien
in custom and history, is created from the fiction that it exists.

Once the myth of identity has been adopted, internal differences and fluc-
tuations in the assigned features come to be seen as signaling deviations in stable identity. Deviations are interpreted by a vulnerable people as emblematic of
cultural disintegration. A reactive identity crisis triggers nostalgic rituals to recapture communal solidarity imagined as lost. Identity work requires mechanisms of self-definition that invariably demand the mechanisms of rejection—
scapegoating of members seen to be deviant from the group. A "logic of domination" is adopted within the group to silence the differences and marginalize
the deviants. Fictions of contaminant invasion from alien presences at the
group's identifying borders furnish the group with a reason for war, an "idiom of
conquest" that justifies external aggressions.

The assertions of tribal identity in their initial anthropological articulations
were often based on the observation of a few random features practiced by a few
individuals. The lack of broad evidence for scientific articulations rarely affects
their acceptance as "truth" by the general public because, in the modern era, the
scientist constructs and administers over the edifice of knowledge. The meanings assigned by scientific observers generally become the meanings accepted
by society at large. They will eventually become actively adopted by the group

they are meant to describe, and the assigned features may even come to be defended as essential to the group's identity and crucial to its survival.

Many people all over the globe still remain convinced of the notion of a hierarchical human world, where biological and historical evolution may be accurately measured by the color of people's skins. To these hardnosed believers, I offer the brilliant but economical argument of Albert Memmi from his important work *Racism*:

> There are no pure races, nor are there even homogeneous biological groups. Were there any, they would not be biologically superior. Were they biologically superior, they would not necessarily be superlatively endowed or culturally more advanced than others. Were they that, they would not have any God-given right to eat more than others, to be better housed, or to travel in better conditions.[8]

When the Europeans finally pulled out of their overseas possessions, they left behind just what the anthropologist claimed to have originally found—a vast mass of disconnected, fragmented, dispersed, alienated groups, each suspicious, confrontational, and hostile with regard to the others.

# Notes

1. George Marcus and Michael Fischer, *Anthropology as Cultural Critique* (Chicago: University of Chicago Press, 1986), ix–x.

2. See also John H. Bodley, "Anthropology and the Politics of Genocide" in *Domination, Resistance and Terror*, Carolyn Nordstrom, Jo Ann Martin, eds. (Berkeley: University of California Press, 1992), 37–54.

3. Salman Rushdie, *Imaginary Homelands* (New York: Viking Press, 1991), 9–21.

4. John S. Mbiti, *African Religions and Philosophy* (New York: Frederick A. Praeger, 1969).

5. Samuel Baker, *Albert Nyanza* (London: Macmillan, 1898), 153.

6. Lucien Lévy-Bruhl, *Primitive Mentality*, Lilian A. Claire, trans. (London: Allen and Unwin, 1923); *The Notebooks on Primitive Mentality*, Peter Rivière, trans. (New York: Harper and Row, 1975).

7. Lévy-Bruhl, *Primitive Mentality*, 61.

8. Albert Memmi, *Racism*, Steve Martinot, trans. (Minneapolis: University of Minnesota Press, 1994), 19.

# Chapter 8
# Religio-Medical Constructions
# of Africans

Neither generosity nor subtlety have characterized Western discourses about Africa, whatever their ethnic or disciplinary source, whatever their economic, political, or religious motivations. From the outset of European colonial penetration of the African continent, the political economy in Africa rested upon chilling metaphors of decadence, darkness, and death. Colonial systems of production as well as religious projects of social reproduction depended upon these metaphors. Tales about a dark, strange otherness which challenged and frustrated well-intended European civilizing processes provided a convenient whitewash for sanitizing colonial exploitations, territorial usurpations, and evangelical missions across the continent. The first explorers' images of dark jungles, dark forests, dark huts, and dark bodies afforded sensational reading in the home country and they confirmed in advance the claims of the first colonial invaders and their anthropological accomplices regarding the existence of dark bodies, disease-ridden and dangerous, and dark souls morally rotting out of the purifying light of civilization and beyond the redemptive embrace of Christian evangelism.

I have described an objectification mechanism, introduced by earliest Western warrior societies and still frequently employed in modern societies, that serves most effectively during times of crisis to render comprehensible the threatening unknown. This mechanism accomplishes meaningfulness because it facilitates sorting the unfamiliar over against the familiar in simple polar categories. Categories of good/evil, pure/contaminated, friend/enemy, and natural/unnatural provide the logical framework for this sorting mechanism. These "two containers," in Walter Burkert's words, can be most successfully rallied to make sense of threatening phenomena.[1] Since the home site of identity is almost always experienced as safe, comprehensible, and sacrosanct, the alien becomes the target of a "demonizing gesture" that assigns the unknown the concomitant negative categories—threatening, irrational, and profane.

The dark continent of African legend and the African people's dark skin fa-cilitated the "demonizing gesture" by providing in advance particularly dark metaphors that continued to feed upon the uncertainties and fears of the first European explorers and the later colonial settlers, who felt surrounded by a vast sea of threatening otherness. The dark metaphors grew into radically dark myths that sought to describe and explain the strange alien land of Africa and its in-habitants.

## 1. African Meets Christian Religious Myth

Africans were at first understood by Europeans as innocent decadents, simply bereft of civilization's moralizing services. After the accounts of Samuel Butler and many of the earliest European arrivals, the reigning view of African peoples was more menacing and malevolent than the metaphor of "innocence" could communicate. On account of the moral overtones to the explorers' degrading descriptions, Europe's colonizing venture into Africa could not help but involve an aspect of evangelism. After all, what are good people to do with the morally rotten, if not to reform them or confine them to hell?

The re-*form*-ation of decadent souls fits well the Christian perception of the saint's designated task upon the earth. The Christian understanding of the drama of human existence as the unfolding of the god's plan renders in the Christian mind a certain vision of history: people fall from grace because they are human, and prone to moral error; they suffer because their evils draw upon them natural consequences in a morally significant universe (or because the god is a judg-mental god who punishes sins); their suffering purifies them of their evil and brings them back to the god. The Christian worldview posits history as a three-dimensional drama—fall, suffering, and redemption.

In this view of history, the worst brutality can be stomached by Christians without sacrificing their good consciences. Africans are like any other infidels, fallen souls, or heathens. Suffering is both morally necessary and indeed in the infidels' best interests, as only through the redemption of suffering may lost souls earn their way into the god's good graces. The redemptive mission of Christian evangelists is an altruistic mission that is served by colonial brutality, just as the colonists, with their brutal and suppressive practices, are in turn served by the Christian view of history. Tsenay Serequeberhan states: "Conven-iently, European colonial consciousness saw itself in the image of fulfilling both the demands of God and the requirements of civilized human existence."[2]

The onslaught of white Europeans in Africa was duty-bound to include zealous evangelists eager to herd the "heathen" Africans into the religion of Christ. E. S. Atieno-Odhiambo reports, speaking of the Luo tribes of Kenya: "At the beginning a lot of people joined in; it looked like almost the whole land had. People were walking from as far as Kadimo to Maseno just for the sake of re-ceiving the Holy Communion."[3] Africans were quick to welcome the Christian missionaries because they already held a view of the cosmos as ordered and overseen by a single deity, and Christianity's message of a human family fit neatly into their communal self-conception and their larger vision of social reality.

The oral histories of African tribes, as remembered and chanted by the tribal elders and included in the education of youths during initiation rites, allude back in time to original syncretisms with neighbors and mark out the historical breaks from that unity. The tales tell of the separation or formation of original tribes, recalling to the most exact detail some offense among family members that resulted in a split within clan connections, or some marriage or political union that joined disparate families into a new unity. The African worldview being utterly social in its character and cosmic in its scope, Christian principles of universal love and familial affiliation corresponded comfortably with their prior perceptions of reality. Placide Tempels states:

> The Bantu cannot even conceive of . . . the human person as an independent being standing on his own. Every human person, every individual is as it were one link in a chain of vital forces: a living link that establishes the bond with previous generations and with the forces that support his own existence.[4]

Bénézet Bujo corroborates this statement, adding that this cosmopolitan attitude applies to the entirety of modern black Africa.[5] Bujo explains: "The clan is first of all a kinship of blood, but . . . the community as such goes beyond this relationship to embrace all human beings."[6] This, asserts Bujo, explains why politicians in modern African states refer to each other as "brother" and "sister."[7] We see this practice continued religiously today among the diaspora of Africans around the world.

Just as the Arabs, conquering their way across northern and eastern Africa since the eighth and ninth centuries, had been successful at evangelizing Africans, Christianity too was readily welcomed on the continent because the new religion had considerable consonance with traditional belief systems. The Africans had long been monotheists, longer indeed than the Europeans. In theory, the fit between African tradition and the Christian humanistic ethical code was a good one. However, the earliest attitudes and practices of the Christian settlers had to have struck indigenous Africans as oddly ungracious. African people, so deeply committed to an ideal of the familial nature of the human world, had to have been struck by the ironic paradox of the Christian message of love espoused by the same people who beat, insulted, and humiliated them. If all people are children of the god, why, the Africans must have wondered, do the missionary teaching primers depict only white children at the feet of the savior? Why are the only black-skinned figures in their books the devils and demons menacing at the gates of hell?

Despite the grave incongruities between the lofty theory of Christian ideals and missionary preaching, and the daily practices of the missionaries and settlers, the African people welcomed the new religion as readily as they welcomed the white intruders. That welcome can be understood as fulfilling the customary African social prescriptions for hospitable reception of visitors. Welcoming newcomers and showing them respect are considered morally necessary components of decent behavior in the African *ethos* of universal humanism.

## 2. Health Crisis in Africa

Another reason for the African people's ready acceptance of Christian missionaries was that the evangelists offered practical benefits that could improve their lives considerably. The earliest missions of Jesuits and Franciscans served as sanctuaries for those natives fleeing slave hunters. Later, the missions responded to the need for medical services for the African natives.

In the early decades of colonial rule in Africa, hospitals and dispensaries were maintained and medical provision oriented entirely for the care of Europeans. From the beginning of foreign settlement on African soil, protecting the lives of the continent's colonial inhabitants and especially the colonial soldiery was the European medical community's overwhelming priority. Curative services for Africans were rare even into the early decades of the twentieth century. It was not until after the Second World War that most missions arose to serve the African patient.

In the middle to late nineteenth century, the social disruption resulting from wars and the trade in slaves, along with the new germs imported from the European continent into vulnerable African communities, culminated in wide epidemics of diseases like smallpox, meningitis, plague, and sleeping sickness. These diseases exacted a frightening toll on the health and lives of African workers, especially the vast armies of human porters and migrant workers constantly taxied across the interior in response to the shifting demands of colonial industry and agriculture. The epidemics were soon recognized as a threat to the entire colonial enterprise, since dwindling populations meant shortages of healthy bodies and thus endangered the cheap labor base upon which the enterprise depended for its success.

Renewed outbreaks of epidemic diseases in the African labor populations constantly threatened to upset the fragile economic and political balance of the early colonial state. Of much greater concern to the colonials, however, was the health of the European populations on the African continent. As the natives fell more and more frequently ill, they began to be seen, and openly described by the medical community, as a reservoir of deadly disease, a threat to healthy European bodies and indeed to "civilization" on the continent. The frequency and intensity of pandemic contagion led to the "great campaigns" where populations were forcibly quarantined and inoculated *en masse* to keep their diseases from spreading to the colonial populations.

By the 1950s, the diseases had reached epidemic levels of fatality among the entire population—African and colonial. It was finally generally recognized that unprotected and untreated African populations frustrated the most diligent efforts to keep European communities disease-free. Christian missionary doctors stepped in to satisfy the need for medics who would condescend to treat diseased black bodies, not so much because their Christian consciences had finally begun to feel empathy for the sick and dying Africans who shared their faith. Missionaries began to recognize the untapped value of the mission hospital for the gleaning of souls. Only with these realizations was the health of the African afforded focused concern.

Colonialist entrepreneurs had long recognized that healthy bodies provided greater exploitative potential. Sick bodies proved poor labor machines that could drag diseases across the continent and infect disparate colonial communities. All along, for the good of the colonial enterprise, there had been posted, at focal points along the migrant labor routes, the simplest contingent of medical staff to check for infected bodies and send them home to their villages instead of on to the next colonial post. By the mid-twentieth century, these station points would also offer convenient sites to heal souls while missionary doctors screened infected bodies.

The first mission hospitals were often attached to colonial transport stations for indigenous laborers or served directly colonial mines or farms. The medical "care" offered at these mission posts challenges the meaning of that generally altruistic term. The native laborers, already accustomed to being herded from place to place, had their bodies prodded and poked, inspected and analyzed, weighed and measured like herd animals. In mass examinations, the clinic doctors helped to determine the value of the laborer in the colonial marketplace. The less healthy workers were weeded out and sent back to their villagers to infect their families.

In the labor posts, there existed a broad range of healing practices, many methods of reading symptoms, often contradictory accounts of the patterns of disease incidence, and varying modes of interpreting those patterns. In some cases, the patients were even assigned medical profiles and awarded medical histories and records, in the absence of medical records describing prior conditions or treatments. What is significant about the medical profiles produced by these mass medical service stations is that they tended to distinguish their patients' medical conditions and to predict propensity to disease by reference to the patients' tribal identity. This had already become the accustomed practice long before the onslaught of the great epidemics, during which blame for disease incidence would be attributed to unhealthy and morally decadent tribal custom.

Not until well into the twentieth century, after the close of the Second World War, did church missions finally build hospitals and begin to provide consistent medical care for the Africans. Traditional healing methods continued alongside the new "white magic" of European practitioners. The missionary doctors and nurses, with their black bags full of ointments and pills and their painful needles full of strange potions, were readily accepted by the Africans and enthusiastically trusted with curing and warding off the new diseases that had arrived with the Europeans. Doctors evangelized; evangels healed. It was a

strange new medical magic of bizarre new therapies, promising to cure both
body and soul of the diseases plaguing African societies.


## 3. African Notions of Health and Illness

The African notion of illness and the prevention and cure of diseases favored the
African embrace of the new white *waganga* (witch doctors). Their own healing
beliefs and practices caused the African people to generally credit European
doctors with a wealthy endowment of the special gifts and powers that were
traditionally counted upon to remedy the curses of bodily and mental ill health.
In the African general understanding, disease happens in individuals and communities because something is out of synchronicity in the community at large;
something ethically wrong has been committed that needs to be put right.[8] The
sick person (*mgongwa*) becomes ill because something is amiss within the
community. The community is plagued by discord that must be healed if the
village is to be well again. Social integrity may be disrupted by jealousies or
resentments among the villagers or from one of the ancestors, or discord may
visit the village from the outside because of the jealousy, dishonesty, or resentment of some neighbor.

For African communities, a *special* person, endowed with *special* connection to the ancestors and the god, must be called to intervene in social crises, if
the original crime is to be righted and the communal (and psychophysical) dysfunction healed. True to the profound communal focus of African peoples, the
traditional method of curing the ills of the person coincided exactly with the
practice of curing the ills of the community. The effective cure proves broadly
multifunctional. A specialist is called in to cure any dis-*ease* that arises, whether
the disease is manifest as a physical illness of an individual, a mental collapse of
a mind, a communal plague, or a disruptive conflict that ruptures relations
within the family or between the god and the community at large.

The African understanding of disease is demonstrated by observing an ancient ritual still practiced today by the Shona tribe of Zimbabwe. The Shona
believe that, if the god sends lightning to strike the hut of a family, the tragedy
has occurred because the god is punishing a misdeed of one of the family, or has
been seduced into that devilry by a jealous or resentful neighbor. The god must
be appeased and the neighbor's malevolence thwarted. This is achieved by
bringing the *mganga* (witch doctor) to the scene of the demolished hut to
cleanse the area of any remaining ill will. Before the family can return to its destroyed hut and salvage the belongings inside it, the *mganga* enters the hut, and
decontaminates the polluted area by repeating purifying words and songs, and
performing magical ceremonial dances over the burned-out site.

The witch doctor performs these functions with great flourish, as a public
demonstration of power. One common spectacle of *mganga* power coincides
with the African belief that lightning is caused by a malevolent intervention

from a god or resentful ancestor. It is thought that the lightning leaves behind, in the ravaged hut, receptacles of ongoing misfortune, "eggs" that continue to carry ill chance. The *mganga* is called to a lightning-struck hut and is the only one permitted to enter inside. The *mganga* searches the site of destruction, and then emerges from the burnt-out hut, displaying proudly the dangerous "lightning eggs" he has found in the hut. The magician-doctor repeats a few magic phrases over the "eggs" to negate their evil power. Then, concealing the purified eggs safely inside his pocket, the doctor welcomes the family back into their now-secure hut, collects payment, and then disappears.

The ritual of the "lightning eggs" is still practiced in rural Zimbabwe, so one need not stretch one's imagination too far to imagine how easily the Christian missionaries of several centuries past—with their claimed special connection to the god, their magical potion-drugs, their exotic technical medical phrases, and their terrifying yet spellbinding hypodermic needles—might have been readily accepted as special magical personages with supermundane powers that could ward off misfortunes and cure the evils that might disrupt the patient's body or plague the body communal.

Despite the negative imagery attached to the dark bodies of the African patients in the missionary discourse, the Africans quickly embraced the Christian message and accepted European doctors, their evangelizing hospitals, and the missionary schools. Since the colonial medical officers refused for centuries to treat the bodies of the indigenous, the Christian missionary doctors were fervently welcomed by the natives as a means to battle the epidemics of disease that they had been long suffering. The evangelist doctor's expertise was the only option to the witch doctor's art for curing black African bodies in the interior of the continent. Often, in times of sickness, both traditional and European forms of medical practice were sought by the Africans, to be extra careful against the new lethal diseases. The missionary-teacher-medic and the young and the old sick African bodies soon become strangely connected bedfellows.

## 4. Jungle Doctor Myths

The jungle doctors and the missionary medics, no less than the anthropologists and the colonial settlers and rulers, readily accepted the general, notably ambiguous portrait of the continent and its inhabitants: mysterious, seductive, beautiful beyond imagination, but deadly, morally ailing, and decayed. Megan Vaughan states: "In the late-nineteenth and early-twentieth-century, East and Central Africa Europeans still perceived of themselves as grappling with a wild and uncontrolled environment, of which Africans were an integral part."[9] Rumors of deathly practices, bloody rituals, and appalling sexual excesses, spawned by the earliest explorers, continued to rule the European imagination both in the home countries and abroad in the colonies, and were especially persuasive to the missionary medic, whose evangelical mission was formulated in the light of these reports.

Before their arrival in Africa, the Christian zealots were already themselves "infected" with a highly popularized prejudice that would dictate in advance a perception of the land and its inhabitants as mutually diseased and rotting—a virtual wellspring of deadly infection. These dark rumors provided a self-justification for colonial intrusion and a double justification for the body and soul healing work of the religio-medical practitioner. V. Y. Mudimbe notes a similar "infection" distorting thinking among the missionaries and insinuating itself into missionary discourse. He states: "Missionary speech is always prede-termined, preregulated, let us say *colonized* . . . [with the conviction of] God's desire for the conversion of the world."[10]

The attitude of missionary doctors toward their African patients tended to parallel the religious philosophy of redemptive history. Sinners need to suffer if they are to be brought unto the god. The European doctors' conviction that the natives were physically ill because they were morally wanting fully frustrated positive attitudes toward, and healthy relationships with the native peoples. As "sinners," Africans were construed as paradigmatic candidates for redemption through suffering. The myth of redemption through suffering can be called upon to justify all kinds of brutality. Missionaries generally see themselves as composing the "army" of god's servants, and since "God is rightly entitled to the use of all possible means, even violence, to achieve his objectives," the mission-aries' commitment to peace and love could become infected with dangerous qualifications, when faced with a threatening mass of "heathen" otherness. [11]

From David Livingstone to Albert Schweitzer, the white doctor in Africa came to compose the paradigm of Western heroism. Since the nineteenth cen-tury, a kind of cult had arisen around the figure of the jungle doctor. Jungle doc-tor cults developed in the home countries and spread across the reading and the newsreel-watching world. The spectacular beauty of the African landscape pro-vided a dramatic setting for any adventure, but when propping up tales of great white *médecins* embroiled in an inhospitable environment infested with disease, wallowing in filth, entrenched in barbarism, superstition, and immorality, that breathtaking backdrop furnished a perilous setting for fascinating jungle doctor sagas.[12]

The popularity and the pocketbooks of the jungle doctor-writers had always been well served by embellishing their tales with exaggerations of the dangers and malevolence of the peoples and lands of Africa. The later testimonies of the Christian missionary doctors could only be taken by their enthusiastic audiences as more reliable in their details and more dedicated in their commitment to truth than the accounts of the early explorer-medics. A general Christian European prejudice asserted that none could know more intimately the truest and darkest secrets of African bodies and souls than those agents of god who tended the bed-sides and the confessionals of the natives.

The fact of the missionary doctor's ulterior motive of collecting and saving souls no doubt gave the medical discourses even greater credibility in Christian audiences on the African continent and in Europe. Despite their remarkable popularity and the high regard in which missionary doctors were held during the colonial period, religio-medical myths, like colonial myths in general, tended to express more about the prejudices and character frailties of the mythologizer than about the objects of their denigrating discourses. The religio-medical practitioners brought their own self-doubts, weaknesses, fears, and biases to their encounter with the African indigenous. The missionaries' perceptions of the African natives were exaggerated by their insecurities and prejudices.

To appreciate the way medical myths were damaging to the Africans, it is necessary to attend to the evolving varieties of biomedical discourse that arose to express the missionaries' experience of the native population. I am indebted to Vaughan for her thorough treatment of the medical community's confrontation with their African patients, in *Curing Their Ills: Colonial Power and African Illness.*[13] Drawing upon an enormous breadth of historical documentation, from court records to fund-raising posters to medical journals and jungle doctor cartoons, Vaughan elucidates how the medical community added a palpable credibility to the already plentiful negative reports of the African continent and its peoples. By rephrasing descriptions of African decadence and debauchery in the technical terminology peculiar to medical discourse—images of disease and infection and deadliness—the medics were able to market their racial prejudices as irrefutable medical fact.

The many varieties of colonial myths were never monolithic or stable in their content or forms, and none of the mythical inventions about Africa and Africans were without their discipline- and occupation-specific self-contradictions. This is also true of the biomedical discourses on Africa and the Africans. Reports by jungle doctors reflect the ambiguous feelings professed by earliest explorers of the continent. Doctors experienced a deep and haunting simultaneous fascination and loathing. Clearly, the medical missionaries concurrently feared and romanticized their strange patients and the exotic land in which they were immersed. There existed tantalizing reasons to popularize the loathing. Africa was, for the jungle doctor, no less than for the ruler, the colonial clerk and the anthropologist, a place where careers could be jump-started to stardom, where reputations could be quickly and gloriously cast. The more deadly the metaphors, the greater the heroism, the greater the hero, and the greater the claim to fame.

The methods employed by the missionary doctors in the twentieth century epidemic campaigns offers much insight, not only into the general European terrors and prejudices toward the Africans, but into the bedside manners of the missionary medics toward their African patients. Witness A. Zahra's report to the *Bulletin of the World Health Organization* on the yaws campaign carried out in Nigeria in the 1950s. The passage describing the inoculation sessions, aptly described as "the sausage machine," bears repeating:

> Young children are stripped of all clothing and adults retain only a loin cloth [or] short underskirt. They present themselves in turn before the examining doctor or assistant, who examines the patient systematically from head to foot, not forgetting the inspection of hands and fingers (both sides), armpits, soles of

feet, genital region (for children), and the medial view of the tibiae. . . . A pole
is fixed in the ground next to the examiner to give support to the patient when
the soles of his feet are inspected. . . . The dose is chalked on the back of the
patient over the right scapular region. Since a dry piece of chalk cannot be used
for long because of the grease and dirt which quickly collect on it, it is previously soaked in water, and then used lightly. The chalked dosage may not at
first show clearly, but the figure soon dries and becomes distinct. . . . An assis-
tant administers the prescribed dosage, as chalked on his back, deeply and in-
tramuscularly into the upper and outer quadrant of the right buttock. [14]

Eerily reminiscent of Franz Kafka's "In the Penal Colony," this passage indicates how European missionary prejudices about their patients were, quite
literally, inscribed upon the African body.[15] As upon a passive lump of flesh
without intelligence, will, or feelings, the European doctor plied his profession
without care for the humiliations or the pain his methods inflicted. The African
experience of Westernized medicine included intrusive, assembly-line-style distribution of painful inoculations, administered without consent or explanation to
nameless, numbered bodies, marshaled in silent, half-naked files by military
personnel, speaking about the recipients in the third person as though the patients had no minds to question the procedure, no souls to offend, no characters
to shame.

There was remarkably little resistance to the campaigns, even where certain
of the practices contravened ancient tribal prohibitions and customs of decency.
This may have been because the campaigns were administered in the "military
fashion" typical of the colonial ruler, and so were probably seen as an extension
of powerful colonial rule. The lack of resistance may also indicate that the African subject, by the time of these forced inoculation projects, was successfully
reconstructed into passive laboring bodies, well educated to the fact of colonial
ownership of their bodies. There were some rare cases of resistance, but these
were readily contained. Men who misbehaved in urban areas were quickly labeled schizophrenic, subdued, and shuffled off to lunatic asylums.

African women almost invariably trusted the white Western doctors and did
as they were instructed. This dutiful submissiveness was interpreted as proof
that African women lacked adequate development of a separated self to render
self-awareness. This gender prejudice on the part of Europeans also accounts for
the fact that African women were rarely accounted "mad" in the colonies:
women were believed to have no individual "self" to become psychically ill.
The prejudices attached to women tended to display the same ambiguities as
other myths about the land and people. Women were seen either as the embodiment of a happy primitive ignorance, sexually unfettered, utterly without self-
consciousness, free from rational capacity, untouched by worldly concerns, mere
carefree reproducers of bodies. On the one hand, they were often found innocu-
ous and merely amusing for their ingenuous and happy sexuality. On the other
hand, women very often elicited reactions of horror and loathing, and were seen
as highly dangerous but shameless repositories of sexual diseases, due to their

unbridled sexuality, diseased temptresses in fertility cults and other "dark" practices.[16] African women were discounted altogether or feared and loathed by Europeans.

The historical literature suggests that, during this period of raging epidemics, the general discourse on the native Africans turned particularly dark in its metaphors, but the literature does not clarify the role that religious prejudice played in this darkening. Africans had previously been perceived by the foreign observers as an undifferentiated mass, an animate extension of a generally perilous environment. The new threat of disease and the moralizing explanation for disease invented by Christian missionary medics brought into distinction individual traits that had previously been compressed and diffused in the European imagination into a monolithic notion of "African" difference. The new interpretation dictated that individual Africans be diligently scrutinized, examined, and surveyed so that the infected and the infectious could be adequately controlled and contained.

## 5. Medical Myths Become Culturally Specific

The focus of the Christian missionaries' concern and the morally significant language that they introduced into discussions of disease incidence brought into focus tribal variations in African identity. The African patient's ethnic background and connections came to be associated, in the mind of the missionary doctor, with the incidence of disease, and thus the various African tribes came to be distinguished in terms of propensity for physical decay. These propensities, projected the European religio-medical healers, had to be a result of decadent tribal practices. Souls that are rotting outside the purifying light of Christian faith ultimately make for rotting bodies as well. J. P. Odoch Pido offers the following example of missionary discourse on disease when he tells how disease was explained to the Acoli tribe: "European Christian missionaries taught Acoli that venereal diseases are for sinners, and sinners are not people."[17]

The significance of this shift in the conceptualization of disease cannot be overrated. Its effects were wide-ranging and abiding, both for the individual African patients and the treatment that African bodies would receive, and also for the general possibilities for community among the exploited African population. Early colonial discourses tended to describe Africans solely in terms of *racial* difference, as an extension of an undifferentiated and generally threatening environment. The shift in religio-medical myth to a focus upon tribal difference had the severely damaging consequence of allowing patterns of tribal behaviors and customs to be blamed for the incidence of certain diseases.[18] Distinct tribal practices began to be seen, by African and by European, as morally diseased and thus physically and spiritually contaminating. Configuring African bodies as differently diseased from group to tribal group did not save the natives from the general fate of being understood by Europeans as masses of diseased bodies. But once those diseased bodies were seen as undifferentiatedly diseased across the tribe, Africans could be accounted "tribally blameworthy" for the illnesses from which they suffered. Their tribal customs and social rituals could be interpreted as more and less diseased.

Another sad consequence of this new way of accounting for disease incidence was that it profoundly discouraged curative medicine. Given the harmful connection made between disease patterns and ethnic practices, the neglect of public health care programs for African patients could be readily justified, and public treatment schemes for existing diseases could be justifiably downgraded.[19] The new medical prejudices hindered European desire to foot the expense of curing those "self-sickened" tribes. Medical campaigns could remain minimal and simply curative in nature, since prevention became the responsibility of the Africans. The native populations needed to cast off their diseased practices if they wanted to live healthy lives. The medical discourse served the colonial mythology, in another respect as well. Ethnic proneness to disease provided a medical rationale for rigorous segregations of the indigenous in slum reservelands far from the purified communities of decent European folk.

Worst of all, for the Africans, the new medical myths dictated the collapse of tribal pride and solidarity, since individual tribes could now be located and demonized as diseased social environments, the dissociation from which became utterly necessary to anyone valuing health and morals. The description of disease occurrence in terms of tribal membership highlighted, for the Africans themselves, the distinctness of their various communities and the divergences in traditional practice separating those communities.

When the African native, oppressed and exploited, threatened with strange foreign illnesses, most needed to band in loyalty to the tribal neighbor, the new self-understandings of social differences and the association of diseases with those differences, eclipsed the fact of their greater membership in the community of the oppressed, and increased the alienation that separated their similarly suffering and exploited bodies. Individual African groups began to share in the European terrors of mixing with certain decadent others from other tribes that might well practice the debauched customs of which they had heard tell. Worse, one tribe could purify its own image by singling out others as blameworthy for the general misperceptions about decadent African practices. With the missionary medic's testimony that Africans were the cause of their own misfortunes, there no longer existed the need to blame the European invaders for their wretchedness. The fault for every unhappy circumstance of the downtrodden African life, corralled into overcrowded quarantined villages, diseased and hungry and filthy, could be placed squarely on the shoulders of colonial victims themselves.

The claim of pathology as "natural" to the African—disease constituting the form of his cultural difference from Europeans—displaced attention from the environmental and economic causes of disease. Concern lapsed from the appallingly unsanitary conditions in which the African villagers and their migrant laborers were housed, the meagerness of their diets, and the exhausting nature of their work. When diseased family members were sent home from the migratory camps and epidemics struck the home villages, there were forced examinations, forced inoculations, forced quarantines and segregations. Sometimes entire African villages were relieved of their huts, their crops, and their possessions in the name of medical emergency. All that they owned was set to flames meant to purify the area of diseases.

In the mid-twentieth century, the missionary medic came at last to the interior of the continent to heal the African body of its ailments, but their new, highly moralizing medical descriptions of disease incidence and their new notions of disease causality on the basis of tribal custom worsened conditions for the Africans. In blaming the natives for their disease incidence, missionary medics eclipsed the real social problems facing Africans and occluded the desperate need for social reforms in the colonies. The new medical discourses obscured the generally destructive effects of urbanization and industrialization, and they masked the multiple sins of the migrant labor system which led to the division of families, the breakdown of cultural unity, and the rampant spread of diseases among the indigenous.

The shift in focus from race to culture in the discussion of African disease is significant because it demonstrates that the European medical community in Africa was never without its peculiar prejudices, preoccupations, and biases. Africans were held blameworthy for their illnesses by the community of those who best understood how diseases function and spread. Missionary doctors were a trusted source of information on the Africans and their decision to blame the Africans for their wretchedness instead of question the influx of disease that accompanied European entry into the continent had enduring effects for the accepted myth surrounding African communities. The connection between suffering and sin is a typically Christian connection, but the universal acceptance of that prejudice across the medical community *en bloc* demonstrates the tendency of the most seductive religious prejudices to affect the mindset of scientific communities as well.

In Africa, the collapse of the African body and the fragmentation and dissolution of African cultures was attributed to Africans. The varied myths claimed that African moral decay was the determining factor in their physical decay. Just as so many other indigenous peoples fell by the wayside of imperialist adventures of "progress," the Africans were blamed for their general wretchedness; Africans simply failed to give up their decadent cultural practices and adapt to modern civilizing processes. The jungle doctor served the colonial project by blaming the high incidence of African disease on the primitiveness of African bodies, the essentially diseased nature of African cultures, and the more or less morally diseased traditions practiced in the African world.

Throughout the slow development of Western medical services in Africa, traditional African healing systems remained remarkably resilient alongside the new "white magic" of the European medical practitioner. Of course, both the African witch doctor (*mganga*) and the old village midwife (*mkunga* or *mchawi*) were simultaneously scorned and feared by European doctors. These native practitioners and the archaic natural methods they employed to heal the sick were seen, by Europeans, both as emblematic of, and as source of the continuance of, the ignorance and superstition of the African native.

The heroic figure of the European "jungle doctor," with bible in hand and serious medical manner, and toting the formidable black bag of instruments and the vials and needles of chemical potions, was counterpoised in the European imagination against the image of the African medicine man, decorated with feathers, clad in animal skins, adorned in face paint and carrying a bag of pebbles and bones. This was clearly, for the European, a battle of "civilized" rationality against superstition, of science against magic, of white health and progress against black sin and disease. However, Vaughan offers these very positive comments regarding African health and healing systems that contradict, in sweeping terms, the negative images we have come to take for granted:

> Africans . . . have maintained a degree of control over health and healing in their communities which many late-twentieth-century Europeans and North Americans, oppressed and alienated by biomedicine, regard with envy. . . . Biomedicine . . . offered little in the way of a conceptual challenge to African ideas about health and healing, the continuities in which are more remarkable than the fractures.[20]

The missionary doctor saw the African as the product of a certain environment, as a practitioner of certain cultural traditions that promoted or resisted disease. The African could be differentiated, categorized, labeled as any other object of scientific research. Witness the results of civilized medicine on the African population: Africans were not thought to be frustrated or depressed by any of this—though they occasionally went "mad"—because they were not seen to possess adequate self-awareness to suffer psychic fragmentation or dislocation. African minds with their individual thoughts, desires, fears, and anxieties were not relevant to the medical treatment; indeed these were rarely acknowledged as existing in the case of such primitive and collectively oriented beings.

The lack of any serious medical attention to the epidemics that plagued Africans can be directly attributed to the prejudices of the missionary doctors and the peculiar myths that oriented the ambiguous care they extended to their African patients. One wonders if the world, even now, in the clarifying light of retrospection, has managed to locate the real cause of African disease and death where it truly belongs: with the arrival of the European invader and the economic and social changes that those invaders wrought upon indigenous peoples.

Africans get sick, as other peoples get sick, because their immune systems come under physical and emotional stressors. New contacts with new diseases imported from foreign lands coupled with domestic conditions of abject poverty, unsanitary living conditions, forced mobility for the sake of filling labor needs across the colonies, and lack of either preventive or curative medical care all contributed to vulnerability to disease. Changing patterns of disease incidence reflected changing patterns of poverty and dislocation, and differentials in the treatment of African peoples by different employers and by different colonial regimes. African people, as all people, get sick more readily when they are displaced and dispossessed, unhappy, maligned by others, when they have unhealthy self-images, and low self-esteem.

Africans became sick because they abandoned those traditional customs and practices that had previously and very effectively kept them healthy and happy. They likely became sick because they were faced with new germs and new viruses transported from foreign shores. But Africans were convinced, by their social superiors, the civilized European, that disease was a function of their racial identity and a function of their differentiated but sickly cultures. Disease was who they were, not what they suffered. Africans were pressed by invading forces across the defining boundaries of their tribal and familial selves. Deeply social beings, Africans were thrown, by overwhelming historical forces, into an individualistic, competitive, rat-race capitalist world and, that dehumanizing lifestyle took its toll upon their health and happiness.

The industrialized modern world has been hard on the mental wellbeing and physical health of all inhabitants, its urbanizing, competitive, and alienating forces dehumanizing the members of societies at all echelons of power. But those who occupy the lower classes of a society invariably reap the worst effects of the system, and their abjection is measurable most clearly in the society's health indices. Africans found themselves, within a generation, forced from their timeworn lifestyles of earthbound belonging and neighborliness into the most abject conditions at the base of the social ladder of a foreign value system. We may assume that it was a most predictable consequence of this alienating situation that people fell sick in one way or another. When they did, the missionary doctor was there, with the needles, the moralizations, and the prayerbook, to explain the disease by blaming the victims. As the colonies, one by one, fell more and more into economic crisis, chronic underfunding took its toll upon all resources within their systems, and ultimately the European patient came to be as deprived of responsible medical care as the African patient had been deprived all along.

## Notes

1. Walter Burkert, *Creation of the Sacred* (Cambridge, Mass.: Harvard University Press, 1992), 24 & ff.

2. Tsenay Serequeberhan, *The Hermeneutics of African Philosophy* (New York: Routledge, 1994), 59.

3. E. S. Atieno-Odhiambo, "Luo Perspectives on Knowledge and Development" in Ivan Karp and D. A. Masolo, *African Philosophy as Cultural Inquiry* (Bloomington, Ind.: Indiana University Press, 2000), 244–258, 250.

4. Placide Tempels, *Bantu Philosophie: Ontologie und Ethik* (Heidelberg, 1956), 67, as cited in Bénézet Bujo, *Foundations of an African Ethic* (New York: Crossroads Publishing, 2001), 86.

5. Bujo, *Foundations*, 85.

6. Bujo, *Foundations*, 86.

7. Bujo, *Foundations*, 86.

8. Bujo, *Foundations*, 120.

9. Megan Vaughan, *Curing Their Ills: Colonial Power and African Illness* (Stanford, Calif.: Stanford University Press. 1991), 38.

10. V. Y. Mudimbe, *The Invention of Africa* (Bloomington: Indiana University Press, 1988), 47-48.

11. Mudimbwe, *Invention*, 47–48.

12. Vaughan, *Curing*, 158–178.

13. Vaughan, *Curing*, 158–178.

14. "A Yaws Eradication Campaign in Eastern Nigeria" in *Bulletin of the World Health Organization*, Vol. 15, 911–935, 933–34, cited in Vaughan, *Curing*, 51.

15. Franz Kafka, "In The Penal Colony," *Franz Kafka: The Complete Stories*, Nahum N. Glatzer, ed. (New York: Schocken Books, 1983), 140–167.

16. Vaughan, *Curing*, 109.

17. J. P. Odoch Pido, "Personhood and Art: Social Change and Commentary among the Acoli" in *African Philosophy as Cultural Inquiry*, 105–135, 126.

18. Vaughan, *Curing*, 158–178.

19. Vaughan, *Curing*, 158–178.

20. Vaughan, *Curing*, 24; cf. "But what was the Disease? The Present State of Health and Healing in African Studies" in *Past and Present*, Vol. 124, 159–179.

# Chapter 9
# Philosophical Constructions of Africans

Western attitudes of supremacy, which culminate in the attempt to annihilate black culture and black histories by annihilating African bodies and African memories of their traditions and histories, could be ascribed to a general cultural bias, burgeoning during an historical era of unprecedented national pride and imperialism. The intellectual roots of this supremacist worldview are deeply embedded in the racist orthodox religiosity of evangelical Christendom and in the prevailing social scientific theories of human evolution that guided anthropological research. But the most disturbing underpinnings of colonial and empirical violence are located in the philosophical ideas of the time that fed the ethnocentric megalomanias of the imperialist powers and provided the rational foundations for justifying the colonial enterprise.

## 1. Ancient Roots of Hierarchical Ordering

The roots of those philosophical ideas extend in full logical and symbolic resonance from a mammoth history of philosophical ideals, ontologies, and epistemologies dating back millennia. As far back as Plato with his positing of a higher, *more real* world of pure ideas, philosophers were promoting notions of hierarchical orderings that were morally significant.[1] According to this schematic of being, the higher up the ontological ladder one finds oneself, the more perfect and *morally elevated* one is. Moral and ontological hierarchies, as the ones found in Plato's mythological musings, impose an ethical barrier between the human world and divine perfection, with the purpose of ensuring against the transgression most shunned in the ancient world—*hybris*, understood as arrogance or overblown human pride. As long as the human world is located well below the summit of the ladder of being, humility is encouraged. As long as ontology is morally significant and hierarchical in form, plenty of ontological room remains for striving toward moral improvement from lower positions on the ontological scale.

The best ideas over time show their flaws and the previously unforeseen dark effects of a theory come into view as they find their way into practice. Despite Plato's best intentions to ensure the philosophical seductiveness of the ethical quest, hierarchical orderings that are morally significant have a hazardous underside. In time, this unfortunate lining inevitably shows itself: raising the ontological bar high above the human head trivializes humans as lesser beings, and degrades earthly life. Ontologies promote the notion of a "fallen" human world, alienated from a primal home and cast adrift from the divine parent group. Ontologies, as well, trivialize the violences of earthly "cave" life, and play down the sufferings of mere bodies. Hierarchical ontologies promote a "two-worlds worldview" that casts earthly existence as a testing ground for hardy souls, where suffering becomes ethically necessary to the accomplishment of the salvational quest.

Plato's ontological and moral hierarchies unfold over the millennia of human speculation into various and more dangerous forms. In the modern era, the notion of an ontological scale altogether discards its originally humbling aspect and abandons its ethical quest. Plato's downgrading of human wisdom in relation to the perfect wisdom of the gods simultaneously means the downgrade of earthly life in relation to a lost paradisal existence. Over time, this devaluation unfolds as downgraded body, sensory information, and passion's knowledge, and, ultimately the import of bodily sufferings pales beside the marvelous workings of a human reason understood as a perfect chip off the divine block.

## 2. Modernist Hierarchies of Being

Eventually, the gods become unnecessary and are dismissed from the lofty helm of the cosmic ship, as human reason reaches unlimited heights of *hybris* and imagines it could probe successfully the deepest secrets of the universe. This evolution in philosophy's metaphysical constructions raises the reliable data of scientific inquiries above the fragile concerns and defective knowledge supplied by perceiving and suffering subjects. In the long run of philosophical inquiry, the ethical quest of ontological hierarchies paves the intellectual road to an arid rationalism that reaches a decidedly dangerous peak among European philosophers during the time of colonial expansion.

The father of modern philosophy, René Descartes, provides the explicit ontological reformulations upon which Enlightenment thought is founded.[2] Descartes redefines the rational, isolated mind as the primary substance of the human animal, when he redefines human beings as disembodied "thinking things." The consequence of Descartes' *cogito ergo sum* ("I think; therefore I am") is that nothing is so certain as the human mind, no information so reliable as the mind's ideas.

The human mind becomes, with Descartes, the veritable Archimedes' point of certitude upon which is founded the edifice of human knowledge. Even the god in Descartes' ontological schema depends upon human reason to establish independent existence. Descartes' neat analogy of the world to a machine means that the planet that serves as nurturing parental womb to the human creature is reduced to a mere clock wound up by a god who then abandons the world to its own mechanical devices. In his robe and his slippers, sitting by his fireside, Descartes could hardly have seen ahead in time to the way that his musings would fulfill themselves in the cruel realities of Enlightenment rationalism, and the triumph of technological knowledge, colonial expansion, and imperial excess.

Benedict de Spinoza is generally accepted as continuing in the rationalist tradition begun with Descartes. In my more sympathetic reading Spinoza recognizes the dangerous path that philosophy is assuming with Descartes.[3] Spinoza reacts against the Cartesian celebration of the merely rational and his mechanistic understanding of the world by asserting a radical monism that reformulates the way the world is envisaged. His system heals together again the bodies and minds that had been torn asunder in Cartesian philosophy. Struck by the amoral madness of the burgeoning capitalist world that surrounds him, with its multiplex religious and monarchial power nodes, and its frenzied materialisms, Spinoza attempts to reconstruct being to defuse its dangerous symbolics.[4]

My reading of Spinoza is favored by the fact that it explains more adequately why Spinoza, a quiet, austere, scholarly man, was found scandalous by many of his contemporaries. Spinoza's metaphysics, termed by David Hume, somewhat ironically, as a "hideous hypothesis," would not have been found so hideous to Spinoza's contemporaries had he remained within the reigning rationalistic formulations and maintained a rigid hierarchy of being.[5] Spinoza denies the hierarchical nature of existence by construing God as another name for nature, and the god's power as wholly cumulative. That is, the full measure of the god's power is calculated, by Spinoza, by taking the sum of the combined powers of all the parts of the god's creations. God is not, as with Descartes, limitless being, but a being limited to the sum of the powers of beings.[6] In a scandalously non-hierarchizing and ontologically liberating move, Spinoza renders the god's potency dependent upon the ability of individual creatures to reach the fullness of their potentialities, by being freed to fulfill their utmost possibilities for self-realization.

For Spinoza, being is God and God is nature, and the power of the whole cannot exceed the sum of the powers of the parts. This ontologically liberating claim serves a democratic politics as well. States are only as strong and legitimate as they are liberal and democratic; kings are only as powerful as their peoples are allowed the freedom to extend and develop their talents; churches are only as godlike as they permit their constituents free expression and thought. The metaphysical system of Spinoza is a grand monism, but Spinoza's metaphysics, as the grand mythological constructions of Plato, serves his ethical task: the defusing of the very ground of the power politics that govern and oppress every aspect of human life during his time.

Spinoza, persecuted at every turn by the various power nodes of the highly hierarchical capitalist world of his time, is intent upon dismantling Descartes' hyper-rationalistic metaphysics and disarming the dangerous ontologies of mind, knowledge, and power. Spinoza is painfully aware of the difficulties of persuading powerful kings and popes to humble themselves to his ethical vision. He closes his *Ethics*:

> If the road I have shown to lead to [virtue and wisdom] is difficult, it can yet be discovered. And clearly it must be very hard when it is so seldom found. For how could it be that it is neglected practically by all, if salvation were close at hand and could be found without difficulty? But all excellent things are as difficult as they are rare.[7]

Spinoza's metaphysics seeks to defuse being of its dangerous hierarchical aspects and philosophy of its arid rationalisms, by redefining being as a great chain, and redefining evil as mere subjective prejudice. In the end, a metaphysic *per se* admits of being as a great power structure that, even as a chain distributing the goodness of the god to each of its contributing parts, maintains the potentially dangerous structure of a hierarchy. Where a hierarchy is posited, rankings and orderings follow and the designation of some beings as more worthy than others cannot be avoided.

Spinoza's hypotheses are found utterly scandalous by many contemporary scholars; Gottfried Wilhelm Leibniz sets out to "correct" the troubling indignities of Spinoza's worldview, seeking to remedy the fragility of a god robbed of free will and dependent upon the solidarity of earthly creatures for fulfillment of power. To this end, Leibniz stresses the power and the goodness of a god that could conceive of a world of fullest creative variety, filling every potential gap in the chain of being with the richest diversity of life forms. The argument, echoing Descartes, requires the reintroduction of an ontological hierarchy, and explicitly moral rankings of the beings populating that scale. With Leibniz's metaphysics, degrees of greater and lesser excellence will once again separate the god's creatures, and determine the greater and lesser possibilities for worlds. Leibniz states:

> From the conflict of all possibles demanding existence, this at once follows, that there exists that series of things by which as many of them as possible exist; in other words, the maximal series of possibles . . . in the nature of the universe the series which has the greatest capacity exists. . . . The sufficient reason of God's choice [concerning what will and will not be permitted to exist] can be found only in the fitness or in the degrees of perfection that the several worlds possess.[8]

## 3. The Human World Becomes Hierarchical

Notions of the plenitude of being come to their fullest and most dangerous fruition in the Enlightenment philosophies of the eighteenth century. Immanuel Kant states:

Human nature occupies as it were the middle rung of the Scale of Being . . . equally removed from the two extremes. If the contemplation of the most sublime classes of rational creatures, which inhabit Jupiter or Saturn, arouses his envy and humiliates him with a sense of his own inferiority, he may again find contentment and satisfaction by turning his gaze upon those lower grades which, in the planets Venus and Mercury, are far below the perfection of human nature.[9]

What is curious about this passage is that it echoes very closely the theme of the famed treatise of Blaise Pascal, "The Misery of Man without God" in *Pensées Les Provinciales*.[10] Such discourses had grown popular at this time of scientific and philosophical categorizations as an attempt to resolve the problem of the ambiguous place of the human being in the vastness of the cosmos. They stem from concerns issuing from the troubling new boundlessness of the cosmos since Galileo Galilei and Isaac Newton and the challenges that boundlessness poses for certain knowledge in the natural sciences.[11] Pascal makes the vast continuity of being an occasion for a meditation upon the insignificance and undue arrogance of humankind and their puny cognitive powers. Caught in the midpoint of an infinite chain of realities so utterly beyond the capabilities of human reason, the frail human creature will never be capable of understanding fully any aspect of the world. Whether looking upon the smallest parts of simple things or gazing out at the vast horizons of the universe, human may believe themselves masters of the universe but their knowledge founders helplessly between the two extremes.

Kant's treatment of the question of the proper human place in the cosmos demonstrates the renewal of a wild *hybris* that proves more generally typical of Enlightenment philosophy than the humility of a Pascal. The vastness of the universe for Kant becomes the occasion to meditate upon human powers and to undercut human humility. He suggests that any allegation of the inferiority of the human species be answered with reflection on human abilities. The "lower grades" of being only exist, he implies, to illuminate human perfection.

Kant's aim is not merely to reserve superiority for the human species over other "possibles" across the vast distances of an infinite universe. He reveals himself as a pivotal spokesperson for European ethnocentrism and a precursor of colonial attitudes, when he asserts that truly fundamental differences separate the kinds *within the human world* as well. Kant states: "fundamental is the difference between the two races of men [black and white] and it appears to be as great in regard to mental capacities as in color."[12] Though Kant explains the differences between races as "fundamental" and more profound than the color of skins, he offers a sympathetic explanation for the original racial divergences within the species.

In *Concerning the Various Races of People*, Kant accounts for the emergence of the distinct racial divisions by indicating unique natural causes bearing upon each group according to their geographical location on the planet.[13] Blacks, he speculates, emerged because the African sun, blazing upon their originally white skin for centuries, tanned it that darker color.

The superiority complex of white European civilization spans the continent and the English Channel. David Hume, one of the most important of English philosophers, marks whites as utterly distinct from all other races; he states of the Africans: "I am apt to suspect the negroes, and in general all the other species of men (for there are four or five different kinds) to be naturally inferior to whites. There never was a civilized nation of any complexion than white."[14]

The Enlightenment represents the culmination of Descartes' elevation of the rational mind over fleshy bodies and the planet. It composes a period when the leading philosophers seek to make reason the absolute ruler of human life. So assured are Enlightenment thinkers of the magnificent possibilities of the human mind that they think reason can be counted upon to shed the light of knowledge upon anything it encounters. Philosophical mappings of the great chain of being, then, offer a double benefit to the European thinkers of the era. The chain itself could be rallied to prove the intellectual prowess of the species over all but the most heavenly beings. But the positing of some human groups as more advanced along the chain than others permit those winners in the ontological race to imagine themselves teetering on perfection. The European philosophies of the Enlightenment era culminate in the overblown nationalisms that eventually culminate in the ontological fantasies of an Adolph Hitler, and they fan an ethnocentric pride that overflows from Europe across the globe in imperialist violences.

The Enlightenment mission to trace the great chain of being and to plot human societies along its length finds its most blatant expression in the phenomenology of Georg Wilhelm Friedrich Hegel. Hegel, like Kant, construes African blackness as proof of their mental inferiority. In his *Lectures on the Philosophy of World History*, Hegel states:

> The characteristic feature of the negroes is that their consciousness has not yet reached an awareness of any substantial objectivity—for example, of God or the law—in which the will of man could participate and in which he could become aware of his own being. The African, in his undifferentiated and concentrated unity, has not yet succeeded in making this distinction between himself as an individual and his essential universality, so that he knows nothing of an absolute being which is other and higher than his own self.[15]

Hegel's project in the philosophy of history is to explain the idea of history as the intervention of an unfolding and divine reason into the world. Through reason, humans come to know and ultimately transform their reality in an uninterrupted dialectical movement from thesis and antithesis, to a higher level synthesis, which at each stage implies not so much a resolution of the conflicting truths of subjects but the advent of a new conflict raised to a higher level of reality. Through the dialectics of contradictions resolving themselves only to arise anew, culture is born and moves toward perfection, unfolding organically.

For Hegel reality does not simply *have* a logical structure; it *is* logical structure unfolding into its excellence. Reason *is* history. For Hegel, one need only note the cultural differences in the world to witness reason unfolding into its differing historical moments. The world's various cultures mark the notches of development of an unfolding reason along the great chain of being. In Hegel, the Cartesian *cogito* becomes governor of the world, and since every governor needs its subordinates, the Africans serve nicely as the primal point of reason's initial moment of unfolding. Since Africans could not extend themselves sufficiently high up Hegel's great chain of being even to boast "an awareness of any substantial objectivity," they could be said to be "primitive," having no history, no culture, and no development. They had missed the evolutionary chain; they had no reason of any account. Africans have no history in the light of which they might make sense of new happenings, claims Hegel. For them, life cannot be understood or figured out; it is simply "a succession of contingent happenings and surprises."[16]

Hegel exemplifies the spirit of his times. The seventeenth century saw Europe in a state of intellectual revolution, spurred on by the example of Newtonian discoveries in science. Assured of the vast powers of the human mind, and certain of the superiority of their own cultural station on the great chain of reason, philosophers too forgot Socrates' warnings against arrogant pride. Civilization came to be understood, by philosopher and non-philosopher alike, as epitomized in white European culture. Without a doubt, philosophers served the cause of the slaughter and exploitation of African peoples. Though the ancient philosophers accounted themselves "physicians of the soul," healing the unhappiness of the sick psyche and ethically nursing it toward the "good life," European philosophers were deeply implicated in the wounding of the African *psyche*.[17]

## 4. Phenomenology Undercuts Hierarchy

The notion of a "great chain of being," which ultimately culminates in the Hegelian logic of reason's unfolding into lesser and greater forms of reasonable being, served well the colonial and empirical projects of our ethnocentric European forefathers. Given the philosophical climate of the colonial era, hardly surprising is the fact that we find philosophers such as Kant and Hegel speaking of the "lower grades" of being, and Claude Levi-Strauss employing the language of "savages" and "primitives" as easily as had the anthropologists and the colonial powers.[18] For the effects that this usage had upon its victims we may look to phenomenology's account of the lived experience.

Phenomenology gained in popularity after the Second World War because its investigations of being ceased to make claims of a certain absolute or scientific "truth" but, rather, sought to understand what subjects are thinking when they do the things—sometimes horrific, sometimes exemplary—that they do.

Once the world had witnessed the Nazi genocide and knew what violences could be justified by references to racial and cultural elevations, philosophers knew they had to rethink the very bases upon which rest their speculations about being and beings. Emil Fackenheim states: "The Holocaust is the rupture that ruptures philosophy."[19]

Phenomenologists begin to challenge Enlightenment assumptions that human knowledge can be certain and reliable, demonstrating that every subject, however advanced or limited in intelligence, believes its reality postulates to represent true real features of an objective world. Phenomenologists also dispute Western, liberal, existentialist definitions of human subjectivity as autonomous and radically free, and extend the meditation upon freedom to naïvely highlight the violences that may proceed from the greatly valued commodities of knowledge and freedom.[20]

Western philosophy betrayed the African segment of the human world, even as it betrayed the lofty ethical and humanitarian ideals upon which the art was originally founded. However, a curious fact of the early twentieth century is that, while the philosopher was off gazing at human others through the lens of hyper-rational theory, the turn of the twentieth-century European artist, was extending more sympathetic attentions to the "primitive art" flowing in from the colonies and finding its place in the Louvre. The artists of Europe provided the impetus that helped to turn public opinion around to the valuation of things African. Pablo Picasso, for one, fell in love with African art forms and their influence shows up in his cubist period work. African motifs are most clearly evident in his *Women of Avignon.*

Art historians may argue that appropriations of non-Western art were in line with the formalistic thinking that governed the art of the era as much as it governed philosophy, rather than any signal of an attempt to deal with political issues. However, the keen eye of the artist is undoubtedly able to cut through the ethnocentric hierarchizing propaganda as certainly as the best artists have always been opposed to the rule-bound sterility of the academy. The influence of African art on Pablo Picasso, Vincent Van Gogh, Amedeo Modigliani, Constantine Brancusi, Henri Matisse, and, by extension, on the cubists and the impressionists, has been grudgingly admitted by most specialists in modern art theory.[21] This influence demonstrates that, in art as in philosophy, there exists a tension between the Apollonian formality of the academy and Dionysian creative forces (witches, monsters, aboriginal works, and "primitive art"), which are key concepts in Friedrich Nietzsche's *Birth of Tragedy.*[22]

The lived experience of centuries of denigration and colonial politico-economic abuse effectively erased African subjectivities—*as African*, that is, tied to the land and each other in the multidimensionality of time. Erased is the sacredness of ancestral lands, erased the genealogical ties that bound tribes, and erased the narrative traditions that linked neighbors, clans, and families. Alienated by centuries of dislocation, extended family connections eroded, along with the ritual life that supported the weak and the aged. Gone are the slow-forged democratic ways distinctive to Africans.[23]

Extinguished is the existential security of a homespace where spiritual life opens into religion and philosophy. This explains why we witness a veritable philosophical silence from the continent over the colonial period.[24] Collapsed is the sacred village life where possessions, labor, new marriage promises, and ancient ancestral ties render a rich density of being to stand firm against the threatening flux of daily existence with its disconcerting flux and flow. Emmanuel Levinas tells that the responsibilities and bonds peculiar to the lived home space give birth to freedom as "a relation of life with an *other* that lodges it, and by which life is *at home with itself.*[25] With robust village life patterns effectively erased and traditions and sacred lands despoiled, mutual dependencies with environing others across the African continent were despoiled. The disappearance of those mutual dependencies, essential to the carving out of individual lives, eroded people's possibilities for "the sovereignty of enjoyment."[26]

In traditional African tribal life, Africans had well understood that individual freedom is a function of communal being, that identities harden in the social context of responsibility to the young, to the old, and to the ancestors. Colonial rule and its concomitant atrocities and exploitations, its "habitus of war," and its denigrating myths, had effectively cut off individual selves from mutual support systems with those environing others that could give subjectivity its social density and communal texture. The African subject has been robbed of the tribal and familial "samenesses" whose proximity carves out those differences that permit singularity of being, the "samenesses" so important for freedom, identity, and the unfolding of generosity and ethical life. The colonial era leaves the African subjects *not at home* with each other. Tsenay Serequeberhan affirms the condition of postcolonial subjects, with the striking statement: "African humanity is anxious and does not find itself at home."[27]

With the struggles for independence, the possibilities for free thought in Africa reopened. African spirituality and philosophy again, like a phoenix, took rise on the continent of Africa. At first it began almost apologetically, asking questions about African identity, and comparing African logical modes with Western philosophical models. Slowly African philosophers began reclaiming, from a variety of angles, the worth of African symbols and categories, and traditional understandings of society, ethics, embodiment, and mind. Africanist discourses began by redeeming African traditions, setting them free from the oppressive yoke of denigration and humiliation that bound them. The first Africanist philosophy and literature passionately expressed the importance of traditional thought systems and beliefs as unique and valuable contributions to the tapestry of human life.

Then philosophical discourse from Africa turned from descriptive and edifying treatise to self-critique, challenging traditional thought against non-African models. Nationalist and Pan-Africanist philosophies dared African thinkers to overcome their competing parochialisms. Philosophers, often themselves trained in the West, echoed Western challenges that African philosophy be more than simple cultural anthropology and become rigorous. Finally, in the last decade, African philosophy has come fully into its own and taken up its mission, unapologetically, forgoing new paths of self-understanding that challenge the past, question the present, and with self-confidence faces the future to define and take up specifically African modes of philosophizing.

# Notes

1. Plato, *Symposium* 210 & ff.; *Phaedrus* 242d & ff.
2. René Descartes, *Discourse on Method*, I. 3; *Meditations on First Philosophy*, III.
3. Wendy C. Hamblet, "The Disarming of Being: The Metaphysics of Benedict de Spinoza," *Prima Philosophia* (Cuxhaven & Dartford: Traude Junghans Verlag, January–March, 2001).
4. Hamblet, "Disarming."
5. David Hume, *A Treatise on Human Nature* (1739), IV, 5.
6. Spinoza states in *Ethics*: "Particular things are nothing else than modifications of attributes of God, or modes by which attributes of God are expressed in a certain and determined manner," A. Boyle, trans. (London, U.K.: J. M. Dent, 1925), Book I, Prop. XXI, Cor.
7. Spinoza. *Ethics*, Section V, Prop. XLII, n.1.
8. Gottfried Wilhelm Leibniz, *Monadology*, ed. Nicholas Rescher (Pittsburgh, Penn.: University of Pittsburgh Press, 1991), 54.
9. Immanuel Kant, *Allegemeine Naturgeschichte und Theorie des Himmels* (1755), 133, cited in Arthur O. Lovejoy, *The Great Chain of Being* (Cambridge: Harvard University Press, 1936), 193; see also Immanuel Kant, *Essay on Man*, First Epistle.
10. Blaise Pascal, *"Misère de l'Homme Sans Dieu"* in *Pensées Les Provinciales*, (Paris, France: Bookking International, 1995), Article II, 31–71 (translation mine).
11. See Martin Heidegger, "Modern Science, Metaphysics and Mathematics" in *Martin Heidegger: Basic Writings*, David Farrell Krell, ed. (New York: Harper and Row, 1977).
12. Cited in Tsenay Serequeberhan, *The Hermeneutics of African Philosophy* (New York: Routledge, 1994), 61.
13. Immanuel Kant, *Concerning the Various Races of People*, published as *Von der verschiedenen Rassen der Menschen* (Germany, 1775) as cited in A. Lovejoy, *The Great Chain of Being*, 194.
14. *Great Thinkers of the Western* World, Ian P. McGreal, ed. (New York: Harper Collins, 1992), 266. Hume quoted in Richard H. Popkin, "Hume's Racism," *The Philosophical Forum*, Vol. 9, nos. 2–3, 213.
15. G. W. F. Hegel, *Lectures on the Philosophy of World History: Introduction*, Hugh Barr Nisbet, trans. (Cambridge, U. K.: Cambridge University Press, 1989), 177.
16. Hegel, *World History*, 176.
17. See Martha Nussbaum, *The Therapy of Desire* (Princeton, N.J.: Princeton University Press, 1996), 13–47.
18. Claude Levi-Strauss, *Myth and Meaning: Cracking the Code of Culture* (New York: Schocken Books, 1995).
19. Emil Fackenheim, *To Mend the World: Foundations of Post-Holocaust Jewish Thought* (Bloomington, Ind.: Indiana University Press, 1994), 191, 200, 249–250.

20. See, for example, Emmanuel Levinas, "The Ego and the Totality" in *Collected Philosophical Papers*, A. Lingis, trans. (Dordrecht: Kluwer Academic Publishers, 1993), 25–46.

21. Charles Harrison and Paul Wood, *Art in Theory 1900–1990* (Oxford, U.K.: Blackwell, 1992), 62–121.

22. Friedrich Nietzsche, *The Birth of Tragedy and the Case of Wagner*, trans. Walter Kaufmann (New York: Vintage Books, 1966), BT 1–10.

23. E. Levinas, *Totality and Infinity*, A. Lingis, trans. (Pittsburgh, Penn.: Duquesne University Press, 1969), 152–174.

24. Cheikh Anta Diop, *Precolonial Black Africa*, Harold Salemson, trans. (New York: Lawrence Hill Books, 1987); *Civilization or Barbarism: An Authentic Anthropology*, Yaa-Lengi Meema Ngemi, trans. (New York: Lawrence Hill Books, 1991); Henry Olela, *An Introduction to the History of Philosophy: From Ancient Africa to Ancient Greece* (Atlanta, Ga.: Select Publishing, 1980).

25. E. Levinas, *Totality*, 165 (emphasis Levinas').

26. Levinas, *Totality*, 164.

27. Serequeberhan, *Hermeneutics*, 9.

# Chapter 10
# African Self-Identity
# after Colonialist Myth

Human beings are namers. We make sense of the confusing data of our worlds by placing names upon new things as they arise in our experiences. Names permit subjects to categorize things, to analyze, compare, and recognize them when they appear in our proximity once again. The ability to name the entities that form the furniture of human lifeworlds is crucial to people's mental health and to their ability to cope with the change and flux that always threaten on the horizons of the known.

## 1. A Phenomenology of Naming

A wealth of philosophical attention has been afforded to exposing the violence of naming. From Walter Benjamin to Emmanuel Levinas, naming is recognized as fundamentally appropriative in nature.[1] In a section of *Totality and Infinity* provocatively entitled "Element and Things, Implements," Levinas speaks of the way in which subjects, terrorized by the chaos of meaninglessness that threatens in the formlessness of the "elemental" in which beings are always already immersed, seek to carve out, through the "extraterritoriality" of the domicile, familiar territory where "sovereignty" can be accomplished.[2] The domicile offers escape from the meaningless chaos of existence. The domicile is constructed through the cognitive and representational acts of "knowing" and "naming."

In another important work, the essay "The Ego and the Totality," Levinas exposes the consumptive nature of these cognitive processes.[3] Introducing highly provocative terminology to emphasize his point, Levinas posits simplest everyday identifications and representations as "violational" acts. Cognition and representation compose the ways that merely "living" beings, to be distinguished from "thinking" beings, "consume" difference, although these acts of cognitive grasping are always perceived by the subject as "innocent." For Levinas, understanding and representing objects are not harmless descriptive enterprises, but they involve violent acts, drawing in proximate self-determinative aliens and denying their right to self-determine by imposing subjective meanings upon the objectified other. The alien, suffering this consumptive imposition, is no longer alien and no longer self-determinative. The alien becomes an aspect of the perceiver's subjectivity—*my* mother, *my* friend, *my* country. Order is wrenched from chaos and a sense of "worldliness" accomplished for subjects when they perceive and understand their objects, while these same subjective exercises rob aliens of their self-naming rights.

For Levinas, a living being is to be distinguished from the more ethically aware—"guilty" on Levinas' terms—"thinking being," not by overcoming subjective violence—since this is impossible—but by becoming aware of one's subjective effects upon others, by proceeding with the caution of one who is cognizant of the violence of subjective life. Most people think it an act of grace to take an interest in knowing their neighbors; Levinas insists that thinking beings admit that their connections with others, however beneficent, are not selfless acts of generosity; they always serve the "identity work" of the subject.

Knowing is a process appropriative of others. A subject, as a living being, thereby violates everyone and everything it touches, perhaps most especially its intimates—family, friends, and neighbors—as these are the ones in the alien proximate most taken for granted as *fully* known.[4] With those we love, it is our deepest wish, and often our strongest conviction, that we know them through and through. But, demonstrates Levinas, in the representative movement of "knowing" the other and assigning the other a meaning—my mother, my friend, my neighbor—the other is gathered up by a "side presented to me" and the infinite unknown beyond my meanings is denied to the object of my definitions.[5]

Others are infinite unknowables for Levinas because their meanings extend endlessly—into infinity—beyond the "sides" that provide the superficial knowledge that others can appropriate in cognition.[6] Subjective naming thus never does accomplish its desired end; the enterprise always ultimately represents a cognitive and representational failure. But it represents an ontological failure as well, because naming acts do not ensure a *firm world* for the subject; existence remains in flux. The acts, like naming, meaning to secure world from chaos, are appropriative and violational of proximate others. The metaphor of consumption may seem unduly and exaggeratedly negative, especially when applied to knowing and naming our loves and our neighbors and friends. But Levinas means to highlight the barren authoritarianism of the Western notion of the free and autonomous subject.

Levinas ultimately softens the severity of this metaphor when he opens room in the cognitive process for the object's escape from the appropriative grasp of the name. In emphasizing an "infinite depth" of meaning impenetrable by the subject's cognitive grasp, Levinas leaves room for the object's *self*-meaning beyond the "sides" appropriated by knowledge. In actuality, despite how hard subjects try to assign defining limits to objectified others, the others drift endlessly away into their own private worlds.[7]

Levinas, in his phenomenological account of the violence of naming, is addressing his critique to the violator—the namer. His object is to grant exposure to the violent nature of living being in the hope of opening the consciousness of Western subjects, often so relentlessly bent upon exercising their coveted freedoms that they endanger the freedom of others. Levinas' hyperbolizing discourse on merely living subjectivity is meant to make thoughtless subjects into "thinkers" who are hyper-sensitive to their potential for negligent totalization. This is not to suggest that, for Levinas, we can, once aware, choose to do otherwise. On the contrary, to live is to seek meaning, to seek to "know" the world. This explains why living being, though utterly violational in structure, remains, for Levinas, always "innocent" violence.[8]

The violence is inevitable and continues even across the threshold of awareness that opens living being into thinking being, apprised of its voracious ways. We cannot do otherwise but name and know and violate, but, in helping us to recognize the violence of our meaningful appropriations, Levinas hopes that we may become "guiltily" appropriative, rather than "innocently" so. For Levinas, feelings of guilt signify that one recognizes an ethical debt to the neighbor. That debt is the prime relation of all human beings. The god dictated, in a time before time, that each person is the "brother's keeper." Perhaps if we become adequately guilty in this way, the violences we cause by taking other people for granted, though never fully avoidable, can be minimized or at least executed under apology.

As much as the philosophical treatments of naming, by Levinas and many other postmodern philosophers, have proven valuable and effective in exposing the violences at work in cognitive processes, they have only exposed what we might call a universal and inevitable violence, a mutual situation that holds generally as a relation among all living beings. These accounts allow that the violent world of human relations still manages a kind of just balance among mutual offenders enacting mutual appropriations, since we all know and name and mutually violate, especially in our most benign and loving encounters.

I fear that the victimization is trivialized with Levinas' optimistic insistence on the ultimate escape of the appropriated other into the unbounded depths of self-definition beyond the sides grasped by the knowing subject. We could even say that the fact that the sides are self-presented implies the object's advance permission to the appropriation.[9] This failure to capture a robust sense of the profound depths to which the subject's violational processes can reach into, and impose upon, the well-being of proximate others—the utter cannibalism of some subjects—obliges my regret that current philosophical accounts of identifying processes, valuable as far as they go, still fall far short of their ethical mark.

In the reality of actual human relations, within the infinitely complex webs of worldly power relations that describe a person's limits and possibilities, the most profound and violent appropriations hold between the dominant and the oppressed. The identifying and representing processes through which the dominant lay claim to the subordinate tend not to be mutually balanced but to be unilateral and coercive. Moreover, in the most extreme of these worst cases, once the unilateral appropriation is accomplished, all hope of escape is terminated. Then the appropriative maneuver can take a fatal reverse turn and the dominant subject's denigrating namings may become self-fulfilling prophecies whereby the victim appropriated not only endorses the abuses suffered as justified and inevitable. The victim may, for a time, take on the characteristics assigned in the dominant discourses.

The most voracious subjective consumptions result in a most profoundly effective tyranny, a tyranny that reaches into its objects and reconstructs their subjectivity. People can be victimized in such radically intrusive ways that they come to see themselves as guilty—and the tyrants as justified—in levying the horrifying crimes they suffer. Clear and distinct identifications compose the fundamental and primary implement without which the violences of inquisitions, crusades, enslavement, colonization, conversion at gunpoint, and every form of ethnic purification cannot be accomplished. Identifications are utterly necessary for the accomplishment of every atrocity, from enslavement to genocide.

## 2. Phenomenology of the Named

According to Georg Wilhelm Friedrich Hegel, Friedrich Nietzsche, and Karl Marx, truths are temporal entities, coming to birth and passing away with the turn of consciousness that inevitably occurs over time. Bad things, as much as good, must pass away as inevitably as they have come into being. Oppressive systems, tyrannies, and colonial imperialist regimes are doomed to eventual collapse, however powerful they may be in their heyday. The most powerful social actors within the oppressive system confidently believe that, unless another external power enters their domain and drives them out, their reign over the powerless will be limitless. However, as the above philosophers of history have shown, the change in the guard comes about inevitably with the turn of consciousness within the system. The participants, the powerful and the disempowered, generally come to the eventual realization that the reigning reality postulates of their world are wearing thin and the political truths that hold the whole intact will soon collapse from within.

In the throes of the oppressive phase of oppressive systems, the myths that maintain the system may be utterly dense and opaque to all participants. One must wonder: what maintains the vigor of the system? How do a handful of mediocre clerks with unremarkable powers hold in their inferior hands the lifeblood of masses of people? In his wonderfully insightful little book, *The Colonizer and the Colonized*, Albert Memmi offers a compelling Marxist interpretation to explain the mystery of how the undistinguished few come to rule the sometimes remarkable many.[10] Applying to the problem of colonial oppressions Marx's insights regarding the nature of the forces that drive the marketplace, Memmi reinterprets the colonial regime as an arena entirely typical of general human modes of engagement. He highlights the ways in which both the powerful and the disempowered come to be altered over time by their membership in arenas of power.

Memmi contends that colonial systems are based upon injustices which cannot help but dehumanize all who participate in those abject situations. Since colonial privilege is the *raison d'être* of the colony and since privilege is never disconnected from affluence, the violences of colonial intrusion are primarily economic. As a Marxist, Memmi is also convinced that the economic dimension of existence is not extraneous to, but foundational of, the lifeworld. The injustices are many-sided and contaminate every level of the people's lives, extending far beyond the merely economic.

The importance of the politico-economic inequalities of an unjust system cannot be overstated. While remaining cognizant of this importance, the current project concerns itself with the profound and destructive effects of the social and *conceptual* hegemony that the ethnocentric Europeans exercised over the indigenous peoples. Economic hardships can be borne together and can even create a sense of community among the afflicted. The politically dominant can shift over time, without altering the day to day lives of the citizens under their thrall. But the daily insolences and open contempt, the deep humiliations must have gnawed daily at the victim populations, corroding steadily but certainly their sense of human dignity. The continual ill treatments must have broken their spirits as much as scarred their bodies.

The cruel colonial tactics for holding sway over masses of indigenous peoples altered the kinds of subjects the Africans had been, and predetermined the kinds of subjects they became. Their abjections set the limits of their future possibilities and established the existential burdens they would bear into those futures. At best, the indigenous were robbed of their sense of worth. At worst, they were programmed to become the kinds of people who had abused them and to repeat the violences they had suffered.

Primo Levi illuminates, in his descriptions of the Nazi death camps, that few can resist adopting the logic of the system in which they are immersed.[11] All systems have a profound influence, for good or for ill, upon the people under their thrall. Cruel and dehumanizing systems, systems dedicated to the utter suppression of the masses, have been shown to exercise a brutalizing effect on their victim populations, existentially shaping them after their own hardened and twisted forms. At Auschwitz, insists Levi, the good died soon after entry into the camp. Their moral character soon proved a hindrance to survival under those austere conditions. The rest of the populace became, by slow but steady undermining, morally eroded by the hunger, exhaustion, and hopelessness, militating in favor of the terrifying argument put forth by Georges Bataille that the identity of every victim is substantively equivalent to the victim's "enraged torturer."[12] Every oppressed person would, if possible, levy tortures upon the torturer.

Levi contends that in inhumane systems, all participants, albeit to varying degrees, grow to mirror the system that oppresses them. Each will eventually become degraded by the conditions of abjection to the point of stealing the shoes from living corpses, trading in comrades for extra rations, and vying for the coveted positions as local minions of the sadistic power that keeps them all in terror and abjection. Little by little distinctions between the victim and the executioner erode until all members of the sick society resemble each other, each sinking to the moral level of the lowest person in the shared culture of violence.

The colonial system, as the Nazi lager, was so deeply and fiendishly corrupt, it was enormously difficult for the oppressed to live normal healthy lives and maintain moral vigor. Under the constant threat of selection and the daily rations of humiliation, exhaustion, and hunger, the twisted pathologies and cruel methodologies of its power nodes eventually reached all the way down through the system, infecting the least of its members and inclining them all in turn to visit their frustrations upon those beneath them. This was the only available outlet for the fury evoked by the wanton cruelties of the system. Few who live under inhumane conditions can evade their disfiguring effects.

Not only the victims but the perpetrators grow increasingly affected by their immersion in oppressive systems. Memmi explains how the colonizers themselves, even those with nobler ideals who initially, at least theoretically, reject the inequities of the colonial system, find their noble ideals daily eroded by the brutalizing situation. They cannot escape the stark fact that their privilege depends upon, and is directly purchased by, the degradation of other peoples. Memmi is insistent that the powers in the colonial world are not blind to the cruel realities of their situation, despite the denigrating myths they spin to justify their cruelties. He holds that they can hardly avoid the brute fact of their own illegitimacy. As foreigners claiming to bring the benefits of civilization to underdeveloped peoples, the invaders are daily faced with the contradictions of their claims, contradictions punctuated by their overwhelming privilege beside the reality of the natives' wretchedness.

As the good died first in Auschwitz, those colonists burdened with conscience cannot long bear up under the weight of the colonial task. The sight of hungry and ragged children, the hopeless eyes of the impoverished are proof every day of the injustices of the system that affords their privilege. When dominance is purchased through violent conquest and continued by exploitation and oppression, perpetual brutalities are necessitated indefinitely. Order is maintained only by keeping the oppressed in a state of misery, ignorance, and dependence. The morally sound can hardly live with the tangible fruits of their privilege. They have to internalize mythical explanations for the cruel situation or they have to give up their pretense of moral soundness and admit their tyranny.

The few of strong character and conscience soon find the colonial situation unbearable, and return to the home country, refusing on moral principle the privileges the colony extends to them. The colonials that remain slip into a general malaise that comfortably blinds them to the miseries, the ignorance, and the deprivations their privilege afford to the indigenous. This, according to Memmi, soon leads to a situation where a relatively small contingent of mediocre people remains to rule the colony. Frustrated clerks who have little hope of distinguishing themselves in the more competitive arena of the home country climb the colonial ladder of success with greater swiftness and ease, once those of conscience abandon their colonial posts.

This situation immediately raises the question thus posed by Jean-Paul Sartre: "How can an elite of usurpers, aware of their mediocrity, establish their privileges?"[13] Oppressions become utterly necessary. A degraded base of humanity serves the purpose, as crucial to the justification of the privileges of the mediocre as to the continuance of the colony, of elevating the mediocre to the lofty heights they so desperately crave. The actual reasons for the oppression cannot be publicly disclosed as this would be self-defeating. Like most structural violences, purposes are concealed and mystified in a mythical veil. The repressive policies and the cruel conditions in which the indigenous are kept are recast as moral necessities without which the degenerate would fall back into their "savage" and "primitive" ways. Through these ever evolving cultural myths, the conqueror becomes the savior, saving the savages from their beastly, filthy, morally bankrupt ways. Material and social oppression becomes justified through conceptual oppression.

The colonial invaders offer as proof of their superiority the fact of their easy defeat of the indigenous. The easy conquest of simple societies is not so surprising. For Africans, as for ancient Greeks and for many simple island societies, to turn away a stranger in need is unthinkable. There exists a practice in many tribes that, if a baby is discovered on the boundary of the village, the child is considered to be a gift of a god. The baby is taken in and raised as one of their own. The newcomer is, in some social arenas, believed to be a reincarnation, one of the living-dead ancestors. The imperative of welcome to the newcomer is indicated in the Swahili word *mgeni*. This rich word means *all at once*—visitor, guest, foreigner, and stranger.

The African reaction to the arrival of the strange, foreign, white-skinned invader was likely one of curiosity and wonder. In some places there was bloody warfare before the European could establish rule on the continent. But, for the most part, European entry was peaceful. The African indigenous would have been predisposed to welcome newcomers with gifts of food and crafts. This common law of generosity to *wageni* (strangers, guests) is most certainly a social, if not divine, imperative. It remains such today in the greater part of Africa, despite the ravages of colonial violence upon traditional ways.

We can be sure that the open generosity of Africans was misinterpreted by the imperialists as a signal of good-natured foolishness. One might speculate a less generous secondary reaction to the European, once it became clear that the European visitor brought seizure of lands and scattering of peoples. One can imagine that resentment and resistance soon came to replace the original risky unqualified generosity traditionally extended to the stranger. Harsh lessons are quickly learned once the full effects of an unqualified welcome are witnessed: families and tribes, once contiguous, were dislocated; their traditional bonds in trade and intermarriage frustrated; the ancient land routes of the nomadic tribes were disrupted; "shared ownership" of lands within broad tribal constellations were swept away by foreign settlers.[14]

One fact that consistently amazes scholars of violence is that a comparably small locus of power is often able to control and manipulate masses of victim peoples and bend them to their will. Often a single person or a very diminutive group is able to hold sway over entire nations and to conscript not only the collaboration of common citizens, but even the willing cooperation of the targeted groups. Why the Jewish deportees, for example, filed peacefully into the trains destined for the death camps is inexplicable. Incomprehensible too is the fact that, in the famous videotapes of mass executions, condemned prisoners run feverishly from the wagons to their places in the execution lines at the summit of the mass graves where Nazi firing squads stand in wait for them. Similarly, onlookers can barely believe that Hutu mothers turned in their half-Tutsi children as "traitors" (by blood) to the cause of Hutu emancipation. Traditional analyses of violence cannot resolve these shocking paradoxes.

The paradox is further exacerbated by the prevailing notion of violence. Many people believe that atrocities compose anomalies that only occur when the normally healthy relations of human societies break down. Conflict is seen to represent a mere lapse in the otherwise benevolent relations people enjoy. Subjects find especially difficult the admission that violence is integral to their own family's or culture's or nation's ways of engaging with others. Only by objectifying and distancing the phenomenon of cruelty, expelling it outside of "natural" socio-cultural processes and human realities can we render our lives sensible and meaningful. Violence is rarely recognized, nor even suspected at the home site of identity.

Because of the prejudice afforded the home system, common persons, as much as social scientific scholars, often fail to acknowledge the most pervasive violence when it occurs in their own social contexts. Oppression is inherent in hierarchical systems *per se* but is difficult to recognize in one's own site of existence. It is the express function of hierarchical systems and their *modus operandi*. In order to maintain the power relations that typify hierarchical social structures, the system puts in place legitimate violences to impose and oversee the inequities that maintain rank and keep order among the citizens.

The notable exceptions to the more common hierarchical systems are the social structures typical of many simple indigenous societies. African systems, before colonization, were remarkably egalitarian. For this reason, they were also extraordinarily stable and decidedly democratic in structure. Tribes often lived for centuries alongside others, trading and intermarrying with each other with very little conflict. African precolonial systems, in many instances, were very low conflict sites. How could the traditional Africans have expected, given their customs and their cultural norms that some strangers would be unfriendly, and their methods of engagement bloody and oppressive?

The curious African native might have been inspired with awe at first sight of the swaggering Europeans, formidably armed with their modern weaponry, so ostentatious in their dress, so sophisticated in their cultured mannerisms, so powerfully arrogant in their mediocrity. Only a small leap of faith would position the African for the adoption of the white man's myths and then to an emulation of the customs and behaviors that won Europeans their abundant privileges. Once the colonial system was in place and the European lifestyle ceremoniously displayed, Africans could be easily convinced by the European invader's logic: Africans did live lowly and beastly existences in comparison with the haughty strangers.

Bruce Lincoln tells, in *Myth, Cosmos, and Society*, how, in ancient hierarchical cities in the Indo-European tradition, wars and raids were a seasonal occupation of the guardian class and one that bore rich booty in slaves and produce for the soldiers and the priestly rulers. The essential superiority of the powerful and violent were visibly manifest in material superiority, which convinced the commoners, living like paupers alongside them, that the gods had predestined the superior soldierly and priestly types for rule over the beastly and ignorant masses.[15]

The few Africans who enjoyed any degree of wealth or any minor honors among the indigenous soon joyfully adopted the ostentatious idiosyncrasies of the European conqueror. Speaking of the Jewish ranks of the Tunisian colonized, for example, Memmi explains:

> Their constant and very justifiable ambition is to escape from their colonized condition. . . . To that end they endeavor to resemble the colonizer in the frank hope that he may cease to consider them different from him. Hence their efforts to forget the past, to change collective habits, and their enthusiastic adoption of Western language, culture and customs.[16]

The adoptions included, of course, the arrogant manners, the flamboyant dress, the pretentious, affected ways, and, the stony glares and the open contempt at the abject poverty of their comrades in oppression. The adoption of the myths of the dominant socio-political forces can also be witnessed in the realm of cultural narratives circulated among the victim subgroups. Mineke Schipper tells that, in the Congo, for example, circulating among the natives was a myth explaining the visible political and technological superiority of the white man.[17]

The Congolese tell that, in the beginning of things, god the father had two sons, Manicongo and Zonga. He loved the two equally. But he decided to test them by sending them forth to do a task. He told them to rise early in the morning of the following day and to bathe in a nearby lake. Zonga, the youngest, was obedient and bright. He stayed up the whole of the night to be certain not to oversleep. At daybreak, he was at the lakeside, diving into the waters as he had been instructed. To his astonishment, once he entered the waters, his skin was transformed to a pure white as a signal that he had won the god's favor. The second brother, Manicongo, was not nearly so attentive to the direction of the god. He awoke later that morning, partook of a good meal, danced and made merry throughout the morning, and then took a nap.

When Manicongo eventually arrived at the lakeside, the waters were drying up. He tried to throw himself into the lake before it altogether disappeared, but he was far too late to fulfill the god's demand and swim in the receding waters. Only his palms and the bottoms of his feet were bathed in the purifying waters; he remained black and without the favor of the god. The god then praised his youngest son, rewarding him for his obedience to the task by letting him choose whatever he wanted from the father's riches. Zonga chose paper, pens, telescope, rifle, and gunpowder. That left little reward for the recalcitrant son. A few copper bracelets, sabers, a hoe, and bow and arrows were Manicongo's prizes. In the wisdom of the god, the two brothers were separated, Zonga crossing the ocean to become father of the white peoples, Manicongo remaining in Africa to father the African peoples.[18]

One might wonder at the way that victimized peoples readily accept declarations of their inferiority and adopt the negative "truths" of their oppressors. They may even revere the powerful and come to adopt the cruel behaviors that they themselves had previously suffered. Why do people who are maligned by powerful others fail to develop a "camaraderie of the oppressed?" Why, instead of banding together, do the downtrodden tend to envy and mirror the arrogant ways of their oppressors? The answer is simple. The more coercive the system, the more coercive the measures generated to monitor and control behavior among the subordinate masses. A repressive, coercive, hierarchical system creates an ethos that, before long, holds sway throughout the entire system, spawning analogous cruelties from the summit to the depths of the system.

Once the violence becomes institutionalized, it invades every arena of power relations, growing more overt and wanton here, more subtle and hidden there, but always and everywhere present. The brutality from above seeps down through the system, generating, in broad sweeps across the society from the privileged to the most oppressed, institutionalized processes of extracting favor, avoiding labor, and accessing goods and services. When violence becomes institutionalized, assumptions about the legitimacy of violence become generalized. Then violence can come to govern modes of interaction among the various strata of the society. Often highly developed, elaborate ideological and ontological postulations, and justifying myths, burgeon forth and circulate, and then fully developed ritual systems emerge to reinforce the new truths of the system. Emmanuel Eze explains:

> There is a zone charged with the energy of myth and utopia. But between the truths that myths in their fictional energy impose at the very depths of our being, and the more objective truths provided by scientific and philosophical analysis, it is the field of the imaginary representations that carries the heaviest weight in the determination of conduct and collective orientation. Thus when this "zone"—the zone of the social imaginary—is "distorted" or "diseased" and "inflamed," then, our actions and "knowledge" become systematically distorted as well.[19]

The mirroring we often witness in the oppressed is not an uncomplicated reflection of culturally significant phenomena. It is a complex and mottled affair, where phenomenal truth is confounded with mythical illusion. Little attention has been given, outside of autobiographical accounts, to the effects of the demonizing gesture. Little analysis has been afforded the effects of performative rituals of dominance and oppression. Whippings, beatings, rapes, and humiliations, in truly sickened oppressive societies, can become pervasive everyday practices, and since these cruel social rituals require explanation, denigrating myths mushroom forth to justify the sufferings of those individuals and subgroups who have been objectified and victimized. Murder leaves telltale corpses; beatings leave bodily scars. But demonizing myths have much deeper effects, and can persist even across the threshold of death, infecting the life-worlds of subsequent generations.

Myths tend toward reification and realization in denigrated peoples through a highly complex process of mirroring and assimilation. Objectified and demonized people absorb the negative representations assigned to them and can begin to experience and exhibit a self-loathing. People tend, under the influence of poor self-esteem, to abandon their traditional ethical codes, discard their customary social prescriptions, and abandon their moral identities. In the worst cases, people turn against their friends and families so convinced are they by the prevailing claims that people such as they are unworthy. Rwandan neighbors, for example, took their machetes and hunted down fellow villagers with whose lives their own had long been intertwined in deeply connected communities. Hutu mothers were known to turn in for execution their husbands, and even in rare cases their half-caste children, once they had been convinced that all Hutus were demonic. Once denigrating myths are spun, their mirroring and assimilation tend toward exponential increase even in the oppressed themselves.

All forms of knowledge arise in subjective context, as the phenomenal furniture of a social world; all knowledge arising in the context of this world is socially constructed. What is often missed is that the knowledge that forms social "fact" is socially *constructive* as well. New political and social subjects eventually emerge in response to pervading myths. People's thought worlds eventually incorporate fractures and resistances into their new identities. Victims emerge from the demonizing gesture as carefully self-crafted replicas of the truths communicated in cultural myths.

Abner Cohen, in *The Politics of Elite Culture*, explains:

> According to Marxist or conflict theory, the power mystique is a subtle, particularistic ideology developed by a privileged elite to validate and perpetuate their domination and thereby to support their own material interests. The cult consists of various techniques of mystification, implicit in philosophy, religion, art, drama, and lifestyle, to persuade the masses that it is only natural for this power elite to rule and this is in the best interests of the society as a whole.[20]

Cohen reaches this conclusion by extending the claim made by Karl Marx and Friedrich Engels in *The German Ideology*: "The ideas of the ruling classes are, in every epoch, the ruling ideas; that is, the class that is the dominant *material* force in society is at the same time its dominant *intellectual* force."[21]

Status in oppressive systems is justified and enforced through essentialist arguments of natural graduations in human being. Mobility among the strata of these societies is utterly impossible, so there tend to be great gnawing gaps, in rigorously hierarchical systems, between social worth and the living conditions afforded the haves and the have-nots. The ideology of "natural" gradations is further justified by its own visible effects. When one cannot protect one's family from arbitrary beatings, sexual violations, insults, and humiliations, this powerlessness tends to be so emasculating, so dehumanizing, that it creates, in the victims, at least for a time, the appearance of the very qualities they are purported to possess—cowardliness, apathy, resignation. These qualities confirm for the oppressors the rightness of their diagnosis of their victims, and suggest victim comfort with their abjection and acceptance of the justness of their fate.

The only outlet available to the downtrodden to express their humiliations and their frustrations is to adopt the violent ways of the systems under which they have suffered and to turn their own limited powers upon those beneath them on the social scale. Thus there tend to develop, within oppressive systems, patterns of arbitrary and capricious violence from the upper latitudes to the lowest. Wanton cruelties take on familiar forms at every depreciating level, throughout the full span of the system.

Once the indigenous are convinced, by the powerful ruling logic, that all social order is essentially hierarchical, once they accept that leadership is a specialization for which the foreign invaders are particularly suited, reasonable people will be prepared to enter enthusiastically into the social contract and to exchange their freedom of thought for acceptance in the group. They will surrender their civil liberties for the good of the whole society. When a leadership is not only respected and admired, but deeply feared, it is most natural for even the most oppressed to content themselves, at least for a time, with the position in society assigned to them. For a key example of this tendency, Cohen refers to the caste system in India, where people "are so content with the status assigned to them by the ideology that a low caste individual would not want to change to a higher caste. The society is so programmed by the blueprint of the *varna* that peace, tranquility and order are [understood to be] the blessing of all."[22]

Lincoln argues that propaganda in rigidly hierarchical systems posits governance of the community as the natural right of a "rational deliberative group" guided by transcendent realities and backed by a warrior class. This propaganda composes an ancient and persuasive ideological apparatus traditionally called upon to justify and support coercive regimes throughout the Indo-European world.[23] The priestly classes propagate such myths to justify their domination as a god-given right and an ethical necessity encoded in the fundamental structure of reality. Rigorously stratified, hierarchical regimes of this type have ruled great expanses of the human world since archaic times. They continue to hold sway even today in many modern societies.

African natives, as with so many victims of the onslaught of "civilization," fell easy prey to the persuasive logic of the systems that oppressed them. As foreign as this repressive, hierarchically-ordered type of political system was to traditional African politics, the foreigners who imported the cruel systems composed the governing political and moral voice. Alternative understandings of the human world were summarily dismissed as outdated, backward, and savage. John S. Mbiti laments:

> Modern change has brought many individuals in Africa into situations entirely unknown in traditional life or for which that life offers no relevant preparation. . . . [S]udden detachment from the land to which Africans are mystically bound, and the thrust into situations where corporate existence has no meanings, have produced dehumanized individuals in the mines, industries and cities. The change means that individuals are severed, cut off, pulled out and separated from corporate morality, customs and traditional solidarity. They have no firm roots any more. [Africans] are simply uprooted but not necessarily transplanted. They float in life like a cloud.[24]

The European conqueror, with the aid of an assembly of ethnocentric clerks, missionary bigots, and scientific and medical personnel, achieved changes in Africa and its peoples that have proven manifold and far-reaching. None of these changes reaches so far and deep as the myths whereby Europeans justified their presence in Africa. Exposing the falseness of denigrating myths, demonstrating their distance from historical and cultural fact, or revealing the functions that originally motivated their creation cannot undercut the power of the governing reality postulates to hold sway over cultural and psychic realities in victim populations.

Neo-Darwinist and Enlightenment discourses undergird European ethnocentrism which in turn undergirds the various discourses of the anthropologist, the colonist, the medical practitioner, and the religious missionary. Colonial, anthropological, religious, and medical myths slowly eroded African traditional systems and reconstructed proud, independent African societies into powerless, slavish, dependent societies. Little did the foreign myth-makers realize, as they embroidered their tales of superiority upon the African mind, that their embellishments of African vice, corruption, and disease might, under their powerful tutelage, become self-fulfilling prophecies. As Hannah Arendt attempts to illustrate, in her account of the political, discourse tends toward reification when it enters the public sphere.[25] Truth becomes powerful and takes on a life of its own once it enters the public sphere; denigrating discourse about exotic, seductive Africa and its formidable, degenerate black inhabitants grew powerful in African minds and reshaped the self-consciousness of the powerless and denigrated peoples of the continent.

Power begins with, and operates through, speaking subjects. Social identity in social hierarchies is fixed by superiors in the society, and individuals, especially those lower on the social scale, are not able to achieve individuating subjective status except in very local representations of the self, in family, clan, or tribal connections that may persist. The person remains indefinitely powerless, without political or social voice, in the larger arena of the social world. Docile bodies serve as appropriately obedient beasts of burden, agricultural utensils, mining tools, or robotic cogs in the military machine. As long as people feel powerless, their incapacity remains a self-fulfilling prophecy. However, once the

denigrating myths that have been applied to them take root in their own consciousness, those myths may awaken strange internal powers, dark and ancient
powers.

## 3. The Mythical Tide Turns

The most "docile bodies" can reach a grave enough pitch of frustration that seductive representations of deep dark inner powers can overtake their sense of
disempowerment. Sooner or later, the disparate and alienated tribes, split by
colonial invasion and anthropological descriptions, come to recognize their
powerlessness as resulting from their victimization by a tyrannical system. At
this time, the victim population grows increasingly capable of confronting the
dominant myths. Local webs of meanings arise to dissolve the denigrating fictions. The illusions of just and natural dominance are bared as cheap excuses for
tyranny. New leaders crop up to contest the imagery, new heroes exemplify traditional values, and new hopes arise that concomitantly raise the existential possibilities of the masses of the oppressed, possibilities that had not hitherto come
into view.

The initial period of postcolonial identity work for the African peoples remained fixed according to a romantic vision of a precolonial age, symbolic of
purity in contrast to a corrupted and destructive Europe. Identity work in the
devastated cultures was largely nostalgic and reactionary. Neither pristine
memories of a precolonial paradise nor rejection of the negative qualities of the
oppressor suffice to fill the void of healthy self-meaning or redeem the lost self-
esteem of the colonial victims. African peoples could not move toward an active, salubrious recreation of their cultural selves until they resolved the newfound crisis of absent or negative cultural meanings, and the corroded and denigrated self-identifications.

Abundant historical grounds may exist for belief in a synchronous African
identity. Plenty of evidence may be cited to demonstrate that Africans once
thought in similar ways, raised their families in similar ways, administered their
people in similar ways, shared fundamental notions about world, time, and
space, worshipped the same ancestral and divine entities in similar ways, and
coexisted, for the most part, according to equally peaceful and democratic traditions. But, post-independence, the differences that had so long been assigned to
them and that had so powerfully reified during the colonial period suddenly presented identity and security issues, even between contiguous groups that, during
the precolonial period, had shared common lands and customs, had intermarried
freely, and had well-established ties in trade.[26]

The vast diaspora of African peoples, on the African continent and spread
about the globe, yearned to identify with each other through a unifying "black
consciousness." But the basis of that commonality in the wake of the colonial
period was no longer clearly marked out. We find in the postcolonial era a

plethora of African tribes, nationalist groups, and pan-Africanist spokespersons all struggling differently with the question of identity.

The colonial era had torn apart a rich web of human connections. Recognizing the artificiality of mythically imposed definitions or the dialogical character of identity work does break the stranglehold of the powerful over the powerless. Nor do such recognitions aid in easing the iron grip of imposed and prejudicial characterizations once they have become accepted and reified in their victims. Unveiling the processes of identity work does not unmake the ethnicities formed from arbitrary identifications.

Once the stranglehold of external oppressions has been broken or has met a natural demise as in the case of the colonial withdrawal, there exists no guarantee that the peoples released from their grip will easily take up their places alongside each other in positive, neighborly relations, even if it had largely been the case that they had done so in a distant past. Often, as has been demonstrated, ethnic groups, fragmented, isolated, vulnerable, and detached, go on to seek self-definition through internal suppression of differences. They can continue to operate according to the logic of domination that they have come to understand. They attempt to re-empower themselves through external aggressions, rebounding the violences they have suffered. They can go on to seek self-determination in ways that are pathological and violent.

Cultural myths establish the parameters of the belonging. The symbolic messages of those myths can, and often do, have highly persuasive power across the boundaries of legitimate identity, insidiously creeping into social assumptions across the wide, diverse arena of the society. Even those who are directly victimized by the myths may join in their acceptance and their affirmation. This ability of the wildest myths to solicit support from all levels of society is counterintuitive, though it is indisputably a feature remarkably commonplace, especially in rigidly stratified and harsh social settings.

This is because the surface content of the myths is not the essential problem. The problem lies deeper, as Maurice Bloch has shown, in the *symbolic* content and the underlying *logic* that configures those mythical expressions.[27] Those deeper ideological and ontological messages remain diligently at work endorsing the status quo of power and reaffirming the system's violences as legitimate and necessary. Rituals (beatings, humiliations, expulsions, and murder of the alien) arise to articulate and purge the emotional energy aroused by the hidden but powerful messages evoked in the myths.

Cultural myths thus rearticulate legitimate patterns of social dependence. They reassert as rightful the relations of power that bind, in mutual interdependencies, the dominant to the powerless subpopulations. This process, in turn, anchors the ritual traditions and the socio-economico-political institutions that rank the population according to an order deemed grounded in "natural" distinctions of talent and worth. The system will dish out privilege and deny opportunity according to "naturally" just desserts. Myth is an essential ingredient in communal management. It allows the legitimate to be marked off from the illegitimate, the privileged from the common. The least member of the social order finds her rightful place in the system of the belonging, which protects her against the en-croachment of alien powers. For reason of this protection, the lowest parties on the social scale are often the strongest proponents of the system, as they feel most palpably the threatening fragility that the system keeps at bay. Myth is a system's way of maintaining the illusion that the prevailing might is right.

## 4. Ironies of African Identity Reconstruction

The sad irony of the African identity reconstructions ought not be missed. The precolonial African tribe was arguably the mode in which differences peacefully gathered in stable, meaningful unities of difference. Far from the rigid racial categorizations that Westerners have generally taken them to be, tribes are fluid categories linked to, and altering with, family connections, livelihood, geographical location, fluctuating allegiances among interwoven communities, and colonial occupation of African lands. New identities were created during the white European presence; for example, the "Coloreds" were invented in South Africa as whites and Khoisan mixed. In many parts of Africa, tribal names vary with changing economic status. KhoiKhoi pastoralists who lose their cattle would become a hunter-gatherer and take on the San identity. A San who gains cattle becomes a KhoiKhoi pastoralist.

Tribes are composed of fluctuating identity relations. Within any given tribe, there exists a vast dispersion of subdivisions, connected yet self-contained. Tribes are composed of clans. In some tribes, clans lived in separate sections of the land; in others, they are entirely intermingled. Subclans or "gates" that share common ancestors six to eight generations into the past provide localized arbitration of clan matters. The family composes the units within the gate and extends to include ten to a hundred members. A family sometimes includes several wives per husband. A further subdivision occurs in the household or the several households that form a village. The village counts houses, gardens, fields, cattle sheds and granaries, cows and other livestock, as well as the circle of huts occupied by those immediately related through blood and marriage.[28]

Kinship extends horizontally across all these many internal divisions, and vertically to include the departed ancestors of four to six generations back and the yet-to-arrive household members that have not yet been born. The tribe composes a chain of identity that offers many and simultaneous sites and levels whereupon selfhood is established. These sites and levels of identity are not hierarchical in any usual sense of the term, because not grounded upon differences in wealth but upon differences in age, the responsibilities that come with age, and upon wisdom demonstrated and prestige earned within the group. The chain of command is social, rather than individualistic, councils of elders and family bands, rather than monarchs and tyrants.

The welfare of each individual within the social group is guaranteed by the concentric webs of responsible overseers. The traditional African tribe composes a colorful tapestry of human life, certainly not without the usual tensions and complexities ever attendant upon human interaction, but hardly the discrete entities of anthropological creation and colonial myth. The alien invaders levied a great injustice upon the African peoples when they labored to corrode, through myths of inferiorization, the complex and integral interwovenness of the African world.

Despite the grim consequences of colonial naming enterprises on African subjectivities, Africanists believe the damages to be surmountable with focused and protracted identity work. Recapture of lost histories, suppressed cultural practices, and self-naming practices is seen as achievable by many Africans. Independence will ultimately allow the denigrated peoples of Africa the "turning of consciousness" that permits the mythical illusions of natural dominance to be bared as just that—illusional and mythical.

When consciousness opens, then local webs of meanings will be able to arise and overtake and dissolve the webs of significance that previously held the cruel systems in sway. Mbiti expresses this as a hope: "On the surface tribal solidarity is disrupted but beneath lies the subconscious mind of the traditional *Zamani*. Nationhood scratches [only] on the surface, it is the conscious mind of modern Africa. But the subconscious of tribal life is only dormant, not dead."[29] The myths that, a year or generation earlier, justified all aspects of the politico-socio-economic arrangements even to those most oppressed within the system, will suddenly glare forth as injustice. Then local self-representations will grow strong enough to challenge the oppressors' truths.

For the Africans, the oppressions were long-lived and the damages are deep. It may well take a great while before they can break entirely free of the conceptual tyranny imposed upon them, and before they can finally recognize that the denigrating myths of the colonists were mere cultural constructions. When they see the colonial systems and the truth postulates that justified them as mere apparatuses of degradation, their collective consciousness effectively turns toward independence and the ousting of the foreign invader.

This is not to say that once the yoke of oppression is lifted and the victim populations freed, the victims are immediately released from the influence of the oppressor. Regimes of power and their methodologies and practices live on in social assumptions, codes of behavior, systematic practices, and structural traditions of the society long after the oppressor has been vanquished.

Traditional models of power relations within social groups tended to adhere to a top-down structure, a hierarchical patterning of relations. A powerful leader or sovereign coerces the lower echelons of power who, in turn, oppress those below them on the power scale. Those at the foot of the social ladder have no social inferiors; so they tend to victimize each other, an abject criminal class that feeds upon itself and bleeds forth in and out of the criminal justice system.

More refined models for the understanding of how power functions apply a center-periphery model. According to this model, central powers, on the basis of morally significant social meanings, define, through internal processes of differentiation, those beings who belong as legitimate citizens and those who fall to the margins. This model, however, is an oversimplified representation of how power relations work within a social arena. Institutional power does exist as a center-peripheral or top-down force within social structures. The power exercised by power nodes is important, not simply for its external coercive influence. That power is important precisely because it captures the cultural imagination of the group and controls the internal forces that are rooted in and that compose the complex meaning systems that dictate social obligation and self-understanding.

Traditional models for understanding systematic power relations ignore the complex interconnectedness of the human world, and the importance of the historical in shaping understandings of self and world and in establishing the ideals which guide everyday thought and behavior patterns in individuals and cultural groups. Individuals and cultures are always already defined by their relations within larger identity structures, and are always already embedded within power systems that monitor and dictate the forms in which they are mutually rooted. Power relations operate and replicate their forms, precisely because locating and rationally confronting the truths upon which the systems rests proves virtually impossible.

It is almost unattainable to step outside one's home system of thought—one's "common mental world" in Walter Burkert's terms—to gain a healthier perspective upon its truths.[30] Cultural coexistents, at every level, share the myths of the system, but in ways peculiar to their differentiated positions within the system. All members of the social group, from its privileged to its marginal, share a certain trust that the inequalities of the system exist for the sake of the collective good. They absorb these myths, understand them, and apply their hidden ideological and ontological messages in individual and sub-culturally specific ways.

People become infected with the logic of their systems, and that logic can orient their modes of being-in-the-world long after they have achieved their freedom from oppression. The patterns of behavior, the methodologies of power, the violence-legitimating ideologies, and the ontological assumptions of natural gradations in human being can remain as living instruments that orient the logic and cultivate the *ethoi* of the newly independent nations.

Freedom is celebrated. New myths—counter-myths to the denigrating historical discourses of colonial voices—will burgeon forth to offer counter-truths to militate against previous colonial truths and to demonize colonial mythologizers. New counter-myths will crop up to illuminate the evils of colonial enterprise and to name as evil the European conqueror. In the short run of history, counter-myths will replay the recent history of violences, by turning the naming upon the namers. In time, naming practices will escape the reactive phase, and begin to create anew. They will nostalgize and reclaim the long-forgotten past of traditional life and even perhaps help to broaden the people's vision to a unified "African" family.

In people whose subjectivities have been reshaped by the violence of repressive systems, violence comes to serve as a functional aspect of their lives, and will continue to be employed under new historical circumstances. They may continue to be used across socio-economic and political boundaries, and infect the newly independent nations. This may linger as open practice, or as a proneness to future violence to be reenacted when people feel powerless or threatened or when other means of social intercourse break down. The violences people have suffered under past regimes will rebound in new violences against each other and against new perceived enemies in the post-oppressive lifeworld.

The violence enacted upon indigenous peoples by their civilized conquerors was not socially muted, not conceptually subtle. It was a starkly brutalizing fact of everyday existence. Without a doubt, those violences suffered were the cause of myriad pathologizing effects for the victims. Violence invades a people's self-consciousness and erodes their adaptive social rituals till it becomes a way of life that is difficult indeed to throw off. The greatest damage that cultural violences cause is the victim people's loss of their meaningful lifeworlds where subjects have been robbed of their subjectivity.

Constructs of identity are absolutely essential to conceptualization of resistance and processes of socio-political reconstruction. Revolution may free the oppressed from the yoke of their material miseries; revolutionary identity is however an unfolding phenomenon that only very slowly breaks free of the violent past to take on adequate cohesiveness to compose a social force. Generations may be required before that force grows strong enough to heal the wounded self-images of denigrated peoples. In the earliest stages of the reconstructive process, identity work is much like story-telling. Subjects must begin with the oppressor's truth, then progress to a dialectical encounter with that truth.

This stage composes an often violent self-othering where the faults of the oppressor are hyperbolized and the self is reconstructed in a negative dialectic, in contradistinction from this monstrous other. Only very slowly can the psychically wounded move on to less negative and polar conceptual ground where they may find themselves in positive characteristics according to ideals and goals free from the stigma of past violences, free to carve out healthy homes and reconfigure friendly relations alongside their neighboring others.

Rarely do the psychically healthy feel the need to console themselves with swaggering confirmations of their worth. Rarely must they pamper their egos with overtly aggressive demonstrations of their power, violent identity work. Rarely do the strong have difficulty existing alongside strong neighbors; they value their enemies as their friends and slights roll off their backs like water. As Nietzsche has shown, when the powerful are fully secure and self-confident, they risk becoming too generous of heart, too compassionate toward their "inferiors." At this point, for Nietzsche, the strong have passed over into the "decadent" and "sickly" stage of their power, even as Hegel's master grows soft and dependent upon his slave to complete the simplest of his daily activities.[31] Nietzsche states:

the noble man lives in trust and openness with himself . . . incapable of taking one's enemies, one's accidents, even one's misdeeds seriously for very long . . .

no memory for insults and vile actions done him. . . unable to forgive simply because he—forgot. Such a man shakes off with a *single* shrug many vermin that eat into others; here alone genuine love of one's enemies is possible.[32]

The strong in character are rarely troubled by the terrors and suspicions, the pettinesses and jealousies that plague the fear-ridden, abused, and neglected. Once people establish a sense of powerful self and the self-confidence to face the neighbor squarely, their relations in the human world can take a healthier turn. But years, decades, and lifetimes may pass before individuals convinced of their inferiority can regain their sense of worth. And it can take generations for cultures whose traditions and customs have been degraded, abandoned, and forgotten to carve out wholesome self-images and find their way to salubrious modes of coexistence once again. Decades may pass before oppressive systems are able to reconstruct and humanize their institutions, and decades more may be required for people, brutalized and humiliated, to act out their pains and terrors and find themselves again as valuable individuals within creditable social groups taking their rightful places within a human world.

# Notes

1. Walter Benjamin, *Selected Readings*, Marcus Bullock and Michael W. Jennings, eds. (Cambridge, Mass.: Harvard University Press, 1996), Volume 1, 62–74; 82-86.

2. Emmanuel Levinas, "Enjoyment and Representation" in *Collected Philosophical Papers*, A. Lingis, trans. (Dordrecht: Kluwer Academic Publishers, 1993), 130–34.

3. Levinas, "The Ego and the Totality" in *Collected Papers*, 25–46.

4. Levinas, "Enjoyment and Representation" in *Collected Papers*, 25–46.

5. Levinas, "Enjoyment," 131–132.

6. Levinas, *Totality and Infinity*, A. Lingis, trans. (Pittsburgh, Penn.: Duquesne University Press, 1969), 134.

7. Levinas, *Otherwise Than Being or Beyond Essenc*, A. Lingis, trans. (Dordrecht: Kluwer Academic Publishers, 1991), 131–132.

8. Levinas, *Totality*, 134.

9. Levinas, *Totality*, 131.

10. Albert Memmi, *The Colonizer and the Colonized* (Boston: Beacon Press, 1991).

11. Primo Levi, *The Drowned and the Saved*, trans. Raymond Rosenthal (New York: Vintage Books, 1989), 38.

12. Georges Bataille, "Reflections on the Executioner and the Victim" in *Yale French Studies: Literature and the Ethical Question*, No. 79 (Yale University Press, 1991), 15–19.

13. Memmi, *Colonizer*, xxvi.

14. See Jean-Loup Amselle, *Mestizo Logics: Anthropology of Identity in Africa and Elsewhere*, V. Y. Mudimbe, ed., Claudia Royal, trans. (Stanford: Stanford University Press, 1998).

15. Bruce Lincoln, *Myth, Cosmos, and Society* (Cambridge: Cambridge University Press, 1986), 164 & ff.

16. Amselle, *Mestizo Logics*, 15.

17. M. Schipper, *Imagining Insiders: Africa and the Question of Belonging* (London: Cassell, 1999), 30–55.

18. Schipper, *Insiders*, 31–32.

19. E. Eze, *Postcolonial African Philosophy, A Critical Reader* (London: Blackwell, 1997), 8.

20. Abner Cohen, *The Politics of Elite Culture: Explorations in the Dramaturgy of Power in a Modern African Society* (Berkeley: University of California Press, 1981), 5.

21. Karl Marx, Friedrich Engels, *The German Ideology*, C. J. Arthur, ed. (London: Watts, 1970), 64.

22. Marx, Engels, *Ideology*, 6.

23. Lincoln, *Myth*, 153 & ff.

24. John S. Mbiti, *African Religions and Philosophy* (New York: Frederick A. Praeger, 1969), 219.

25. Hannah Arendt, *Between Past and Future: Eight Exercises in Political Thought* (New York: Penguin Books, 1977), 153–155.

26. See Jean-Loup Amselle's excellent treatment tracing how "chains" of connected societies were "disarticulated," especially nomadic herding groups (the Fulani, Bambara, Mandingo, Senufo, Minyanka, etc.), *Mestizo Logics: Anthropology of Identity in Africa and Elsewhere*, Claudia Royal, trans. (Stanford: Stanford University Press, 1998).

27. Maurice Bloch, *From Blessing to Violence: History and Ideology in the Circumcision Ritual of the Merina of Madagascar* (Cambridge: Cambridge University Press, 1986); see also *Prey into Hunter: The Politics of Religious Experience* (Cambridge: Cambridge University Press, 1992).

28. Mbiti, *African Religions*, 100 & ff.

29. Mbiti, *African Religions*, 222.

30. Walter Burkert, *Creation of the Sacred: Tracks of Biology in Early Religions* (Cambridge, Mass.: Harvard University Press, 1996), 24 & ff.

31. G. W. F. Hegel, *The Phenomenology of Spirit*, A. V. Miller, trans. (Oxford: Oxford University Press, 1979), B. IV. A, 111–119.

32. Friedrich Nietzsche, *On The Genealogy of Morals*, I, 2.

# Chapter 11
# Conflict of African and Colonial Identifications

Cultural understandings of self and world begin in childhood, long before culture is recognized or given definition. This fact explains the propensity in each of us for ethnocentrism, where that term denotes a narrowness of worldview in which one's own cultural group is ascribed a self-evident central position amid others. *Qua* central, one's own culture is assumed dominant, legitimate, and exemplary. The characteristics of the home group are valued positively over differences of other groups that are measured negatively against the dominant virtues.

Growing to understand who we are and what the world is generally involves gleaning information provided by experience and by example from the environing cultural milieu. This information, although gathered at first in the broadest strokes, is taken as truth about the world, and not as the viewpoint of an individual, as local eccentricity, or anomaly of taste. The correctness of the home view—its ways of intercourse and exchange, its mannerisms and codes of etiquette, its eccentricities and its singularities—is guaranteed in advance, while counterviews are discarded as deviant. Culture is the main mediating instrument of continuance for diverse individuals combined within a shared space. The bureaucratic structure of the home group, its symbolism and mythology, the peculiarities of its features, and its unique social practices give definition and identity to individuals and to the group *qua* totality; these factors render a sense of wholeness, permitting the security of a closed meaning system and an atmosphere of belonging.

Stability and integration describe the lived experience of the home cultural space in the experience of those who belong. Yet, if we could step outside the phenomenological viewpoint for a moment and assess the situation from a "scientific" analytic standpoint, we would see a gaping breach between the lived experience of the subject and a sociological consideration of cultural identity. Cultures are not closed meaning systems. They are not stable entities with fixed characteristics. Cultural identity, as individual identity, is constantly in flux. The factual chaos of everydayness is concealed from the subject's phenomenal sight and buried beyond the horizons of local meanings that give the comforting illusion of world.

Local meanings that render a sense of world are ever under reconstruction. The lifeworld is continuously on its way to order, but never fully arrives. This non-arrival, this continual postponement of order, results from the constant reformulation of the meaning parameters of the lifeworld in confrontation with new information: new data and new exemplars arise in the environment and raise paradoxes and contradictions with regard to the old schemata of meanings. As new phenomena appear, the truth parameters of the lifeworld are constantly tested and retested; then the reigning truths are adjusted to fit the new data and to accommodate the new information. The horizons of the lifeworld are in continuous re-creation in order that the illusion of stability and meaning can be maintained. Chaos is suppressed or banished to alien cultural soil.

A gesture of distancing and objectification gives comprehensibility to the strange other that suddenly erupts upon the horizon of the comfortable subjective world. A mechanism of differentiation sorts the new data into already given meaning categories, categories already given within the ethnocentric, subject-centered lifeworld. This mechanism begins as a benign curiosity that genuinely desires to understand the infinite otherness of proximate beings. Inevitably, the conceptual grasp becomes thwarted in its quest for certain knowledge of the proximate unknown. When thwarted, the investigator feels disturbed and begins to exaggerate the malevolence and potency of the being alluding understanding. As unknowable otherness confronts the subject, the lifeworld is shaken to its very depths. The subject is forced to revert to the most archaic meaning-sorting "rituals" to reinstate order in the shattered lifeworld. Then, the investigative probe can "turn dark" and trigger a mechanism I name the "demonizing gesture."[1]

## 1. Western Hierarchical Identifications

Walter Burkert explains how the archaic, ritualized meaning-sorting mechanism came about and how it functions to make sense of chaotic social worlds.[2] Burkert, a classical philologist and anthropologist of religion and culture, combines historical and philological research with biological anthropology. This rich combination of methodologies and points of entry to the subject of human community produces remarkable results. Burkert had long held the classical Greek tradition to have utmost and profound importance for the intellectual and cultural development of the West. However, his investigations into classical thought ultimately caused him to conclude that the classical tradition is not an isolated cultural irruption unto itself but is permeated with symbols and practices from archaic epochs that may, he speculates, prove prehistoric in origin. These symbols and practices continued to exercise an irresistible hold over

Greek society well into the classical era, long after the cultural meaningfulness of those practices had vanished.

The sacrifice ritual is one such pervasive anomaly that Western anthropologists of violence believe lingered precariously across the Western lifeworld. This ritual continued to accompany festivals, seats of oracles, athletic games, cult gatherings and other mystery ceremonies, theater festivities, state ceremonies, and funeral services long after that ritual had any meaningful resonance with those events. The uncanny endurance of this ritual led Burkert to a second startling insight: rituals function in such a fashion that they do not require belief or understanding to remain operative and effective across vast expanses of time and changing historical circumstances.

The persistent and culturally unsupported functionality of myth can be explained by attending to the history of ritual in the Western tradition. Ritual comprises the preverbal medium of communication, more primitive and ancient than speech. According to Burkert, modern sorting mechanisms that give meaning to cultural lifeworlds even today are themselves archaic in origin, enduring in the forms of durable ontologies and ideologies that have been bequeathed by archaic rituals. In their original forms, archaic rituals transmitted, through enduring cultural performances of determined series of repeated actions, ontological and ideological messages that communicated to participants their rightful and necessary places and functions in the lifeworld.[3] Since those "messages" remain functional in the classical Greek world, and down into the modern lifeworld, looking to archaic ritual practices is crucial to the discovery of the kinds of functional messages that are being communicated to us and through us to our children.[4]

Burkert looks to the distant past of the species to the rich palette of ritual life in early hominoids, rituals that centered about life's most significant functions—hunting, warfare, and mating, the search for food, dispositions for fear or flight, aggressive display and sexual customs. Burkert is convinced that many of these early rituals have been bequeathed to modern humans, unaltered in ideological and ontological content across millennia of evolution. Burkert believes that the symbolic content, functional logic, and tone of seriousness have been transmitted from ancient murder rituals to modernity through an uninterrupted chain of tradition, a tradition of meaning-sorting mechanisms.[5]

All ritual tradition Burkert holds to consist of condensed, systematized information whose function is to keep ordered and finite the conceptual system of the participating community.[6] Ritual traditions employ strategies of negation, and class-inclusion and -exclusion to achieve this cognitive purpose. These strategies convey to and through bodies patterns and analogies of reality meanings that reduce the confusing data of life so that a simplified system of cultural meanings can orient the lifeworld. A reduction of complexity enables subjects who would otherwise feel vulnerable and powerless amid the infinite complexity of their environments to better function by supplying them with an ordered cognitive environment, a "common mental world."[7]

One very effective way sorting rituals achieve this reduction of complexity, according to Burkert's theory, is by positing dual meaning containers that allow

definitions and identities to hold true for people across the cultural landscape.[8]
Cognitive meaning-sorting containers classify and organize data into fundamental categories that are morally significant—good or bad, right or wrong, ours or
foreign, pure or impure, sacred or profane, friend or enemy. Where data or entities fall into the more positive categories, the truth horizons of the lifeworld,
momentarily confused by the foreign, are quickly and easily repaired. But where
new experiences or phenomena cannot be sorted out and understood, they fall
into more negative categories.[9]

From these various sortings, hierarchies are constructed and links of causality are forged so that reality is reduced to simple and general concepts—clear,
discrete, essentialized ideas—that bring sense and meaning to the individual life.
A radically over-simplified, polarized worldview is the result. No matter how
democratic Western political structures claim to be, how devoted to equal freedoms and rights Western leaders may claim to be, Western systems have, from
the advent of the Western state, remained rigidly hierarchical in nature, grossly
unequal in economic and political rights, and doggedly convinced of their systems' superiority in comparison with non-Western systems.

Burkert has demonstrated that a simplified, polarized worldview continues
to function most effectively as an orienting system in Western lifeworlds. Generally, a symbolic marker of highest meaning, an "ultimate signifier" (god,
chief, king, father) is placed at the summit of the hierarchy because this enables
the meaning system to resolve even the most thorny of human dilemmas. The
belief in a transcendental signifier permits the believer to leave to the god's infinite wisdom those troubling paradoxes of life; it provides legitimate leaders as
placeholders for the god to govern and bring to order human communities, and it
authorizes appropriate punishment strategies to contain those darker phenomena
that nag and gnaw at the horizons of the lifeworld.

Meaning-sorting rituals continue to prove functional in modern Western societies. They prove useful in justifying wars of aggression and inequitable distribution of goods within their societies and across the globe. The meaning systems that are employed by the dominant powers in Western states also prove
useful to those unfortunates who come to be confined to the horizons of the
lifeworld, since meaning systems can effectively help the oppressed as well to
make sense of the thornier issues of their lives. Who, more than the marginalized, more desperately need the system to give sense to their impoverished, abject existences? Who, more than the marginalized, need the promise of a godly
savior and a transcendent gift system to resolve the paradoxes of their lives: that
some humans are more human than other humans; that some values are not
valuable; that some histories are not truly histories; some cultures, though
steeped in tradition and millennia old, are not truly cultured.

Who, more than the wretched need a system that can sort out the mystery
that civilization involves the most oppressive domination, the most insecure
conditions, the most unjust distribution of goods and dignity? With meanings in
place, the beatings, the tearings apart of families, the cruel migrations of labor
work, the exploitation, the epidemics that ravage their families (for which they

themselves are somehow to blame)—all the misery and degradation, the absurdity and the suffering can be brought into moral equilibrium by positing a transcendent overseer, a god, to whom all must ultimately concede, and the promise of a transcendent gift system that balances the cosmic ledger in a final accounting.

Ritual's ordering processes convey and communicate the collective representations of a culture. These meanings are conveyed across each successive generation as the time-honored traditions of the society at large. Through ritualized meaning-sorting mechanisms, a common mental world of clear and distinct meanings has come to be shared by cultural groups in the West even across multicultural landscapes. Hierarchical patterns of social and political arrangements and unequal practices of provisioning remain constant across Western societies and demonstrate that the meaning systems that governed in militaristic societies millennia ago in the Western tradition remain operative and functional today.

Those rituals persist because rituals *per se* comprise "the very epitome of cultural learning," argues Burkert.[10] The fact is not merely that meaning-sorting rituals are self-reinforcing through the powers of repetition and resonance. The persistence of ritual messages in the West are attributed to the manner in which these rituals are made to resonate in the bodies of participants. Ritual learning, historically, involves the body. It involves the performance of repeated sequences of actions. Those actions, in the Western tradition, composed largely bloody and murderous performances. The violent ritual practices are etched into the young performers by the harshest forms of intimidation. Where memories are painful, humiliating, or anxiety-ridden, learning proves most indelible.[11]

Ancient ritual practices in the West centered about animal as well as human sacrifices, painful purgatorials, and excruciating physical mutilations. When the dominant teach the subgroups the "truths" of their world through whippings, beatings, rapes, humiliations, tortures, and murders, the learning is bound to be deep. Terror, humiliation, and pain are certain to leave indelible scars.

Western rituals of dominance, like these bloody events and practices, are most effective and instructive because they require full bodily participation and activate the full range of emotional responses. These cruel events tended to be practiced over and over, all down the pecking order of the society, from the highest echelons of power through to the bottom of the social heap, etched into each successive generation, of subgroup and dominant elite, a sense of the inviolability of the current traditions and the rightfulness of the current power nodes.

For Burkert, ritual's time-honored meaning-sorting mechanisms evolve and mushroom into the entire range of accepted truths that constitute the Western lifeworld. Ideological messages, ontological assumptions, denigrating myths and myths of legitimation, and the full array of ritual practices that evolve to convey and reinforce all of these are spawned mutually and become complexly entangled with each other. Whether these truths are accurate matters not in the least. They still function to provide a common and meaningful lifeworld for the social group. "Two sign systems, ritual and language, [come] to reinforce each other,"

Burkert explains, "to form the mental structures that determine the categories and the rules of life."[12]

Anthropologists of violence are convinced that the cruelest practices, from the most heinous physical tortures to the denigrating mythical fabrications that humiliate and undermine the identity of the oppressed, are embedded in Western cultural practices and narratives. Murder is altogether final. But in some ways murder is more kind than other oppressive practices because murder offers closure for the victim, an end to the humiliation and pain. Tortures alter bodies permanently, but psyches may remain intact. Denigrating myths may seem at a glance to be less cruel because less detrimental. But the social fact is that denigrating cultural myths eat most deeply into the person and spread across entire cultures. They often reconstruct the social realities of subjects and of subjected populations. Often the denigrating myths become self-fulfilling prophecies, as permanent as any scars, and more inescapable than death.

Myths are recorded and transferred across populations in rigorous and tangible practices, in rituals of domination and oppression, and in a society's stories, songs, and artistic images. Subjective identities form within the cultural confines of ritual and myth, and are expressed in the self-narratives of the subgroups. The myths spun by the dominant powers of Western societies to justify their oppressions of foreign others and to legitimate their dominance over foreign territories and peoples have become deeply embedded facts of Western identity that are glorified and nostalgized. Their violent methods often come to be accepted as appropriate within the oppressed population as well.

The subject, in the lived event of the moment, can rarely recognize that its culture, its narrative myths, and its social rituals are ethically absurd, and detrimental to the varieties of subjects under the thrall of these social realities. Rarely can a subject perceive and acknowledge that cultural narratives and practices have overwhelming influence upon the kind of person a subject becomes or what the subject believes and values. Identity is lived as active, spontaneous, autonomous, and radically ahistorical. The critical blindness of subjects to the institutionalized powers of socio-cultural and political realities occurs because the mobility and variability of self is not seen well from the inside of life's event. This forgetting is made possible because the passive, historical aspects of the lifeworld are, as it were, at the subject's back. Self comes into relief only in distinction with other individuals. Identity is nothing if not relation; it is relation between self and world, and between self and other selves, whether animate and inanimate, friend and foe, similar and alien.

Western notions of subjectivity understand individuals as radically isolated and free, as though the very subjectivity of Western subjects were of central import to the "human" drama. Phenomenological treatments, as those of Emmanuel Levinas, demonstrate that, in the West, a subject's freedom is lived as untouched by historical forces or by environmental and human influences. This living as though an island permits the subject a secondary freedom, a freedom from the concern of its effects upon others, a freedom from responsibility.[13]

Levinas works to illuminate and undermine the sense of empirical faultiness and moral gravity accorded Western notions of subjectivity. Only in those moments when subjects reflect upon existence thoughtfully and think self in relation to others, can they discover their truest selves, according to Levinas. A subject may live its freedom as an uncompromised and secure domicile set apart from the world, but, because the walls of that home space are composed of relations in the world, a subject never truly enjoys the isolated sanctuary it imagines itself to enjoy. Without essence, the subject is nothing if not radically inter-relational, formed in association with, and over against, who and what it is not.

## 2. African Phenomenological Identifications

Phenomenology works to illuminate the fact that, contrary to Western rationalist assumptions, the boundaries between self and alien are crucial to a subject's sense of identity. The boundaries that mark off difference render a sense of singular self, a clarified self-image and a distinguishable singularity, which issue in an illusion of stable identity, though in reality the self and all of its identifying boundaries are ever mobile, fluctuating, shifting, gaping, constantly in need of repair, and continually being challenged, altered, and manipulated by changes in the environing world.[14] A subject's "identity work" is a perpetual affair. The forces of self-production are highly developed in human beings, although the self-constructions are largely carried on behind the scene at the outer frontiers of self-awareness. The many and various alien forces that are drawn upon in the process of identity work are not readily recognizable as necessary and valuable contributors to the task by subjects within the Western worldview. Convinced as we are of our subjectivity as radically free and autonomous, we become caught up in the living experience of *self*-production and pursuit of our dreams and happiness, that otherness not only falls away as necessary to identity work, but looms on the horizon of that work as threatening to its completion.

The environing historical, and inter-relational forces responsible for the subject's sense of unique identity are much more deeply appreciated within the African worldview. For thousands of years before the colonial period, the bulk of African social and political forms remained naturally democratic and non-hierarchical in structure, according to African historians. Africans remained gathered into small tribal societies of pastoralists and hunter-gatherers, peacefully inter-trading and intermarrying with their neighbors. This long, stable, peaceful past is jarringly different from European history that, from the time of the first Western empire of the Greeks, tended to cultivate in people a military ethos and a love of more rigidly ordered community. The distinction between Western and African societal and political forms may be explained to a large degree by the fact that African societies did not reach the formidably overpopulated state that as a rule caused early Western city-states to erect grain silos, form standing armies to protect the stores, then employ those armies in proud displays of aggressive overflow upon their neighbors' territories. Rigidly strati-fied societies of peasants, military professionals, and priestly leaders separated by vast discrepancies in economic lot would very early have given rise to ques-tions about justice and unequal desert; from earliest times these questions would have been answered with references to family trees, to distinctions between good and lowly birth, and to divinely ordained political forms.

In Africa, however, people gathered in small kinship groups that tended to struggle with internal challenges, such as how to ensure fertility to mothers and the sacred soil, how to keep the fragile newborns alive, and how to feed the clan in times of drought. Thus small tribal societies developed ritual traditions that were more internally focused, practicing fertility rites, rites of passage, and rites of initiation into community service and responsible leadership. Having avoided the violent ritual traditions of war and the rigid social stratifications fed by booty, African societies (with the notable exception of a few oversized African kingdoms) remained free from the class paradoxes that gave rise to pretensions of birth and family bloodline. Instead, Africans tended to share a hearty recogni-tion of the value of communal identity, the importance of the social context to vigorous individual development, and an appreciation for the interwovenness of human life with the natural world.

## 3. A Clash of Identity Systems

Though identity is actually a gift from without, the Western experience of the radical (non-Western) other is rarely one of beneficent donor. Confrontation with the alien often is radically disconcerting to Western subjects. Perhaps this is because the Westerner remains in the thrall of the Hegelian dialectic, con-vinced by a myth of history as progress that implies that the most prosperous and technologically advanced peoples are also the most morally advanced. They believe that, because Western prosperity is sought by all human beings, Western civilization must be the best.

The dark underside of this ethnocentrism states that non-Westerners must be other-than-best, perhaps the worst. However humbly and benignly the alien presents itself, it represents to the culturally ignorant observer a discomfiting presence that is experienced as threatening. The more foreign to the subject's ways of being, the more intimidating and hostile otherness appears, menacing from beyond the borders of self, from the utter darkness beyond the horizons of "world." The stranger cannot be penetrated by cognition, difference cannot be made mine (my mother, my friend, my neighbor), so the strange looms menac-ingly before the ethnocentric observer and grows exaggerated, both in potency and malevolence.

This discomfiting situation calls forth a psychic defense mechanism com-mon in the West, a phenomenon that social scientists name "dehumanization." According to psychologists Viola W. Bernard, Perry Ottenberg, and Fritz Redl, dehumanization composes "a defense against painful or overwhelming emotions [that] entails a decrease in a person's sense of his own individuality and in his perception of the humanness of other people."[15] Ironies abound from this defensive mechanism. This force is most natural, and originally composes a positive and adaptive device in difficult and threatening situations. The device is a psychic mechanism designed to warn the subject of impending dangers in the environment. The mechanism has the maladaptive propensity of inserting itself into situations where danger does not lurk, functioning as an alienating force that wedges between people and alienates cultures. The psychological safety device can actually create dangerous situations where, under more temperate forces, camaraderie and coalition prove the most reasonable consequence.

Persons convinced of their own superiority may experience painful or overwhelming emotions when confronted by an unknown. Ethnocentrism assumes sameness is morally significant and imagines the other as exaggeratedly potent and malevolent, more demonic, less human, and more of an immanent threat than the alien actually is. The sense of being faced by a subhuman and threatening other, a monster, activates in the subject a counter-force to combat these crushing emotions; the intimidated subject can, under the effect of this delusion of monstrous presence, behave less humanly toward others. People generally assume that a person's humanity is measured by one's ability to emotionally connect with others, to be a feeling member of a human world where compassion and concern guide thoughts and actions. Where dehumanization is at work, the subject treats other humans inhumanely, thus becoming less of a social animal and more of a mere animal, a beast. Dehumanization is a double-edged sword that cuts into the humanity on both sides of its event.

A subject gains a sense of singular self, of unique identity, in confrontation with the alien. The ethnocentric subject, the arrogant Western subject, feels threatened by that confrontation. According to Western anthropology, people have developed cognitive and "re-present-ative" processes in order to organize confusing empirical data and impose a comforting sense of world where chaos has emerged. Polar oppositions function in service of this task. Negative impressions of others render positive impressions of self. The more we feel assured of the inferiority of the different on a scale of human being, the more we can feel superior, guaranteed of our own humanity, ironically at the very moment when our humaneness most falls into question.

Home sites of identity—self, family, culture, nation—compose internal and operative environments that manifest thought and action patterns dictated within shared universes of meanings through shared symbols and the logical connections between those symbols. These shared mental worlds give horizons of reality. In the Western tradition, with its military underpinnings in the Greeks and its ethnocentric illusions encoded in Western anthropology and Enlightenment philosophy, the shared mental world has grown more confrontational over time, more arrogant with power and prosperity. The polarizing mechanisms developed in the Western world to sort and order new phenomena in the field of empirical reality have grown increasingly negative and aggressive. Western dichotomizing gestures of inclusion and exclusion that sort the belonging and expel the non-belonging have gained an overblown sense of infallibility in the modern era. As a result, Western moralizations now assume greater moral authority than time-worn traditions of international law that have historically been called upon to guide global conduct.

Millennia ago, Plato established for the Western world that the rational is equivalent with the good.[16] This assumption logically demands the corollary that the senseless and irrational or incomprehensible are bad. Westerners have boasted superior civilization from Plato's time to the present day. That self-assurance has developed into a civilizational arrogance that has also spanned millennia, fulfilling itself in civilizing missions, in imperialistic ventures across the globe, and in shameless slaughters of others seen as less human.

The irony is clear: the one who sees the self as morally superior runs the greater risk of falling into the evil feared and condemned in others. History has proven that the dichotomizing gesture that names the neighbor monstrous and evil is likely to fulfill itself in the moral demise of the namer. The mechanism of dehumanization reveals more about the namer than about the object named. Our individual or cultural narratives of the alien expose the fears, insecurities, and weaknesses of the home site more than they expose the moral failings of others.

Albert Memmi has noted that the racist logic underpinning colonialist systems expresses this irony. Where a belief in the superiority of one's own race is cited to assure privilege and rights of domination over other peoples, the frequent consequence is that the best characters among the colonialist population cannot live with the absurdity of this claim, the oppressions that it seeks to justify, or the denigrating myths that keep the system logically afloat.[17] The impossibility of good people abiding by such absurdities, according to Memmi, leads to a situation where only small pools of mediocre clerks remain to run the colonies. The harshness these clerks displayed in managing the indigenous tells us more about the insecurities and weaknesses of character of the clerks than about any innate failing in those they oppressed.

Racism occurs when biological traits are called upon to define a human group, and then groups are ordered into a hierarchical scale of graduations labeled more or less natural.[18] These so-called natural traits are then employed to justify social, economic, and political inequalities. Differences constructed at the home site of identity (belonging/non-belonging, reasonable/irrational, good/evil) reveal nothing of the essential traits of the named. The racial other to the powerful colonial forces rarely emerges from the naming process as simply different but as different from the good and the belonging. The home site of identity generally being experienced as safe and loyal and pure, the other by virtue of the otherness is necessarily configured as unclean, unsafe, and treacherous.

When foreign systems of meaning do not meet with the logic of the home system, people often opt to the conclusion that the other system is irrational and meaningless. Westerners are wont to juxtapose myths with fact, truth, and reality, as though there were only one reality, one universe of meaning. We see our own reality constructions as truth and those that deviate from ours as clearly myth. This juxtaposition represents from the beginning a false dichotomy. Myths, from the inside of their lived experience compose and express the universe of facts that provide the reality postulates that configure worlds. They function as the "truth" horizons of the lifeworld for good or bad.

The universe is a moral universe for all folks. In the Western tradition, the universe is moral because it is rational. Since definitions of rationality are constructed at the home site of identity, only Western style, scientific, hyper-rational postulates are moral. The colonialist logic that claims Europeans are logical and rational while Africans are pre-logical and irrational fit neatly within the given system of meanings already long-standing in the Western tradition since the Greek ancestors of the Western world named all non-Greeks *barbaroi*. Westerners share a worldview that is essentially ethnocentric, militaristic, rationalistic, hierarchical, and governed by the scientific myth of progress. Enlightenment philosophers and Christian evangelist missionaries extend this cultural arrogance into a totalizing and hegemonic vision of a natural cosmic order under the directorship of a just and rational god unfolding a divine plan for cosmic justice through appointed Western leaders whose rightfulness to rule is signaled by their god-given wealth and their birthright as Westerners.

Precolonial African societies, for the most part, avoided the arrogance, ethnocentrism, and imperialism that developed in the West because their agricultural and pastoral methods dictated that populations would remain stable and there would be no need for territorial confrontations with neighboring peoples. Without competition as a decisive factor in their societies, they did not develop along the structural pattern of class hierarchies.

They tended toward the development of natural democracies, and stratifications in the group depended on distinctions of age and reputation for wisdom. People are understood to come to human fruition the more that they take up their rightful tasks and responsibilities toward others less powerful than they. African society developed in ways that are deeply egalitarian, in distinction to the radically hierarchical capitalist democracies of the West. The African worldview issues in a healthier, more responsible, and richer sense of self than individualistic Western liberal understandings. For the African, a person becomes a full human being only by becoming a full participant in the social world. This means taking on the responsibilities of caring for the young, the weak, the sick, and the elderly, as well as assuming the duties of home and village (pedagogy, defense, and material) and the ritual obligations to the living-dead (libations, genealogies, and care of the gravesites).

Every human being, even the dead, is understood to move from the full life of the *Sasa* toward the *Zamani* of the past, a spirit world where individual distinction is lost. This conception of time demonstrates that the family unit, not the individual, is of fundamental import in the African sense of world. Forgotten ancestors can grow malevolent when, retired from the active memory of the society, they lose their individual personalities. This belief supports the significance of family relations and suggests the need for a wealth of children, since a person's own continuance after death depends upon his family's fidelity to the rituals of remembrance. This latter cultural truth clearly plays into the hands of colonial oppressors who require an expanding workforce of cheap labor to support their privileged lifestyles. Colonial oppressions made life for the Africans more difficult every day, convincing them of the common sense of increased birthrates as replacement for the dead and failing family members. These practices promoted cultural myths of the beastly sexuality of the natives and of their absurd propensity to further impoverish themselves by having many children.

The African worldview envisions the "I" as emerging only within the "we" as the individual finds a place within the social world of rights and responsibilities. This worldview clashes at a fundamental logical level with the individualistic autonomous Western notion of subjectivity and with the Western view of the world as a collection of competing selves gathering according to social contracts to foster their self-serving passions. The foundational logic of the Western worldview clashes dramatically with the African. The self-understandings, the values that dictate attitudes, and the virtues governing appropriate behaviors within those clashing worldviews positioned the Africans from the start for exploitation, and the colonialist for tyrannical rule.

The European imaginary configured the African native as an inferior being to be subjugated and brought into the rational light of civilized being. Rarely did the colonists try to help the Africans along the road to any of civilization's benefits, not to political adeptness, nor economic prosperity, nor social well-being. The relationship was merely exploitative. Many African tribes prior to colonialism had never known subjugation; they had always been self-governing.[19] Many African nations had maintained exemplary democratic and egalitarian political institutions since ancient times, and yet their skills withered and eroded in the light of their mythologized incapacity for anything beyond sex and meaningless labors.[20] Rarely were Africans permitted the slightest hand in the running of the affairs of the colony. Subjugation and exploitation was the sole fate of Africans across the continent on the argument that they were essentially inferior, incapable of handling the challenging tasks demanded in modernized nations.

Differences within a cultural space are multifarious in nature but always, essentially, differences in power. The European invaders explained colonial differences in terms of superiorities and inferiorities in rationality and moral worth. The problem with the equation of the good and the rational is that the worst violence is generally fully rational—at least according to the agent's logic. Violent people are often highly adept at inventing reasons for their violences. Worse, violence in the hands of legitimate authorities is generally construed in advance by the dominant as much as by the oppressed of the society as legitimate violence. The logic is seductive. Often people who have suffered under that logic go forth from their abjection, applying the identical logic to order their private worlds. Children who are beaten often turn to physical punishments in rearing their own families. Beaten wives will turn to their children and assert their limited authority in cruel and violent ways. One of the greatest powers of violence is its ability to beget itself. But this power is no great mystery. It is entirely reasonable.

# Notes

1. Wendy C. Hamblet, *The Sacred Monstrous: A Reflection on Violence in Human Communities* (Lanham, Md.: Lexington Books, 2004), 45–60.

2. Walter Burkert, *Structure and History in Greek Myth and Ritual* (Berkeley: University of California Press, 1979); *Homo Necans: An Anthropology of Ancient Greek Sacrificial Ritual and Myth*, Peter Bing, trans. (Berkeley: University of California Press, 1983); *Creation of the Sacred: Tracks of Biology in Early Religions* (Cambridge, Mass.: Harvard University Press, 1996); *Savage Energies: Lessons of Myth and Ritual in Ancient Greece*, Peter Ling, trans. (Chicago: University of Chicago Press, 2001).

3. Burkert, *Creation*, 18–19.

4. See Hamblet, *Sacred Monstrous*, 7–30 for a full account of this tradition.

5. Burkert, *Creation*, 22.

6. Burkert, *Creation*, 22 & ff.

7. Burkert, *Creation*, 22 & ff.

8. Burkert, *Creation*, 27 & ff.

9. Burkert, *Creation*, 27 & ff.

10. Burkert, *Creation*, 29.

11. Burkert, *Creation*, 29.

12. Burkert, *Creation*, 29-30.

13. Emmanuel Levinas, "The Ego and the Totality" in *Collected Philosophical Papers*, Alfonso Lingis, trans. (Dordrecht: Kluwer Academic Publishers, 1993), 25-46.

14. Levinas, "Ego," 25–46.

15. Viola W. Bernard, Perry Ottenberg, and Fritz Redl, "Dehumanization" in *Sanctions for Evil*, Nevitt Sanford, Craig Comstock, eds. (San Francisco: Jossey-Bass, 1971), 102.

16. Plato, *Republic* 6.504e ff., cf. 6.505 & ff., 508b & ff., 7.517b & ff., 534b & ff.

17. Albert Memmi, *The Colonizer and the Colonized* (Boston: Beacon Press, 1967), 45–76.

18. Memmi, *Colonizer*, 45–76.

19. John S. Mbiti, *African Religions and Philosophy* (New York: Frederick A. Praeger, 1969), 27–29.

20. Chancellor Williams, *The Destruction of Black Civilization: Great Issues of a Race From 4500 B.C. to 2000 A.D.* (Chicago: Third World Press, 1987), 21, 26.

# Chapter 12
# Savage Is as Savage Does

During times of crisis, people find themselves cast adrift from the governing truths of their worlds. To reestablish self-definition and stabilize their cognitive worlds, they reinstate the distinctions that separate them from others. When their self-image comes under challenge, they restore their identity parameters and reaffirm their dominant myths in order to confirm who they are, and what unique qualities render them morally worthy and their unique existence necessary. The requisite "identity work" is accomplished in a great many instances by casting the group's ideal self-image over against the constructed image of a radical other—a non-belonging person or subgroup within the larger social group or perhaps an alien group neighboring to their own. We can be certain that we are *we* because we are not *they*.

Social constructions or myths concerning group identity are almost always morally significant, granting moral superiority to the home group to the moral disadvantage of the non-belonging. In order to achieve an "inside" of social belonging, every social group must have its outsiders. The outsiders provide the morally negative image beside which the group will construct its morally positive self-image. The distinction between insiders and outsiders may be fuzzier and less defined where the community is more peacefully oriented and does not perceive itself to be under threat. But, in times when crises occur and social disruption demands explanation, the outsiders suddenly come into relief as different and offer themselves up to the insiders as convenient scapegoats for explaining social disruption.

Historically, insiders and outsiders seem to matter less to people who live simply and securely. Only where societies feel themselves threatened do researchers note identity work that comes to expression in violent rituals of expulsion and exclusion. Many anthropologists of violence believe that, as long as communities remain small and self-sufficient—as a great many indigenous tribal populations did before they were colonized—those groups do not develop rituals of exclusion and countercultural rejection. Instead, as long as people do not feel threatened by neighboring forces, they tend to maintain religious beliefs that

posit the familial nature of the human world, and they tend to express those beliefs in social rituals that welcome neighbors and strangers as extended family.

When communities grow to overblown sizes, they tend to develop political
systems that are hierarchical in nature, and order comes to be maintained by
tighter social constraints and monopolization of violence by the rulers of the
system and their designated minions of coercion. With greater size and power,
the community begins to adjust its economics and politics; it begins to stockpile
its food produce and other resources, which in turn brings into necessity the
maintenance of a standing army to protect these stores. At this point in the evolution of communities, members begin to relate differently to each other; internal patterns of competition over resources and honors begin to split the
neighborly solidarity of the citizen ranks.

With these fundamental changes in social relations come changed attitudes
toward outside groups. People begin to see those groups living around them not
as friendly neighbors but as competitors for resources, including land that grows
scarce with internal competition. The community begins to prey upon the lands
and resources of their neighboring peoples now seen as malevolent outsiders;
they see as just and prudent the presentation of a strong image to the outside
world. Thus is the ideology of *Realpolitik* born! Strong leaders, large armies,
and forbidding weaponry become seen as crucial to the protection of the community's interests and for deterring encroachment by outsiders. War rituals
come into practice along with a more fevered nationalism, obsessions with domestic security, secret police, secrecy in internal affairs (in case the neighbors
are listening), and intelligence-gathering missions beyond the state borders.

These fundamental changes in the relations of insiders to insiders as well as
that of insiders to outsiders comes about only once the community has grown to
a very large size. This pattern of state evolution explains many of the historical
differences separating Western states from, say, African ones. The overpopulated lands of Europe tended to overflow in violent paroxysms upon each other
and eventually onto foreign lands like Africa and the New World, whereas the
indigenous folk who inhabited those worlds tended to still operate according to
an ethos of neighborly relations; they tended to welcome newcomers and travel-
ers as guests and visitors to their communities. Eli Sagan and Jared Diamond
write persuasively about the geographical, demographic, and economic forces
that ultimately drove European cultures to develop "guns, germs, and steel"
while the indigenous cultures remained peaceful agriculturalists who stayed put
on their lands and developed fertility rites instead of rituals of murder.[1]

Western colonialist and imperialist history leaves Western nations today in
control of the planet, politically, and economically. Western truth too reigns
supreme. Although that supremacy has been won largely through the power of
guns, germs, and steel, Western interpretations of historical, political, economic,
and philosophical truth hold privileged positions in the conflicting truths that
necessarily make up a human world. Western powers disseminate their interpretations of world across the planet, not simply as one interpretation among many,
nor as the best among conflicting truths. Western interpretation claims its own

truths as those of a civilized human world. From their position of privilege at the summit of global power and wealth, their truths are credited to be the only civilized truths; alternative viewpoints are named as inferior, uncivilized, and false. The bearers of these alternative viewpoints are similarly named inferior, uncivilized, and faulty of mind.

# 1. Savage Rituals

The naming of others as inferior, whether subhuman, savage, or uncivilized, is the legacy of an ethnocentric arrogance quasi-pervasive of the European world during the modern era. Inferiorizing others is a manifestation of the defensive mechanism that social scientists call "dehumanization." The mechanism of dehumanization is deployed to achieve a specific purpose: to raise oneself above others by inferiorizing them. The use of this psychological device then tends to reveal more about the subject employing the mechanism than about the object of denigration. This chapter investigates what the continued employment of the mechanism of dehumanization, over decades and centuries, reveals about the European rulers, settlers, anthropologists, evangelists, medics, and philosophers of the colonial period. I hope to disclose the psychological weaknesses that drive the politically powerful to dehumanize the powerless, already cowed by whip and gun. This disclosure is important not only for a clearer understanding of African history, but for an understanding of the forces that continue to drive global politics and to undermine possibilities for economic success and political freedom in the third world today.

Social scientists tell that dehumanization stems from fear. White Europeans understandably experienced feelings of grave peril in the face of strange new experiences—the dark and mysterious African and the beautiful but perilous lands of Africa. Fear of the unknown can be abated if one can study and come to understand the object and dispel its threatening mystery. Fearful feelings can frustrate this process and may not permit a fair rendering of the unknown. Fear colors the subject's perceptions and shapes the accepted knowledge of the feared.

Fear of the African continent, pronounced "dark" by earliest European explorers, prepared the colonial adventurers for an initial experience of the strange new land and its strange dark inhabitants as perplexing, frightening, and intimidating. The colonists felt endangered at finding themselves for the first time in a small minority, surrounded by vast numbers of physically and culturally different people who better understood how to survive the strange and intimidating environment. When people find themselves in a minority situation for the first time, they experience their differences keenly; they feel out of place and incongruous. Their identity comes into stark relief—as starkly jarringly discordant. People who have lived abroad from their homelands among radically different others for any length of time are familiar with the grating terror that grips people who find themselves overwhelmed by a vast sea of common otherness. The frightened minority almost invariably experience a phenomenon psychologists name "culture shock," a syndrome which represents a negative stage in the assessment of their situation, and one that that renders mere difference as disturbingly, horrifyingly different. The stranger feels swallowed up by the sea of differences and nostalgic for the familiar. Under culture shock, the most benign human differences can appear culturally and morally wanting.

The most robust psyches suffer a period of culture shock after an extended stay in a foreign land very different from their own. Stereotyping the features that characterize the menacing mass of difference, and constructing definitions that make sense of the strangers are typical reactions to the overwhelming feelings that accompany culture shock. Exaggerating the potency and malevolence of the strangers is another common reaction. The negative stage of culture shock often subsides uneventfully once the newcomers begin to understand their neighbors, learn the customs, and forge meaningful relationships that heal the cultural rift that renders them estranged. If one can make friends, learn the strangers' ways, and assimilate at least to some degree, the result is generally toleration and appreciation of cultural difference. People often find that the features found threatening in strangers are adaptive and comprehensible in the context of the human world in which they are lived. Human communities share many common features—common struggles, challenges, life dreams, values, joys and sorrows, triumphs and frustrations. People of very great cultural differences can locate satisfying points of connection and agree on a great many weighty things, when they make the effort to know each other.

Africans were from the beginning generally curious about the new white people who had entered their world. Lacking in the technology of sophisticated armaments, they proved rarely a true threat to the European arrivals on the continent. This lack mattered less in configuring European perceptions of the natives than did the colonial's perceptions of themselves and their situation. What mattered most was the colonials' perception of themselves—of being superior or inferior to the native population, of being self-confident or diffident, and of having or lacking feelings of moral certitude about their elitist existence in the colonies at the cost of great misery to the local populations. One explanation given for the wantonly abusive treatment of Africans by European invaders asserts that fear and feelings of being overwhelmed and unworthy of the challenge configured the colonials for strong arm tactics. Questions of self-worth caused the Europeans to experience the African people in an exaggerated way, their experience of the African peoples pessimistically embellished in proportion as the colonials felt threatened.

Albert Memmi believes that the colonists' fear in the face of the African natives stemmed from a general weakness of character and intellect on the part of the European intruder. The colonials, according to Memmi, were largely inferior or mediocre clerks escaping the more rigorous competitive arena of their homelands. Africa served well as a conveniently distant mat under which could be swept a multitude of European misfits, defectives, and mediocres.[2] The less competitive arena of African affairs provided ample opportunity for success to those who had not proven successful in the more challenging environment of the home country; Africa also provided a convenient stage upon which petty and frustrated individuals could avenge themselves upon the world and assert themselves as powerful. The clerks could feel superior and powerful by dehumanizing their social inferiors in the colonies.

Dehumanization is a simple adaptive procedure that hardens individuals for effective action where they might otherwise become paralyzed by fear and confusion, faced with something overwhelming and perhaps impossible to endure. In the lived experience of the mediocre colonial clerk, there was much that appeared as threatening, bewildering, and impossible to endure.[3] Much research by social scientists shows that perpetrators are often looking to empower themselves, elevate themselves above their own felt mediocrity, when they practice abuse of innocent others.

Memmi claims that European inferiority shaped colonial perceptions of the Africans and triggered the mechanism of dehumanization. Other specialists offer a different explanation of abusive behavior toward innocent victims. Some researchers theorize that innocence invites its own abuse. I do not find that blaming the victim is a compelling response to violence; nor is it helpful in understanding why perpetrators act as they do or why they often act conscience-free.[4] This theory offers interesting corollaries. Compelling evidence is beginning to emerge that suggests that perpetrators of violence do not simply suffer from feelings of inferiority. This evidence suggests that abusers most often suffer from superiority complexes that distort their sense of their own abusiveness on the assumption that their superiority grants them the moral privilege to act freely in relation to other people perceived of having lesser value.[5]

In *Evil: Inside Human Violence and Cruelty*, Roy F. Baumeister gives a powerful treatment of the causes of violent behaviors. He states: "Multiple studies with a variety of research methods found plenty of evidence of low self-esteem among the *victims* of bullies, but little or none among the bullies themselves."[6] Psychologist Dan Olweus, who spent years studying childhood bullies, confirms that there is no indication that bullies are hiding anxiety and insecurity under a tough exterior, as psychologists and psychiatrists have generally assumed to be the case.[7] Bullies seem to have an inflated idea of their worth. Evidence indicates that a substantial number of abusive people practice dehumanization of weaker people for the power trip of watching others cower and suffer.

Some among the colonizers were merely petty and resentful mediocres, but others felt deeply powerful in their elitist positions. Akin to the pitiless guards, doctors, and *kapos* of the Nazi lagers, the colonials practiced brutality simply because they found themselves in a position where they could do so without negative consequences. One is reminded of anthropologist Maurice Bloch's assertion that, among the Orokaiva "Pig People" of Papua, New Guinea, violent rituals culminate in aggressive displays and overt violences against neighboring tribes in proportion as the group feels powerful enough to succeed without reprisals.[8]

The fact that white European invaders could, in the name of civilization, seize foreign lands, and exploit, displace, and slaughter the inhabitants of those lands suggests that the notion of civilization has been misunderstood from its inception. Civilization does not signify cultural superiority or moral righteousness; it signifies nothing more than a greater abundance of guns, germs, and steel.

## 2. Genealogy of "Civilization"

Most people feel secure that the terms they employ in everyday discourse are meaningful and useful. Socrates' primary philosophical project resides in the attempt to draw to the attention of the Athenian population that the words they used and the definitions they assumed clear had broken free from their social anchors. The meanings of critical ethical terms—justice, beauty, goodness— had, with the inevitable alterations that transfigure all social realities over time, slipped from meaningful relevance with current social conditions. The terms of popular discourse lagged behind historical realities and had come to betray their original utility. Socrates urged the Athenians to take up their terms anew, to test the meaningfulness and functionality of the terms they take for granted, and question whether those terms continue to serve toward resolving current ethical dilemmas.

Civilization is a term that has been in use for millennia. Most people of the Western tradition assume they understand intimately what meanings have become attached to the word. Since much blood has been shed under the rubric of civilization, the philosophical challenge to test the meanings of our terms seems appropriate.

The term "civilization" has a lengthy history and there have existed the usual twists and turns in popular usage of the term. The term nevertheless is invariably taken as a positive concept: people consider it better to be civilized than not. The history of this prejudice can be traced to the intellectual roots of the Western world in a common bias shared among the ancient Greeks. The Greeks named themselves citizens (*politēs*) of Hellenic city-states (*poloi*) whereas all non-Greeks were named collectively barbarians (*barbaroi*).

Aristotle in the fourth century B.C.E. extends and explains this distinction. Aristotle insists that the *polis* (the Greek city-state) is more desirable than the *ethnos* (non-Greek ethnic community) because the *polis*, due to its solid and centralized structure, permits the effective communications across the city necessary to political activity among the citizenry.[9] Since human beings are political animals for Aristotle, any individual not part of a political community (*polis*) was less human, more animal, than Greek citizens. There exists good reason for Aristotle to broaden the Greek distinction between *politēs* and *barbaros* into the *polis/ethnos* distinction; Aristotle is himself an alien to the Greek peninsula. He is nevertheless a wellborn citizen of a privileged family from a complex and rich civilization on the mainland; Aristotle's father Nichomachus served as court physician to the king of Macedon.

The concept of civilization is, with the Greeks, couched in the notion of the active political life of human agents in a free society. The civilized are political rather than apolitical. The English term "civilization" has a common meaning-history. It hails from the Latin word *civitas* (a union of citizens, a state, or commonwealth). Cicero echoes the Greek prejudice for societies of the Greek style—centralized, hierarchical, and unified—when he distinguishes between civilized states and barbarous tribes. Cicero elevates the Roman-style state above the non-Roman by naming the Romans civilized.[10] At this point in the history of the term, civilization begins to signify something different from a community where there exists the possibility of citizen engagement in political activity, as was the tradition in ancient Athens. With the Romans, civilization is a term describing the state that enjoys a highly centralized political structure. The centralized state is civilized because it enjoys the leadership of a monarch or a Caesar who can impose power and the common rule of law over the entire stretch of the empire's territories.

Cicero's superior *civitates* follows the Aristotelian tradition in favoring the city of Rome and other cultural centers over the various loose groupings of ethnic populations sprawled about the extensive territories of the Roman Empire. Civilized people, for Cicero, means Roman citizens who dwell in urban regions of the empire, in the city—*civitas*; uncivilized folks denotes those who inhabit rural settings. The civilized are the "citified." The civilized are members of a tightly organized, firmly ruled city, in opposition to those country folk who live where power structures are kinship-based, in rural settings that have weaker political organization. That is, for Cicero and the Romans of his time, communities are deemed civilized to the extent that they are more rigidly ranked class societies where rights and prerogatives are unevenly distributed and top-down coercive power keeps the structure intact; communities are deemed uncivilized where they are less socially and politically stratified, more egalitarian and naturally democratic, and where power is structured according to kinship relations and order is maintained by councils of elders.

The designation civilized has implied, from the beginning of its use, a human community that is more evolved in its organization in the direction of a more rigid, more stable structure. That stability is purchased through the abandonment of individual freedom to the power of the king or priest, and to the monopolization of violence by authorized minions of state power. Order is a value held supreme since the ancient Western world, because through the order of civilization, the annoying cacophony of individual citizens exercising their individual freedoms is replaced by the single commanding voice of the power elite backed by the armies and the domestic police.

The central assumption that maintains order within the more civilized power structure is the belief that moral authority is identical with the politically strong. That belief abides in civilized communities across the vicissitudes of historical change because the belief satisfies, for powerful and powerless alike, a fundamental human need that is crucial to the formation of a powerful identity: the need to believe that we are distinct human beings and that our distinction has moral worth. Humans need to know that their existence has value because they add something of unique moral quality that stands out from the faceless human mass. Whether the civilization is Greek or Roman, whether the community is a tiny *polis* nestled in the hills or a gargantuan empire, all the members of the political structure, from the most powerful to the most oppressed, can find existential satisfaction by looking out from the familiar upon their strange neighbors and affirming: ours is better than theirs.

The distinctly Western preference for the ordered and highly structured over the loosely ordered and freely associated is a preference as old as Western civilization itself. The concomitant prejudice that explains the differences between the two organizational models as an evolutionary difference with moral implications composes a second prejudice as old as the Western world. In the most archaic tradition of the ancient Greeks, an integral and divine lawfulness is assumed to order all beings in time. The governing assumptions of the ancient Greek worldview affirm: one is better than more than one; simplicity is superior to multiplicity; plurality represents commonality, mediocrity, and an embarrassment of riches, without which the world is better off. According to this set of assumptions, the universe is a holistic, harmonious, single entity under a common rule of law imposed from within.

The ancient Greek worldview asserts the universe as one, coherent, cooperative, and purposeful *cosmos* instead of *chaos*. It declares that all things function according to a single divine underlying reason that steers them and guides them in harmonious relations in the direction of systematic development. Things evolve, moving in a reasonable and better direction over time. God or Nature (*Physis*) is good, healing, and orderly, from the breath of life (*pneuma*) that enlivens the individual body to the all-soul (*psyche pantos*) that "has care of all things un-souled (*apsychou*)."[11] Bodies naturally move toward their proper destinies, organically unfolding according to inner and appropriate ends (*teloi*). Acorns grow into oak trees and not swans, and they always become the best oak trees that they can possibly be, given the limits of the environing system in which they find themselves. In the ancient worldview, justice names the inner balance that guarantees the integrity of the thing and maintains each thing in harmonious relations with the whole field of the thing's being.[12]

The Greek assumption of the superiority of the rigidly stable and unchanging "one" over the complexity and annoying, embarrassing changeability of the "many" reaches its most explicit articulation in Plato's definition of justice as the organization of the messy multiplicity of parts under its natural ruler, reason. Plato names the highest excellences in his worldview "forms." Forms are stable, unchanging realities that exist eternal and ageless in the rhythms of the heavenly bodies and in the changeless minds of gods.[13] Aristotle and Plato both affirm that good things are stable. Human communities deserve to be preserved precisely to the extent that they provide a stable space where citizens may flourish, but Aristotle believes they deserve existence to the degree they persist unchanged.

Western philosophers have not stopped to question whether order and stability are appropriate goals for communities where human differences are to gather freely. Perhaps chaos names the healthy state of affairs when people are allowed to freely mix and yet remain their unique selves. Conflicting ideas and traditions and belief systems compose the inevitable reality of relations in a multicultural world. The existence of conflicting truths evidences a healthy society; it does not, in the minds of tolerant people, evidence the need for a resolution of the conflicted realities of the group, nor their assimilation into a single uniting truth.

From the emergence of the first cities, the civilized way of life has amounted to the suppression of differences within the social structure for the sake of rendering a unified and ordered whole. Solidarity in earliest states was achieved by installing a strong monarch or priest, backed by a powerful warrior class. In the quest for stability and sameness, a Leviathan is born. In tribal societies, relations among the so-called *barbaroi, ethnoi,* or uncivilized operate within kinship traditions of cohesion. There is no such thing as a crime against the state or against society; there are only crimes against human beings.[14] Tribal groups "consider that disputes between its members should be settled by arbitration."[15]

In contradiction with the prejudiced historical use of *civitas* that claims only the citified as "civilized," Eli Sagan asserts, in his *At the Dawn of Tyranny,* that civil peace prevails only in smaller populations no larger than a tribal group. Tyranny dawns in human societies when the group forms into a state. Arbitration of differences and negotiations between conflicted peoples cease to be settled in peaceful face-to-face conciliatory rituals. The state represents, in Sagan's account, a social group so distended that the possibility of negotiation and reconciliation between individual members of the group disappears. Overgrown societies develop centralized mechanisms of social control and strategies to ensure cohesion despite the internal contradictions of subgroup identities.[16] With the advent of the state, "an end [is put] to self-help in matters of punishment, compensation, and revenge."[17] This explains why Max Weber claims the state to assume a monopoly on legitimate force in any society.[18]

An inspection of the history of *civitas* serves to illuminate the ironic fact that, though people generally associate a full range of positive qualities with the term "civilized," those associations represent a faulty view of the reality of human civilizations. Civilization is a term that a social group or state attaches to itself once it has abandoned the more peaceful, democratic features typical of smaller, rural societies and assumed a monopoly on violence to order and stabilize itself and assure its longevity. Internally, minions of state power are put in place to apply the system's might and suppress the citizenry and keep them in their respective places of subordination. Armies and political magnates apply the power of the system externally to satisfy the territorial needs that are ever expanding with the state's growing population. Human sacrifice, war, and tyranny

arise with the advent of *civitas*, according to Sagan.[19] A mere gloss at recent
history serves to ratify Sagan's conclusions about the brutality of civilization.

## 3. Genealogy of "Savagery"

Our consideration of the ambiguities associated with the term civilized has compelling implications for those terms denoting civilization's opposite, uncivilized,
barbarous, or savage. Since the designation of civilized is, upon closer histori-
cized scrutiny, revealed to be a term by which members of rigidly stratified societies named themselves politically and morally superior to their rural
neighbors, the terms designating uncivilized prove equally ethnocentric. The
term "savage" is addressed to a human being "living somewhat like an animal in
an uncivilized, primitive way; a crude, boorish person; a person of extreme, unfeeling, and brutal cruelty; a barbarian."[20] The term is employed to describe
people who behave in less citified ways. "Savage" can be used as a verb to express the enactment of extreme acts of violence by persons less citified and
therefore less subjected to the rule of law.

Sagan demonstrates that citified persons are far more likely to practice violence against their countryfolk. States compose larger units of power whose first
distinguishing features include the monopolization of violence in the hands of
the powerful or their authorized minions. In states, we evidence the first examples of extreme intraspecies violence—human sacrifice, political tyranny, and
war. Although state authorities have a monopoly on violence, the everyday practices of members of communities tend in a short time to mirror the practices of
the powerful. People at the lowest levels of the societies soon take up the distinguishing features of the power nodes of the society into their own lives, enacting
ordering violences as righteous wherever they are the ones in power.

This mirroring is as true in family relations—parents ruling more harshly
over children, husbands over wives—as it is in the world of production—
masters lording their power over slaves, and managers over workers. People in
non-kinship groups tend in matters of moral responsibility to replace individual
struggles of conscience with robotic submission to laws and other state institutions of control, while societies built upon family relations tend to hold out
longer against state practices. The rigidly stratified state and its policies of tyranny ultimately tend to break down the ethical relations of individual members
and kinship groups and replaces face-to-face relations with abstract notions of
justice, universalized rules of behavior, and rituals of appropriate punishments
for social deviants. The state dehumanizes its members.

A musing on the various meanings of these savages, those who are said to
stand outside of membership in the dehumanizing entity of the state, is useful.
The first definition—"living somewhat like an animal"—suggests the possibility
of recognizing a savage by a display of animal behaviors. Fyodor Mikailovich
Dostoevsky offers a brilliant response to the charge that animal behaviors are

less morally evolved, crueler, than human behaviors. In his novel *The Brothers Karamazov*, Dostoevsky has Ivan Karamazov, his philosophical aspect, state: "People talk sometimes of bestial cruelty, but that's a great injustice and insult to the beasts; a beast could never be so cruel as a man—so artfully, so artistically cruel."[21]

Philosophers and social scientists have often noted that the violences of animals are effectively "innocent" compared to those of human beings. Konrad Lorenz, animal behaviorist, points out that when animals tear apart other animals for food, they do not show signs of aggression or enjoyment of the violence itself. Animals do not lust after blood any more than humans do when they discover a roast of beef in the refrigerator.[22] Animals do not display the physiological signs that would warrant our labeling their hunting methods as cruel or aggressive behavior. Animals kill innocently, without sadistic intent or subterranean motives, without shame or remorse. Under normal circumstances, animals simply kill to eat or to protect their young. As Ivan Karamazov declares, our difference from the animal world is what is shameful: humans are often artfully and artistically cruel. Witness the medical experiments of the Nazi death camps, the products (soap, buttons, lampshades) made from parts of human bodies.

The white invader deemed the Africans savage for their deficiency in polite (that is, European-style) manners. The African was savage because ignorant of appropriate codes of conduct practiced in European cities and thought, by their white practitioners, to be appropriate to all peoples of the world. By African standards, the same could be said of the whites. African tradition embraced a wealth of social ritual foreign to the white invaders. For example, as I have remarked, there exists in Africa since ancient times the belief in a divine decree that stands above the petty rules of the human world, a rule that demands that waylaid strangers be welcomed, fed, and helped on their way. White Europeans violated that African standard.

European myths at first painted the African as simultaneously savage and innocent. A primitive innocence served as both explanation for, and manifestation of, the African's alleged hyper-sexuality. Ultimately the Africans lost their reputation for primal innocence once colonial doctors and missionaries named them blameworthy for the epidemics of sexual diseases that swept the continent from the moment of the Europeans' arrival. The colonials would deem the Africans guilty of savagery, if they dared to resist in any fashion the exploitation or control that was being exercised over them.

Let us consider the term "savage" under its aspect of primitiveness. To be primitive is a temporal designation. It simply means chronologically first, "primal." Europeans attached the term "primitive" to peoples to indicate that no evolution had occurred within African societies. Africans had no history. Europeans believed Africans to resemble the first humans who occupied the earth. So Africans were thought to be retarded in development, not only technologically and politically as states, nor socially and economically as social groups, but biologically and genetically as human beings. Africans were, with the single disparaging word "savage," reduced to people whose bodies and minds had never evolved to full potential, and whose traditions and societies remained backward and undeveloped over millennia. Where Europeans cited changes to their societies (albeit changes generally brought about through bloody conquest) as proof that they are historical beings, Africans and other simple indigenous societies were deemed to be comprised of simple-minded folk incapable of glorious histories, daring conquests, or empire-building.

The distinction between historical and ahistorical peoples implied in the distinction between civilized and savage presupposes a myth of progress, a prejudice of the Western world. The myth of progress rests on a faulty assumption: that all changes are for the good. The myth presupposes that historical changes chart moral advances as well; that all changes better the human world. Since Charles Darwin's claim that the fittest creatures are favored for biological selection while the least fit fall by the evolutionary wayside, Westerners have granted the notion of fitness an aspect moral significance.[23] The fittest live on because they are the fittest. But they are not necessarily the morally best. In the extreme life-challenging conditions of the Nazi death camp, one thing became clear to Holocaust survivor Primo Levi: the good die first.[24] Despite the empirical evidence of histories of imperial civilization, Westerners have remained under the thrall of this myth, deeming politico-historical changes necessary to the development of morally superior social and political forms, and crucial to the improvement of life conditions.

A popular maxim asserts all change as good. Change is change. Change is never guaranteed as good or bad. Rarely is the most perspicacious thinker able to predict with any degree of accuracy whether a certain change will turn out to be good in its manifold historical effects in the world. Life's changes sometimes bring successes and triumphs, sometimes evils and suffering. Generally changes bring a mixture of all these effects.

No sound reason exists to support the further popular prejudice that the complex lives lived in industrialized societies are superior to the simple lives of tribal communities. Much is gained with the advances of technology, to be certain; the benefit of medicines is self-evident and the blessing of dishwashers and washing machines few will deny. Yet many of the people in industrialized societies today live lives of wretchedness and affliction. The technological advances advertised broadly across the society only serve to indicate to the poor of those societies the vastly inequitable distribution of goods, services, and opportunities. Forgotten materially, many citizens of the richest nations of the world do not benefit from Western prosperity; they feel isolated, alienated, superfluous, and dehumanized.

These characteristics—materially wretched, isolated, alienated, superfluous, and dehumanized—can in no way be applied to the precolonial African world, as a vast body of recent scholarship has convincingly demonstrated.[25] The presupposition that Africans lagged behind other peoples before the colonials ushered them into the modern world has, nevertheless, been a patent prejudice applied to them from the arrival of the first invaders, and one that continues to plague Africans today. There persists since colonial times a mantra of prejudice:

"You belong to a race without history, without traditions, without inventions or artifacts of any value. You have no worthwhile heritage toward which you may point with pride." This ethnocentric mantra liberal white authors, educators, and a handful of persuaded black disciples continue to chant across the globe today.[26]

The myths of African savagery are far from the historical truth. Recent research attests that the original peoples of Africa were once the leading people on earth, pioneers in the sciences, medicines, architecture, writing, and stonework.[27] Africans, historians now seriously speculate, sailed the oceans to discover the Americas long before the white Europeans found their way across.[28] Africans arrived at the concept of a single deity as creator of the universe several thousand years before Abraham. This fact renders credibility to Chancellor William's theory that the early wandering Hebrews, so plentiful in archaic Africa, may have received many of their religious notions from Africans.[29]

The colonial myths about the Africans were correct in one most important respect: African "primitives" did remain relatively unchanged over millennia. Their socio-political systems were exemplary models of natural democracy. Williams demonstrates that Africans enjoyed widespread, synchronous, remarkably stable, democratic social organizations that predated the founding of Athens and the existence of Greece. Williams states: "a single constitutional system prevailed throughout Black Africa, just as though the whole race, regardless of the countless patterns, lived under a single government."[30] Local remnants of these original systems remain in many places intact, still profoundly and genuinely democratic, despite the history of brutality that African communities have suffered. Europeans could not understand or recognize the deeply democratic ways of the Africans, since European systems were, and are, rigorously hierarchical in structure and prepared the European poorly for recognition of purer democracy.

Williams recounts the story of a European explorer who was outraged at an African king who kept the explorer waiting for weeks for a response to the exploring party's request to study the African countryside thereabout. The Europeans were scandalized at being denied even a brief audience, because they noticed that, while the whites were left to wait, the king entertained "any black that wandered in from the countryside." What the whites failed to understand was that the African king was anything but an autocratic sovereign as is typical in Western political worlds. African kings did not enjoy the right to receive the strangers, not even socially, without the permission of the local council of elders and without the presence of at least three senior elders. To decide upon a matter as important as a petition to conduct explorations within their sacred lands, a full council of state had to be called.[31]

This account helps to demonstrate that the Europeans, with their rat-race lives and their rich evolving—unsettled, unstable, unpredictable—histories, consistently mistook as primitive savages those people whose cultural and political ways were foreign to their own. What Williams's explorers interpreted as a failure in appropriate decorum toward European guests testified to the complexity of the checks and balances that maintained the equilibrium of power in African tribal systems of authority and control.

Recent continent-wide research into traditional African systems reveals similar patterns of shared leadership throughout all African institutions.[32] The European failure to understand the political and cultural differences between themselves and their African others, coupled with the unqualified European ethnocentrism, retarded the European ability to appreciate the fundamental and harmonious beauty of African traditions. With the reigning cultural myopia, Europeans could only interpret the dark stranger as savage in the sense of the second definition: "a crude boorish person or a barbarian."

Definitions for savage people can only find meaning from a reference point that is relentlessly ethnocentric and hierarchical. The connotation barbarian issues from a similar position. Barbarian is a term traceable to the ancient Greeks; all peoples who were not Hellenic were named barbarians. Whether Persian prince, Cretan mystic, or Macedonian philosopher, all who hailed from lands outside the Greek peninsula earned the label of *barbaros* by reason of their external origin and by the strange sound of their tongue to the Greek ear (*bar-bar*). Europeans took up the term as boor; the Dutch use *boer*. These terms echo the Greek disgust for the upstart nouveau riche who worked for a living instead of enjoying old money and old honorable family name. Boor also echoes the European disgust for people from rural areas; boor means a farmer, peasant, or farm worker, and is connected to *bouwen*: to build or to cultivate. Anyone who labors in fields or on the construction site composes a boor because a laborer cannot know the polite customs of city society so is, by city standards, "a rude, ill-mannered person."

One is deemed ill-mannered by reference to a particular culture's standards of polite behavior. Arabs belch after meals to show their appreciation. An Englander leaves in disgust if such behavior occurs at his table. Italians clear their plates and empty their glasses, so their hosts know the meal was appreciated. Kenyans are obliged by custom to eat a full meal at every stop upon their journeys, whether they can stomach another bite or no. Zimbabweans require that guests leave a little on the plate to demonstrate that the feast has been more than adequate. Illness of manners can only be pronounced from inside an established cultural lifeworld where local practices are deemed the only ones appropriate and healthy for universal human use.

From whatever angle an attempt is made to understand the term savage *as a noun*, ultimately one must fall back to an ethnocentric position to grant the word any meaning. Since all cultures have unique perspectives about what constitutes appropriate manners, what constitutes "civilized" behavior, and what forms of government, social customs, and rearing patterns for their children are valuable and worthy of practice, people will sort others on a scale from savage to civilized accordingly as they find those foreign others more and less attuned to the values that they values they hold in high esteem and practice in their homespaces. We tend as human beings to value those who are like us and to demonize as savage those most deviant from our social norms.

# 4. Savagery as Cruelty

If the term savage has any meaning whatsoever, the meaning must be found in the final definition of the term, which reads: "a person of extreme, unfeeling, and brutal cruelty."[33] This meaning is different from the others in that it is not founded upon cultural or ethnic presuppositions. This meaning is robust and positive. Without reference to peculiar socio-cultural meanings, the definition of savagery as cruelty is both descriptive and prescriptive. It rests on the assumption that human behavior ought to be above that of the beasts of the field; it assumes that human behavior ought to be feeling, compassionate, and humane. Savagery entails a willful and wanton enactment of brutality onto another being. Savagery can only be accomplished where an object exists, where there is a "savaging" of others. To deserve the name of "savage," one must perform certain kinds of actions, display certain kinds of behaviors that are not simply inappropriate but wantonly, even murderously, cruel.

Analysts of violence suggest a distinction in types of harmful action. René Girard, for example, distinguishes between the "good violence" of social ritual such as legal rules, criminal punishment, and war (by definition obsessively regulated); and the "bad violence" of unbridled murder, as exemplified in bloody feuds that carry over multiple generations and pollute all whom the feud touches, directly or indirectly.[34] Girard names social and legal-political violence a manifestation of "the sacred" in the human world. The god of the society is thought to be revealed in these rituals, granting blessings to chosen disciples and punishments to outsiders to the preferred group.[35] One is tempted to agree with Girard, given the frequency that wars, death penalties, and other legitimized violences are undertaken by nations in the modern world under the blanket sanction of the god's approval.

Savagery comes in different forms and exacts differing tolls on its victims. Bodies may be savaged by torture and other direct violences; entire peoples may be psychologically and physically savaged by war. Many people are psychologically and materially savaged by the structural violences of economic or political oppression. One thing is uncontested across the broad landscape of scholarly theory about violence, and ratified in the common perception and usage of the term "violence": savagery is about cruel action; it designates manifest harm, physically or psychically afflicted upon people, and willfully intended.[36] Savagery is about performance that involves unfeeling, brutal, senseless harm to others. People savage other people when they act cruelly toward them. Agents of such actions are the ones who compose the true savages. Savage is as savage does. The conceptual collapse of the other definitions leads us to the indisputable conclusion that savage action—intentional cruelty to others—remains the only true indicator of savagery. Such action remains the only definition that holds meaning across the cultural landscape.

Any serious consideration of the meaning of the term "savage" culminates in a disturbing corollary. Our European forebears, fervent, god-fearing, daring people who braved the distant shores of unknown lands to import (their particular brand of) civilization to indigenous peoples across the globe, behaved toward those simple peoples in the most cruel and barbaric ways. They unremittingly claimed to be bringing culture, development, and evolution to the people whom they encountered. But altruism was never a motive in colonial invasion. The greater number of people the colonials encountered were simply slaughtered *en masse* in the name of the king and the god. Those remaining alive were enslaved, exploited, and robbed of their lands, resources, pride, and histories. If savage is as savage does, then we are bound by historical evidence to the conclusion that it is precisely those who believed themselves to sit at the summit of the moral and human universe who compose the savages of the human world.

Aimé Césaire, in his *Discourse on Colonialism*, arrives at a similar conclusion. He observes: "Europe is unable to justify itself either before the bar of 'reason' or before the bar of 'conscience'. . . . Increasingly it takes refuge in a hypocrisy that is all the more odious because it is less and less likely to deceive."[37] When Europe undertook to carve up the world of foreign others, to slaughter and enslave the inhabitants, and to strip-mine the continent's resources, European civilization proved itself on its own moral terms backward, and regressive. Europe proved incapable of pursuing its imperial designs and fulfilling its entrepreneurial conquests while yet keeping faith with the central tenets of its own democratic liberal heritage. Christian Europe could not fulfill the demands of its god or meet its own requirements for civilized human existence. European civilization proved savage on its own terms.

Phenomenologically, subjects, when looking down their noses at others, lose sight of the fact that the human objects they witness are also subjects in their own right, with peculiar strengths and weaknesses, powers and faults, cultural customs and eccentricities. It also suggests that the witnessing subject loses sight of a fundamental phenomenological truth: the radical alterity of other subjects, and the impossibility of entering the home space of another person's identity except by the existential burglary against which Emmanuel Levinas warns.[38]

The savagery suffered by Africans during the colonial era has left its mark upon African societies and upon individual African psyches. The violence of that era can be witnessed to rebound in private and family lives throughout the African diaspora and in the domestic and foreign affairs of African nations today. Neocolonial violences replace the old colonial oppressions and broaden from the African continent to engulf the entire third world. Those violences too can be expected in time to rebound across the globe, as the poor struggle to emerge onto a world stage economically and politically rigged for their failure.

The next chapter traces the effects of European savagery on African peoples as they work free of their historical abjection. These examples describe but a few reboundings of colonial violence on the African continent today. But these samples are meant to signal a vaster potential for rebounding violence than one book can foretell. Present economic policies and trade legislation effectively marks the transition from nation-state relations to corporate global rule. That transition means that, no matter how humane individual states may become, the continuing prosperity of the already prosperous is guaranteed, along with the continuing degradation of the downtrodden of the earth. This situation dictates that even those countries not yet oppressed by the strong-arm tactics of the United States and Europe will one by one fall victim to the poverty, degradation, and misery that will ensure future reboundings of violence across the globe.

# Notes

1. Jared Diamond, *Guns, Germs, and Steel* (London, U.K.: W. W. Norton & Co. 1999); Eli Sagan, *At the Dawn of Tyranny* (New York: Knopf, 1985).

2. Albert Memmi, *The Colonizer and the Colonized* (Boston: Beacon Press, 1991), 52.

3. Viola W. Bernard, Perry Ottenberg, Fritz Redl, "Dehumanization" in *Sanctions for Evil*, William E. Henry, Nevitt Sanford, eds. (San Francisco: Jossey-Bass, 1971), 102-124.

4. Wendy C. Hamblet, "The Reasonableness of Cruelty" in *Appraisal*, Vol. 4, No. 4 (October, 2003).

5. Rollo May, *The Power of Innocence: A Search for the Sources of Violence* (New York: Norton and Co., 1972).

6. May, *Innocence*, 152.

7. D. Olweus, *Aggressive Behavior: Current Perspectives* (New York: Plenum, 1994), 97–130; see also Roy Baumeister, *Evil: Inside Human Violence and Cruelty* (New York: Henry Holt, 1997), 128–168.

8. Maurice Bloch, *Prey into Hunter: The Politics of Religious Experience* (Cambridge: Cambridge University Press, 1992), 195.

9. Aristotle, *Politics* 3.1.1274 b32–33.

10. *Cassell's Latin Dictionary* (New York: Funk & Wagnalls, 1957), 100.

11. Plato, *Phaedrus* 246a (translation mine).

12. Plato's justice, as depicted in the *Republic* and the myth of the Feast of Being in the *Phaedrus*, is a careful balance among the soul's rational, passionate, and appetitive elements (*Phaedrus* 247d ff.; *Republic* 368e).

13. Plato, *Statesman* 286d; *Hippias Maj.* 289d, 292d; *Philebus* 51b ff.; *Parmenides* 130b.

14. Eli Sagan, *At the Dawn of Tyranny* (New York: Alfred A. Knopf, 1985), 244.

15. Sagan, *Dawn*, 245.

16. Sagan, *Dawn*, 247.

17. Sagan, *Dawn*, 247.

18. H. H. Gerth and C. W. Mills, *From Max Weber* (New York: Oxford University Press, 1958), 134.

19. Sagan, *Dawn*, 249.

20. *Webster's New Universal Unabridged Dictionary* (Cleveland: Dorset & Baber, 1979), 2nd Edition, 1612.

21. Fyodor Dostoevsky, *The Brothers Karamazov*, Constance Garnet, trans. (New York: Doubleday, 1995), 220.

22. Konrad Lorenz, *On Aggression*, Marjorie Kerr Wilson, trans. (New York: Harcourt, Brace, and World, 1966), 241.

23. Charles Darwin, *The Origin of Species: By Means of Natural Selection or the Preservation of Favoured Races in the Struggle for Life* (New York: Bantam, 1999).

24. Primo Levi, *The Drowned and the Saved*, Raymond Rosenthal, trans. (New York: Vintage Books, 1989), 11–21.

25. Basil Davidson, *In Search of Africa: History, Culture, Politics* (New York: Random House, 1994); Cheikh Anta Diop, *Precolonial Black Africa*, Harold J. Salemson, trans. (Brooklyn, NY: Lawrence Hill Books, 1987); *Civilization and Barbarism*, Harold J. Salemson, Marjolin de Jager, eds., Yaa-Lengi Meema Ngemi, trans. (Brooklyn, NY: Lawrence Hill Books, 1987).

26. Davidson, *Search*, 3 & ff.

27. Chancellor Williams, *The Destruction of Black Civilization* (Chicago: Third World Press, 1987), 49–52.

28. Ivan Van Sertima, *They Came Before Columbus* (New York: Random House, 1976).

29. Williams, *Black Civilization*, 34.

30. Williams, *Black Civilization* 21.

31. Williams, *Black Civilization* 21, 31.

32. See note 20, this chapter.

33. See note 10, this chapter.

34. René Girard, *Violence and the Sacred*, Patrick Gregory, trans. (Baltimore: Johns Hopkins University Press, 1979), 14, 52.

35. Girard, *Sacred*, 52.

36. See for example Ron Rosenbaum, *Explaining Hitler: The Search for the Origins of His Evil* (New York: Random House, 1999).

37. Aimé Césaire, *Discourse on Colonialism* (New York: Monthly Review Press, 1972), 9.

38. Emmanuel Levinas, *Totality and Infinity*, A. Lingis, trans. (Pittsburgh, Penn.: Duquesne University Press, 1969), 66–67.

# Chapter 13
# Rebounding Violences

We burn with desire to find a solid seat and a last constant firmament from which to erect a tower that reaches the infinite [*une tour qui s'élève à l'infini*]; but the foundation cracks and the earth opens onto the abyss.

Blaise Pascal[1]

People rarely know the extent and depth of the effects they have upon unsuspecting others as they pursue their projects and erect their *tours à l'infini* across the face of the earth. One fact must be admitted. Though people in the West give lip service to human rights across the globe, Western ways of being-in-the-world, guided by democratic-capitalist ideals of individualism, freedom, and autonomy, have evolved little from the arrogant imperialisms of their forefathers or from the militarism of the Greek ancestors. Though Westerners are generally quick to point a moralizing finger at the developmental backwardness of the third world, most are remarkably silent on the moral viability of their continuing privileges, their lion's share of the common feast of our planet.

Ethnocentric arrogance continues to limit relations between the West and their less fortunate neighbors in the global marketplace. Ethnocentrism persists in restricting diplomatic effectiveness in Western dealings within the international community, and continues to frustrate peace efforts and humanitarian labors across the globe. Ethnocentrism serves to preclude our full and accurate understanding of the violence of the past, including those of the colonial era that I am seeking to highlight in this work. Scholars can count the corpses, document the scars, calibrate the numbers of the dislocated, figure the percentage of collapsed families, establish the divorce rate and number the fatherless children, track the speed of urban flow and abandonment of the countryside, and reckon the proportion of homes struggling beneath poverty line. But these data are mere numbers. Numbers do not capture the lived reality of long-term sufferings.

How can that which cannot be counted be appreciated: how people and cultures have been disconnected from their heritages and set adrift from their destinies? Of what glorious futures and noble histories have Western imperialist projects—*tours à l'infini*—robbed other populations as their powerful civilizations made their way to their first world status? How have indigenous populations been permanently touched by the experiences of foreign invasion, repressive rule, extreme poverty, and exploitation? How can the scholar gauge how the courses of indigenous histories have been forever ambushed; how people once proud and great have been psychically altered? What are the human or dehumanizing results for the victim people cast from their sacred soil that harbors their ancestors? What remains when families have been torn apart, heroes forgotten, histories lost, and ancient traditions trampled and ridiculed as primitive and savage?

Experts on violence, such as genocide scholar/psychologist Ervin Staub, tell that violent histories continue to promote violent responses in people long after the apparent close of their events.[2] Violence begets violence and persecution rebounds into the victim's future encounters with people perceived as threatening. In his *The Roots of Evil*, Staub traces the emergence of psychic factors that lead people in the direction of extreme violences like genocide. He draws upon the example of those who have experienced the rigors of war to demonstrate that those who have witnessed, suffered, or perpetrated violent actions continue to live in the thrall of a violence-legitimating view of reality long after their removal from the bloody scenes of the crimes. Staub states:

> The persistent stress and intense danger that soldiers experience in combat have many long-term effects . . . [manifest in] posttraumatic stress disorder. . . . The veterans often lack goals; they have lost a sense of self, identity, meaning, control. They give the impression of being "empty shells." Other symptoms are easily stimulated anger and rage and sensation-seeking, the need to engage in dangerous activities. They have lost faith in legitimate authority. They no longer believe that the world is a benign, orderly, and controllable place or that they themselves are worthwhile to relate to.[3]

## 1. Rebounding Violence

History witnesses that violent events have myriad long-term effects, many of which are disastrous because they groom people in favor of future violence. Suffering through radically violent times tends to leave witnesses, victims, and perpetrators shaken and insecure about the fundamental goodness of the world and their human neighbors. Violence tends to position all those it touches for an unhealthy fascination with radical movements or dynamic leaders. Strength, and often simple raw might, comes to be seen as crucial to everyday security in a threatening world, so mighty leaders, flamboyant promises, and radical projects promising a "new world order" can appear very attractive to people whose sense of security has been eroded.

In the wake of violent histories, involving oneself with radical movements and mighty leaders can also impart a sense of significance where a void has been hollowed out in one's sense of self-worth through suffering, denigration, and abuse. Submerging the self in a powerful group, joining the ranks of a forceful movement, and swearing allegiance to a dynamic leader permit people to escape their vulnerable, threatened, limited, individual identities and to assume a group identity where they can feel powerful and important. Dynamic groups and leaders tend to offer fresh ideologies that can offer escape from the conceptual confusion that violence tends to create in its victims. Attachment to a strong group identity renders renewed comprehension of the world, new meaning to their existences, and new direction and purpose to their actions.

Strong group identities are generally formed by radical polar opposition to some other group or ideology. Since the home group or ideological position must be configured as the best, alternative identities are generally demonized in hyper-moral terms, so in a post-violence world an individual's identification with a strong group tends that person in favor of future violent activity, by intensifying feelings of belonging while providing a highly visible enemy. The rise of dynamic new leaders with radical plans for new world orders is quite common in the aftermath of extended histories of violence.

Having a visible enemy is most important for people who have suffered through violent histories. Trauma leaves victims plagued by feelings of vulnerability and low self-esteem which render them prone to the mechanism of scapegoating, which locates easily identifiable enemies and makes ready sense of the chaos of experience. The psychological mechanism of scapegoating permits a sure identification of the cause for the chaos which in turn permits the distressing feeling of vague anxiety about an unspecified danger (typical features of the worldview of victim populations in the posttraumatic world) to be replaced by a rational plan to rid the world of an identifiable enemy. Impoverished, humiliating lives and low self-esteem can be elevated to a sense of superiority and entitlement to abuse. Other persons or groups can be devalued and blamed for one's troubles.

People who have lived through terrifying and brutalizing life conditions continue to be stalked, long after the closure of those histories, by uncontrollable and horrifying recollections, as well as recurrences of terrifying dreams. These tend to obstruct the path of healthy identity work and frustrate attempts at sound relationships with others, long after the close of the violence. People who have suffered through violent histories experience a numbness, a lack of healthy responsiveness, to external events and people. They can go to extreme lengths of self-evasion and diminished sense of responsibility to escape the memories of the mangled bodies and the horrifying sense of unpredictability that continues to stalk their daily existences.[4]

To deal with the persistent terrors that loom up out of their past, people of violent histories tend to anaesthetize themselves against pain and fear by hardening up inside; their capacity for horror diminishes; their sensitivity to others becomes blunted. Human beings become less connected to their fellows, less caring, less vulnerable to pleas for mercy and compassion. People who have lived through difficult life situations become hardened and desensitized. Often they show signs of being dehumanized in their dealings with others.

Violence changes people profoundly and, at least for a time, makes them more prone to violence. This fact underpins my claim that violence tends to rebound within communities and then outward upon neighboring others. The tendency of violence to rebound across victim communities and into their neighboring worlds suggests one possible indicator of the extent of the damage that has been caused to the African peoples by the centuries of colonial abuse. Since Africanist scholars assert that precolonial African was a synchronous network of neighboring villages, practicing varied forms of "natural democracy" that was exemplary in its egalitarianism, the degree of the damage of the waves of continental rape by European invaders may be roughly gauged by the degree that African people and systems have altered from their original peaceful forms.

Far from the practice of popular modern myths that measure the savagery of the African people by recurrences of violence on the continent, I suggest that the difference between the original ways of coexistence and the violent interactions of today offer the sympathetic student of history an indication of the extent of the damages that have been created by those violent histories. In this chapter, I gloss the historical landscape of the last century and consider some of the most notorious violences, in an attempt to demonstrate how those brutalities qualify as reboundings of colonial violence resulting from abuses suffered by the African peoples in those areas.

Staub and other social scientists agree that victimization leaves people with a personal sense of vulnerability and a worldview that promotes violent responses. Violence tends to rebound upon others because violence begets violence over time. Given the rebounding nature of violence and the vast variety of abuses that Africans suffered, I find not at all surprising that violence continues to rebound in the encounters among African countrymen and with their global neighbors. The violences of their past will likely haunt African futures for some time to come.

Thus is the painful, agonizing process of reconstructive identity work carried out. These abused peoples must reclaim their pasts, reconnect with their heritages, and come to terms with their colonial past. They must salvage their self-esteem as individuals and as cultures. They must transform the repressive systems bequeathed to them by their colonial masters into systems that mirror their deeply democratic pasts and are more closely fitted to African ways. Most difficult of all, they must find how to break free of the dialectic of us against them if they are to find themselves again in healthy, positive, non-dialectical ways. Until African people feel safe in their homes, unthreatened by their surroundings, and unexploited by the global economy, violence will likely continue to rebound, flaring into myriad and terrifying forms across the African continent and beyond.

I trace historical examples that I believe to compose violent reboundings. I hope that these examples may offer insight into a more general phenomenon prevalent in subgroups in societies where people have been generally but unequally exploited. I argue that the invaders' common strategy of divide-and-conquer results in unequal exploitation that turns subgroup against subgroup, creating resentments and discontent among the ranks of the oppressed. These resentments may have been temporarily eclipsed by the presence of the more visible white enemy, but later, upon removal of the colonialist forces, the resentment of the divided African populations would arise anew and flare into projects of vengeance. I contend that the European tactic of divide-and-conquer continues to have devastating effects for subgroups, once unequal in repression, who must face each other as equals in the post-independence world. The phenomenon of unequal oppression frustrates the formation of communities among the oppressed and positions people to repeat the violences of their abusers, even after the oppression has been overcome.

We have been witnessing for decades varieties of rebounding violences across the African nations that composed the earliest colonies. The observer can hardly find this remarkable, given the fact that this is where the continental rape began, and given the radical variety of its forms. Where slaves were rounded up *en masse* by their tribal neighbors deploying firearms and powder that the Portuguese supplied, no height or number of proverbial good fences can quickly make for good neighbors or repair the patterns of enmity that have been forged across centuries. Since no other commerce could compare in profit yield to the slave trade, no others were developed for a long while. Violent beginnings set in motion cycles of retaliatory carnage that are still rebounding today in Angola and the surrounding nations.

## 2. Rebounding Violence in Rwanda

The 1994 genocide in Rwanda has, for many Western onlookers, provided the superlative living proof of the "savagery" attributed to all Africans. Though only a small, tight group of military elites provided the ideological and material motivations to support uncompromising Hutu domination in Rwanda, the brutal and bloody executions were largely carried out by ordinary people. Tutsi and moderate Hutu opponents were listed, their houses marked out, and the gendarmes, the native rural police trained by the French, were sent in to do the dirty job. But the numbers of those designated for erasure being so great—ten percent of the population!—the task turned out to be herculean. Ordinary peasants were forced to join in house-to-house hunts. Often they were ordered to massacre their neighbors or be massacred themselves. Men, women, and children, babies and old folks were slaughtered *en masse* with the crudest of weapons: household implements and farming tools.

After the fact of the murders, the civilian executioners offered in explanation: "What would you have done? Either you joined in the massacres or you were yourself massacred!"[5] The majority of the survivors' stories bear out the sad truth that the government purposely set in motion what was, within the population at large, an almost spontaneous movement to wipe out the internal enemy. The mass murders were conducted across the country in small villages where everyone knew each other and recognized each other by tribal identity. Ordinary villagers turned upon their friends and their neighbors, and in some cases their own Tutsi husbands, wives, and half-caste children. Many did reap material benefits in the loot robbed from the victims' homes, but, for the most part, the motivation for the murders lay in decades of tribal resentment, fanned for years by ideologies of demonization of the Tutsis and their Hutu sympathizers as devils tormenting and infecting decent Hutu folk.

How do people begin to turn on each other and to hate their neighbors to such a fanatical degree that they can massacre women, babies, and old folk without distinction or compunction? Military and political leaders provided the ideological base for the murders, but people are not unthinking dupes. The ideologues must provide a narrative that has some resonance in the people's experiences, that echoes in their psyches, and that speaks to their deepest fears and resentments, perhaps reawakening old sufferings they have endured. There exist many crucial factors that promoted this kind of hatred that will never come into the light of understanding. But a mere gloss over the recent history of Rwanda provides ample food for causal thought.

In 1918, under the Treaty of Versailles, the German colony of Rwanda-Urundi was named a protectorate under the governance of Belgium. The two territories of Rwanda and Burundi were to be administered separately under two different Tutsi monarchs. This fact may not appear particularly shocking until we realize that tribal identities are far more fluid than most people appreciate. If we grant stable identity, as did the colonials, then we must appreciate the further fact that the Tutsi composed only fourteen percent of the population. Another important factor has been treated in detail by Mahmood Mamdani in his enlightening book *When Victims Become Killers*. The Belgians proceeded to establish their power over the people of Rwanda by reconstructing and enforcing political identities out of the already mythically constructed tribal distinctions among the people.[6]

Both the German colonists (before the seizure of their colonies after the First World War) and the Belgians (after the seizure) greatly favored the Tutsi over the Hutu, extending to the Tutsi the privileges of Western-style education, positions of authority, and jobs that were denied to the other eighty-five percent of the population. The typical colonial divide-and-conquer strategy for governance of the colonies made use of the Tutsi minority to enforce rule over the rest of the population. In order to accomplish the division necessary to the domination of the Rwandan population, the Europeans first needed to redefine Hutu-Tutsi identities and relationships, and to enforce these redefinitions in the minds of the people. This was no small feat.

The difference between the Hutu and Tutsi was originally understood by the Rwandan population as a distinction of class and occupation. Originally, according to the people's lore, a single tribe came to be split into two identity divisions dependent upon whether the family's job was pastoral or agricultural. Borders of that social distinction were as fluid as tribal borders tended to be elsewhere throughout Africa. As one's occupation or social status varied, so did tribal identities fluctuate. Over generations, any original firm division separating the two identity groups had been lost through intermarriage and cultural inclusion. Tutsi and Hutu had become integrally interwoven. This is demonstrated by the fact that, before colonial rule, local chiefs arose not by distinctions of superiority of class, wealth, or occupation but according to which individual elder was held by the local population to be the wisest elder of the village.

Where any original tribal differentiations had all but eroded, the governing European colonials were faced with the important task of reconstructing those divisions. Antiquated social and occupational distinctions were redefined as distinctions of race. Rwandan subjects were re-sorted according to racial distinctions, in consonance with a racial myth popularized by anthropologists at the time—the Hamitic hypothesis. This hypothesis, applied to the Rwandans, stated that the Tutsi were a non-indigenous people who had migrated to Rwanda via the rivers from Ethiopia or from the east. Tutsis were reconstructed as alien to "Black African" peoples. The importance and probable motivation behind this shift in the formulation of political subjectivities lies in the divide-and-conquer strategy typical of colonial rule. The Tutsi, through this reconstruction, were posited as having a civilizing, Caucasian influence among the black-skinned, thick-lipped, spiral-haired Hutu.

The Hamitic hypothesis was not articulated with reference to the populations of Rwanda and Burundi only. It was rallied across a wide area of territory and colonial thought to explain all signs of life more akin to European-style civilization. Bantu Africa was seen to be more advanced where monotheistic belief was noted, where the use of iron and other material was noted in the crafting of artifacts, and where statecraft had developed along hierarchical lines instead of according to the general democratic patterns practiced across much of Africa. According to the Hamitic hypothesis, the Tutsi, the Bahima, and the ruling stratum of Baganda were Hamites. Where Africans were identified as browner-skinned, they were named more civilized and connected with Arab, rather than black African, identity.

The identity-reconstructions established through the Hamitic hypothesis served well the divide-and-conquer policies of the colonials in Rwanda and elsewhere across the continent. In Rwanda, the interpretation of the Hamitic hypothesis had uniquely racial overtones. Mamdani explains:

> The important point is that only the Tutsi—not the Bahima elite, nor the Baganda, nor any other group considered Hamitic—were constructed as a race as opposed to an ethnic group. Only in Rwanda and Burundi did the Hamitic hypothesis become the basis of a series of institutional changes that *fixed* the Tutsi as a race in their relationship to the colonial state.[7]

Various ethnicities can blend together and form viable communities. But racial distinctions are interpreted as distinctions of breeding and, according to the prevalent anthropological theories of the era, are decidedly hierarchical. To peoples whose identities are intimately tied to the land, differences of race imply notions of "rightful belonging." One becomes seen as the home group with a rightful claim of belonging to the land, and others are seen as alien, possibly defiling the places whose sacredness is long-standing. With racial reconstructions of identity, the Hutu could be seen as truly Rwandan, the Tutsi as invaders from afar.

One of the difficulties that had to be sorted out in the case of Rwanda was how these redefinitions would be practically imposed. The identity reconstructions were often not visibly evident; the physical attributes assigned to the different tribal distinctions simply did not match the visible evidence at hand. Hutu did not always have darker skin or curlier hair. Tutsi were not always tall. The problem called for more solid evidence than was visually available. To this end, a system of sorting was accomplished in the 1926 introduction of a system of identity cards. This practice, as contemporary genocide scholars know and repeatedly highlight, often composes an important factor leading up to genocide. With the introduction of identity cards, the Tutsi were reconstructed as a different race from the Hutu, as members of the Hamitic race rather than black Africans.

The Belgian colonial reforms of 1926 to 1936 worked diligently to apply the new schema of racial distinction invented by the colonials. Where local villages were complex intermixtures of Tutsi and Hutu and where the wisest men of the villages served as local chief, Hutu leaders were ousted from local leadership. Even decidedly Hutu villages were no longer allowed to choose a leader from among their local chiefs. All villages had to be ruled by the more "European-like" Tutsi chiefs. The Hutu were lumped together into a single mass of indigenous peoples alleged by the colonials to require the more civilizing influence of governance by their racial superiors, the Tutsi.

The consequences of the colonial reconstruction of political identities upon communal integrity within the villages of Rwanda were devastating. Identities split along racial lines. To the black Hutu, the brown-skinned Tutsi were seen as foreigners who had invaded the true Rwandans. Tutsi were seen as foreign allies whose privilege was backed by the white invaders' firepower. Tutsi, raised by the colonials to elevated social and occupational ranks and placed in positions of rule over the Hutu, were seen as foreign enemies of the native majority, collaborators in a colonial plot to subordinate and humiliate legitimate Rwandans. The Belgian reforms rendered the reconstructed Tutsi-Hutu relationship a double subordination for the Hutu, political as well as biological. But they also reconstructed the privileged few as collaborators in the misery and abjection of the disenfranchised many.

The denigrated and subordinated Hutu stewed long in these prejudicial juices. Not for fifty years did they challenge the theory of inferiority of Hutu peoples. Then, suddenly the Hutu were prepared to defy the prejudices and the alien invaders with violent action. Not until 1957 did the Hutu in Rwanda form the PARMEHUTU, the Party for the Emancipation of the Hutu. From that moment, the forces of resentment, resistance, and rebellion were unleashed and violence was inevitable. In 1959, the Hutu rebelled against the Belgian colonial power and their Tutsi collaborators. At this point, 150,000 Tutsis saw the writing on the wall and fled to neighboring Burundi, where the Tutsi monarchy was still in control. A year later, the Hutu won municipal elections organized by the Belgian rulers, and the Belgians withdrew from the country in 1961–1962.

From this point onward, the story continually darkens, with more and more Tutsis forced to flee from Rwanda to Burundi. Hutus began as early as 1963, immediately after the Belgian withdrawal, to act out their decades of resentment and suppression in the slaughter of their tribal others. The massacres reached their apex in the 1990s when the Rwandan army began to train and arm civilian militia and promote the idea of sending the Tutsis back to Ethiopia via the rivers. Over the course of a hundred days from April to June 1994, 800,000 Tutsi and moderate Hutu were slaughtered by their countrymen, many of them dumped in those rivers associated with their arrival—until the waters flowing out of Rwanda were literally clogged with corpses!

The number of victims was so great because the United Nations leadership and the entire international community (especially Belgium, France, and the United States) failed completely in their responsibilities during this horrific period.[8] Had the U.N. Security Council used the term "genocide" to describe the situation in Rwanda during their discussions of the situation on April 30 of 1994, they would have been obliged by international law to intervene in the hostilities and to "prevent and punish" the perpetrators. But they chose not to use the morally and legally binding term of genocide. Instead they spoke of genocide-like acts and civil war. Even talk of "crimes against humanity" failed to move the powers of the United Nations to intervene in the massacre.[9]

The term was employed only hundreds of thousands of murders later, after the corpse count was so high as to make ludicrous any denial of genocide. Even then, international aid was slow to follow. Arguments raged in the international community over who would pay the bill to provide the military equipment and troops for the intervention. The United States, self-proclaimed champion of the oppressed, was conspicuous in its stalling, arguing with the U.N. about the cost of providing the necessary heavy-armored vehicles to support a peacekeeping mission in Rwanda. No sign of U.N. deployment was manifest by the end of June, when the greater compass of the killing was completed.[10]

Undeniable laws of causality govern the flow of events in the empirical world. Even so, the configurations of their flow, especially when those events involve human affairs, interests and emotions, are so convoluted and complex that no amount or degree of historical analysis can guarantee any certain understanding of the mystery of their causal connection. One can only speculate within the broadest margins of error why worldly events take the courses that they do. In the odd case, however, there exists a history that seems to predetermine an inexorable outcome.

The genocide in Rwanda is one such clear-cut case. A glance across the seventy years of Rwandan history leading up to the massacres renders almost predictable the likelihood that the indigenous population of the country would split into fearsome enemy identities. The Rwandan community of interwoven identities was reconstructed as two distinct alienated subgroups, redistributed socially, economically, and politically, elevated and subordinated according to the ruling ideology. There is little doubt that such rigidly hierarchical distinctions would split the population violently and ultimately culminate in their tragic confrontation. Resentments were formed and fostered by the German conquerors, and then the Belgians added the indignity of racial dogma that cemented the division between the peoples as biological, rather than ethnic.

The colonial strategy of control—divide-and-conquer the enemy—proved an effective imperialist tactic and certainly a well-practiced one during the imperialistic era. By reconstructing tribal identities on the basis of race and then choosing those named Tutsis as local rulers, Tutsis became collaborators in colonial rule. By affording to that minority greatly preferential treatment, and by affirming, on a naturalized basis, their elevation into a political, social, and economic elite, the Europeans assured that the Tutsis would be seen as instrumental to Hutu oppression. They would come to be directly aligned with their Caucasian partners-in-crime as cause of the wretchedness and the repression of the Hutu. Resentments against the Germans, and then later the Belgians, were similarly focused upon their Tutsi collaborators and perhaps amplified precisely because these previous tribal brothers were now seen as aliens invading their midst.

Given this history of reconstructed political subjectivities, the hatreds that ignited into genocide become less of a mystery. Institutional and ideological winds fanned the glowing embers of resentment, and the smoldering animosity eventually burst into violent flame. It is far too simplistic an explanation to merely cite savage tribalisms as the cause of the genocide, though many Westerners continue to do that. The sufferings and deprivations dished out by the colonial masters through their racially elevated accomplices prepared the Hutu people well for a violently retributive future.

Foreign masters bent upon their own power and privilege turned a single oppressed population into enemies and killers. Decades of racial myth and colonial abuse convinced the Hutu that their tribal others were strangers from another region and not true Rwandans. Tutsi were not only infecting Hutu society and contaminating their tribal purity; they were imposing illegitimate foreign rule upon the indigenous people, the true Rwandans. When the Europeans finally pulled out and independence arrived, the identity reconstructions persisted. Nationalistic motivations and solidarity movements were unable to provide sufficiently unifying forces to mend the divisions and heal the stark rifts between the people. The Hutu remained convinced that foreign powers still infected the purity of their indigenous home so long as Tutsi remained on Rwandan soil.

Since the genocide, professional therapists, such as Staub, have attempted to analyze the hatreds and defuse their racially configured ideological bases, in the hope that the two alienated groups might reconnect as tribal fellows.[11] By helping the Rwandans to rediscover their deeper identity as comrades in oppression, by helping them to relive those horrific massacres to recognize that both groups have equally suffered, both have seen loved ones slaughtered, both have known terror and pain, Staub has realized a certain success in reconnecting the two groups as bedfellows in suffering. Working first with the young student populations, both Hutu and Tutsi, in their school settings, Staub and his colleagues made such impressive strides in advancing these alienated peoples toward a sense of newfound unity, that during the summer of 2002, Staub and his colleagues were asked to return to Rwanda to perform a similar healing magic with the governing officials, in preparation for the proposed democracy to be instituted in the next several years.

## 3. Southern Africa's Rebounding Violence

Southern Africa exemplifies the phenomenon of the rebounding of colonial violences in ways peculiar to the abuses that were suffered there. Scholars such as Leroy Vail have made great progress in explaining the recent burgeoning of tribal identifications since independence across southern Africa. In *The Creation of Tribalism in Southern Africa*, Vail and his colleagues make the case that Westerners cannot comprehend African resistance to Westernization. Bound within the Western worldview that favors their own political forms, Westerners are baffled by the African failure to welcome the breakdown of their traditional societies.[12] The Western prejudice sees African traditions as parochial, divisive, and retrogressive beside Western political forms seen as evolved and modern. Thus Westerners fully expected that:

> [g]reater access to education, improved communications, and the shifting of people from the slumbering "traditional" rural sector to the vibrant modern industrialized sector by the beneficent forces of economic growth guaranteed that ethnic loyalties would fade away.[13]

The guarantee that ethnic loyalties would fade away remains unfulfilled, and many Westerners continue to explain this failure by claiming that Africans, being doggedly backward, are incapable of appreciating the benefits of the more progressive Westernized systems. To the eternal dismay of Western observers, many people across southern Africa have fallen back to the countryside and reclaimed their ethnic/tribal identities cast aside temporarily in the fervor of nationalist movements toward independence. For many Westerners, this reclamation stands as further proof of the incorrigibly tribal nature of the African peoples, and this essential tribalism is called upon, again and again, to explain any conflict that arises to disrupt national unity.

I am arguing that African nationalist movements, precisely because they were shaped in reaction to colonial oppressions, often offer an unhealthy, overly simplistic, radically polarized foundation for carving out postcolonial identities. The nationalist identity remains locked within the dichotomy of us victims versus those oppressors. That identity may have proven useful for the framing politico-economic demands during movements toward independence, but it has no substantive philosophical content, no existential appeal, no meaningful connection with the everyday lives of postcolonial Africans.

As long as Africans remain trapped within a dichotomous counter-identity, they remain disconnected from their truer selves and their cultural heritages, and stuck in an unhealthy reactive mode of existence. Their traditional worldviews, and the customs and institutions that form their cultural roots had, in many cases, been abandoned and lost to memory by the close of the colonial period, since the colonists had been highly successful in convincing the indigenous peoples that they had neither histories, nor cultures, nor heroes or leaders of any real consequence, no traditions worth maintaining. Independence forces strive to replace the lost markers of identity with nationalist identity claims, but the nationalist identities are often experienced as foreign and artificial, as alien as colonial reidentifications had been.

In Southern African states, postcolonial nationalist loyalties retain little direct connection with the everyday lives of African people living in postcolonial states. They compose largely false constructions that fail to serve the compelling intellectual, social, and political needs and visions that arise for the people once they are freed from foreign control and oppression. Unfamiliar with everyday experiences, falsely imposed identity reconstructions fall to the wayside of identity work if they fail to satisfy existential requirements for the healing of broken selves and cultures in the wake of violent histories.

Nationalist movements seek a clean break from foreign influence. Yet postcolonial political and economic institutions in the new independent nations tend to mirror the colonial forms, and, like the colonial regimes, they continue to realize and extend the benefits of the system only to the political elites, while the common people realize little substantial life improvement. For most of the people in the postcolony, there ensues little practical enhancement over their colonial lives. The fruits of independence reach few of those who most need benefit. The economic development promised to the masses, when development occurs at all, tends to remain to the advantage of the dominant elites who step into the colonial ruler's political shoes. The fervor for nationalism and Pan-Africanism generally tended to die out as a natural consequence of the disappointments that ensued with the discovery that the bureaucratic organization of postcolonial states meant little change for the mass of the populations in the new independent nations.

Post-independence dissatisfactions and disappointments soon draw people back to their ethnic home places, to tribal connections and family attachments whose deeper bonding forces provide empathetic communities in which to share and voice their frustrations. Sometimes these sites of belonging meld into happier units that assuage the disillusioned. At other times and circumstances, such communities fester into pockets of resentment. Often, in southern African states, the communities of tribal belonging grow into formal sites of opposition to the new political powers, as those powers come to be seen as artificial constructs rooted in, and maintaining the foreign oppressive methods of, the colonial era. Many postcolonial conflicts have had their genesis in these renewed sites of belonging and the overzealous identity work that arises therein to express resentments.[14]

Tribal consciousness remains alive in southern Africa because tribalism is promoted by continuing resentments against the inadequacies of the political and social structures that, bequeathed from the colonial era, remain in sway in the new nations. Many of the postcolonial regimes remain repressive elitist regimes just as they had been under colonialist rule. The failure of the new regimes to provide more egalitarian opportunities to the various subgroups of the new nations, their incapacity to fulfill the economic and social demands of all parties, and their inability to satisfy the people's existential needs for the reclamation of lost histories and traditions and the meaningful reconstruction of postcolonial identities, has in many states culminated in anarchist reactions in the population. These responses are largely answered in the same manner in which colonial insurgence had been met—with repression. The new nations thus tend to repeat the errors of their colonial predecessors.

Traditional customs were in many instances beaten and shamed out of the people during colonial times. Many tribal practices had fallen into disuse. Kinship and tribal loyalties were eroded during the frequent displacements, and finally collapsed with the wars of independence that pitted colonial armies of conscripted Africans against African independence forces. However, in the new postcolonial nations, tribal consciousness suddenly came alive again, often expressed in new hyper-aggressive factionalisms. John S. Mbiti argues that the tribal roots of African culture were never really forgotten during the colonial era, but lay dormant within the African subconscious, waiting to be reawakened. "On the surface tribal solidarity is disrupted but beneath lies the subconscious mind of the traditional *Zamani*. Nationhood scratches on the surface, it is the conscious mind of modern Africa. But the subconscious of tribal life is only dormant, not dead."[15]

One universally alienating factor for Africans during the colonial era was the arbitrary geographical borders that had been drawn by the colonial invaders, borders that held no practical or mystical meaning in terms of African connections with the land. Into the postcolonial era, borders were destined to remain fixed in the colonial fashion, and Africans would remain unable to identify with the land through the meaningless borders of their countries. Thus national identity has been a difficult goal for many countries to achieve. The failure to identify beyond the tribal level has been disruptive of larger unities, but instrumental in luring people back from alienating cities to their native geographical spaces and the ancestral lands of tribal belonging.

During the colonial era, the Europeans tended to draw and highlight tribal divisions among the peoples of Africa because these distinctions served the success of their divide-and-conquer tactics. The differences played out by the colonials over time came to be reified in the self-identities of the Africans. The colonial power relations often implicated one subgroup in the oppression of others. Employers showed preference to one ethnic group and positioned them in superiority over others, in order to maintain their hierarchically structured workforces in a constant state of disunity and competition. The worst cases mirrored that in Rwanda as the employers over time constructed an alienated class within the varied population of the oppressed. Over time, a class system was fully functional along tribally and racially-constructed foundations, firing long-standing divisions and resentments among the various groups within the labor community.

The entire migrant labor system employed widely across southern African territories institutionalized the practice of urbanizing laborers while leaving their families bound to the countryside. This was accomplished in a number of ways. The families of migrant workers were not permitted to accompany the laborers to the various work sites across the countryside. Laborers in the city were forced to limit the length of time that they remained in the city; there existed explicit regulations against the transfer of rural families to the city. In any case laborers were paid too little to make urban migration of the entire family a viable option, especially given the extendedness of African families. Through these practices, the colonials ensured that few of the laborers felt at home in their work sites, whether stationed at urban or rural migrant sites of labor. The workers continued to think of the rural area as their home.

The transitory nature of urban and rural labor sojourns kept family identities centered in the rural lands. Labor practices also meant that the people were generally able to maintain their tribal connections, keeping alive their mystical relationship with the sacred lands of the ancestors and their practice of the ancient beliefs and ritual customs of their local groups. Transitory labor practices, because they drew together a diversity of tribal identities into a common labor force, also made inevitable for the displaced laborers the formation of hyper-idealized stereotypical images of their homelands and their cultural roots. These many factors, experts agree, explain why tribal ideological movements have their roots in rural, not urban, areas.[16]

Another important factor that not only kept tribal consciousness alive all through the colonial era but continues to maintain it today is the fact of the uneven development of educational facilities, employment opportunities, and medical, sanitation, and other resources. The colonials were not committed to equal treatment or equal resources for the Africans under their rule. During the struggles for independence and after the struggles had been won, petty bourgeoisie rallied along tribal lines to maximize their political voice and increase their chances for access to resources and power. These consolidated sites of loyalty continued in the form of tribally significant competitivisms long after independence, always further exploited by ambitious, upwardly mobile elites striving to secure their own narrow interests.

The myths of the colonials, in all their myriad forms, contributed to the rebirth of ethnic loyalties, because their zealous claims that Africans had no histories, traditions, or customs of any value were bound to force reactions in the denigrated peoples that overvalued their cultural roots, hypostatized their cultural identities, invoked visions of a lost past, and glorified long-dead leaders and heroes. The hyper-valuation and romanticization of tribal identities provided a sense of tribal concord that ultimately helped the oppressed to reject and over-come their wretched, impoverished circumstances.

Tribal identity, in Africa as everywhere, is largely a social construct.[17] This does not mean however that cultural differences are meaningless constructions. Cultural identity constructions give meaning to individual lifeworlds and pro-vide a site for self-realization. Especially during difficult life situations, mean-ings can be sought by reforging connections with idealized pasts. Such recon-nections can prove instrumental in moving people past present humiliations.

Africans of the modern era have lived through rapid changes. Their cata-pulting into the contemporary globalized world has left Africans, as it often leaves Westerners, feeling atomized, rootless, disconnected, and confused. Until the 1989 collapse of the rigid cold war world divided into two highly visible hyper-identities—Western capitalist democrats and Soviet communists—it had been easy to find one's place and to define one's ideological allegiances. In the wake of the Soviet collapse, there reigned the general belief that global solidar-ity and liberal freedoms would replace the dichotomous ideological standoff. That dream has been disappointed at every turn. Instead there has ensued a flood of ethnic conflict across the globe. Ethnic divisiveness is a quasi-universal post–cold war phenomenon, not a phenomenon exclusively African.

Chances are that modernizing forces (urbanization, industrialization, com-moditization, and capitalist competitivism), those very civilizing forces in which the imperialistic Europeans took such pride, create the conditions that corrode healthy self-identity and fire ethnic conflict. Nostalgic tales of great traditions, magnificent heroes, and glorious histories crop up to heal the feelings of isola-tion, causing agendas for self-determination to arise. Calls for a return to a glo-rious past have a deeply human appeal across vast cultural landscapes. The ap-peal is all the more understandable for societies whose sense of worth has been called into question by denigration. Ethnic regeneration projects become fash-ionable in the modern era because they promise connection among monadic consumers thrust into the alienating global marketplace.

Accounts of migrant labor practices in southern Africa, whether in the min-ing camps of Witwatersrand, Zaire, or Zambia, in the plantations of Mozam-bique or south Malawi, or in the farms and ranches of Zimbabwe, demonstrate disputably that the isolating effects of capitalist colonialism gives rise to sharper and sharper differentiations among peoples, replacing earlier African synchro-nicity and egalitarianism. The differences in privilege dished out across the cul-tural landscape by the colonial employers eroded former friendships among in-dividuals, families, and tribal groups. The chronic absence of laborers, generally male members of families, from the countryside for long periods of time eventu-ally resulted in the collapse of families and the disintegration of cultural groups. Furthermore, as children became educated in Westernized mission schools, many were taught to despise their traditional ways and so became alienated from their countrified parents, understanding them as backward by Western standards. Where there had previously existed links of trade and intermarriage, political allegiances, clientage relationships within and among lineages, and continuities of religious belief and social custom, there stood radically isolated peoples.

After the dust of the collapsing colonial world and the struggles for independence had settled and people returned to their families and lives, national loyalties ceased to exercise a compelling tug upon their hearts. Once freed from the yoke of colonial oppression, people expected their lives to grow better, but in most cases Africans found their hopes for a better life dashed. Slowly the inadequacies of the new regimes became painfully evident and the common people faced overwhelming dissatisfactions and disappointment. This led to renewed interest in the tribal loyalties, in traditional customs and histories, in the lands that represented home. In many cases, the return to ethnic loyalties has fired old resentments and divisions, and corroded the dreams of pan-African unity. Old tribal conflicts arise anew as life conditions for most Africans remain very difficult.

Another factor that must be calibrated in, if the effects of colonial violences are to be fully understood, is the conscription of anti-independence armed forces from the ranks of the colonized. Whites rarely entered the battlefields themselves! They wielded a powerful persuasion toward colonial complicity in the fact that, had the struggle for independence failed, those loyal to the Europeans would have been rewarded generously as more civilized than the rebels. Since the struggles for independence led eventually to independence, after the dust of battle had settled, in many countries like Zimbabwe, the closure to European rule was celebrated by all, but the wars had not left the varied African population on friendly terms with each other.

## 4. Rebounding Violence in Zimbabwe

The colonial experience in British Rhodesia is another example of the process of dehumanization from which the independent state of Zimbabwe continues to suffer. In 1888, Cecil Rhodes, British capitalist, and Charles Rudd, Rhodes's business partner, received the blessings of the British monarchy to invade Matebeleland and Mashonaland and the surrounding areas that would come to be called Rhodesia. These were lands rich in minerals, especially gold, so they made a perfect colonial target. The white mercenaries led a bloody invasion in 1890 and began thereafter to draw white settlers to the lands with the promise of 6,000 acres each and full rights to the gold on those lands.[18]

Eight years later, a unified front of the native Shona and Matabele staged an armed resistance, the first *Chimurenga*, in an effort to liberate their lands from foreign control. But they were no match for European weaponry. The valiant uprising ended with the African people being forced off the lands of their ancestors into barren, isolated reservelands, or condemned to labor in slave-like conditions on what were now private white farms.

Until 1965, the white minority regime held absolute sway. When Ian Smith declared independence from Britain, the native peoples saw their opportunity. The forces of the Zimbabwe African People's Union (ZAPU) and the Zimbabwe African National Union (ZANU), under Joshua Nkomo and Robert Mugabe respectively, united as the Patriotic Front and launched the second *Chimurenga*. This culminated in the negotiations for the Lancaster House Agreement of 1979 that laid the foundations for the 1980 Constitution of the new independent country of Zimbabwe.

One might imagine the case of Rhodesian colonization closed thereafter, with a happy ending for all, but the actual result of the liberation was typically disappointing from the point of view of justice for the historical victims of abuse. The post-independent era has not gone as the Africans had hoped largely because the redistribution of lands, which was supposed to have occurred over the first ten years of independence, was frustrated at every turn. This is largely because the redistribution was fashioned on a willing-buyer, willing-seller basis, and because the various parties' acceptance of the plan was accomplished on condition of the promise of British funding.[19]

This condition meant that the colonial master held the purse strings of the operation, and continued to hold sway over the land negotiations. When white farmers proved reluctant to give up their most arable holdings, the Zimbabwean government, concerned about maintaining British funding, was in no free position to pressure the white farmers to do justice by the agreement. The newly independent nation desperately needed the aid promised by Britain, as they found themselves financially unprepared for the huge costs of buying out the white farmers at the "fair market price" clause of the agreement.

From the early 1980s, the World Bank and the International Monetary Fund further limited the effectiveness of the new government by imposing the usual "structural adjustment" program on the newly independent nation.[20] Their demand in the case of Zimbabwe was typical of demands upon other developing nations: Deflate your currency, open your public patrimony to penetration by neocolonial business opportunists, and sell off your public works to wealthy foreign investors. Do not waste your money on costly infrastructural improvements or social programs!

In a country without clean water, without rural power, with only the most rudimentary school systems featuring painfully underqualified teachers, and with no hospitals throughout the vast reserve areas where the majority of people eek out their meager existences, the restrictions imposed by the typically short-sighted capitalist wisdom of global monetary forces dictated that the vast percentage of the people saw little improvement in their lives from colonial days. The new country, stepping into the global arena, was immediately crushed by International Monetary Fund and World Bank structural adjustment policies.

Laboring under the new constraints, Zimbabwe was hardly in a position to cater to the needs of its neglected people. Zimbabwe, in the heart of the "breadbasket of Africa," was suddenly not able to feed its people. Zimbabwe was transformed into a neo-colony strictly restricted to the production of cash crops for export in order to meet the hard currency demands of its debt-repayment schedule imposed by the global monetary powers. The largely white commercial farmers, far from having returned the lands to the native peoples as had been promised, were growing cash crops like tobacco for world markets and raking in super-profits!

Robert Mugabe did not give up his hope for the independent nation. In 1992, the Land Acquisition Bill targeted the large-scale commercial farmlands for redistribution to landless Africans, mainly homeless war veterans who had been promised returns on their soldierly investment in independent Zimbabwe. The redistribution was limited by the continuing fact of Britain's financial pledges but it was becoming increasingly clear that those monetary promises were as fragile as the redistribution promises had proven. Britain's pledges of compensation to the newly independent nation proved typical of colonial pledges across the continent. Britain had guaranteed forty-four million pounds to the resettlement program at its outset, but a mere five years later, in 1997, when the Labor Party came into power in Britain under the conservative Tony Blair, the British cut off the promised funding.

By 1999, Zimbabwe and Robert Mugabe had had enough. Mugabe began the direct confiscation of commercial farmlands, redistributing the latter from the whites to the Zimbabwean peasants. Moreover, Mugabe scandalized the capitalist powers of the world when he openly rebelled against the policies of the International Monetary Fund and the World Bank, causing Zimbabwe, in 1999, to become declared in default of its loans. The loans were terminated and soon the global monetary powers revoked Zimbabwe's membership.

Land crises as in Zimbabwe are not confined to that particular site of colonial abuse, but exist as well in South Africa, Namibia, Mozambique, and many other countries of Africa. U.S. and British powers remain adamant in their fervor to halt the agrarian revolutions that seek to redistribute African lands among the landless indigenous. Whether the redistribution of ancestral lands is so passionately opposed by the Western capitalist powers because it fans an old paranoia about communism or because it limits the possibilities for neocolonial plunder by largely British and U.S. big businesses remains a matter of debate.

Zimbabwe provides a typical case for charting the long-term effects of colonial abuses and neocolonial extensions of colonial exploitation through global trade policies. As the new millennium dawns on the peoples of Zimbabwe, as on the various peoples of that region, fondly named the Breadbasket of Africa, famine is widespread and growing exponentially every year. Former white officials of the colonial government, including Ian Smith, former leader of white-ruled Rhodesia, still own thousands of acres of the best land in Zimbabwe. Of those white farmers forced from their lands in Zimbabwe in the recent land seizures—a situation generally seen as scandalous in the West—a good many moved next door to Mozambique and bought land at bargain basement prices after a white-led mercenary army had devastated that country.

The export economy forced by World Bank and International Monetary Fund policies effectively determines that, along with social programs, food for the native peoples becomes a non-priority. To understand the fragile economic equation in Zimbabwe today the scholar must consider broken colonial promises and the changing weather patterns of the continent, which scientists now link directly to the smokestacks of Western industrial giants. Famine in the rich African breadbasket is less a mystery than generally thought.

Zimbabwe is currently the target of Western imperialist aspirations as one of the coveted "fixer-upper nations" for capitalist penetration. Blair and George W. Bush remain critical of Zimbabwe for some of the same reasons they are hostile to Iraq, Iran, North Korea, Palestine, Venezuela, Cuba, and the Philippines. These countries form a rogue group of independent nations that refuse to play the global trade game. They are hostile toward the persistent attempts of Western big business to strip-mine their countries' resources and to yoke their hungry people as underpaid slave-wage laborers.

Western neo-imperialists are targeting Zimbabwe in a global smear campaign ostensibly as a reaction to the land seizures in that country. One concealed reason for the frustration of the extreme capitalists of the West toward Zimbabwe's Robert Mugabe may be Zimbabwe's role in providing military assistance during the crisis in the Democratic Republic of Congo in 1998. The Southern African Development Community (SADC) provided armed forces to support Laurent Kabila who led the government of the Congo after the fall of the CIA puppet Mobuto Sese Seko.[21] Kabila, who obdurately denounced neo-imperialist intervention in his country and in the region, required Zimbabwe's aid in resisting an invasion, backed by the United States and Britain, from Uganda and Rwanda. Given these conditions and the powerful Western opponents to Kabila, it is no great mystery to learn that Kabila was assassinated in January, 2000.

Colonialism appears, to the uncritical eye of the general population of the West, as a long-dead relic of an unfortunate imperialistic past. World leaders, most people happily believe, no longer sit in public forums and openly carve up the far reaches of the planet for their individual and national profits. But experts on globalization and the attendant rhetoric of "development" tend not to share this optimistic view. Big business, they contend, with the aid of the World Bank and World Trade Organization policies, ultimately generate the same devastating effects for third world nations as colonial exploitation had previously exacted. The third world, rich in resources, gets poorer and poorer each year in what fair trade movement spokespersons are calling "the race to the bottom" that pits one poor country against another, one exploited workforce against the next, to compete for the favors of the richest big business interests in the world. [22]

Zimbabwe is a glaring case in point for the study of neocolonial struggle. The case of Zimbabwe is especially dear to me because, during the 1980s, when Canada was involved in diverse programs of aid to needy third world nations, I volunteered as a teacher in a Canadian-built and maintained college in the reservelands of rural Zimbabwe. Canada, under the auspices of the World University Service of Canada and the Canadian International Development Agency (CIDA), enlisted, through Canadian universities, teachers and other professional specialists to work in various capacities in the underdeveloped rural areas of the newly independent nations of Africa as well as other struggling nations of the third world. My husband, a historian, and I, a budding philosopher, welcomed the opportunity for a firsthand experience of Africa, so we volunteered our varied expertise to the development of the new nation of Zimbabwe, pledging several years as teaching fellows at notoriously deficient local wages in a rural mission college.

From the earliest moments of our placement in the mission school of rural Zimbabwe, it became clear to us that there existed a great deal of resentment among the native population directed against white people in the country; curiously, the presence of white foreigners, even those engaged in generous aid projects, was found as objectionable as the persistent old colonial faces of white Zimbabweans. This tension was being generally exploited by nationalist forces within the country and fanned into flames where there existed a political or economic profit to be made from such fanning. Open public preaching often with racist overtones and directed against alienated social elements was common. Color and racial difference were openly marketed as the cause of many of the country's social and political problems. For the Canadian contingency of teacher conscripts, many of whom had left behind not only family and friends, but substantial jobs with higher pay, to spend a few years of our lives aiding a developing nation, drastically impoverished of educated or technically trained personnel, there reigned a shared bewilderment at the open racism and anti-Western prejudice that met us in this fair young land. My studies in the structure of violence over the past decades have helped me to understand what baffled me during those years: white skin provided a highly visible enemy against which the newly independent nation could posit and solidify its postcolonial identity and heal inter-tribal divisions.

At the mission college where my family and I were stationed, one could regularly hear over the local radio, in public speeches, and in the daily college addresses by the black African headmaster of the college, discourses demonizing white foreigners as parasites in the country. Mission teachers who had come to Zimbabwe in aid programs such as ours were being targeted in postcolonial propaganda campaigns as infiltrating the country under concealed imperialist agendas. One story depicted imported humanitarian aid workers as "stealing" jobs and living space from Zimbabwean professionals because of over-population in the foreigners' skyscraper-strewn cities. Zimbabwe was suffering a professional crisis and begging the international community for assistance. Professionals were being seduced from first world universities and workplaces to fill the gaping void of adequately prepared teachers and other professionals, sponsored largely by gifts from humanitarian organizations, international aid foundations, and governmental development programs of more affluent nations. Nevertheless, local propaganda declared that aid programs were the work of corrupt white neocolonials who aimed to return Zimbabwe to white control, take over the country once again, and bleed it for their own advantage. A foreign stranger could say little to dislodge these fears in the local peoples.

I recall being baffled, mystified, and at times appalled by the profundity of the students' ambiguously fascinated hatred for all things Western, given the fact that many of them were arriving at the college straight from the rural area with no previous experience or connection with any white Westerner before their arrival at the mission school. They were outwardly polite but barely disguised their deep resentment for their teachers, though most of the teachers in the mission schools are Marist monks, a Catholic teaching monastic order dedicated to building schools, training teachers, and providing education for the underprivileged in rural areas of the world. The Marists had braved the rural lands of Rhodesia during the 1940s to bring fine mission schools, water, electricity, and of course their religion to the far reaches of the country.

Part of my mystification hailed from my utter lack, at that time, of a studied knowledge of the harmful effects of historical European interventions in African countries. I came to learn, during my years in Zimbabwe, that race had become a functional myth and racial ideology a political tool in the new Zimbabwean nation. The myth of race helped frustrated African elites to deflect challenges to their effectiveness for rule in the new nation, in the face of a collapsing economy and a corrupt bureaucracy. Demonizing white farmers and professionals from the international community had been burgeoning across the Zimbabwean countryside over the years since independence. Pervasive denigration of whites served to repair black African self-images in the country.

The young male students at the mission college where I was stationed assured me that they were well acquainted with the practices of white Western folk. They knew that overflow populations from Western nations were scouring the earth to escape their grossly overcrowded homelands. Pictures of the towering skyscrapers of Western nations had convinced the young students that the West had run out of space. Westerners were once again flooding to third world nations to steal fresh homelands and arable farmlands for their private use. The students were not to be dissuaded from their certain conviction that even mission teachers as we, who worked for meager salaries in the wilds of the African bush where their own teachers refused to go, were but greedy capitalists out to take advantage of them.

It is clearer to me now, after my decades of study of violence, that white foreigners and white Zimbabweans provided a conveniently visible enemy whose starkly demonized image permitted the easy reconstruction of black African identities in the postcolonial era. The propaganda about the insidious infiltration of corrupt minorities in their country served current political purposes of rebuilding national ties and overcoming tribal factionalism in the postcolonial era. Despite the ties we as teachers inevitably forged with individual students, discourses demonizing white folk continued to be vociferously expressed throughout the country and welcomed in school speeches.

The loud denouncement of whites served a second purpose: it occluded a more troubling, more subtle horror that crept through the countryside. The demonization of whites was serving a sociological purpose, conveniently displacing aggression rooted in inter-tribal resentment that had been festering since the colonial era, the legacy of the divide-and-conquer politics of colonialism. Persistent resentments found expression as questions of authentic identity: who are the true Zimbabweans, now that the white Rhodesians are marked as non-belonging? A renewed postcolonial tribalism was slicing the country in two factions.

Despite the nagging racism that undermined trust at our college, we eventually won the confidence of the students by declaring a new Hiking Club. This invention furnished us with a convenient excuse to spring the students, always suffering from desperate feelings of imprisonment during their three-month school terms, from their boarding houses to the nearby river for day hikes and overnight camping excursions. In this venue of relative freedom, the students began, slowly at first and then later fevered and impassioned, to share horrifying childhood memories of the years when Zimbabwe was embroiled in its independence war.

Their dark tales also explained why their resentment of black Africans was more profound and resolute than their resentment of alien whites. The persisting resentments that divide the populace in the postcolonial period remain a legacy of the divide-and-conquer tactics of the British Rhodesian powers during the colonial period. But deepest and most ripe were the inter-tribal wounds opened during the independence war period. Those wars had been brutal and ugly, and had pitted neighbor against neighbor, and tribe against tribe. Those black Africans who had been conscripted into the Rhodesian army to subdue the rebel forces who had fought for independence provided easy postcolonial enemies.

Once trusted, my family and I found ourselves privy to tales recounting painful memories of the horrors that the college students and their families had suffered during the wars of independence. In every case, it was tribal others, not whites, who were hated unconditionally and blamed for the atrocities that generally characterized the period of the struggle for independence. Wanton, horrific, ingenious tortures had been practiced by African against African. These tortures were inscribed in the memories of these youths. They did not seem to recall with great resentment that white Europeans had usurped their lands and treated them like beasts of burden. They recalled only that their tribal enemies had been partners in the colonial crimes.

One particularly grueling story told how bands of armies, first from one side of the independence struggle and then the other, had in turns invaded their village. The father, a farmer in the reservelands and having no role in the independence struggle, was accused of supporting the white farmers. With sadistic pleasure, the black soldiers, conscripted into the colonial armies and fighting in support of the whites, made the old man dig his own grave under the incentive of their whips and taunts. Then, to the horrified screams of his family, the soldiers burned out the old man's eyes. As the old father, delirious, struggled to feel his way along the village floor to the gray pit he had dug for himself, the soldiers compelled his loved ones to beat him to death with trunks of small trees as he crawled his way to the pit, where he would be buried alive if the family had not been diligent enough in their labors.

Stories and memories akin to these leave the Zimbabwean postcolony in suffering and division. The miseries that the people had undergone at the hands of white Europeans during the colonial period created very strong racial prejudices in the minds of the black African population. Far more intense and deeply engrained were the post-independence resentments among the tribal factions. In the post-war period the atrocities of the independence wars were still fresh and painful. So too were the prejudices that affirmed that whites are more civilized than blacks. That popular belief dictated that the atrocities of the war would more readily be seen as the inventions of enemy black Africans, and not as direct orders of the colonial Europeans. After independence, then, hatreds against white colonials were soon refocused upon alien tribesmen. Politically motivated myths arose to purify the Shona tribe of any implication with the ruling whites, and to reconstruct the Matebele and other smaller tribes, not only as instrumental forces in keeping the European colonial stranglehold over the natives but as responsible for the war atrocities.

By the 1980s, racially based enmities pitting blacks against whites were on public display at local levels of the country to re-boost national confidence and heal the divisions among the warring tribes. Rarely did evidence of this scapegoating practice reach the press, though, since such practices would surely endanger investment and aid from rich Western nations. As teachers in the rural area, my family and I came to be regularly called upon by minority (non-Shona) students, members of the Matabele and other less powerful tribes, to protect them from the cruel beatings dished out in the dormitories. My fiery Sardinian husband, with the subtle charm and wild-eyed appearance of a Charlie Manson, made it his private mission to end the beatings, which he assumed to be the handiwork of the generally drunken Shona headmaster, known for his regular "virginity tests" administered to the handful of local girl students. The story has an ironic conclusion: the culprit behind the student beatings turned out to be an overzealous Spanish monk who, with the full knowledge and support of the monks and the headmaster, believed he was doing the only thing possible to keep half-savage young men in tow. The plan was quite ingenious, if barbaric. The monk conscripted henchmen from among the senior students and established a coercive age-based hierarchy to undercut divisive tribal divisions among the student body.

I contend that we witness the rebounding of the violences of the colonial era and the atrocities of the independence wars in the current land redistribution program pursued by Mugabe. To the great dismay of Westerners and Africans alike, Mugabe is committed to ousting white farmers from their lands, though the white farmers are African-born descendants of the colonials and have no home country to which they could return. The land-redistribution program helps to keep public attention in Zimbabwe upon racial differences and so it serves well the postcolonial goal of healing divisions between blacks and blacks. The violences associated with the ousting of the whites can be seen as direct reboundings or counter-violence brought about after decades of seething frustrations in the exploited community of oppressed, black, colonized peoples.

During my years in Zimbabwe in the eighties, tribal tensions were kept under wraps, as Western generosity ran high and Mugabe paraded racial conflict as mended and colonial hatreds as cured. However, among my students, the resentments of the independence war period clearly smoldered on. We mission-teachers easily noted that those young men who were least successfully integrated into the mission community were those who were markedly physically different (taller, thinner, and darker-skinned) from the majority of the student body (robust, brown-skinned, medium-height Shona).

Occasional reports arrived from a sibling Marist Brothers mission in the Ndbele north, telling of bloody raids by the national armies upon the local populations. Tribal tensions were more subtle but still evident during the army's routine inspections of the countryside near our mission. One day a Matabele family would occupy a hut on a nearby hill, keeping mostly to themselves and living quiet, isolated lives. Eventually, the soldiers would tour the area and, the next morning, the family would be gone. Nothing would be asked of the disappearance by neighboring villagers; no explanation would be offered.

Postcolonial conflict in Zimbabwe centers around the issue of land. The peoples' alienation from the soil of their ancestors during the colonial period brought the postcolonial attention of African peoples back to the land. We can glean from the example of Zimbabwe that the refocus upon the land is about righting historical wrongs. Redistribution is a healing phenomenon. In many instances, the renewed focus on the land rekindles old tribal hatreds. Some people simply want to reclaim their traditional identities and recover the lands of their forefathers, but others are simply voracious capitalists or political hopefuls, anxious to make their fortunes or to fortify their political careers.

The land, as meeting point of time and space, presents postcolonial Africans with an ancient focal point for self-rediscovery, reclamation of cultural pasts, and a dimension of existence around which to make peace between the hyper-futuristic Western capitalist ideals and the sacred, time-honored traditions of African heritage. In large areas of southern Africa today, conditions for people remain much as they had been during the colonial era. In some places, conditions have worsened, as they have in Zimbabwe as a result of the land redistribution reforms. Migrant labor, so disruptive of family and culture, is still the dominant practice, and the attitudes of the people toward that system remain unaltered in their dissatisfactions.

The failure of the new nation-states to provide the necessary welfare measures to support a fully urbanized population is promoting in many people a renewed preoccupation with the lands of their tribal homes. Land and rural life is slowly becoming valued once again. As living expenses remain lower in the rural areas, the homeland is regaining its existential worth, regaining its rich mystical meaning—as a place of origin, a point of identity reference along life's journey, a restful respite from the migrant labor camps, and as a destination for future retirement. But this new focus on the land can clearly take people in one of two opposing directions: it can be healing and bring them together to share the sacred soil, or it can be a source of conflict that reawakens old resentments.

The return to the land offers the African a means to reclaim histories and traditions. It is the land that resolves the conflicts dividing the Westernized youth educated in white European schools and traditional elders who want a return to a lost African world. The past of tradition meets the future of global market projects in the African notions of time and space: for the traditional African, the past *is* the future; no paradox exists in African minds between the two dimensions of time. Life's journey leads forward from childhood through adulthood toward old age, but culminates, with death, in a passage back to one's roots in the spiritual reunion with the ancestors and with the god. As the newly independent nation steps into the global marketplace, African traditionalism can provide the healing time that is needed to nurse the wounds of colonial division.

Africans are not backward simply because they do not move forward in the same ways that Westerners do. Postcolonial African nations enter the new global era and step onto the world stage. They cannot retreat from global forces that pull them into the market fray, but they are not necessarily bound to Western patterns of development, Western behavior codes, or Western-style institutionalization. Africans are not predestined to repeat Western mistakes. The return to the land that has been occurring across southern Africa points the way to an alternative future where authentically African ways of dwelling might be carved out anew. Perhaps the most modern of the first peoples of the earth are not determined to follow the dark fate of Western nations. What the future holds for the people of Africa, in terms of their relationships to the land and their relationships to each other, depends upon the effectiveness of postcolonial identity work to see beyond their histories of abuse and violence.

# Notes

1. Blaise Pascal, from *"Misere de l'Homme sans Dieu"* in *Pensées des Provinciales* (Paris: Bookking International, 1995), Article II, 31–71 (translation mine).
2. Ervin Staub, *The Roots of Evil: The Origins of Genocide and Other Group Violence* (Cambridge: Cambridge University Press, 1989).
3. Staub, *Roots*, 47; see also A. Egendorf, C. Kadushin, R. S. Laufer, G. Rothbart, L. Sloan, *Legacies of Vietnam: Comparative Adjustment of Vietnam Veterans and their Peers*, Vol. 1 (Washington, D.C.: U.S Government Printing Office, 1981); P. J. Wilson. "Conflict, Stress and Growth: The Effects of War on Psychosocial Development among Vietnam Veterans" in *Strangers at Home: Vietnam Veterans since the War*, C. R. Figley, S. Leventman, eds. (New York: Praeger Press, 1980); K. E. Fletcher, "Belief Systems, Exposure to Stress, and Posttraumatic Stress Disorder among Vietnamese Veterans" (Ph.D. diss., University of Massachusetts, Amherst).
4. Staub, *Roots*, 50 & ff.
5. Mahmood Mamdani, *When Victims Become Killers: Colonialism, Nativism, and the Genocide in Rwanda* (Princeton: Princeton University Press, 2001), 221 & ff.
6. Mamdani, *Victims*; see also Bill Berkeley, *The Graves are Not Yet Full* (New York: Basic Books, 2001); Scott Peterson, *Me Against My Brother* (New York & London: Routledge, 2000).

7. Mamdani, *Victims*, 35.

8. Samantha Power, *A Power from Hell* (New York: Basic Books, 2002), 329–390.

9. Power, *Power*, 329–390.

10. Power, *Power*, 329–390.

11. Ervine Staub, *The Psychology of Good and Evil: Why Children, Adults, and Groups Help and Harm Others* (Cambridge: Cambridge University Press, 2003).

12. Leroy Vail, *The Creation of Tribalism in Southern Africa* (Berkeley and Los Angeles: University of California Press, 1991), 10.

13. Vail, *Tribalism*, 1.

14. Jack David Eller, *From Culture to Ethnicity to Conflict* (Ann Arbor, Mich.: University of Michigan Press, 1999), 17 & ff.

15. John S. Mbiti, *African Religions and Philosophy* (New York: Frederick A. Praeger, 1969), 222.

16. Vail, *Tribalism*, 10.

17. See Albert Memmi, *Racism*, Steve Martinot, trans. (Minneapolis: University of Minnesota Press, 2000).

18. Vail, *Tribalism*, 118–146.

19. Vail, *Tribalism*, 118–146.

20. Clever Mumbengegwi, "Macroeconomic and Structural Adjustment Policies in Zimbabwe" in *International Political Economy* (Palgrave-MacMillan, 2002).

21. J. D. Hargreaves, *Decolonization in Africa* (London, U.K.: Longman, 1988), 182.

22. See film by Jeremy Brechter, *Global Village or Global Pillage*, Washington, D.C.: World Economy Project, 2000; see also www.villageorpillage.org on February 27, 2007).

# Chapter 14
# African Philosophical Therapy

The best philosophy, according to the ancient tradition following Socrates, composes *therapeia*, a curing, a tending, a fostering of health, a nurturing in sickness, or a medical treatment.[1] Philosophy is therapy, not for the body but for the soul. Socrates was executed as an old man of seventy, leaving behind an oral philosophical tradition, a philosophical method of argumentation, and a practice of rigorous analysis of concepts and meanings. But he left behind no writings. For a written record of Socrates' philosophical therapy, the student must turn to Plato's corpus. Plato depicts Socrates in action as he leads his students to question their deepest assumptions, to "give birth" to their ideas, and to test them for validity in the court of their highest ideals.[2]

In the *Republic*, Plato has Socrates name philosophy's most crucial work discussions of "the right conduct of life."[3] Socrates is pictured in some Platonic dialogues caught up in sheer abstraction, his thoughts flying off in lone pursuit of ethereal heights. But in most of the Platonic corpus, Plato pictures Socrates at his work in the bustling marketplace of Athens, the most thriving intellectual, cultural, and trading center of the ancient world. Socrates tells the Athenian court, in his defense recorded in Plato's *Apology*, that the philosopher is a gift sent from the gods to keep the lumbering horse of the state from trampling on justice. Philosophy's work is "the highest welfare of your souls" Socrates explains to his fellow Athenians.[4]

Socrates is explicit: philosophers meditate upon the highest things—beauty, justice, and goodness. But they must not be permitted to "linger there" but must "go down again among those bondsmen and share their labors and their honors, whether they are of less or of greater worth."[5] Plato describes the city as a dangerous cave where philosophers, at great risk to themselves, must battle ignorance and false truths and prizes to rescue the few bright souls. Philosophy, for Socrates, is not the arid speculation of lofty ideals. It is the perilous return to the marketplace to practice therapy upon the lost souls of the city.

I understand philosophy, in the wake of the collapse of the great Athenian Empire, to continue the tradition of philosophy as therapy in three distinct schools stemming from Socratic practice; these schools—Epicureans, Skeptics and Stoics—are named the Hellenistic Schools of Philosophy. In the disillusionment that followed in the failure of great city-states to provide a healthy environment for the cultivation of justice in their citizens, the philosopher returned to Socratic tradition to provide therapy for the soul, to cultivate justice one soul at a time.

These traditions sought social and political functionality for their art, addressing the most pressing and painful problems of human life. They grappled with the reality of human misery, fear of death, the ambivalent passions, love and sexuality, violence and aggression. Though they still practiced careful argumentation and developed rigorous definitions of lofty ideals, though they retired their arguments from the bustling marketplace to the gardens of their private retreats, the Hellenistic schools concentrated their efforts upon "the right conduct of life," developing meticulous programs of ethical practice that could bring its apprentices peace, tranquility, and justice in the midst of a morally collapsing world.

Sadly, the Hellenistic Schools of Greece and Rome have largely fallen by the wayside of Western philosophical practice. Hellenistic ethics have received little attention since the fourth century C.E. They are only rarely studied in general history of philosophy programs of the West. The therapy of souls that, by rigorous attention to ethical practice, can bring consolation and healing in the worst of human miseries has largely fallen into disuse in the Western world in favor of spectacular analytic displays of clever argument.

## 1. Philosophical Healing in Africa

Socrates calls upon philosophy to heal the human illness of injustice, to provide the therapy necessary to heal the wounded soul. The art of philosophy, however, can be deployed to wound as quickly as to heal. Enlightenment philosophy goes hand in hand with the prevailing social Darwinist evolutionary theories and with religious ontologies to supply justifying narratives to the colonizations and imperialisms of the modern era. One is reminded of the multifold and self-contradictory meanings contained in the ancient Greek word for medicine—*pharmakos*. *Pharmakos* refers to medication or medicine, all manner of potent tonic, magical words, songs or antidotes, or any type of therapy that acts as a remedy or preventative to ward off the disease of body and soul. But the word also signifies an elixir that poisons or destroys. *Pharmakos* names the hemlock that Socrates was sentenced to drink to execute himself.

In African belief, the *mganga* or medical magician is similarly credited with having special powers that inquire into the causes and the cures of destructive or unusual states of being or events. The *mganga* can be called upon to kill or to cure; hence the *mganga*'s ambiguous reputation even in the African interpretive world. Africans fear the *mganga*, but they never fail to show him respect.

During the long eras of European imperialism and colonialism, the values and ideals, and metaphysical visions expounded by European philosophers demonstrated that Enlightenment celebrations of the powers of the human intellect, begun in the sciences, found expression and amplification in the philosophical writings of the time. Europeans, across every discipline, agreed that Europe was the center of the intellectual universe and the cultural gem of the god's creative project. The Eurocentrism of the philosopher and the scientist conjoined with capitalist projects for extracting the wealth in resources and labor from the lands and bodies of supposedly less evolved societies.

Christian consciences were far from appalled by these exploitive projects. The popes were full allies of the conquering monarchs, prompting and aiding the colonial undertakings to full fruition. The Christian worldview affirmed that the god demanded that the savages be evangelized and civilized. The failure of the natives to submit their lands to foreign rule and their bodies to exploitation brought about their slaughter as readily as did their failure to submit to the biblical attack upon their souls.[6]

Philosophy, a human endeavor, was actively practiced across the African continent from time immemorial. Many of the ideas that are foundational to Socratic thought have their origin in philosophical traditions that emanated from Africa centuries before. Postcolonial African philosophy, however, has taken up a special set of tasks. Arising like a phoenix out of the smoldering ashes of colonial ruin, African philosophy has demonstrated the healing power for which the art of philosophy was known in the ancient world. I contend that the evolving forms assumed by African philosophy since its re-inception in the 1930s evidence that African philosophy has been working through a plethora of "identity dysfunctions" that compose the legacy of colonial abuse. African thinkers have been doing important work that serves the existential needs of Africans everywhere: liberating African minds for healthy identity work and reclaiming African traditions and institutions from the ashes of the colonial experience.

African philosophers are struggling, throughout the closing decades of the twentieth century, with the crucial task of decolonizing African thought and freeing it from its previously felt need to fit with, break with, or respond to Western modes of rationality. Tsenay Serequeberhan states, in his *The Hermeneutics of African Philosophy*:

> African humanity is anxious and does not find itself at home. It is this felt anxiety, this absence, this gap between *actuality* and *ideality* which today calls forth and motivates the struggle, at various levels and in differing forms, against neocolonialism, and simultaneously, out of the exigencies of this struggle, provokes the reflections of African philosophical hermeneutics.[7]

African philosophy arises anew to serve the existential needs of African peoples in the wake of colonialism, to express the African people's right to free existence, to self-determination, and to valorization for their positive contribution to human civilization. Important identity features rendered questionable in the colonial myths that emerged to justify colonial oppression over African peoples. But African philosophers are at last speaking their own truths, and are thereby providing that therapy for the soul most needed in the postcolonial African world. African philosophers are giving meaning to the existential existences of Africans on the continent and, in this way, African philosophy is helping to heal the African mind-set torn brutally by colonization.

The path that African philosophy takes, since its inception in the 1930s, confirms not only the richness of African cultural tradition and the profundity of African philosophical talent, but the multifold effects of colonial violence. Where subjectivities have been erased, where histories have been obliterated, where cultures have been condemned as decadent there is need for fevered and extreme posturing to defend the conceptual parameters of a lifeworld. Many people have suffered colonization and slavery. Many have been oppressed by foreign dictators. But only the Africans have come away from these experiences with concerns about their value as human beings, about the fitness of their mental capacities, about the moral worth of their cultural practices and institutions, about their ahistoricality—indeed, about their very right to continued existence. This explains why African philosophy in the postcolonial era is driven by what we might call a will to defend, the varied articulations forming attempts to reclaim and revitalize traditional belief systems and to reinstate African societies as legitimate cultural forms.

## 2. Ethnophilosophy Redeems Tribal Identity

Earliest African philosophy was shared across African social groups, passed down from elders to the young of each new generation, transmitted and preserved in verbal genealogical records, shared mythologies, wise sayings, the memory of the elderly, traditional proverbs, stories and living religions and socio-political structures of the African peoples. Because of the lack of written records to formalize these philosophical traditions and because of the lack of specific authors to whom the original ideas could be attributed, Europeans tend to interpret African philosophical activity as absent from the continent before its confrontation with the Western world through colonization.

Ethnocentric European philosophers, as Lucien Lévy-Bruhl, ascribed this lack of (Western-style) philosophy to the supposedly unevolved primitive mentality of the pre-logical African mind.[8] Formal and written African philosophy began to flourish again in the wake of independence in many African nations and by Africans in diaspora. This earliest phase followed in the rigid analytic tradition of Western philosophy, a tradition many philosophers say is dying—albeit a very slow death—under the challenge to its ethical viability posed by postmodern philosophers of the Continentalist tradition.

The long centuries of colonial slaughter and abuse had obliterated the bodies, the political alliances, and the sacred territorial holdings of African peoples.

But colonialism had also obliterated African histories, their cultural traditions, and their prolonged and deep intellectual customs and practices. The African philosophy practiced during colonial times composes highly Westernized interpretations of African culture. Even when the philosophy is sympathetic to African causes, the tone is apologetic and the purpose remains the exculpation of the "prelogical" mentality of Africans by Western rationalistic measures. These philosophies as ethnic apologetics are known as African ethnophilosophy.

I see African ethnophilosophy responding to a deep anxiety in the African people in the late colonial era. Philosophers on the African continent seek to revalorize the African peoples whose right to life, freedom, and inclusion in the human world had been placed in question by the European world. The first wave of African philosophy strives to reassert the positive contribution to human civilization historically made by African peoples. Ethnophilosophy is philosophical therapy that works to uproot the colonial prejudicial reality postulates that had justified colonial oppressions.

Ethnophilosophy, occurring between the 1930s and the 1960s, serves an existential need in a brutalized people; it represents a stage in evolving identity work carried out in the wake of victimization. That identity work, however, is markedly obsessive, its overzealous apologetics typical of the highly reactive identity work that generally attends the shattered self-images of victim populations. The philosophical therapy of the late colonial period remains locked within a logic of apology because ethnophilosophy continues under the thrall of Enlightenment prejudices that linger on the African continent at this time, well entrenched in the minds of African thinkers educated in the Western tradition.

I am claiming African ethnophilosophy to compose an explicitly substantialist stage in African philosophical work because it represents a return to the "thing in itself" in the tradition of Kant and Husserl.[9] First European, then African, ethnophilosophers seek to redeem the denigrated cultures and histories of African societies by charting a return to a "glorious black past" through highly nostalgized re-evaluations of African social beliefs and practices. The ethnophilosophers simply translate African social traditions into philosophical nomenclature.

Ethnophilosophy appears a sickened stage of African identity work. But it is an utterly crucial one as well. When souls have been wounded, individually or *en masse*, they must redeem themselves again, reclaiming their autonomy and their self-esteem by recovering control of their own identities. They must tear back their subjectivities from the dominant powers that have governed their interpretation, and they must reaffirm their right to carve out the details of their own distinctiveness. Much of ethnophilosophy in Africa is concerned to accomplish two crucial tasks: to trace metaphysical and epistemological continuities between African thought systems and Western philosophy, and to trace radical discontinuities between the traditional African lifeworld and the European colonial lifeworld. This reclamation emphasizes the *ethos* of generosity, welcome and life valuation that left Africans vulnerable to foreign invasion, in distinction from the European colonial worldview where autonomous subjectivity revels in the power of its own reflective image by inventing a savage other over against which to posit its own superiority.

In the earliest forms of African philosophy, there exists much evidence of African attempts to escape the continuing hegemony of Western categories of thought. Challenges to historical interpretations abound, along with articulation of more authentic formulations of African self and community. Early African philosophers seek to deconstruct colonial representations of Africans and re-place the denigrating colonialist imagery with positive expressions of African selfhood. The new self-images, still highly essentialized, remain continuous with the dominating philosophical order. That is, African thinkers assert the civilized status of African ideas by proving the congruousness of their thought systems with those of the West. Others cast African ideas in polar opposition to a de-monized radical enemy, the evil white colonialist. One of the ways African thinkers show their departure from Western conceptual hegemony is in describ-ing their political orientation as socialist, rather than capitalist. The new self-descriptions include sketches of unique brands of socialism peculiar to Africa, such as that articulated by Julius Nyerere, which revalorizes African culture by positing its orientation as fundamentally communal and focused on social wel-fare, to be positively compared to Western capitalist greed.[10]

The first philosophers accepted into the Western world as African philoso-phers are, ironically, neither Africans nor philosophers. Earliest African phi-losophy composes philosophy about Africa, carried out by Europeans living among the Africans, mostly theologians and anthropologists who formed part of the colonial train. These philosophers attempt to articulate what they recognize as an identifiable and definitive worldview among Africans. The objective of their philosophies is twofold: to have African social traditions redeemed as wor-thy of inclusion in the human world, and to have African lived philosophy in-cluded as worthy of the name philosophy. Their argument is that some lived philosophies display features that are unmistakably philosophical.

The most important of these early thinkers was Placide Tempels, a white Franciscan missionary, who studied and recorded the behavior patterns and the language of the Shabu Baluba of Zaire, among whom he lived and served as a mission priest for years. Tempels' project is to write for colonials and especially missionaries to demonstrate to Europeans that African systems of thought and belief exhibit a systematicity and a defining logic of their own that might qualify their inclusion in the world's true philosophies. In his primary work, *Bantu Phi-losophy*, Tempels unfolds the philosophical underpinnings of the everyday be-liefs and practices of the Bantu peoples. He demonstrates that their worldview has a definite ontological structure, envisioning the universe as a vast field of vital forces or life forces, which he termed *force vitale*.[11]

Human beings, *muntu*, occupy the center of this field of invisible realities, because the vital force is supreme in humans. To be wise, among the Bantu, is to know the forces and their effects, and to be capable of explaining everyday, as well as special, events in terms of the *force vitale*, that is, capable of giving metaphysical explanations for the physical events that occur. Specialists in the form of diviners and magicians hold sway in their communities for having precisely this capability. Since the universe is the outward manifestation of an inner dynamism of forces, names acquire a special significance for the Bantu, both as signs of inner strength and as the expression of connections with the forces of others, including the dead ancestors. D. A. Masolo confirms: "By acquiring a name, every person becomes a link in the chain of forces linking the dead and the living genealogies."[12]

Ultimately, Tempels sympathetic reading of the Bantu belief system can be called duplicitous. While insisting upon its inclusion in the body of true philosophy and carefully articulating a systematic ontological vision that governs everyday beliefs and behaviors, ritual practices, and ethical understandings in Bantu societies, Tempels concludes that Christian beliefs and scientific knowledge form the paradigm of rationality, while African "traditional religious belief systems and magical explanations of life are the paradigm of irrationality . . . marked with [religious] darkness and [epistemological] ignorance."[13]

Ethnophilosophy composes a kind of defensive apology for African thought systems. The first stage of African philosophy can be considered to be seeking self-empowerment for African peoples through nostalgic reclamation of their histories. Insofar as those reclamations compose over-essentialized and static descriptions of dynamic groups, they tend to repeat anthropological errors and to reassert the European categories that served in colonial abuse. Ethnophilosophy maintains a foundational assumption consistent with Hegel's notion of the universality of being; it maintains the notion of an inherent coherence to the natural and human order that allows differing thought systems to be expressed in universal terms according to some fundamental unifying logical principle, and to be hierarchically ordered.

African ethnophilosophy remains faithful to the assumption of a natural order of things (people, events, and history), failing to recognize that hierarchical ontology, with its inherent rankings and orderings, serves to legitimate abuse of different others instead of fostering acceptance of cultural difference. Early Western-style African philosophies remain lodged in an apologetics for still inferiorized African rationality. The merely descriptive accounts of the lived philosophies of tribal life are ultimately always measured against Western-style idealized abstractions of metaphysical formations. The accounts fail to answer to challenges that only the West can boast rigorous form and methodology. Ethnophilosophy leaves African intellectuals defensive about their philosophical prowess.

The first attempt at African ethnophilosophy repeats the anthropological and theological categories according to which African cultures and beliefs are traditionally denigrated. Little doubt exists Tempels adheres to Lévy-Bruhl's concept of the "prelogical" and that Tempels's project is governed by, and suits well, the expectations of its intended audience of European colonials and missionaries. That Tempels is a thinker in firm solidarity with the colonial powers is clear from his statement: "our civilizing mission alone can justify our occupation of uncivilized peoples."[14]

Later African ethnophilosophers attempt to break free of this universalizing feature by employing a logic more pluralistic in its assumptions and approach. Melville Herskovits, an anthropologist who is a pioneer of African studies in the United States, argues for a cultural relativism born of a "respect for differences" and an "affirmation of the values of each culture" whereby philosophy becomes more generous in its categories and seeks to understand and harmonize goals, "not to judge or destroy those that do not dovetail with our own."[15] The second phase of ethnophilosophy is more generous in its approach, but, perhaps because of its anthropological approach or because it is undertaken by non-Africans, African societies, no matter how philosophically expounded and positively extolled, remain exotic specimen under the observer's microscope, rather than a viable subject of philosophical discourse and a worthy participant in philosophical dialogue. Few African philosophers, with the exception of Alexis Kagame and John S. Mbiti, engage in the ethnophilosophical debate during this earliest stage of African philosophy.

## 3. Negritude Philosophy Redeems Racial Identity

Simultaneous with ethnophilosophy emerges another universalizing trend in African philosophy. The "negritude movement" seeks a reformulation of African identity based on common fundamental cultural features seen to connect the disparate peoples of the African continent and the African diaspora. Launched during the 1930s in the Latin Quarter of Paris by young black students from Africa and the Caribbean, negritude draws its inspiration from the African American "Harlem Renaissance" and writers like W. E. B. Du Bois, Langston Hughes, Claude McKay, Sterling Hayden, Countee Cullen, Paul Vesey, and James Weldon Johnson. Negritude claims of a common cultural base serves well during the difficult era of independence struggles and in the early life of the newly independent states, providing a crucial thread of African unity to disparate peoples torn apart geographically, culturally, and politically by their cruel histories.

Negritude philosophers such as Léopold Senghor and Aimé Césaire struggle to overcome the latent Eurocentrism embedded in reigning African philosophical trends by the European and European-trained Africans who had founded African philosophy as a formalized study during the colonial era. Negritude philosophy offers a discourse of solace to Africans feeling isolated, culturally detached, and displaced across the globe, but since negritude is a reactionary movement, which overturns and reclaims Eurocentric denigrations of African phenomena, it continues to employ colonial categories to measure the worth of those phenomena. For example, negritude celebrates the value of a typically African rationality, but continues to employ Eurocentric measures to argue for its worth. This posited African mentality then has difficulty coming out ahead when weighed according to the reigning (Eurocentric) calibrations of appropriate rationality and rigorous systematicity.

Senghor, late in his life, offers the following account of his awakening to the importance of a peculiarly Africanist discourse that escapes colonial categories of moral and intellectual worth:

> In 1936 . . . [w]e had no lack of arguments with which to attract our fellow Africans and Negroes of the African Diaspora to the Renaissance of Black Culture. . . . His interest peaked by a review he read in the journal *Les Cahiers du Sud*, Aimée Césaire bought one of Frobenius' major works, *Histoire de la civilization africaine*. It was a translation, published by Emmanuel Gallimand, of *Kulturgeschichte Afrikas*. After having read it, Césaire passed it on to me, and I still have that copy with his name on it in my library. To understand the joy which took hold of us as we read this book, it is necessary to go back in time— to the instruction given in the "white man's schools," public or private, in the colonies.[16]

Senghor and Césaire find in Frobenius's critical German romanticism a way to translate an Africanist apologetic into a new glorification of African cultural heritage. Consequent to his new philosophical awakening, Senghor attempts to turn the Eurocentric discourse inside out with his theory of the "civilizational complementarity of races." Senghor figures the "Negro [as] the man of Nature," loving, feeling, sensual, profoundly connected with the land in the immediacy of earthly sound, smell, rhythms, and forms. He places this image of the "natural" African over against the European with his "discursive reason." The essentialist renderings of the distinction between European and African are once again founded on the basis of racial difference, so once again the dichotomy reasserts the idea of abiding essentialized natural kinds of human beings. Fast in the Hegelian tradition, Senghor re-establishes the categories that Europeans had applied to Africans to justify their oppressions.[17]

No matter how congruous a mix the complementary races might make in the grand scheme of cosmic being, ultimately, there exists little distinction between the *Africanité* of Senghor and the racism of Lévy-Bruhl. Africans may be no less human for their immersion in a state of nature, but, according to Senghor's own final accounting, the "proper characteristic of Man is to snatch himself from the earth . . . to escape in an act of freedom from his 'natural determinations.' It is by liberty that man conquers nature and reconstructs it on a universal scale, that man realizes himself as a god; this is freedom."[18]

On Senghor's terms, Africans lack the "proper" characteristics of real human beings. Should Africans acquire the determinative characteristics, the "conquering," "reconstructing on a universal scale" and their confusion of themselves with gods, one would be hard pressed to distinguish them from the European colonials, without reference to race or color. Although Senghor's "Negritude was always seen as the intuitive or romantic counterpoint to the West's sterile rationalism and scientific, material society," as Richard H. Bell describes, yet there is no missing the unmistakable Hegelian ring to Senghor's insistence on a "civilization of the universal."[19]

The nationalistic poet Césaire serves an important phase of African self-discovery and identity reclamation, but ultimately his philosophy proves an equally unfortunate platform for establishing an Africanist position that can persevere beyond early independence struggles. His *Discourse on Colonialism* focuses upon the problem of recovering lost African histories.[20] The prime difficulty for African philosophy, in Cesaire's calculation, is facing the problematic of the new kinds of subjectivities that colonial denigrations had constructed—ahistorical beings. The charge that the native Africans are primitives had robbed Africans of their humanity precisely because human beings have memories and genealogies, undeniable evidence of histories. Human beings take up their destinies and throw themselves toward their futures. They act. The downtrodden apolitical masses are reduced to beasts of burden, in Cesaire's account. The fundamental concern of postcolonial Africans, he claims, must be to retake the initiative and enter the dialectic of history by taking up the counter-violence that their prior negation as historical subjects evokes.[21]

## 4. African Philosophy Escapes Colonial Logic

The next wave of African philosophy remains reactive, composing a "self-critical stage" in African thought. Its intention is to pose a challenge against the approach and methodology of the various strains of ethnophilosophy that was thought to be unnecessarily apologetic for African differences from the West. African thinkers of the 1970s and 1980s are beginning to recognize that ethno-philosophy is insufficient, both to the task of philosophy *per se* and to the existential needs of postcolonial Africans. African philosophy must not simply confine itself to definitions of how, and to what extent, African traditions exhibit those features of "civilization" denied them in colonial discourse.

African thinkers of the self-critical strain agree that African civilization can prove its worth more convincingly when African philosophers extend their inquiries beyond the task of locating vague philosophical components in traditional African cultures. Since a huge feature of colonial myth had been its challenge to the African mentality as "prelogical" and incapable of abstract thought or systematic shrewdness, self-critical philosophers recognize the need for African philosophers to step outside colonial categories and extend their analyses beyond reactionary discourses of identity. They note the futility of mere nostalgic and purified discourses seeking to redeem the value of traditional African life. Self-critical philosophers attempt to produce a bona fide philosophy of culture that is capable of self-critique. African philosophers, they reckon, need to develop a schema of peculiarly African standards that can be called upon, in place of Western hyper-rationalist ideals, to evaluate African belief systems and customs.

This phase of African philosophy seeks to become truly philosophical by reconceptualizing its mission as an active critical engagement with the biases of its own thought. The self-critical strand of African philosophy reflects upon and attempts to transcend the logical paradoxes embedded in African worldviews and systems of thought. Thinkers of this tradition raise such questions as the relation between race and culture. They investigate the appropriate role of intellectuals in newly independent African nations. They also seek to chart the implications of global forces in the reconstruction of African culture, seeking to understand the effects of the clash of indigenous and global epistemologies upon African modes of knowledge-production, and to flesh out problematic definitions of development promoted by big business giants and accepted by the global community.

Self-critical philosophers recognize the implications for stagnation and collapse encompassed in the faulty definitions of development accepted in the global marketplace. They are committed to analyzing what constitutes true development in the African context, and they seek to understand how such true development might be pursued and measured, and what its costs and obstacles would be.

Thinkers such as Peter O. Bodunrin Adeniji, Kwasi Wiredu, and Henry Odera Oruka advocate a universalist approach.[22] For them, African philosophy must oppose traditional beliefs and folklore, and raise above African particularities to the level of universal discussion before addressing concerns and priorities peculiar to African socio-political contexts. Wiredu, in *Philosophy and African Culture*, applies and affirms the Western prejudice against the lived philosophies of Africa. Wiredu holds that traditional African philosophy only begins where the "bald dogmatic assertions of traditional belief" meet with the activity of Western-style philosophical reflection and argumentation. Wiredu argues that only thought that adheres to the rigorous analytic style of the West—the fruit of a reasoning and logical process—can be named true philosophy.[23]

A second strain of this phase, represented in the work of Paulin J. Hountondji, F. Eboussi Boulaga, and the idealist Marxists Marcien Towa and Amilcar Cabral, favor a dialectical approach to the new philosophy.[24] African philosophy, argues Hountondji, needs to carve out its own intellectual space within the global discourse. Philosophy, he asserts, is "a perpetual movement, a chain of responses from one individual philosopher to another across the ages."[25] African texts need to be taken up and criticized to usher their inclusion into the history of philosophical dialogue. For this to occur, four criteria must be met. African philosophy must be (1) written, not oral, in its form; (2) rigorously scientific; (3) produced by thinkers who are of African geographic and ethnic origin; and (4) purely dialectical in its form.[26]

The self-critical stage of African philosophy is largely reactionary, opposing itself to ethnophilosophy. It is also reactionary in its obsessive drive to overcome Western philosophical standards for measurement of the value of African philosophy. Ultimately, these thinkers nevertheless remain loyal to Western analytic assumptions and philosophical standards. Hountondji demonstrates this faithfulness in his insistence upon a strict dialectical form and his refusal of metaphysics, moral philosophy, and religious inquiries as legitimate philosophical forms. The loyalty of early African philosophers to the Western tradition of philosophy is not so difficult to understand since most of these thinkers were themselves trained in universities committed to the Western tradition.

With the 1990s, African thinkers are freeing themselves from self-defensive or critical obsession with their cultural and philosophical pasts, and their work takes on a new focus that is self-determinative. I call this phase of African philosophy the "existential" stage since problems of freedom, responsibility, and the role of the individual in the postcolonial nation have come to the foreground of philosophical discourse. Wiredu, Hountondji, Mudimbe, K. Anthony Appiah, Amy Gutmann, and Masolo head an impressive parade of African thinkers who seek to overcome colonial essentialist categories that persist in ethnophilosophy, but also to move beyond reactionary discourses in the shadow of colonial hegemony. These thinkers are seeking to carve out new philosophical territory that is uniquely African, unquestionably philosophical, unapologetic, freshly creative, and yet deeply in touch with the thoughts and beliefs of African peoples in their dynamic, shifting, contextualized realities.

In the past ten years, a growing philosophical refinement and a new subtlety is emerging in African philosophy. Criticism still plays a crucial role in the politics of knowledge. But a new highly rigorous philosophy has emerged. Evident in the late African philosophy of the twentieth century is a deep appreciation for the complexity of the structural modes, the epistemological foundations, and the teleological motivations driving knowledge-production systems. More explicitly acknowledged too is the power of these philosophical factors over cultural creation and transformation. African philosophers in the last decade leading into the third millennium are calling for explanations of reality and analysis of ideas, beliefs, and cultural practices that bring the living social realities of their people to sophisticated levels of conceptual awareness, while remaining true to the everyday experiences of African life.

These thinkers still work against the hegemony of Western conceptual structures that repeat colonial domination and inferiorize African modes of inquiry and expression. They seek to actively maintain the intimate link between theory and the African people's everyday thought. African philosophers are closing the divide that splits academia from social realties at large, a split that characterizes and plagues philosophy throughout the Western world. The African philosophers of the twenty-first century seek very pragmatic goals: to replace the "overdetermination (of people's historical and cultural paths by external forces) with self-determination in both theory and praxis."[27]

Extending themselves beyond essentialist descriptions of their people, beyond polar categories of self-identity, beyond the negative phase of resentful critique of demonic forces troubling their past, African philosophers are reaching a positive phase of self-determination where they are able to achieve practical consequences in healing the effects of a violent past. There is every reason to credit African philosophy with fulfilling philosophy's ancient calling, because unlike Western philosophy's hermetic isolation in the ivory tower of academia, African philosophy's integral connections with the realities of African life means that scholarly discourse maintains the possibility of proving itself truly healing.

Given that the entire direction of formal, written African philosophy has been determined by imperialist and colonial violence, I find it paradoxical that African philosophers rarely address in their work the question of violence *per se*. Little attention has been granted to the nature and forms of violence and its determinative role in human affairs. Perhaps the best work on colonial and post-colonial violence is that of Frantz Fanon who stresses the value of violence in the anticolonial struggle.[28] Another excellent treatment of the effects of colonial violence in Africa is that of Albert Memmi whose corpus composes a brilliant account of the colonial relationship and the nature of colonial abuse.[29]

Remarkably little philosophical energy has been applied to the analysis of the various kinds of violence that are peculiar to African contexts or to the question of the treatments of crime and punishment employed in colonial and post-colonial nations. African philosophers do not question the political and historical grounds for recommending the legitimacy of a punishing authority. Nor do African philosophers give extended analysis to the questions that motivate the current work: how violence has created new postcolonial forms of subjectivity and nationhood.

Fine African therapists of the soul have met with a wealth of success in healing the wounded African self-image and helping the postcolonial African world to carve out uniquely African conceptual and logical categories to express and evaluate the indigenous traditional and evolving systems of thought. Compelling to me, however, as a scholar of violence, is the fact that, while these philosophers develop sophisticated explanations of reality, rigorous analyses of development, agency, and personhood, and thoughtful speculations about African destinies in the global arena, African philosophers do not seem driven to explore the mystery of their past sufferings. They do not afford explicit and prolonged attention to the causes, modes, creative possibilities, and multifold effects of violence upon African subjects, cultures, and nations. While much valuable identity work is being accomplished by African philosophers, one wonders how viable definitions of modern Africa and Africans can ignore the question of the effects of the violent historical and political grounds of African self-becoming. One wonders how theorists of African identity can begin their analyses without first confronting and theorizing the horrors that have configured the African postcolonial world.

## 5. Western versus African Therapy

Socrates warns of the dark caves of earthly states whose truths are controlled by unscrupulous demagogues who manipulate public opinion—spin myths—to suit

their own insidious designs for wealth and power. Postmodern philosophers in
the Western tradition lament the fact that millennia of meditation on the just and
the beautiful and the good could not help to avoid the centuries of colonial and
imperial slaughter that, for them, culminate logically in the brutal madness of
the Holocaust.[30]

There exists little explanatory value in herculean sweeps across the broad
spectrum of human history. Yet, the postmodern philosopher cannot escape the
nagging suspicion that the reasons for Western civilization's moral failure lies
with philosophy's failure to be more morally influential in human affairs over
the millennia since its Western inception. There exists a suspicion that the cause
of Western imperialism may rest deep within the history of philosophy itself.
From the abandonment of philosophy's epistemologically humble, deconstruc-
tionist foundations in Socrates can be mapped the gradual but certain trajectory
of a notion of ontological plenitude that implies the gathering power of human
reason in the world. The metaphysical edifices of the Neo-Platonists overflow
into the notion of a great chain of being.[31] It is only a small leap from the worldview that asserts the hierarchical arrangement of the species of the earth to the
Enlightenment *hybris* that applies ranking to human beings and human societies
as well. That metaphysical tradition logically unfolds into a *hybris* that ultimately celebrates the infinite possibilities of a European reason while devaluing
those whose rational traditions do not conform to the European mold.

Enlightenment philosophy understands human development on the metaphor of the limitless human brain evolving toward its own perfection in resolving the seeming paradoxes of perceptual reality. Minds and brains, isolated entities, invade more and more piercingly the Cartesian mechanistic universe of
isolated "things-out-there" that stand by idly, changelessly, waiting to be penetrated by cognition, and articulated in some objective truth. Modern systematic
philosophy is rooted in the idea that the conceptual relation of subjects to phenomena is analogous to the relation of the perceiver to the object as it occurs in
visual perception. This analogy is confirmed to extend broadly across the disciplinary spectrum by social scientific, and especially the neuro-scientific, fixation
on the study of vision, a dominant focus that persists to this day.[32]

It was not until Friedrich Nietzsche insisted that our valuations and moralizations are a reflection of local "tastes," shaped by time and place and local
prejudices and not certain objective eternal truths, that philosophy began to
question itself again, and the postmodern world emerged.[33] Ludwig Wittgenstein
replaced the metaphor of vision and its reference matrix in language with the
notion of the world as a human construct, as a reality humanly created by a
community of speakers generating families of meaning. Greek philosophy finally takes a humble turn in the tradition of Socratic deconstructive ethics and
sets aside its Enlightenment arrogances and godlike aspirations of certain knowledge.[34]

Cheikh Anta Diop, Henry Olela, and others claim that what we name Western philosophy is African in its origins, that earliest black African influences
reached Socrates and Athens through colonial expeditions to ancient Egypt. If

this is so, one might wonder how African thought systems have avoided the Western trajectory of hierarchization. Why did African thought not culminate in the arrogant ethnocentrisms we find in Enlightenment European thought? The answer to this mystery is clear: both societies begin in the modest deconstructive tradition that promotes humility as the prime ethical value. Western philosophy, soon after Plato, abandons the aporetic stance and its call for *hybris* regarding human wisdom, and pursues instead grand schemas of metaphysics penetrable by reason.

In the modern arrogance of science and reason, Western philosophers force entry to that sacred realm of truth that Socrates reserves only for the gods. They tread a path of certainty that ultimately becomes the quasi-universal destiny of the Western world. African thinkers do not share in this destiny. Ancient African philosophical systems were not put to paper until after colonial rule had ended; the people remained oral in their traditions through most of the twentieth century. This fact is no guarantee that thinking will not go astray into dangerous forms. But Plato warns, in the *Phaedrus*'s long meditation on writing and speaking, that writing is a dangerous medium that easily goes morally astray. Like a bastard son, Plato has Socrates declare, written words run about without the oversight of a careful parent. They can say anything to any audience and cause all manner of chaos in the world.

African philosophies remained for centuries focused upon profoundly social lived realities, shared across entire communities and evolving within those communities. Earliest philosophy in Africa composes a dynamic experience of self, community, and world, coexisting in harmonious balance. As a result, African philosophy did not follow a tradition of arid abstraction of concepts. Nor did it take the form of clever displays of argumentation. Since African communities did not generally assume the dangerous forms of hierarchies of power or wealth, their philosophies did not evolve into gratuitous displays of the superior wit of an intellectual class.

African philosophers in the postcolonial era toil to heal the wounded African psyche of its brutalizing history. That healing has followed a path all its own and yet bears comparison with other discourses that seek to overcome abusive histories; feminist philosophy offers a ready comparison. The path of philosophical healing appears to wind a common course that leads from a labored apologetics of self-redemption from historical denigration, through an often highly aggressive self-glorification that remains reactionary and in obvious respects sickened. The loud and aggressive, boot-stomping feminist provides a solid example of this phase. Finally, however, the victim comes into her own in a self-acceptance that is appreciative of her strengths and thus can afford to enter into a self-questioning.

I have suggested that African philosophy has failed in one respect, in neglecting to dwell directly upon questions surrounding their historical victimization. But perhaps this neglect is not a failure. This neglect may signal that African philosophers have moved past their violent histories, past self-apologetics, and the dialectics of reactionism, and come at last entirely into their own. They now seem focused not upon the past but toward a brighter future. Perhaps, in traditional African fashion, philosophers are simply performing their therapies, cultivating healthier postcolonial souls who may discover themselves anew with greater pride and self-love, enjoy greater freedom from history's horrors, and stride toward futures bright with promise, as the magnificent people that they are. Beacons of grace and pride, the Africans have much to teach the West.

# Notes

1. *Liddle & Scott, Greek-English Lexicon* (London, U.K.: Oxford University Press, 1903), 315.
2. Plato, *Theaetetus* 160de.
3. Plato, *Republic* 352d.
4. Plato, *Apology* 30b.
5. Plato, *Republic* 7.519d.
6. See V. Y. Mudimbe, *The Idea of Africa* (London: James Currey, 1994), 1–37.
7. Tsenay Serequeberhan, *The Hermeneutics of African Philosophy* (New York: Routledge, 1994), 9.
8. Lucien Levy-Bruhl, *The Primitive Mentality*, Lilian A. Claire, trans. (London, U.K.: Allen and Unwin, 1923), 23.
9. Keith Ansell Pierson, Duncan Large, eds., *The Nietzsche Reader* (Oxford, U.K.: Blackwell, 2006), 3–7.
10. See, for example, the work of Julius Nyerere, *Freedom and Unity* (Oxford: Oxford University Press, 1967); *Ujamaa: Essays on Socialism* (Oxford: Oxford University Press, 1968); *Freedom and Socialism* (Oxford: Oxford University Press, 1968); *Freedom and Development* (Cambridge: Oxford University Press, 1973). See also Kwame Nkurumah, *Class Struggle in Africa* (New York: International Publishers, 1975); *Towards Colonial* Freedom (London: Panaf Books, 1979); *Revolutionary Path* (London: Panaf Books, 1980).
11. Placide Tempels, *Bantu Philosophy* (Paris: La Présence Africaine, 1965), 115.
12. D. A. Masolo, *African Philosophy in Search of Identity* (Paris: La Présence Africaine, 1965), 50.
13. Masolo, *Identity*, 47.
14. Tempels, *Bantu*, 115.
15. M. Herskovits, *Cultural Relativism* (New York: Random House, 1972), 33.
16. Léopold Senghor, "The Revolution of 1889 and Leo Frobenius," *Africa and the West: The Legacies of Empire*, Isaac James Mowoe, Richard Bjornson, eds., R. Bjornson, trans. (New York: Greenwood Press, 1986), 77.
17. Léopold Senghor, "The Spirit of Civilization or the Laws of African Negro Culture" in *Presence Africaine*, Nos. 8–10, 52.
18. Léopold Senghor, *On African Socialism*, Mercer Cook, trans. (New York: Praeger, 1964), 65 (emphasis mine).
19. Richard H. Bell, *Understanding African Philosophy* (New York: Routledge, 2002), 25.
20. Aimé Césaire, *Discourse on Colonialism* (New York: Monthly Review Press, 1972).
21. Césaire, *Discourse*, 9. See also Albert Memmi, *The Colonizer and the Colonized*, Howard Greenfeld, trans. (Boston, Mass.: Beacon Press, 1991), 55, 62–65.

22. P. O. Bodunrin, *Lessons of History for the Nigerian Republic* (London, U.K.: Warwick House, 1998); Odera Oruka, *Sage Philosophy: Indigenous Thinkers and the Modern Debate on African Philosophy* (Nairobi, Kenya: Acts Press, 1991); K. Wiredu, *Cultural Universals and Particulars: An African Perspective* (Bloomington, Ind.: Indiana University Press, 1996); Paulin Hountondji, *African Philosophy: Myth and Reality* (Bloomington, Ind.: Indiana University Press, 1983); V. Y. Mudimbe, *The Invention of Africa* (Bloomington, Ind.: Indiana University Press, 1988) and Mudimbe, *The Idea of Africa* (Bloomington, Ind.: Indiana University Press, 1994); D. A. Masolo *African Philosophy in Search of Identity* (Bloomington, Ind.: Indiana University Press, 1994).

23. Kwasi Wiredu, *Cultural Universals and Particulars: An African Perspective* (Bloomington, Ind.: Indiana University Press, 1996).

24. Paulin Hountondji, *African Philosophy: Myth and Reality* (Bloomington, Ind.: Indiana University Press, 1983); F. Eboussi Boulaga, *Christianity Without Fetishes* (New York: Orbis Books, 1984); Marcien Towa, *L'idée d'une philosophie négro-africaine* (Lyon, France: Editions CLE, 1979); Amilcar Cabral, *Unity and Struggle* (New York: Monthly Review Press, 1979).

25. Hountondji, *African Philosophy*, 105.

26. According to Richard H. Bell, *Understanding African Philosophy* (New York: Routledge, 2002), 28–32.

27. Karp, Masolo, *African Philosophy as Cultural Inquiry* (Bloomington, Ind.: Indiana University Press, 2000), 10.

28. Frantz Fanon, *Black Skin, White Masks*, Charles Lam Markmann, trans. (New York: Grove Press, 1967); *The Wretched of the Earth*, Constance Farrington, trans. (New York: Grove Press, 1986). Fanon is a psychiatrist, not a philosopher, born in Martinique, not Africa.

29. Albert Memmi, *The Colonizer and the Colonized*, Howard Greenfeld, trans. (Boston, Mass.: Beacon Press, 1991); c.f. *Racism*, Steve Martinot, trans. (Minneapolis, Minn.: University of Minnesota Press, 1994).

30. Emil Fackenheim, *To Mend the World* (Bloomington, Ind.: Indiana University Press, 1982).

31. Arthur O. Lovejoy, *The Great Chain of Being* (London, U.K.: Harvard University Press, 1964).

32. Leslie Brothers, *Friday's Footprint: How Society Shapes the Human Mind* (Oxford: Oxford University Press, 1997), 66.

33. Friedrich Nietzsche, "The Natural History of Morals," *The Gay Science*, Walter Kaufman, trans. (New York: Vintage, 1974), especially Section 186.

34. Ludwig Wittgenstein, *Philosophical Investigations*, G. E. M. Anscombe, trans. (Oxford: Blackwell, 1953).

# Chapter 15
# Concluding the Savagery

The routine harvest of insult and injury reaped by the people of Africa during centuries of colonial abuse caused the African people to discover facts about the frailty of the human condition better left unrevealed—the vulnerability of human flesh, the defenselessness of social forms against the onslaught of denigrating myth, and the incapacity of an ethos of generosity and welcome to protect against sheer aggression and arrogance. Through beatings, rapes, and myriad humiliations, Africans discovered that unqualified trust in their fellow humans was naïve and foolhardy. Worst of all, Africans discovered the inability of the healthiest mentality and most robust self-esteem to withstand prolonged indignity. Where insults are swallowed and moral outcries suppressed, and where peoples are pushed from sacred lands, where clans are scattered, and tribal solidarity offended, communal resentment eventually gives rise to agendas of revenge that turn the decent into the bloodthirsty. Like a time bomb, the colonial world, from the moment of its birth, ticked away toward a vicious and brutal finale that would not suddenly abate with the advent of independence.

To calculate the damages afforded the colonial victims, one cannot stop at mere corpse counts and inventories of appropriated landholdings. One must consider the disintegration of families by long years of forced labor migration. The debit ledgers must also tally the cultural and artistic losses, the corruption of time-honored traditions, the loss of respect for the elders when children are trained in European-style schools, the effects of the bloody battles that won independence, and the long-term split those wars wedged between Africans conscripted into the colonial armies and those fighting for independence.

Most importantly, the disfiguration of subjects and lifeworlds must be entered into the account of African losses. People change under long generations of indignity, fear, and abuse. People inhabiting oppressive regimes witness that violence is a highly effective tool that imposes order in situations of chaos; it is abundantly functional and proficient at this task. Abused subgroups of the society, once they break free of their masters' stranglehold, generally turn directly to this method to gain control of the power networks of their world. Once the sword is taken up in a cause seen as moral, it is not easily relinquished again when the immediate goals have been achieved. Violence tends to persist in the arsenal of accepted practices of the individual or community, ready to serve new goals as they develop and to endow future ends with the moral purity of past objectives.

Rarely does the practice of violence end with the burying of a people's dead. A short glance across the historical terrain of the last century reveals violence as a commodity that is not ingested without remainder; rather, it spawns endless mutations. Old forms of violence generate new products, and consumers of those products become new peddlers of its recreations. Subjective spaces of identity are transformed, social scripts rewritten, and social action is redressed in the light of violences suffered. The very ways in which self and world are framed within the lifeworlds of the suffering witness that violence and subjectivity become inextricably entwined. There ensues in victim populations an abrupt removal of established practices for conflict resolution, an interruption of traditional contexts for making sense of chaotic events, and a recasting of everyday rituals of social intercourse that blurs boundaries delineating violence from legitimate force. Violence creates, sustains, and transforms patterns of social interactions, restructures the inner world of lived realities, and corrupts the outer world of social and moral meanings.

Violence erodes the connectedness that binds people across generations and across cultural boundaries, corroding the trust that binds the social worlds of friends, family, and neighbors. Even learned reactions to social stimuli have to be unlearned after violent histories. Repertoires of sensory memories have to be reprogrammed from their grounding, brutalizing experiences. In South Africa during apartheid, for example, black Africans had trained themselves not to respond to the cries of torture victims in their housing projects, since response generally caused the respondent to be targeted as traitor or sympathizer. The forced dismissal of a neighbor's woes is contrary to every human instinct. Once learned, the dehumanizing practice taken up during apartheid had to be unlearned in the post-apartheid period.

The ability to survive in zones where radical violence has been the norm often has to do with a people's successful development of the capacity to cut oneself and one's group off from neighbors and to learn to dissimulate, deceive, and defraud. During the centuries of slave trade in the hinterlands of the Ivory Coast, for example, native African populations protected their freedom by working for the slavers. Supplied with guns, they assumed the morally ambiguous role of hunting down their tribesmen and their neighbors. Others escaped the hunters by becoming skilled at ducking out of sight and hiding, keeping to themselves and avoiding their neighbors, and becoming accomplished liars. Some tribes built whole underground villages unknown to their closest neighbors. Ancient African social rituals, such as asking after the health of neighbors and welcoming passersby, drew suspicion and were soon abandoned.

European colonials savaged the people of Africa. That savagery rebounds in manifold ways. Violence effectively rebounds in individuals and in societies that have suffered. It rebounds in ever new directions, serving new purposes, shaping new practices, and providing ever new justifications for harming others. Even when independence has been won and the oppressed have been freed from the tyranny of their past abuses, people do not easily return to their previously peaceful practices; victim people do not easily and simply step back into a lost past and pick up where they had existentially and culturally left off, decades and centuries before.

Pecking orders tend to remain persistent across vast changes in the historical circumstances of a group. The stratifications of ordered societies persist across changes of the political and economic guard. Despite the new faces, the old practices linger; old patterns of abuse and control remain intact. The systems the new independent nations of Africa inherited from the old colonial powers remained, systems designed for the express purpose of repression and coercion of sub-populations. Institutionalized inequalities in wealth, status, and power compose the logic of the regime that underpins every agency in every facet of national affairs, spelling patterns of domination and oppression all the way down the social ladder. Discontent with unequal access to privileges, jobs, education, and other benefits of the system, their hopelessness comes to be expressed in outbursts of violence in the newly independent states, as it had in the colonies.

Sometimes the historical savagery rebounds as a political problem. Some African peoples are loathe to accept in the ruling class of their nation peoples who, in the wake of colonial divide-and-conquer strategies, they now see, not as fellow sufferers in a common "community of the oppressed," but as aliens infecting their nation. Other people seek revenge against their neighbors, as they recall the treachery of those conscripted into the colonial militaries during the wars for independence. The historical savagery rebounds in the city streets, in the villages, and on the political stages of newly independent African nations, where the people carry out their "identity work" to recapture lost dignity, and reclaim lost tribal connections. People continue to suffer from the humiliations they have endured in common, but their painful pasts, as similar as they are, also set them one against another, and set the exploited against the new leaders stepping into old elitist positions and often maintaining the violences encoded within the inherited colonialist institutions.

The African continent of diverse and culturally rich peoples suffered long from physical, psychic, and structural violences imposed by colonial invaders under the rubric of civilization. This meditation centers upon African peoples so abused, but the reflection could have been focused upon any of a plethora of peoples since the dawn of modernity. I could be describing the indigenous populations of half the globe, overrun, slaughtered, and enslaved by foreign invaders as European civilizing projects swept across the globe.

When we look out across Africa, we must admit that very little has changed. The rape of the African continent is still in full swing today. Enrique Dussel observes:

The heroes of neocolonial emancipation worked in an ambiguous political sphere. Mahatma Gandhi in India, Abdel Nasser in Egypt, and Patrice Lumumba in the Congo dream of emancipation but are not aware that their nations will pass from the hands of England, France, or Belgium into the hands of the United States.[1]

Frantz Fanon too affirms: "There's nothing save a minimum of re-adaptation, a few reforms at the top, a flag waving: and down there at the bottom an undivided mass, still living in the middle ages, endlessly marking time."[2]

In the breadbasket of Africa (Malawi, Zimbabwe), people are eating dirt. They are boiling up grass to fill the hungry tummies of their children. Across the African continent, the vast majority of the native population forms a permanent underclass. They are still, in many respects, strangers in their own land. There exists, in so many places, the glaring paradox of indigenous poverty alongside the affluence of white settlers still living like feudal overlords on the best, most arable farmlands. The huge houses of white folk—who consider themselves indigenous after several generations removal from Europe on the continent— just uphill from the run-down shacks of their black servants stand as postcolonial reminders of the past. The undervaluation of African states and peoples in the global reckoning of things continues to haunt the Africans, as deeply as does the ambiguousness of their freedom and independence.

The wise, ancient peoples of Africa, like so many indigenous cultures that have slipped into the oblivion of abuse and neglect, enjoy a deep social conscience that the West, with its ethos of individualism and materialism, can never fully understand. Africans are calling upon their mighty reserve of tradition to muster the solidarity that will free them from their divisive histories. Africa's finest hour does not lie in a glorious past that has been smothered by colonial abuse. I believe Africa's future to lie in the peculiarly African brand of peaceful socialism that keeps faith with the teachings of Africa's great freedom-fighters—Nelson Mandela, Archbishop Tutu, Julius Nyerere, and others. It falls now to the denigrated peoples of the dark continent to demonstrate to the Western world that living humanly is not about material gain or power; it cannot be won by military troops and by "shock and awe" arsenals. Living *humanly* in the African tradition is about village-dwelling in peaceful companionship with folk who are ashamed to possess more than their poorest neighbors.

In the final analysis, the success of the independence struggles in postcolonial Africa must be measured in terms of the new nations' ability to overcome their violent pasts, to recapture their traditions and histories, while avoiding an over-sacralizing reclamation of the past. Africans must learn to heal the ruptures of the new present with its radical split between traditional and modern modes-of-being embodied in the gap between the urbanized African and the rural dweller. Africans must learn to hold firmly together in the face of the sinister neocolonialisms that continue to enslave their peoples, strip-mine their resources, and usurp their lands.

Africa's case is a particular tragedy with unique lingering effects, but, in many regards, the African historical experience symbolizes the new global situation, as neocolonialism increasingly fractures third world communities across the planet, splicing them into the dual extremes of the few who enjoy a life of luxury over against the hopeless many. Where little hope exists for a decent life, there festers a hotbed rife with resentment and riddled with religious fundamentalisms that will eventually magnify into terrorisms of all description.

As I write this less than cheering conclusion to my treatment of the savagery that Africa has suffered, the young nations of Africa step forth from the euphoria of liberation to take their places alongside the entirety of the third world, most of which is quickly and perhaps irrevocably being turned into a vast global slum. The changelessness of indigenous societies that was mythically alleged by Europeans has now become a depressing reality for the vast majority of third world nations. Nothing has really changed for the savaged peoples that linger on the ravaged expanses of rotted colonial splendor. The direct enslavement of history's victims to colonial masters and the dehumanizing structural violences of colonial regimes has simply been replaced by more subtle, more insidious enslavement to new, more cunning masters in neocolonial relationships of labor exploitation and economic dependence.

The indigenous of the Middle East, the South Pacific, and the new world fare no better than the people of Africa. Everywhere, the infinitesimal remainder who survived European projects of civilization, slavery, and the cruelest forms of systematic extermination—burnings at the stake, hackings into dogfood, roasting children on spits—struggle to survive another century of hopelessness.[3] In North America, the indigenous retreat onto reserves where alcoholism rates approach one hundred percent. Or they escape from that hell to join the vast armies of the dispossessed who wander the streets of our brave new world.[4] Corpses are being bulldozed into shallow graves in Jenin; the Holy Land runs in blood. Body bags are piling high in Iraq and Afghanistan. Reports of the United States' use of torture to discipline, extract information, or simply humiliate arrive almost daily from prison camps and war zones around the world; when more convenient, torture is outsourced to client-state terror regimes. No doubt the god would like to help, but is presently occupied, fighting (on both sides, incidentally) of the new global war on terror. We see hunger, disappointment, misery, and hopelessness everywhere we look across the globe, from the poorest of nations to the richest; these maladaptive features slowly fester into criminality, religious fanaticism, and international terrorism.

European empires and neocolonial powers owe Africa restitution for their plundering and their savagery. The United States and other rich Western nations, as heirs to European colonialism, need to get actively involved in protecting ravaged areas of the African continent where people's lives are at risk; they need to place their powerful voices behind humanitarian calls for forgiveness of debt in postcolonial lands; they need to lean heavily upon the World Trade Organization to humanize the rules of global trade and to pressure the World Bank and IMF for reforms of unfair policies that further victimize history's victims.

Former empires cannot help Africans with the slow, painful task of their identity reconstruction. African philosophers labor diligently to work through the wreckage of human lives and recapture some of the great existential losses that compose the legacy of colonial rule in Africa. But progress is necessarily slow, as all worthwhile things tend to be. African philosophers have begun the hard task of identity reconstruction; politicians, religious figures, and other community leaders must take up the torch, empowering people with new and positive self-images, providing suitable exemplars for young folk to emulate, and sketching out suitable new forms of liberation ideology peculiar to African needs.

If violence still flares regularly across the continent and remains persistent in the most unfortunate of African lands, such as the Congo and Sierra Leone, Western witnesses must not attribute this persistence to natural or genetic deficiencies in the people of the African continent. Rather, Westerners must understand that Africans are struggling against overwhelming existential, economic, and political odds to restructure their lives and their cultures after centuries of brutalizing and savage oppression. Westerners must recall that there exists no violence so severe or destructive as imperialism, the single human crime on which rests the current and continuing prosperity of Western nations. If healing comes slowly to Africa, the reason is twofold: colonial myth enjoyed a profound and lengthy reign on the African continent, and philosophical healing is limited to the slow speed at which philosophical ideas seep into the public consciousness, a pace that proves sluggish at the best of historical times.

# Notes

1. Enrique Dussel, *Philosophy of Liberation* (New York: Orbis Books, 1985), 13.
2. Frantz Fanon, *The Wretched of the Earth* (New York: Grove Press, 1968), 47.
3. Las Casus, *Brevisma Relacion de la Destruccion de lao Indies* (1540) cited in Noam Chomsky, *Year 501: The Conquest Continues* (Cambridge, Mass.: South End Press, 1993), 198.
4. Aldous Huxley, *Brave New World* (London: Harper Perennial, 1998).

# Bibliography

Amselle, Jean-Loup. *Mestizo Logics: Anthropology of Identity in Africa and Elsewhere.* Translated by Claudia Royal. Stanford, Calif.: Stanford University Press, 1998.

Arendt, Hannah. *Between Past and Future: Eight Exercises in Political Thought.* New York: Penguin Books, 1977.

Atieno-Odhiambo, E. S. "Luo Perspectives on Knowledge and Development." Ivan Karp & D. A. Masolo, eds. *African Philosophy As Cultural Inquiry.* Bloomington, Ind.: Indiana University Press, 2000.

Baker, Samuel. *Albert Nyanza.* London: Macmillan, 1898.

Bataille, Georges. "Reflections on the Executioner and the Victim." Translated by David Rousset. *Yale French Studies No. 79: Literature and the Ethical Question.* New Haven:Yale University Press, 1991.

Baumeister, Roy. *Evil: Inside Human Violence and Cruelty.* New York: Henry Holt, 1997.

Bell, Richard H. *Understanding African Philosophy.* New York: Routledge, 2002.

Benjamin, Walter. *Selected Readings.* Marcus Bullock and Michael W. Jennings, eds. Cambridge, Mass.: Harvard University Press, 1996.

―――― *Illuminations.* Edited by Hannah Arendt. Translated by Harry Zohn. New York: Schocken Books, 1968.

Berkeley, Bill. *The Graves Are Not Yet Full: Race, Tribe, and Power in the Heart of Africa.* New York: Basic Books, 2001.

Bernard, Viola, Perry Ottenberg, and Fritz Redl. "Dehumanization." Nevitt Sanford and Craig Comstock, eds. *Sanctions for Evil.* San Francisco: Jossey-Bass, 1971.

Bloch, Maurice. *Prey Into Hunter: The Politics of Religious Experience.* Cambridge: Cambridge University Press, 1992.

―――― *From Blessing to Violence: History and Ideology in the Circumcision Ritual of the Merina of Madagascar.* Cambridge: Cambridge University Press, 1986.

Bodley, John H. "Anthropology and the Politics of Genocide," Carolyn Nordstrom and JoAnn Martin, eds. *Domination, Resistance and Terror.* Berkeley, Calif.: University of California Press, 1992.

――*Victims of Progress.* Mountain View, Calif.: Mayfield Publishing, 1990.

Bodunrin, Adeniji P. O. *Lessons of History for the Nigerian Republic.* London: Warwick House, 1998.

Bohannan, Paul, and Philip Curtin. *Africa and Africans.* Garden City, N.Y.: The Natural History Press, 1971.

Bongmba, Elias Kifon. *African Witchcraft and Otherness.* Albany, N.Y.: State University of New York Press, 2001.

Brothers, Leslie. *Friday's Footprint: How Society Shapes the Human Mind*. Oxford.: Oxford University Press, 1997.

Bujo, Bénézet. *Foundations of an African Ethic*. New York: Herder and Herder, 2000.

Burkert, Walter. *Savage Energies: Lessons of Myth and Ritual in Ancient Greece*. Chicago: University of Chicago Press, 2001.

———. *Creation of the Sacred: Tracks of Biology in Early Religions*. Cambridge, Mass.: Harvard University Press, 1996.

———. *Homo Necans: An Anthropology of Ancient Greek Sacrificial Ritual and Myth*. Berkeley, Calif.: University of California Press, 1983.

———. *Structure and History in Greek Myth and Ritual*. Berkeley, Calif.: University of California Press, 1979.

Burns, J. H., ed. *Jeremy Bentham, Collected Works*. London: Athlone Press, 1968.

*Cassell's Latin Dictionary*. New York: Funk & Wagnalls, 1957.

Césaire, Aimé. *Discourse on Colonialism*. New York: Monthly Review Press, 1972.

Chomsky, Noam. *Media Control: The Spectacular Achievements of Propaganda*. New York: Seven Stories Press, 2002.

———. *Year 501: The Conquest Continues*. Cambridge, Mass.: South End Press, 1993.

———, and Edward S. Herman. *Manufacturing Consent: The Political Economy of Mass Media*. New York: Pantheon Books, 2002.

Christie, Kenneth, ed. *Ethnic Conflict, Tribal Politics: A Global Perspective*. Surrey, U.K.: Curzon Press, 1998.

Cohen, Abner. *The Politics of Elite Culture: Explorations in the Dramaturgy of Power in a Modern African Society*. Berkeley, Calif.: University of California Press, 1981.

Coleman, James Smoot. *Nationalism and Development in Africa: Selected Essays*. Edited by Richard L. Sklar. Berkeley, Calif.: University of California Press, 1994.

Daniel, E. Valentine. *Charred Lullabies: Chapters in an Anthropology of Violence*. Princeton, N.J.: Princeton University Press, 1996.

Davidson, Basil. *The Search for Africa: History, Culture, Politics*. New York: Random House, 1994.

De Rivero, Oswaldo. *The Myth of Development*. London: Zed Books, 2003.

Derrida, Jacques. *Writing and Difference*. Translated by Alan Bass. Chicago: University of Chicago Press, 1978.

———. *Speech and Phenomena*. Translated by David B. Allison. Evanston, Ill.: Northwestern University Press, 1973.

Descartes, René. *Discourse on Method*. Translated by John Veitch. London: J. M. Dent, 1996.

———. *Meditations on First Philosophy*. Translated by Donald A. Cress. New York: Hackett, 1993.

Diamond, Jared. *Guns, Germs, and Steel: The Fates of Human Societies*. London: W. W. Norton and Co., 1999.

Dillistone, F. W., ed. *Myth and Symbol*. Norwich, U.K.: Page Bros., 1966.

Diop, Cheikh Anta. *Civilization or Barbarism: An Authentic Anthropology*. Translated by Yaa-Lengi Meema Ngemi. New York: Lawrence Hill Books, 1991.

———. *Precolonial Black Africa*. Translated by Harold Salemson. New York: Lawrence Hill Books, 1987.

Dostoevsky, Fyodor. *The Brothers Karamazov*. Translated by Constance Garnet. New York: Barnes and Noble Books, 1995.

Dussel, Enrique. *Philosophy of Liberation*. New York: Orbis, 1985.

Eboussi-Boulaga, F. "The Topic of Change." Ivan Karp and D. A. Masolo, eds. *African Philosophy as Cultural Inquiry*. Bloomington, Ind.: Indiana University Press, 2000.

Egendorf, A., C. Kadushin, R. S. Laufer, G. Rothbart, and L. Sloan. *Legacies of Vietnam: Comparative Adjustment of Vietnam Veterans and their Peers.* Washington, D.C.: U.S. Government Printing Office, 1981.

Eller, Jack David. *From Culture to Ethnicity to Conflict: An Anthropological Perspective on International Ethnic Conflict.* Ann Arbor, Michigan: University of Michigan Press, 1999.

Eze, E. *Postcolonial African Philosophy, A Critical Reader.* London: Blackwell, 1997.

Fackenheim, Emil L. *To Mend The World: Foundations of Post-Holocaust Jewish Thought.* Bloomington, Ind.: Indiana University Press, 1982.

Falk, Richard. "The World Speaks on Iraq." *The Nation* 281:4. August 1–8, 2005.

Fanon, Frantz. *The Wretched of the Earth.* New York: Grove Press, 1986.

———. *Black Skin, White Masks.* New York: Grove Press, 1967.

Figley, C. R., and S. Leventman, eds. *Strangers at Home: Vietnam Veterans Since the War.* New York: Praeger Press, 1980.

Ford, Clyde W. *The Hero with an African Face: Mythic Wisdom of Traditional Africa.* New York: Bantam Books, 1999.

Foucault, Michel. *Discipline and Punish, The Birth of the Prison.* Translated by Alan Sheridan. New York: Random House, 1995.

———. *The Order of Things.* New York: Random House, 1970.

Gadamer, Hans-Georg. *Truth and Method.* Translated by Joel Weinsheimer. New York: Continuum, 2005.

———. *Philosophical Hermeneutics.* Translated by David E. Linge. Los Angeles: University of California Press, 1977.

Gerth, H. H., and C. W. Mills. *From Max Weber: Essays in Sociology.* New York: Oxford University Press, 1958.

Gill, Leslie. *The School of the Americas: Military Training and Political Violence in the Americas.* Durham, N.C.: Duke University Press, 2004.

Girard, René. *Violence and the Sacred.* Translated by Patrick Gregory. Baltimore, Maryland: Johns Hopkins University Press, 1979.

Griffiths, Ieuan L. L. *The Atlas of African Affairs.* London: Witwatersrand University Press, 1994.

Gyekye, Kwame. *Tradition and Modernity: Philosophical Reflections on the African Experience.* New York: Oxford University Press, 1997.

Hallen, Barry, and J. Olubi Sodipo. *Knowledge, Belief and Witchcraft.* Stanford, Calif.: Stanford University Press, 1997.

Hamblet, Wendy C. *The Sacred Monstrous: A Reflection on Violence in Human Communities.* Lanham, Md.: Lexington Books, 2004.

———. "The Disarming of Being: The Metaphysics of Benedict de Spinoza." *Prima Philosophia*, January–March 2001.

Hamerton-Kelly, Robert G., ed. *Violent Origins.* Stanford, Calif.: Stanford University Press, 1987.

Hamilton, Edith, and Huntington Cairns. *The Collected Dialogues of Plato.* Princeton, N.J.: Princeton University Press, 1961.

Hargreaves, J. D. *Decolonization in Africa.* New York: Longman, 1988.

Harrison, Charles, and Paul Wood. *Art in Theory 1900–1990.* Oxford: Blackwell, 1992.

Haught, James A. *Holy Hatred: Religious Conflicts of the Nineties.* Amherst, N.Y.: Prometheus Books, 1995.

Hegel, Georg Wilhelm Friedrich. *Lectures on the Philosophy of World History: Introduction.* Translated by Hugh Barr Nisbet. Cambridge, U.K.: Cambridge University Press, 1989.

————. *The Phenomenology of Spirit*. Translated by A. V. Miller. Oxford: Oxford University Press, 1979.

————. *Vorlesungen über die Philosophie der Geschichte*. Frankfurt: Theorie- Werkausgabe 12, 1970.

Heidegger, Martin. *Basic Writings*. David Farrell Krell, ed. New York: Harper and Row, 1977.

————. *Poetry, Language, and Thought*. Translated by Albert Hofstadter. New York: Harper-Collins, 1975.

Henry, William E., and Nevitt Sanford, eds. *Sanctions for Evil*. San Francisco, Calif.: Jossey-Bass, 1971.

Herskovits, Melville. *Cultural Relativism*. New York: Random House, 1972.

Hesiod. *Works and Days and Theogony*. Robert Lamberton, ed. Translated by Stanley Lombardo. New York: Hackett, 1993.

Hobbes, Thomas. *Leviathan*. New York: Penguin, 1982.

Hosking, Geoffrey, and George Schöpflin, eds. *Myths and Nationhood*. New York: Routledge, 1997.

Hountondji, Paulin. *African Philosophy: Myth and Reality*. Bloomington, Ind.:

Indiana University Press, 1983.

Hume, David. *A Treatise on Human Nature, Part One*. D. G. C. MacNabb, ed. New York: Fontana, 1970.

Husserl, Edmund. *Ideas Pertaining to a Pure Phenomenology and to a Phenomenological Philosophy*. Translated by F. Kersten. Dordrecht, Netherlands: Kluwer, 1998.

————. *Cartesian Meditations*. Translated by Dorian Cairns. Dordrecht, Netherlands: Kluwer, 1995.

Huxley, Aldous. *Brave New World*. London. Harper Perennial, 1998.

Kafka, Franz. *The Complete Stories*. Edited by Nahum N. Glatzer. New York: Schocken Books, 1983.

Karp, Ivan, and D. A. Masolo, eds. *African Philosophy as Cultural Inquiry*. Bloomington, Ind.: Indiana University Press, 2000.

Keeley, Lawrence. *War Before Civilization*. Oxford, U.K.: Oxford University Press, 1996.

Kennedy, Randall. *Nigger: The Strange History of a Troublesome Word*. New York: Pantheon Books, 2002.

Kirk, G. S., J. E. Raven, and M. Schoefield. *The PreSocratic Philosophers*. Cambridge: Cambridge University Press, 1957.

Laertius, Diogenes. VIII, 77. Kirk, G. S., J. E. Raven, and M. Schoefield, *The PreSocratic Philosophers*. Cambridge: Cambridge University Press, 1957.

Las Casus. *Brevisma Relacion de la Desrtuccion de lao Indies* (1540) cited in Noam Chomsky. *Year 501: The Conquest Continues*. Camrbridge, Mass.: South End Press, 1993.

Leibniz, Gottfried Wilhelm. *Monadology*. Nicholas Rescher, ed. Pittsburgh, Penn.: University of Pittsburgh Press, 1991.

Levi, Primo. *The Drowned and the Saved*. New York: Random House, 1989.

Levi-Strauss, Claude. *Myth and Meaning: Cracking the Code of Culture*. New York: Schocken Books, 1995.

Levinas, Emmanuel. *Discovering Existence with Husserl*. Translated by Richard Cohen and Michael Smith. Evanston, Ill.: Northwestern University Press, 1998.

————. *Collected Philosophical Papers*. Translated by Alfonso Lingis. Dordrecht, Netherlands: Kluwer, 1993.

——. *Otherwise Than Being or Beyond Essence*. Translated by Alfonso Lingis. Dordrecht, Netherlands: Kluwer, 1991.

—— *Ethics and Infinity*. Translated by Richard Cohen. Pittsburg: Duquesne University Press, 1985.

——. *Totality and Infinity: An Essay on Exteriority*. Translated by Alfonso Lingis. Pittsburgh, Penn.: Duquesne University Press, 1969.

Lévy-Bruhl, Lucien. *The Notebooks on Primitive Mentality*. Translated by Peter Rivière. New York: Harper and Row, 1975.

——. *Primitive Mentality*. Translated by Lilian A. Claire. London: Allen and Unwin, 1923.

Lifton, Robert J. "Failures of Identification and Sociopathic Behavior." William E. Henry, Nevitt Sanford, eds. *Sanctions for Evil*. San Francisco: Jossey-Bass Inc., 1971.

——. *The Nazi Doctors: Medical Killing and the Psychology of Genocide*. New York: Basic Books, 1986.

Lincoln, Bruce. *Death, War, and Sacrifice: Studies in Ideologies and Practice*. Chicago: University of Chicago Press, 1991.

——. *Myth, Cosmos, and Society*. Cambridge, Mass.: Cambridge University Press, 1986.

Lorenz, Konrad. *On Aggression*. Translated by Marjorie Kerr Wilson. New York: Harcourt, Brace, and World, 1966.

Lovejoy, Arthur O. *The Great Chain of Being*. Cambridge, Mass.: Harvard University Press, 1936.

Madeley, John. *Big Business, Poor Peoples: The Impact of Transnational Corporations on the World's Poor*. London: Zed Books, 1999.

Mamdani, Mahmood. *When Victims Become Killers: Colonialism, Nativism, and the Genocide in Rwanda*. Princeton, N.J.: Princeton University Press, 2000.

——. *Citizen and Subject: Contemporary Africa and the Legacy of Colonialism*. Princeton, N.J.: Princeton University Press, 1996.

Marcus, George, and Michael Fisher, eds. *Anthropology as Cultural Critique*. Chicago: University of Chicago Press, 1986.

Marx, Karl, and Friedrich Engels. *The German Ideology*. Edited by C. J. Arthur. London: Watts, 1970.

Masolo, D. A. *African Philosophy in Search of Identity*. Bloomington, Ind.: Indiana University Press, 1994.

May, Rollo. *The Power of Innocence: A Search for the Sources of Violence*. New York: Norton, 1972.

Mbiti, John S. *African Religions and Philosophy*. New York: Frederick A. Praeger, 1969.

McGreal, Ian P., ed. *Great Thinkers of the Western World*. New York: Harper Collins, 1992.

Memmi, Albert. *Racism*. Translated by Steve Martinot. Minneapolis, Minn.: University of Minnesota Press, 1994.

——. *The Colonizer and the Colonized*. Translated by Howard Greenfeld. Boston, Mass.: Beacon Press, 1991.

Merleau-Ponty, Maurice. *The Primacy of Perception*. Translated by Nancy Metzel and John Flodstrom. New York: Routledge, 2002.

Mowoe, Isaac J., and Richard Bjornson, eds. *Africa and the West: The Legacies of Empire*. Translated by R. Bjornson. New York: Greenwood Press, 1986.

Mudimbe, V. Y. *The Idea of Africa*. Bloomington, Ind.: Indiana University Press, 1994.

——. *The Invention of Africa*. Bloomington, Ind.: Indiana University Press, 1988.

Mumbengegwi, Clever. *Macroeconomic and Structural Adjustment Policies in Zimbabwe: International Political Economy.* New York: Palgrave-MacMillan, 2002.

Nietzsche, Friedrich. *The Nietzsche Reader.* Keith Ansell Pierson, and Duncan Large, eds. Oxford, U.K.: Blackwell, 2006.

———. *The Gay Science.* Translated by Walter Kaufmann. New York: Vintage Books, 1974.

———. *A Genealogy of Morals.* Translated by Walter Kaufmann. New York: Vintage Books, 1967.

———. *The Birth of Tragedy and the Case of Wagner.* Translated by Walter Kaufmann. New York: Vintage Books, 1966.

———. *Thus Spake Zarathustra.* Translated by Thomas Common. New York: Tudor Press, 1934.

Nordstrom, Carolyn, and Jo Ann Martin, eds. *The Paths to Domination, Resistance, and Terror.* Berkeley, Calif.: University of California Press, 1992.

Nussbaum, Martha. *The Therapy of Desire.* Princeton, N.J.: Princeton University Press, 1996.

Nyerere, Julius. *Freedom and Development.* Oxford: Oxford University Press, 1973.

———. *Freedom and Socialism.* Oxford: Oxford University Press, 1968.

———. *Ujamaa: Essays on Socialism.* Oxford: Oxford University Press, 1968.

———. *Freedom and Unity.* Oxford: Oxford University Press, 1967.

Odera Oruku, Henry. *Sage Philosophy: Indigenous Thinkers and the Modern Debate on African Philosophy.* Nairobi, Kenya: Acts Press, 1991.

Odoch Pido, O. P. "Personhood and Art: Social Change and Commentary among the Acoli." Ivan Karp, D. A. Masolo, eds. *African Philosophy as Cultural Inquiry.* Bloomington, Ind.: Indiana University Press, 2000.

Oliver, Roland, and J. D. Fage. *A Short History of Africa.* New York: Penguin, 1962.

Olweus, Dan. *Aggressive Behavior: Current Perspectives.* New York: Plenum, 1994.

Pallmeyer, Jack Nelson. *School of Assassins: Guns, Greed, and Globalization.* Edinborough: Orbis Books, 2001.

Pascal, Blaise. *Pensées les Provinciales.* Paris, France: Bookking International, 1995.

Peterson, Scott. *Me Against My Brother: At War in Somalia, Sudan, and Rwanda.* New York: Routledge, 2000.

Plato. *Euthyphro, Apology, Crito, Phaedo, Phaedrus.* Translated by Harold North Fowler. Cambridge, Mass.: Harvard University Press, 1999.

———. *Lysis, Symposium, Gorgias.* Translated by W. R. M. Lamb. Cambridge, Mass.: Harvard University Press, 1996.

———. *Statesman, Philebus, Ion.* Translated by Harold North Fowler and W. R. M. Lamb. Cambridge, Mass.: Harvard University Press, 1992.

———. *Theaetetus, Sophist.* Translated by Harold North Fowler. Cambridge, Mass.: Harvard University Press, 1988.

———. *The Republic: Books I–V.* Richard W. Sterling and William C. Scott, eds. Translated by Paul Shorey. Cambridge, Mass.: Harvard University Press, 1969.

Power, Samantha. *A Power from Hell.* New York: Basic Books, 2002.

Radin, Paul. *Primitive Religions.* New York: Dover, 1957.

Ratner, Michael, and Ellen Ray. *Guantanamo: What the World Should Know.* White River Jct., Vt.: Chelsea Green Publishing, 2004.

Redding, Arthur. *Raids on Human Consciousness: Writing, Anarchism and Violence.* Columbia, S.C.: University of South Carolina Press, 1998.

Ricoeur, Paul. *The Symbolism of Evil.* Translated by Emerson Buchanan. Boston, Mass.: Beacon Press, 1967.

Rodney, Walter. *A History of the Upper Guinea Coast 1545-1800*. Oxford: Clarendon Press, 1970.

Rosenbaum, Ron. *Explaining Hitler: The Search for the Origins of His Evil*. New York: Random House, 1999.

Rosenberg, Justin. *The Follies of Globalization Theory*. London: Verso, 2000.

Rushdie, Salman. *Imaginary Homelands*. New York: Viking Press, 1991.

Sagan, Eli. *At the Dawn of Tyranny*. New York: Knopf, 1985.

Schipper, Mineke. *Imagining Insiders: Africa and the Question of Belonging*. New York: Cassell, 1999.

Senghor, Léopold. "The Spirit of Civilization or the Laws of African Negro Culture." *Présence Africaine*. Nos. 8–10, 2004.

———. "The Revolution of 1889 and Leo Frobenius." *Africa and the West: The Legacies of Empire*. Edited by Isaac James Mowoe and Richard Bjornson. Translated by R. Bjornson. New York: Greenwood Press, 1986.

———. *On African Socialism*. Translated by Mercer Cook. New York: Praeger, 1964.

Serequeberhan, Tsenay. *The Hermeneutics of African Philosophy*. New York: Routledge, 1994.

Shaughnessey, James D., ed. *The Roots of Ritual*. Grand Rapids, Mich.: B. Eerdman's Publishing, 1973.

Shaw, Rosalind. "'Tok Af, Lef Af': A Political Economy of Temne Techniques of Secrecy and Self." *African Philosophy as Cultural Inquiry*. Edited by Ivan Karp, D. A. Masolo. Bloomington, Ind.: Indiana University Press, 2000.

Sluka, Jeffrey A., ed. *Death Squad: An Anthropology of State Terror*. Philadelphia, Penn.: University of Pennsylvania Press, 2000.

Spinoza, Benedict de. *Ethics*. Translated by A. Boyle. London: Dent and Sons, 1925.

Staub, Ervin. *The Psychology of Good and Evil: Why Children, Adults, and Groups Help and Harm Others*. Cambridge: Cambridge University Press, 2003.

———. *The Roots of Evil: The Origins of Genocide and Other Group Violence*. New York: Cambridge University Press, 1989.

Stivers, Richard. *Evil in Modern Myth and Ritual*. Athens, Ga.: University of Georgia Press, 1991.

Tempels, Placide. *Bantu Philosophy*. Paris, France: Présence Africaine, 1959.

Tucker, Robert C., ed. *The Marx-Engels Reader*. London: W. W. Norton, 1978.

Vail, Leroy, ed. *The Creation of Tribalism in Southern Africa*. Berkeley, Calif.: University of California Press, 1991.

Vaughan, Megan. *Curing Their Ills: Colonial Power and African Illness*. Stanford, Calif.: Stanford University Press, 1991.

———. "But what was the Disease? The Present State of Health and Healing in African Studies." *Past and Present*. Vol. 124.

Waller, James. *Becoming Evil*. New York: Oxford University Press, 2002.

Weil, Simone. *Intimations of Christianity Among the Ancient Greeks*. Translated by Elizabeth Chase Geissbuhler. London and Henley: Routledge and Kegan Paul, 1957.

Williams, Chancellor. *The Destruction of Black Civilization: Great Issues of a Race from 4500 B.C. to 2000 A.D.* Chicago: Third World Press, 1987.

Wiredu, Kwasi. *Cultural Universals and Particulars: An African Perspective*. Bloomington, Ind.: Indiana University Press, 1996.

Wittgenstein, Ludwig. *Philosophical Investigations*. Translated by G. E. M. Anscombe. Oxford, U.K.: Blackwell, 1953.

Wolfe, Eric R. *Envisioning Power: Ideologies of Dominance and Crisis*. Berkeley, Calif.: University of California Press, 1999.

Wright, Richard A. *African Philosophy: An Introduction.* New York: University Press of America, 1984.
Young, Dudley. *Origins of the Sacred: The Ecstasies of Love and War.* London: Little and Brown, 1992.
Zahra, A. "A Yaws Eradication Campaign in Eastern Nigeria." *Bulletin of the World Health Organization.* Vol. 15.

# Index

# About the Author

**Wendy C. Hamblet** is a Canadian philosopher, alumna of Brock University, Canada, and Pennsylvania State University, U.S.A. Hamblet teaches Genocide Studies and Contemporary World Moral Problems at North Carolina A&T University. Hamblet's research centers about the problems of violence, subjectivity, and identity formation. She is author of *The Sacred Monstrous: A Reflection on Violence in Human Communities* (Lexington Books, 2004) and co-editor (with Richard Koenigsberg, Library of Social Science, New York) of *Psychological Interpretations of War* (New York: *Peace Review*, 2006). Hamblet has authored many chapters in edited volumes of scholarly essays (Rodopi, *Philosophies of Peace; Studia Phaenomenologica* Centenary Volume *Jan Patočka 1907–2007*) and dozens of articles in peer-refereed journals such as *Monist, Appraisal, Prima Philosophia, Journal of the British Society for Phenomenology, Existentia Meletai Sophias,* and the *Journal of Genocide Research*. Hamblet is a member of the faculty of the Genocide and Human Rights University Program (in collaboration with the Zoryan Institute), an active member of The Concerned Philosophers for Peace, International Association of Genocide Scholars, and International Philosophers for Peace (IPPNO), and she serves as editor and member of the Board of Advisors for the Globalization for the Common Good Initiative. Hamblet is also an accredited and practicing Philosophical Counselor and Ethics Consultant, associated with the Paul Maillet Center for Ethics of Ottawa, Canada.